LAND O LAKES®
TREASURY OF
COUNTRY HERITAGE
MEALS & MENUS

CREDITS:

Published in 1994 by
Tormont Publications Inc.
338 Saint Antoine St. East
Montreal, Canada H2Y 1A3
Tel. (514) 954-1441
Fax (514) 954-5086

Recipes developed and tested by the Land O'Lakes Test Kitchens, with assistance from Robin Krause.

Design, photography and production by Cy DeCosse Incorporated.
Recipes and manuscript © 1989, 1990, 1991, 1992 Land O'Lakes, Inc.
Design and photography © 1989, 1990, 1991, 1992 Cy DeCosse Incorporated.
All rights reserved.

LAND O LAKES® is a registered trademark of Land O'Lakes, Inc. and is used under license.

Land O'Lakes, Inc. photograph on page 72.
Minnesota Historical Society photographs on pages 4 (Carl Graff), 152, 280, 348 (Edmund A. Brush).

ISBN 2-89429-591-X
Printed in Canada

LAND O LAKES®
TREASURY OF
COUNTRY HERITAGE
MEALS & MENUS

TORMONT

LAND O LAKES®

TREASURY OF
COUNTRY HERITAGE
MEALS & MENUS

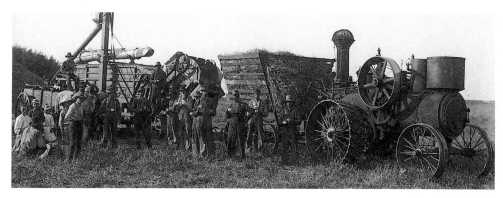

Cooperation has always been an American virtue. We had to work together to settle our wild, new land. And perhaps the true meaning of the American Melting Pot is that after cooperating in work, people from every part of the world sat down together to try each other's foods.

As we ate each other's foods we became friends and, as our children married one another, we became an American family.

It's a family that eats well. Our foods are as diverse and interesting as our people. A true American menu may feature food ideas from Europe at breakfast and Asia at dinner. Considering the varied sources of all these great recipes and the abundance of American ingenuity that's been added, American cooking is a true cooperative effort . . . and the taste can't be beat anywhere, anytime!

At Land O'Lakes, we know about cooperation. After all, we started in 1921 as a farm cooperative and we're still owned and managed by over 300,000 farmers today. We've always taken a special interest in American cooking, the kind of good country cooking that gets handed down from one generation to the next.

In the Land O'Lakes Kitchens, we've taken these classics and tested and retested them with today's new ways of cooking. We've kept your old favorites tasting the same, but we made them quicker or easier. We've included nutritional information for every recipe, and we've added some new ideas and foods we think may be America's favorites tomorrow. This cookbook is Land O'Lakes way of cooperating with and continuing the rich heritage of American cooking. We hope you enjoy it.

Contents

Breakfasts & Brunches 6

Simple Suppers 72

Hearty Dinners 152

Picnics & Barbecues 218

Casual Entertaining 280

Elegant Entertaining............................ 348

Celebrations 398

Index 500

BREAKFASTS & BRUNCHES

Big family breakfasts are as American as Paul Bunyan. Consider his working-day breakfast: 19 pounds of sausage, 6 hams, 8 loaves of bread and 231 flapjacks topped with a pound of butter and a quart of maple syrup.

Although this was a legendary breakfast, real American breakfasts used to be almost as big. In the magazine HOUSEHOLD published in 1884, a writer told city readers that a typical country breakfast consisted of "buckwheat cakes, maple syrup, potatoes, graham gems, coffee, ham and eggs, fried mush, apple sauce and doughnuts."

Today when we gather for an eye-opening meal like that, we call it brunch. This allows us to spread our calories over breakfast and lunch. It's a great way to entertain on a lazy weekend morning with family and your favorite guests sitting and chatting for hours over cups of your best coffee.

On the next pages are dozens of new recipes, delicious reasons for getting out of bed, even on a weekend. And we've taken some traditional recipes and updated them so they're easier to make. Plus we've included some quick new breakfast ideas for busier mornings. We think you'll agree that all of them are really worth waking up for!

BREAKFASTS & BRUNCHES
MENU

Easy & Quick Brunch

*In the summertime, eating is easy with fresh foods from the garden
. . . a tomato/asparagus frittata and fresh fruit with a ginger glaze
served with chocolate chip banana muffins.*

Fresh Tomato & Asparagus Frittata p.51
Ginger Glazed Fruit p.58
Chocolate Chip Banana Muffins p.28

BREAKFASTS & BRUNCHES
MENU

Seafood Lover's Brunch

*Guests will love sailing into this bountiful brunch that features
a flaky crab, mushroom and leek tart. Also aboard are prize-winning
blueberry muffins and sweet and creamy Devonshire-Style fruit.*

Crab, Mushroom & Leek Tart p.48
Prize Winning Blueberry Muffins p.28
Devonshire-Style Fruit p.58

BREAKFASTS & BRUNCHES
MENU

Make-Ahead Brunch

When you want to relax and enjoy your own brunch try this delicious ham, broccoli and cheese strata that you make the night before, then bake while you visit with guests. Serve with baked fruit ambrosia and tender, homemade kolachi pastries.

Ham & Broccoli Strata p.47
Baked Ambrosia in a Cup p.57
Old World Kolachi p.40

Special Occasion Brunch

Poached salmon with a new twist! Salmon fillets are rolled into pinwheels and served on top of cantaloupe and honeydew melon puree. An elegant brunch with fruit tarts, orange and almond filled braided coffee cake and new flavored coffees.

Flavored Coffees p.17   Salmon Pinwheels With Melon Puree p.47
Orange Almond Braided Coffee Cake p.39
Strawberry n' Cream Tart p.66

BREAKFASTS & BRUNCHES
MENU

Rise & Shine Breakfast

For a great eye-opener, serve fresh fruit kabobs to stir up sparkling fruit juices. Next, they'll love tender, fluffy yogurt pancakes with fresh strawberry syrup. The entrée is a delicious Cheddar cheese, bacon and mushroom oven omelet.

Sparkling Juice With Fruit Kabobs p.15
Tender Yogurt Pancakes p.18   Fresh Strawberry Syrup p.25
Cheese & Mushroom Oven Omelet p.52   Assorted Breakfast Meats

Springtime Brunch

Pretty as a spring morning, this colorful brunch pairs an herb-flavored,
creamy chicken, melon and cucumber salad with a rich lemon glazed nut bread.
Cream-filled cone cookies served with berries are a sweet way to end this brunch.

Crisp Cucumber n' Melon Chicken Salad p.42
Lemon Nut Bread p.32
Delicate Cookie Cones With Orange Cream p.68

Sparkling Juice With Fruit Kabobs (pictured)
Mixed Fruit Warmer

Sparkling Juice With Fruit Kabobs

15 minutes

Add sparkle to your favorite fruit juice for a refreshing brunch beverage.

3 cups your favorite juice (cranberry, white grape, cranberry raspberry, orange, apple)
3 cups lemon-lime soda *or* champagne

6 (4 to 6-inch) wooden skewers
1-inch pieces assorted favorite fresh fruit (strawberries, bananas, pineapple, apples, cherries, grapes, etc.)

6 servings

In 2-quart pitcher combine juice and soda. On each skewer place assorted pieces of fruit. For each serving place one fruit kabob in each glass. Pour juice over fruit kabob; serve immediately.

Nutrition Information (1 serving)
• Calories 140 • Protein 0g • Carbohydrate 37g • Fat 0g
• Cholesterol 0mg • Sodium 16mg

Mixed Fruit Warmer

30 minutes

Serve this warm beverage as a chill chaser at breakfast or brunch.

⅓ cup firmly packed brown sugar
2 cups water
1 (32 ounce) bottle cranberry raspberry beverage
1 (6 ounce) can frozen orange juice concentrate

8 thin orange slices
2 cinnamon sticks

8 servings

In 3-quart saucepan combine all ingredients. Cook over medium heat, stirring occasionally, until sugar is dissolved and mixture just comes to a boil (15 to 20 minutes).

Microwave Directions: In large bowl combine all ingredients. Microwave on HIGH, stirring every 5 minutes, until sugar is dissolved and mixture just comes to a boil (11 to 16 minutes).

Nutrition Information (1 serving)
• Calories 150 • Protein 1g • Carbohydrate 37g • Fat 0g
• Cholesterol 0mg • Sodium 6mg

In 1921, at Land O'Lakes first annual meeting, 300 farmer-members attended. Just four years later, Land O'Lakes had 30,000 farmer-members and owners.

Spicy Whipped Cream (pictured)
Flavored Coffees

Spicy Whipped Cream

Serve dolloped on brewed coffee.

1 cup whipping cream
2 tablespoons powdered sugar

¼ teaspoon cinnamon
  Dash nutmeg

1½ cups

In chilled small mixer bowl beat chilled whipping cream at high speed, scraping bowl often, until soft peaks form. Continue beating, gradually adding powdered sugar, cinnamon and nutmeg, until stiff peaks form.

Flavored Coffees

For flavored coffees, start with strong brewed coffee.

Coffee Strength Per Cup

	Coffee	Water*
Weak	1 tablespoon	¾ cup (6 ounces)
Medium	2 tablespoons	¾ cup (6 ounces)
Strong	3 tablespoons	¾ cup (6 ounces)

Irish Coffee: Stir in Irish whiskey and sugar to taste. Top with sweetened whipped cream.

Almond Coffee: Stir in almond flavored liqueur to taste. Top with sweetened whipped cream and toasted sliced almonds. For non-alcoholic almond coffee, use medium brewed coffee. Stir in almond extract and sugar to taste. Top with sweetened whipped cream and toasted sliced almonds.

Mexican Coffee: Stir in coffee flavored liqueur to taste. Top with sweetened whipped cream; sprinkle with brown sugar and cinnamon.

Chocolate Coffee: Stir in chocolate flavored syrup and cream to taste.

Coffee For a Crowd

To Serve	Coffee	Water*
12	2 cups	16 cups
25	4 cups	32 cups

Iced Coffee: Cool coffee; serve over ice. Stir in sugar, cream and/or milk to taste, if desired.

Coffee n' Cream: Stir in your favorite flavor ice cream to taste.

Coffee Condiments

To be served as condiments with hot brewed coffee: Chocolate curls, grated orange peel, orange slices, cinnamon sticks, sweetened whipped cream, brown sugar and your favorite liqueurs.

*Use freshly drawn cold water; do not use softened water.

Peach Melba Crepes

60 minutes

Crepes

1½ cups all-purpose flour
1 tablespoon sugar
½ teaspoon baking powder
½ teaspoon salt
2 cups milk
2 eggs
2 tablespoons butter *or* margarine, melted
½ teaspoon vanilla
2 teaspoons butter *or* margarine

Raspberry Sauce

4 cups sliced peaches *or* nectarines
¼ cup sugar

1 (10 ounce) can frozen raspberries in syrup, thawed, *do not drain*
½ cup currant jelly
1 tablespoon cornstarch

Sweetened whipped cream

6 servings

In small mixer bowl combine flour, 1 tablespoon sugar, baking powder and salt. Add all remaining crepe ingredients *except* 2 teaspoons butter. Beat at medium speed, scraping bowl often, until smooth (1 to 2 minutes). Melt 2 teaspoons butter in 8-inch skillet until sizzling. For each of 12 crepes pour about ¼ cup batter into skillet; immediately rotate skillet until thin film covers bottom. Cook over medium heat until lightly browned (1 to 2 minutes). Run wide spatula around edge to loosen; turn. Continue cooking until lightly browned (1 to 2 minutes). Place crepes on plate, placing waxed paper between each. Cover crepes; set aside. In large bowl stir together peaches and ¼ cup sugar; set aside. In 1-quart saucepan stir together undrained raspberries, jelly and cornstarch until cornstarch is dissolved. Cook over medium heat, stirring constantly, until mixture comes to a full boil (5 to 7 minutes). Boil, stirring constantly, 1 minute. To serve, place ⅓ cup peaches in center of each crepe; roll up. Spoon 2 tablespoons raspberry sauce over each crepe. Top with sweetened whipped cream.

Nutrition Information (1 serving)
• Calories 440 • Protein 9g • Carbohydrate 82g • Fat 9g
• Cholesterol 91mg • Sodium 322mg

Tender Yogurt Pancakes

30 minutes

3 eggs, separated
1½ cups all-purpose flour
¼ cup sugar
¼ cup butter *or* margarine, melted
1 (16 ounce) carton (2 cups) plain yogurt

2 teaspoons baking powder
1 teaspoon baking soda
¼ teaspoon salt

18 pancakes

In small mixer bowl beat egg whites at high speed, scraping bowl often, until stiff peaks form (1 to 2 minutes); set aside. In large mixer bowl combine egg yolks and all remaining ingredients. Beat at medium speed until well mixed. By hand, fold in beaten egg whites. (Small fluffs of egg white will remain in batter.) Heat griddle to 350° or until drops of water sizzle. For each pancake pour ¼ cup batter onto greased griddle. Cook until bubbles form (about 1½ minutes). Turn; continue cooking until underside is light brown (about 1½ minutes). Serve warm.

Variations

Blueberry Pancakes: Fold 1 cup fresh or frozen blueberries into pancake batter.

Pecan Pancakes: Fold ⅓ cup chopped pecans into pancake batter.

Banana-Nut Pancakes: Fold ½ cup (1 medium) mashed banana and ⅓ cup chopped walnuts into pancake batter.

Nutrition Information (2 pancakes)
• Calories 100 • Protein 4g • Carbohydrate 13g • Fat 4g
• Cholesterol 55mg • Sodium 182mg

Peach Melba Crepes (pictured)
Tender Yogurt Pancakes

Cinnamon Apple Baked Pancake

60 minutes

This dramatic oven-baked pancake is filled with cinnamon sweet apples.

Pancake
¼ cup butter *or* margarine
1 cup all-purpose flour
2 cups milk
3 eggs
½ teaspoon salt

Filling
2 tablespoons butter *or* margarine
2 teaspoons cornstarch
1 tablespoon cold water
⅓ cup firmly packed brown sugar
½ teaspoon cinnamon
2 medium cooking apples, cored, sliced ½-inch

6 servings

Heat oven to 400°. In 12x8-inch baking pan melt ¼ cup butter in oven (5 to 6 minutes). In small mixer bowl combine all remaining pancake ingredients. Beat at low speed, scraping bowl often, until well mixed (1 to 2 minutes). Pour melted butter into batter; continue beating until well mixed. Pour batter into hot pan. Bake for 30 to 40 minutes or until puffed, set in center and golden brown. Meanwhile, in 10-inch skillet melt 2 tablespoons butter. In small bowl stir together cornstarch and water. Stir brown sugar, cinnamon and cornstarch mixture into butter. Cook over medium heat, stirring constantly, until sugar dissolves and mixture bubbles and thickens (2 to 3 minutes). Stir in apples. Continue cooking, stirring constantly, until apples are evenly coated and crisply tender (10 to 12 minutes). Spoon filling over hot pancake; serve immediately.

Nutrition Information (1 serving)
• Calories 330 • Protein 8g • Carbohydrate 40g • Fat 16g
• Cholesterol 175mg • Sodium 374mg

French Toast Croissants

30 minutes

French toast served a new way.

Orange Butter
½ cup butter *or* margarine, softened
¼ cup powdered sugar
1 teaspoon grated orange peel

French Toast
⅓ cup milk
2 eggs, slightly beaten
1 teaspoon grated orange peel
¼ cup butter *or* margarine
4 plain croissants, cut in half crosswise *or*
8 (1-inch) slices French bread
Powdered sugar

4 servings

In small mixer bowl beat together all orange butter ingredients at medium speed, scraping bowl often, until light and fluffy (1 to 2 minutes); set aside. In pie pan stir together milk, eggs and 1 teaspoon orange peel. In 10-inch skillet or on griddle melt 2 tablespoons butter over medium heat. Dip 4 croissant halves into egg mixture, turning to coat both sides. Place croissant halves, cut side down, in skillet. Cook, turning once, until golden brown (3 to 4 minutes on each side). Remove to serving platter; keep warm. Repeat with remaining 2 tablespoons butter and 4 croissant halves. Dust croissant halves with powdered sugar; serve with orange spread.

Nutrition Information (1 serving)
• Calories 550 • Protein 8g • Carbohydrate 27g • Fat 47g
• Cholesterol 232mg • Sodium 531mg

Cinnamon Apple Baked Pancake (top)
French Toast Croissants (bottom)

Wild Rice Pecan Waffles (top)
Sun Honey Waffles (bottom)

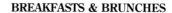

Wild Rice Pecan Waffles

30 minutes

Wild rice and pecans add crunch to this hearty morning treat.

3 eggs
1¾ cups all-purpose flour
¼ cup butter *or* margarine, melted
1½ cups milk
4 teaspoons baking powder
½ teaspoon nutmeg

1 cup cooked wild rice
⅓ cup chopped pecans

Maple syrup
Butter *or* margarine

8 servings

Heat waffle iron to medium high heat. In large bowl, using wire whisk or rotary beater, beat eggs until fluffy (1 to 2 minutes). Stir in flour, butter, milk, baking powder and nutmeg until smooth (1 to 2 minutes). Stir in wild rice and pecans. Pour batter onto center of hot waffle iron. Bake according to waffle iron directions or until golden brown (4 to 6 minutes). Repeat with remaining batter. Serve hot with maple syrup and butter.

Nutrition Information (1 serving)
• Calories 260 • Protein 8g • Carbohydrate 29g • Fat 13g
• Cholesterol 122mg • Sodium 259mg

Sun Honey Waffles

45 minutes

Fresh lemon peel and honey add sparkle to a midmorning brunch or weekend breakfast.

Waffles
3 eggs, separated
1¾ cups all-purpose flour
1½ cups milk
½ cup vegetable oil
2 tablespoons sugar
1 tablespoon baking powder
½ teaspoon salt
2 tablespoons honey
2 teaspoons grated lemon peel

Topping
1 cup whipping cream
2 tablespoons powdered sugar
1 teaspoon grated lemon peel
1 cup mixed fresh *or* frozen fruit (blueberries, strawberries, raspberries, etc.), thawed

Maple syrup

4 servings

Heat waffle iron to medium high heat. In large bowl, using wire whisk or rotary beater, beat egg yolks until light yellow color (1 to 2 minutes). Stir in all remaining waffle ingredients *except* egg whites just until moistened. In small mixer bowl beat egg whites at high speed, scraping bowl often, until stiff peaks form (1 to 1½ minutes). Gently fold beaten egg whites into waffle mixture. Pour batter onto center of hot waffle iron. Bake according to waffle iron directions or until golden brown (4 to 6 minutes). Repeat with remaining batter. Meanwhile, in chilled small mixer bowl beat chilled whipping cream at high speed, scraping bowl often, until soft peaks form. Continue beating, gradually adding powdered sugar, until stiff peaks form (1 to 1½ minutes). Fold in 1 teaspoon lemon peel. Serve waffles with whipped cream, fresh fruit and syrup.

Nutrition Information (1 serving)
• Calories 920 • Protein 15g • Carbohydrate 95g • Fat 55g
• Cholesterol 278mg • Sodium 610mg

Homemade Berry Jam (pictured)
Fresh Strawberry Syrup

Homemade Berry Jam 30 minutes

Smother bread with this homemade jam for a delicious treat; also great for gift giving.

4 cups fresh *or* frozen strawberries, slightly mashed

2½ tablespoons powdered fruit pectin
3 cups sugar

3 cups

In 2-quart saucepan combine strawberries and pectin. Cook over medium heat, stirring constantly, until mixture comes to a full boil (10 to 15 minutes). Stir in sugar. Continue cooking, stirring constantly, until mixture comes to a full boil (3 to 5 minutes). Boil 1 minute. Remove from heat; with large metal spoon skim foam from top. Pour jam into hot sterilized jars. Store refrigerated.

Microwave Directions: In 3-quart casserole combine strawberries and pectin. Microwave on HIGH, stirring after half the time, until mixture comes to a full boil (6 to 10 minutes). Stir in sugar. Microwave on HIGH, stirring every minute, until mixture comes to a full boil (4 to 6½ minutes). Boil 1 minute. With large metal spoon skim foam from top. Pour into hot sterilized jars. Store refrigerated.

Nutrition Information (1 tablespoon)
• Calories 55 • Protein 0g • Carbohydrate 14g • Fat 0g
• Cholesterol 0mg • Sodium 0mg

Variation

Raspberry Jam: Use 4 cups fresh or frozen raspberries, slightly mashed. Add 1 tablespoon fresh lime juice to fruit. Increase sugar to 3½ cups. Prepare as directed above.

Fresh Strawberry Syrup 45 minutes

Special syrup with the fresh taste of strawberries for your pancakes or waffles.

1 pint strawberries, hulled, halved, mashed slightly*

1 cup sugar
¾ cup light corn syrup

2 cups

In 3-quart saucepan place strawberries. Cook over medium heat, stirring occasionally, until strawberries come to a full boil (6 to 8 minutes). Line strainer with cheesecloth; place over large bowl. Pour hot strawberries into strainer mashing with back of spoon to extract juice; discard pulp. Return juice to pan. Add sugar and corn syrup. Cook over medium heat until mixture comes to a full boil (9 to 10 minutes). Boil 1 minute. With large metal spoon skim foam from top. Store refrigerated. Serve over pancakes, waffles or desserts.

*1 (16 ounce) bag frozen strawberries can be substituted for 1 pint strawberries. Increase cooking time of strawberries to 15 minutes.

Microwave Directions: In 3-quart casserole place strawberries. Microwave on HIGH, stirring every 2 minutes, until strawberries come to a full boil (4 to 5 minutes). Line strainer with cheesecloth; place over large bowl. Pour hot strawberries into strainer mashing with back of spoon to extract juice; discard pulp. Return to casserole. Add sugar and corn syrup. Microwave on HIGH, stirring every 2 minutes, until mixture comes to a full boil (3 to 6 minutes). Boil 1 minute. With large metal spoon skim foam from top. Store refrigerated. Serve over pancakes, waffles or desserts.

Nutrition Information (1 tablespoon)
• Calories 50 • Protein 0g • Carbohydrate 13g • Fat 0g
• Cholesterol 0mg • Sodium 5mg

Apple Butter

2 hours

Old-fashioned apple butter tastes heavenly spread on pancakes, waffles or warm bread.

3   pounds (9 medium) tart cooking apples,
   peeled, cored, quartered
½   cup apple cider *or* apple juice
1½ cups sugar
½   cup firmly packed brown sugar

1½ teaspoons cinnamon
¼   teaspoon allspice
⅛   teaspoon nutmeg
2   tablespoons cider vinegar

3½ cups

In Dutch oven place apples and apple cider. Cover; cook over medium heat, stirring occasionally, until apples are very soft (25 to 30 minutes). Place apple mixture in food processor bowl or 5-cup blender container; process until smooth (1 to 2 minutes). Return apple mixture to same pan; stir in all remaining ingredients. Cook over low heat, stirring often, until mixture is very thick (30 to 45 minutes). Serve warm or cold on pancakes, waffles, toast or warm breads. Store refrigerated.

Microwave Directions: *Reduce ½ cup apple cider to ¼ cup.* In 3-quart casserole place apples and apple cider. Cover; microwave on HIGH, stirring after half the time, until apples are very soft (18 to 23 minutes). Place apple mixture in food processor bowl or 5-cup blender container; process until smooth (1 to 2 minutes). Return apple mixture to same casserole; stir in all remaining ingredients. Microwave on HIGH, stirring every 10 minutes, until mixture is very thick (30 to 45 minutes). Serve warm or cold on pancakes, waffles, toast or warm breads. Store refrigerated.

Nutrition Information (1 tablespoon)
• Calories 41 • Protein 0g • Carbohydrate 11g • Fat 0g
• Cholesterol 0mg • Sodium 0mg

Old-Fashioned Pear Conserve

60 minutes

Fresh pear flavor is preserved in this delicate spread for breakfast breads.

2   pounds (8 medium) pears, peeled,
   cored, quartered
2¼ cups sugar
1   (8 ounce) can crushed pineapple in
   unsweetened juice

1   tablespoon lemon juice
½   teaspoon grated lemon peel

2½ cups

Place half of pears in food processor bowl or 5-cup blender container. Process until finely chopped (1 to 2 minutes). Place chopped pears in Dutch oven. Repeat with remaining pears. Stir in all remaining ingredients. Cook over medium heat or until pears are very soft and mixture thickens (30 to 40 minutes). Serve warm or cold on pancakes, waffles, toast or warm breads. Store refrigerated.

Microwave Directions: Prepare pears as directed above. Place chopped pears in 3-quart casserole. Stir in all remaining ingredients. Microwave on HIGH, stirring every 10 minutes, until pears are very soft and mixture thickens (30 to 40 minutes). Serve warm or cold on pancakes, waffles, toast or warm breads. Store refrigerated.

Nutrition Information (1 tablespoon)
• Calories 60 • Protein 0g • Carbohydrate 16g • Fat 0g
• Cholesterol 0mg • Sodium 0mg

Apple Butter (left)
Old-Fashioned Pear Conserve (right)

Chocolate Chip Banana Muffins

45 minutes

Hearty, flavorful breakfast muffins.

¾ cup firmly packed brown sugar
½ cup butter *or* margarine, softened
1½ cups (3 medium) mashed ripe bananas
2 eggs
1 teaspoon vanilla
1 cup all-purpose flour

1 cup whole wheat flour
1 teaspoon baking soda
¼ teaspoon salt
½ cup miniature semi-sweet chocolate chips

1½ dozen

Heat oven to 350°. In large mixer bowl combine sugar and butter. Beat at medium speed, scraping bowl often, until mixture is creamy (1 to 2 minutes). Add bananas, eggs and vanilla. Continue beating, scraping bowl often, until well mixed (1 to 2 minutes). In medium bowl stir together flours, baking soda and salt. Add flour mixture to banana mixture; stir just until moistened. Fold in chocolate chips. Spoon into greased muffin pans. Bake for 18 to 25 minutes or until light golden brown. Cool 5 minutes; remove from pans.

Nutrition Information (1 muffin)
• Calories 180 • Protein 3g • Carbohydrate 26g • Fat 8g
• Cholesterol 45mg • Sodium 156mg

Prize Winning Blueberry Muffins

45 minutes

A hint of fresh lemon zest adds a special flavor to these scrumptious muffins.

½ cup sugar
¼ cup butter *or* margarine, softened
1 (8 ounce) carton (1 cup) dairy sour cream
2 tablespoons lemon juice
1½ teaspoons grated lemon peel
1 egg
1½ cups all-purpose flour

1 teaspoon baking soda
1 cup fresh *or* frozen blueberries (unthawed)

1 tablespoon sugar
½ teaspoon grated lemon peel

1 dozen

Heat oven to 375°. In large mixer bowl combine ½ cup sugar and butter. Beat at medium speed, scraping bowl often, until well mixed (1 to 2 minutes). Add sour cream, lemon juice, 1½ teaspoons lemon peel and egg. Continue beating, scraping bowl often, until well mixed (1 to 2 minutes). In medium bowl stir together flour and baking soda. By hand, stir flour mixture into sour cream mixture just until moistened. Fold in blueberries. Spoon into greased muffin pan. In small bowl stir together 1 tablespoon sugar and ½ teaspoon lemon peel. Sprinkle about ¼ teaspoon mixture on top of each muffin. Bake for 20 to 25 minutes or until lightly browned. Cool 5 minutes; remove from pan.

Nutrition Information (1 muffin)
• Calories 170 • Protein 4g • Carbohydrate 26g • Fat 6g
• Cholesterol 49mg • Sodium 166mg

Chocolate Chip Banana Muffins (pictured)
Prize Winning Blueberry Muffins

Good Morning Muffins (pictured)
Savory Bacon Muffins

Good Morning Muffins
40 minutes

These hearty muffins are made with carrots, coconut and raisins.

½ cup firmly packed brown sugar
¼ cup butter *or* margarine, softened
1 (8 ounce) carton (1 cup) dairy sour cream
2 eggs
1 cup (2 medium) shredded carrots
½ cup flaked coconut

½ cup raisins
1½ cups all-purpose flour
1 teaspoon baking soda
1 teaspoon cinnamon

1 dozen

Heat oven to 375°. In large mixer bowl combine sugar and butter. Beat at medium speed, scraping bowl often, until well mixed (1 to 2 minutes). Add sour cream and eggs. Continue beating, scraping bowl often, until well mixed (1 to 2 minutes). By hand, stir in carrots, coconut and raisins. In medium bowl stir together flour, baking soda and cinnamon.

Add flour mixture to sour cream mixture; stir just until moistened. Spoon into greased muffin pan. Bake for 20 to 25 minutes or until lightly browned.

Nutrition Information (1 muffin)
• Calories 220 • Protein 4g • Carbohydrate 29g • Fat 10g
• Cholesterol 163mg • Sodium 65mg

Savory Bacon Muffins
45 minutes

Great with eggs, these muffins are chock-full of bacon and onion.

6 slices bacon
¼ cup chopped onion
2 cups all-purpose flour
2 tablespoons sugar
2 teaspoons baking powder
½ teaspoon baking soda

½ teaspoon salt
1 (8 ounce) carton (1 cup) dairy sour cream
½ cup milk
1 egg, slightly beaten

1 dozen

Heat oven to 375°. In 10-inch skillet cook bacon until crisp (6 to 8 minutes). Remove bacon; drain on paper towels. Pour off all but *2 tablespoons* bacon fat. Stir onion into remaining 2 tablespoons bacon fat. Cook over medium heat until tender (3 to 4 minutes); cool. In large bowl combine flour, sugar, baking powder, baking soda and salt. In small bowl stir together

bacon, onion, sour cream, milk and egg until well blended. Add to flour mixture; stir just until moistened. Spoon into greased muffin pan. Bake for 18 to 20 minutes or until lightly browned.

Nutrition Information (1 muffin)
• Calories 160 • Protein 5g • Carbohydrate 20g • Fat 7g
• Cholesterol 35mg • Sodium 259mg

Southern Indians invented grits by cooking dried corn kernels so the hulls slipped off. The remaining whole tender hearts they called hominy, *which comes from the Algonquin Indian words,* rockah ominie. *Today hominy grits served with eggs and ham is still the favorite breakfast of the South.*

Orange Raisin Scones

25 minutes

A tender biscuitlike bread, flavored with orange and raisins.

Scones
1¾ cups all-purpose flour
3 tablespoons sugar
2½ teaspoons baking powder
2 teaspoons grated orange peel
⅓ cup butter *or* margarine
½ cup raisins
1 egg, slightly beaten
4 to 6 tablespoons half-and-half

1 egg, slightly beaten

Orange Butter
½ cup butter *or* margarine, softened
2 tablespoons orange marmalade

1 dozen

Heat oven to 400°. In medium bowl combine flour, sugar, baking powder and orange peel. Cut in ⅓ cup butter until crumbly. Stir in raisins, 1 egg and enough half-and-half just until moistened. Turn dough onto lightly floured surface; knead lightly 10 times. Roll into 9-inch circle; cut into 12 wedges. Place 1 inch apart on cookie sheet. Brush with beaten egg. Bake for 10 to 12 minutes or until golden brown. Immediately remove from cookie sheet. Meanwhile, in small bowl stir together ½ cup butter and orange marmalade; serve with scones.

Nutrition Information (1 scone with about 1 tablespoon butter)
• Calories 240 • Protein 3g • Carbohydrate 25g • Fat 15g
• Cholesterol 82mg • Sodium 208mg

Lemon Nut Bread

1 hour 15 minutes

A lemon glaze soaks into this nut-laden bread to add extra moisture and flavor.

Bread
⅔ cup sugar
½ cup butter *or* margarine, softened
2 eggs
¼ cup lemon juice
1 tablespoon grated lemon peel
1½ cups all-purpose flour
1 tablespoon baking powder

⅛ teaspoon salt
½ cup milk
1 cup chopped pecans

Glaze
½ cup powdered sugar
2 tablespoons lemon juice

3 mini loaves (30 servings)

Heat oven to 350°. In large mixer bowl combine sugar and butter. Beat at medium speed, scraping bowl often, until light and fluffy (1 to 2 minutes). Add eggs, one at a time, beating 2 minutes after each addition. Add lemon juice and peel; continue beating until well mixed. In small bowl stir together flour, baking powder and salt. Continue beating butter mixture, alternately adding flour mixture and milk while scraping bowl often, until smooth (1 to 2 minutes). By hand, stir in pecans. Pour into 3 greased 5½x3-inch (mini) loaf pans. Bake for 40 to 45 minutes or until wooden pick inserted in center comes out clean. In small bowl stir together glaze ingredients. Poke holes in top of warm breads with a wooden pick; drizzle glaze evenly over top of breads. Let stand 10 minutes. Remove breads from pans; cool completely. For easier slicing, wrap in aluminum foil and refrigerate 4 hours or overnight. Store refrigerated.

Nutrition Information (1 serving)
• Calories 110 • Protein 2g • Carbohydrate 12g • Fat 6g
• Cholesterol 27mg • Sodium 78mg

Orange Raisin Scones (pictured)
Lemon Nut Bread

Apple Cheese Coffee Cake

60 minutes

Two all-time favorites, apples and cheese, pair up in this moist coffee cake.

Coffee Cake
1½ cups all-purpose flour
½ cup sugar
2 tablespoons butter *or* margarine, melted
½ cup milk
1 egg, slightly beaten
2 teaspoons baking powder
½ teaspoon salt
1 cup (4 ounces) shredded Cheddar cheese
1 cup (1 medium) chopped tart cooking apple

Topping
½ cup all-purpose flour
⅓ cup firmly packed brown sugar
½ teaspoon cinnamon
¼ cup butter *or* margarine, melted

9 servings

Heat oven to 375°. In small mixer bowl combine all coffee cake ingredients *except* cheese and apple. Beat at low speed, scraping bowl often, until well mixed (1 to 2 minutes). By hand, stir in cheese and apple. Spread into greased 9-inch square baking pan. In small bowl combine ½ cup flour, brown sugar and cinnamon. Cut in butter until crumbly; sprinkle over coffee cake batter. Bake for 25 to 35 minutes or until wooden pick inserted in center comes out clean.

Nutrition Information (1 serving)
• Calories 320 • Protein 7g • Carbohydrate 43g • Fat 13g
• Cholesterol 66mg • Sodium 362mg

Apricot Cream Coffee Cake

2 hours

Glistening apricots top this cream cheese-filled coffee cake.

Coffee Cake
1¾ cups all-purpose flour
½ cup sugar
¾ cup butter *or* margarine, softened
2 eggs
½ teaspoon baking powder
½ teaspoon baking soda
¼ teaspoon salt
1 teaspoon vanilla

Filling
¼ cup sugar
1 (8 ounce) package cream cheese, softened
1 egg
1 teaspoon grated lemon peel
1 (10 ounce) jar apricot preserves

Glaze
⅓ cup powdered sugar
2 to 3 teaspoons lemon juice

16 servings

Heat oven to 350°. Grease and flour bottom and sides of 10-inch springform pan. In large mixer bowl combine all coffee cake ingredients. Beat at medium speed, scraping bowl often, until well mixed (1 to 2 minutes). Spread batter over bottom and 2 inches up sides of prepared pan. In small mixer bowl combine all filling ingredients *except* apricot preserves. Beat at medium speed, scraping bowl often, until smooth (2 to 3 minutes). Pour over batter in pan. Spoon preserves evenly over filling. Bake for 45 to 55 minutes or until crust is golden brown. Cool 20 minutes; remove sides of pan. Meanwhile, in small bowl stir together powdered sugar and lemon juice until smooth. Drizzle over warm coffee cake. Serve warm or cold; store refrigerated.

Nutrition Information (1 serving)
• Calories 280 • Protein 4g • Carbohydrate 35g • Fat 15g
• Cholesterol 79mg • Sodium 223mg

Apple Cheese Coffee Cake (left)
Apricot Cream Coffee Cake (right)

Buttery Cinnamon-Nut Bread (top)
Chocolate Mocha Pastry (bottom)

Buttery Cinnamon-Nut Bread

45 minutes

Bread
1 (1 pound) loaf frozen bread dough, thawed
3 tablespoons butter *or* margarine, softened
½ cup sugar

½ cup chopped pecans
1 teaspoon cinnamon

Glaze
½ cup powdered sugar
1 tablespoon milk

10 servings

Heat oven to 375°. Press thawed bread dough on bottom of greased 15x10x1-inch jelly roll pan. Spread dough with butter; prick with fork. In small bowl stir together sugar, pecans and cinnamon; sprinkle evenly over dough. Bake for 18 to 23 minutes or until golden brown.

In small bowl stir together glaze ingredients; drizzle over warm bread. Cut into squares or triangles; serve warm.

Nutrition Information (1 serving)
• Calories 250 • Protein 4g • Carbohydrate 38g • Fat 10g
• Cholesterol 12mg • Sodium 257mg

Chocolate Mocha Pastry

1 hour 30 minutes

Pastry
½ cup butter *or* margarine
1 cup all-purpose flour
2 tablespoons water
¼ cup semi-sweet miniature real chocolate chips

Topping
1 cup water
½ cup butter *or* margarine
1 cup all-purpose flour
1 teaspoon vanilla
3 eggs

Glaze
1 teaspoon instant coffee granules
2 tablespoons warm water
1½ cups powdered sugar
2 tablespoons butter *or* margarine, softened

¼ cup semi-sweet miniature real chocolate chips
1 teaspoon vegetable oil

2 pastries (16 servings)

Heat oven to 350°. In large bowl cut ½ cup butter into 1 cup flour until crumbly. With fork mix in 2 tablespoons water. Gather pastry into ball; divide into 2 equal portions. On cookie sheet pat each portion into 12x3-inch rectangle about 3 inches apart. Sprinkle 2 tablespoons chocolate chips over each half; press gently. In 2-quart saucepan combine 1 cup water and ½ cup butter. Cook over medium heat until mixture comes to a full boil (6 to 8 minutes). Remove from heat; stir in 1 cup flour and vanilla. Cook over low heat, stirring constantly, until mixture forms a ball (about 1 minute). Remove from heat. By hand, beat in eggs until smooth and glossy. Spread half of egg mixture over each rectangle. Bake for 50 to 55 minutes or

until surface is crisp and golden brown; cool completely. (Topping rises during baking and shrinks during standing forming a custardlike layer.) In small bowl dissolve coffee in 2 tablespoons warm water; stir in powdered sugar and 2 tablespoons butter. Spread each cooled pastry with about ¼ cup glaze. In 1-quart saucepan combine ¼ cup chocolate chips and oil. Cook over medium low heat, stirring constantly, until melted (2 to 4 minutes). Drizzle ½ of mixture crosswise over each pastry; pull knife through drizzle lengthwise 3 times to create design. Cut each pastry into 1-inch slices.

Nutrition Information (1 serving)
• Calories 250 • Protein 3g • Carbohydrate 24g • Fat 16g
• Cholesterol 87mg • Sodium 146mg

Orange Almond Braided Coffee Cake

Orange Almond Braided Coffee Cake

3 hours 30 minutes

Tender pastry encloses the moist orange almond filling.

Coffee Cake
1 cup milk
¼ cup butter *or* margarine
1 (¼ ounce) package active dry yeast
¼ cup warm water (105 to 115°F)
3½ to 4½ cups all-purpose flour
¼ cup sugar
1 egg
1 teaspoon salt

Filling
1 (3½ ounce) package almond paste
¼ cup firmly packed brown sugar
¼ cup butter *or* margarine, softened
¼ teaspoon grated orange peel

Glaze
1 cup powdered sugar
2 to 3 tablespoons milk
½ teaspoon almond extract
¼ teaspoon grated orange peel

2 coffee cakes (16 servings)

In 1-quart saucepan heat milk over medium heat until just comes to a boil (5 to 7 minutes); stir in ¼ cup butter until melted. Cool to warm (105 to 115°F). In large mixer bowl dissolve yeast in warm water. Add cooled milk mixture, 2 cups flour, sugar, egg and salt. Beat at medium speed, scraping bowl often, until smooth (1 to 2 minutes). Stir in enough remaining flour to make dough easy to handle. Turn dough onto lightly floured surface; knead until smooth and elastic (about 10 minutes). Place in greased bowl; turn greased side up. Cover; let rise in warm place until double in size (about 1½ hours). Dough is ready if indentation remains when touched. Punch down dough. In small mixer bowl combine all filling ingredients. Beat at medium speed, scraping bowl often, until well mixed (1 to 2 minutes). Divide dough into 2 equal portions. On lightly floured surface roll one portion into a 10-inch square; cut square into three 10x3-inch rectangles. Spread about 2 tablespoons filling down center of each rectangle to within ½ inch of edge on all sides. Bring long sides together over filling; pinch sides and ends tightly to seal. Gently braid 3 filled pieces together to make 1 coffee cake. Pinch ends together to seal; tuck ends under braid. Repeat with remaining portion of dough to make second coffee cake. Transfer both coffee cakes to greased cookie sheet. Cover; let rise until double in size (30 to 40 minutes). *Heat oven to 350°.* Bake for 20 to 30 minutes or until golden brown. In small bowl stir together all glaze ingredients. Drizzle over warm coffee cakes.

Nutrition Information (1 serving)
• Calories 250 • Protein 5g • Carbohydrate 37g • Fat 9g
• Cholesterol 35mg • Sodium 210mg

In 1791, George Washington stopped to see his friend Colonel John Allen. Although Mrs. Allen wasn't expecting guests, she soon rustled up this breakfast: a young pig, a turkey, ham, fried chicken, sausage, waffles, batter cakes, eggs and hot soda biscuits. When Washington sat down at the table he asked only for one hard-boiled egg and coffee with rum.

Old World Kolachi

Tender buttery pastries filled with fruit preserves — just like Gramma's.

1 (¼ ounce) package active dry yeast
¼ cup warm water (105 to 115°F)
3¼ to 3½ cups all-purpose flour
½ teaspoon salt
1 cup butter *or* margarine, softened

1 cup whipping cream
2 eggs, slightly beaten

1 (10 ounce) jar fruit preserves

2½ dozen

In small bowl dissolve yeast in warm water. In large bowl combine flour and salt; cut in butter until crumbly. Stir in yeast, whipping cream and eggs. Turn dough onto lightly floured surface; knead until smooth (2 to 3 minutes). Place in greased bowl; turn greased side up. Cover; refrigerate until firm (6 hours or overnight). *Heat oven to 375°.* Roll out dough, ¼ at a time, on sugared surface to ⅛-inch thickness. Cut into 3-inch squares. Spoon 1 teaspoon preserves in center of each square. Bring up two opposite corners to center; pinch firmly together to seal. Place 1 inch apart on cookie sheets. Bake for 10 to 15 minutes or until lightly browned.

Nutrition Information (1 kolachi)
• Calories 160 • Protein 2g • Carbohydrate 17g • Fat 10g
• Cholesterol 46mg • Sodium 108mg

To Prepare Old World Kolachi:

1. Roll out dough, ¼ at a time, on sugared surface to ⅛-inch thickness. Cut into 3-inch squares. Spoon 1 teaspoon preserves in center of each square.

2. Bring up two opposite corners to center; pinch firmly together to seal.

Old World Kolachi

Dijon Chicken
With Double Cheese Bake

7 hours 30 minutes

An easy do-ahead chicken dish. Prepare the day before, then bake the day of the brunch.

6   cups cubed 1-inch French bread
2   cups shredded cooked chicken
2   cups (8 ounces) sliced ¼-inch fresh
    mushrooms
1½ cups (6 ounces) shredded Cheddar cheese
1½ cups (6 ounces) shredded Mozzarella
    cheese

10   eggs
1⅓ cups milk
⅓   cup dry white wine *or* chicken broth
½   cup chopped green onions
¼   cup Dijon-style mustard
¼   teaspoon pepper

10 servings

In greased 13x9-inch baking pan place bread. Layer with chicken, mushrooms and cheeses. Meanwhile, in large bowl whisk together all remaining ingredients. Pour over layered chicken mixture. Cover; refrigerate 6 hours or overnight. *Heat oven to 325°.* Uncover; bake for 50 to 60 minutes or until set in center. Let stand 10 minutes.

Nutrition Information (1 serving)
• Calories 360 • Protein 27g • Carbohydrate 19g • Fat 18g
• Cholesterol 331mg • Sodium 641mg

Crisp Cucumber n' Melon
Chicken Salad

2 hours 30 minutes

Fresh herbs flavor this creamy, fruited chicken salad.

Dressing
½   cup whipping cream
½   cup mayonnaise
2   tablespoons chopped fresh dill*
1   teaspoon chopped fresh tarragon leaves**
¼   teaspoon salt
⅛   teaspoon pepper
1   teaspoon grated lime peel

Salad
4   cups cubed ½-inch cooked chicken
2   cups cubed ½-inch honeydew *or* cantaloupe
½   cup toasted slivered almonds
1   medium cucumber, peeled, sliced,
    cut in half

6 servings

In chilled small mixer bowl beat chilled whipping cream at high speed, scraping bowl often, until stiff peaks form (1 to 2 minutes). Gradually fold in mayonnaise; stir in all remaining dressing ingredients. In large bowl combine all salad ingredients. Add dressing; toss to coat. Refrigerate 2 hours before serving.

*2 teaspoons dried dill weed can be substituted for 2 tablespoons chopped fresh dill.

**¼ teaspoon dried tarragon leaves can be substituted for 1 teaspoon chopped fresh tarragon leaves.

Nutrition Information (1 serving)
• Calories 460 • Protein 30g • Carbohydrate 10g • Fat 34g
• Cholesterol 121mg • Sodium 291mg

Dijon Chicken With Double Cheese Bake (pictured)
Crisp Cucumber n' Melon Chicken Salad

Egg & Bacon Topped Croissant (top)
Ham n' Apple Bagels (bottom)

Egg & Bacon Topped Croissant

45 minutes

This layered breakfast sandwich is topped with a creamy hollandaise sauce.

Hollandaise Sauce
¼ cup water
3 egg yolks
¾ cup butter, melted
1½ tablespoons lemon juice
Salt and pepper

Croissant
4 croissants, split
Butter, softened
8 slices crisply cooked bacon
8 poached eggs

2 tablespoons chopped fresh chives

4 servings

In 1-quart saucepan whisk together water and egg yolks until frothy. Cook over *very low* heat, whisking constantly, until mixture is thickened (7 to 12 minutes). Remove from heat; very slowly whisk in ¾ cup melted butter. Stir in lemon juice, salt and pepper to taste. *Heat broiler.* Spread croissants with butter; place, butter side up, on cookie sheet. Broil 5 to 7 inches from heat until light golden brown (1 to 2 minutes). On each of 4 individual plates place bottom croissant half; top with 2 slices bacon and 2 poached eggs. Spoon hollandaise sauce over poached eggs; sprinkle with chives. Place remaining top croissant halves over sauce. Serve with remaining hollandaise sauce.

Tip: To keep hollandaise sauce warm place saucepan over hot, not boiling, water. Stir occasionally.

Nutrition Information (1 serving)
• Calories 760 • Protein 23g • Carbohydrate 21g • Fat 65g
• Cholesterol 739mg • Sodium 829mg

Ham n' Apple Bagels

30 minutes

Prepare these cinnamon-glazed bagels stacked with ham, apple and cheese just before serving.

¼ cup butter *or* margarine
¼ cup firmly packed brown sugar
½ teaspoon cinnamon
1 tablespoon water
2 cinnamon raisin bagels, cut in half

1 tart cooking apple, cored, cut into 4 (½-inch) rings
8 slices (4 ounces) shaved cooked ham
8 (3x1x⅛-inch) slices Cheddar cheese

4 servings

In 10-inch skillet melt butter. Stir in brown sugar, cinnamon and water. Cook over medium heat, stirring constantly, until mixture just comes to a boil. Boil, stirring constantly, 1 minute. Remove from heat. Dip cut side of bagel halves in brown sugar mixture. Place cut side up on cookie sheet; set aside. Add apple rings to remaining brown sugar mixture. Cook over medium heat, turning once or twice, until apple rings are crisply tender (2 to 5 minutes). *Heat broiler.* Broil bagel halves 5 to 7 inches from heat until lightly toasted (1 to 1½ minutes). Top each bagel half with 1 apple ring and 2 slices shaved ham; return to broiler. Continue broiling until heated through (1 to 2 minutes). Top each with 2 strips cheese; return to broiler. Continue broiling until cheese is melted (1 to 2 minutes).

Nutrition Information (1 serving)
• Calories 400 • Protein 16g • Carbohydrate 32g • Fat 24g
• Cholesterol 76mg • Sodium 780mg

Salmon Pinwheels With Melon Puree (pictured)
Ham & Broccoli Strata

Salmon Pinwheels With Melon Puree

3 hours

Salmon

3 pounds (1¼-inch thick) salmon fillets, skinned
1 cup dry white wine *or* water
½ teaspoon salt
½ teaspoon coarsely ground pepper
1 bay leaf
1 lemon, thinly sliced
1 cup (1 medium) thinly sliced cucumber

Melon Puree

1 cantaloupe, halved, seeded
1 honeydew, halved, seeded
¼ teaspoon salt
2 teaspoons chopped fresh tarragon leaves*
1 teaspoon grated lemon peel
1 teaspoon grated lime peel

8 servings

Slice salmon fillets lengthwise and slightly on a diagonal into long (1½-inch wide) strips. To form pinwheels, hold down thick end of salmon strip, curl strip around to form pinwheel; secure with wooden picks. In 10-inch skillet bring all remaining salmon ingredients *except* cucumber to a full boil. Add salmon pinwheels. Cover; cook over medium heat, turning once, until salmon flakes with a fork (6 to 8 minutes). Add cucumber slices; continue cooking until cucumber is crisply tender (30 to 60 seconds). Remove salmon and cucumber; let stand 10 minutes. Cover; refrigerate at least 2 hours to chill. Meanwhile, cut half of cantaloupe and half of honeydew into 1-inch pieces. In 5-cup blender container place cantaloupe pieces. Blend on High speed until pureed (2 to 3 minutes). Stir in ⅛ *teaspoon* salt, *1 teaspoon* tarragon and lemon peel. Pour into medium bowl; refrigerate 30 minutes. Repeat with honeydew pieces. Stir in remaining ⅛ teaspoon salt, 1 teaspoon tarragon and lime peel. Refrigerate 30 minutes. If melon puree becomes watery, drain excess moisture through paper towel lined strainer. Remove wooden picks from salmon. Meanwhile, peel remaining halves of cantaloupe and honeydew; slice into very thin wedges. To serve, arrange salmon pinwheels on cantaloupe and honeydew puree. Garnish with cantaloupe and honeydew wedges and cooked cucumber slices.

*½ teaspoon dried tarragon leaves can be substituted for 2 teaspoons chopped fresh tarragon leaves.

Nutrition Information (1 serving)
• Calories 350 • Protein 35g • Carbohydrate 22g • Fat 11g
• Cholesterol 94mg • Sodium 299mg

Ham & Broccoli Strata

9 hours 30 minutes

12 slices white bread
12 ounces sharp Cheddar cheese, cut into ¼-inch slices
1 (10 ounce) package frozen chopped broccoli, thawed, drained
2 cups chopped cooked ham *or* Canadian bacon

3 cups milk
6 eggs
1¼ teaspoons dry mustard
2 tablespoons finely chopped onion

12 servings

With 3-inch cookie cutter cut a design out of each bread slice; set aside. Tear remaining bread into pieces; place in bottom of greased 13x9-inch baking pan. Layer with sliced cheese, broccoli, ham and bread cutouts. In medium bowl beat together all remaining ingredients. Pour evenly over mixture in pan. Cover with plastic wrap; refrigerate 8 hours or overnight. *Heat oven to 350°.* Uncover; bake for 60 to 75 minutes or until set and golden brown. If browning too quickly, loosely cover with aluminum foil. Let stand 15 minutes.

Nutrition Information (1 serving)
• Calories 300 • Protein 20g • Carbohydrate 19g • Fat 16g
• Cholesterol 155mg • Sodium 168mg

Seafood in Patty Shells

60 minutes

Shrimp and crabmeat in a rich and creamy butter sauce served in tender, flaky patty shells.

1 (10 ounce) package frozen patty shells, baked *or* 6 bakery patty shells

Seafood
¼ cup butter *or* margarine
1 cup sliced ¼-inch fresh mushrooms
¼ cup sliced ¼-inch green onions
1 (10 ounce) package frozen deveined cocktail size (1½-inch) raw shrimp, thawed, drained
1 (6 ounce) package frozen crab, thawed, drained

Sauce
¼ cup butter *or* margarine
⅓ cup all-purpose flour
1½ cups half-and-half
¼ cup white wine *or* apple juice
1 teaspoon lemon juice
1 tablespoon chopped fresh dill
¼ teaspoon salt
¼ teaspoon hot pepper sauce

6 servings

Have patty shells ready. In 2-quart saucepan melt ¼ cup butter. Stir in mushrooms, green onions and shrimp. Cook over medium heat until seafood is tender (4 to 6 minutes). Stir in crab. Pour seafood into medium bowl; set aside. In same saucepan melt ¼ cup butter. Stir in flour until smooth and bubbly (1 minute). Stir in all remaining sauce ingredients. Cook over medium heat until mixture comes to a full boil (4 to 6 minutes). Stir in seafood mixture. Continue cooking until seafood is heated through (4 to 5 minutes). To serve, pour ¾ cup creamed seafood into each patty shell.

Nutrition Information (1 serving)
• Calories 530 • Protein 20g • Carbohydrate 26g • Fat 38g
• Cholesterol 147mg • Sodium 759mg

Crab, Mushroom & Leek Tart

1 hour 30 minutes

Pastry
1¼ cups all-purpose flour
⅛ teaspoon salt
½ cup butter *or* margarine
3 to 4 tablespoons cold water

Filling
3 tablespoons butter *or* margarine
2 cups (8 ounces) sliced ¼-inch fresh mushrooms

½ cup sliced leeks *or* chopped onion
1 cup whipping cream
1 (6 ounce) package frozen cooked crab, thawed, well drained
2 egg yolks, slightly beaten
½ teaspoon salt
¼ teaspoon pepper
⅛ to ¼ teaspoon hot pepper sauce

8 servings

Heat oven to 400°. In small bowl combine flour and ⅛ teaspoon salt. Cut in ½ cup butter until crumbly; with fork mix in water. Form into ball. On lightly floured surface roll pastry into 14-inch circle. Place in greased 12-inch tart pan; press into and against sides of pan. Cut away excess pastry; prick with fork. Bake for 12 to 14 minutes or until lightly browned. Meanwhile, in 10-inch skillet melt 3 tablespoons butter. Add mushrooms and leeks. Cook over medium heat until vegetables are tender (4 to 5 minutes). Remove from heat. In small bowl stir together whipping cream, crab, egg yolks, salt, pepper and hot pepper sauce. Stir into mushroom mixture. Pour into baked pastry shell. Bake for 18 to 22 minutes or until set and golden brown.

Nutrition Information (1 serving)
• Calories 400 • Protein 8g • Carbohydrate 18g • Fat 29g
• Cholesterol 161mg • Sodium 524mg

Seafood in Patty Shells (pictured)
Crab, Mushroom & Leek Tart

Quiche Lorraine Squares (pictured)
Fresh Tomato & Asparagus Frittata

Quiche Lorraine Squares

2 hours

Traditional quiche made for a crowd.

Crust
2 cups all-purpose flour
¼ teaspoon salt
⅔ cup shortening
4 to 5 tablespoons cold water

Filling
1 egg, separated
3 cups (12 ounces) shredded Swiss cheese

1 pound crisply cooked bacon, crumbled
¼ cup sliced ⅛-inch green onions
4 cups (1 quart) half-and-half
6 eggs
½ teaspoon salt
¼ teaspoon nutmeg
¼ teaspoon pepper
  Dash cayenne pepper

12 servings

Heat oven to 375°. In large bowl stir together flour and ¼ teaspoon salt. Cut in shortening until crumbly. With fork mix in water just until moistened. Form into ball. On lightly floured surface roll into 16x12-inch rectangle. Place on bottom and up sides of 13x9-inch baking pan; crimp or flute crust. In small bowl beat egg white with fork until frothy; brush on pastry. Sprinkle cheese over pastry; sprinkle with bacon and green onions. In large bowl whisk together all remaining ingredients and reserved egg yolk; pour over bacon and green onions.

Bake for 35 to 50 minutes or until knife inserted in center comes out clean. Let stand 15 minutes.

Tip: Two (10-inch) quiche pans or 2 (9-inch) pie pans can be substituted for 13x9-inch baking pan. Roll pastry into 2 (12-inch) circles. Assemble as directed above. Bake for 30 to 45 minutes or until knife inserted in center comes out clean.

Nutrition Information (1 serving)
• Calories 480 • Protein 18g • Carbohydrate 21g • Fat 36g
• Cholesterol 222mg • Sodium 816mg

Fresh Tomato & Asparagus Frittata

30 minutes

Serve this beautiful egg dish at the table, right from the skillet.

½ pound fresh asparagus spears, trimmed
¼ cup butter *or* margarine
1 cup sliced fresh mushrooms
½ cup (1 medium) chopped onion
6 eggs

8 slices bacon, cooked, crumbled
1 small ripe tomato, sliced
1 cup (4 ounces) shredded Cheddar cheese

4 servings

In 10-inch skillet place asparagus spears; add enough water to cover. Bring to a full boil. Cook over medium heat until crisply tender (5 to 7 minutes). Drain; set aside. In same skillet melt butter. Add mushrooms and onion; cook over medium heat until tender (3 to 4 minutes). In medium bowl beat eggs until frothy; stir in bacon. Pour into skillet. Stir gently over medium heat to cook evenly on bottom (3 to 4

minutes). As egg mixture sets, lift edges with spatula to allow uncooked egg to flow underneath. Arrange tomato slices and asparagus on top. Cover; continue cooking until eggs are set (4 to 5 minutes). Sprinkle with cheese; cut into wedges.

Nutrition Information (1 serving)
• Calories 430 • Protein 23g • Carbohydrate 6g • Fat 36g
• Cholesterol 484mg • Sodium 602mg

Broccoli n' Cheese Oven Omelet

30 minutes

Omelets for six, done the easy way, in the oven.

¼ cup chopped onion
¼ cup chopped green pepper
⅓ cup milk
6 eggs, separated
¼ teaspoon salt
⅛ teaspoon pepper
1 tablespoon butter *or* margarine

2 cups frozen cut broccoli and vegetable combination
½ cup (2 ounces) shredded Cheddar *or* Swiss cheese

6 servings

Heat oven to 325°. In medium bowl stir together onion, green pepper, milk, egg yolks, salt and pepper. In large mixer bowl beat egg whites at high speed, scraping bowl often, until stiff peaks form (1 to 2 minutes). Fold egg yolk mixture into egg whites just until mixed. In 10-inch ovenproof skillet melt butter. Pour egg mixture into skillet. Cook over medium heat until edges begin to set (3 to 4 minutes).

Remove from heat; bake for 10 to 15 minutes or until puffed and eggs are set in center. Meanwhile, prepare frozen vegetables according to package directions; drain. Spoon vegetables on top of omelet; sprinkle with cheese.

Nutrition Information (1 serving)
• Calories 160 • Protein 10g • Carbohydrate 6g • Fat 11g
• Cholesterol 291mg • Sodium 254mg

Cheese & Mushroom Oven Omelet

45 minutes

Cheddar cheese, bacon and mushrooms fill this popular breakfast entrée.

2 tablespoons butter *or* margarine
2 cups (8 ounces) sliced fresh mushrooms*
6 eggs
⅓ cup milk
2 tablespoons all-purpose flour

⅛ teaspoon pepper
1½ cups (6 ounces) shredded Cheddar cheese
¼ cup (6 slices) crumbled cooked bacon

6 servings

Heat oven to 350°. In 10-inch skillet melt butter; add mushrooms. Cook over medium heat, stirring occasionally, until mushrooms are tender (4 to 6 minutes); drain. Set aside. In medium bowl combine eggs, milk, flour and pepper. Beat with wire whisk or fork until frothy. Stir in *1 cup* cheese, bacon and mushrooms. Pour into buttered 9-inch square baking pan. Sprinkle with remaining cheese. Bake for 20 to 25 minutes or until eggs are set in center.

*1 (4 ounce) can sliced mushrooms, drained, can be substituted for 2 cups (8 ounces) sliced fresh mushrooms.

Microwave Directions: In 9-inch pie plate melt butter on HIGH (30 to 40 seconds). Stir in mushrooms. Cover with plastic wrap; microwave on HIGH, stirring after half the time, until mushrooms are tender (2 to 3 minutes). Drain; set aside. In medium bowl combine eggs, milk, flour and pepper. Beat with wire whisk or fork until frothy. Stir in *1 cup* cheese, bacon and mushrooms. Pour into same pie plate. Microwave on HIGH, stirring after half the time, until eggs are set in center (3½ to 5½ minutes). Sprinkle with remaining cheese. Let stand 2 minutes.

Nutrition Information (1 serving)
• Calories 290 • Protein 17g • Carbohydrate 5g • Fat 22g
• Cholesterol 321mg • Sodium 393mg

Broccoli n' Cheese Oven Omelet (pictured)
Cheese & Mushroom Oven Omelet

Spinach-Filled Puff Pancake

45 minutes

This oven pancake is the perfect dish for a hearty spinach and cheese filling.

Pancake
2 tablespoons butter *or* margarine
⅔ cup all-purpose flour
¾ cup milk
2 eggs
½ teaspoon salt

Filling
2 tablespoons butter *or* margarine
1 teaspoon chopped fresh dill*

¼ teaspoon pepper
2 cups (8 ounces) sliced ¼-inch fresh
    mushrooms
1 medium onion, cut into ¼-inch rings
½ cup red *or* green pepper, cut into ½-inch
    pieces
1 (10 ounce) package chopped frozen
    spinach, thawed, well drained
1 cup (4 ounces) shredded Cheddar cheese
                                        6 servings

Heat oven to 400°. In 9-inch glass pie plate melt 2 tablespoons butter in oven (2 to 4 minutes). In large bowl combine flour, milk, eggs and salt. Using wire whisk or rotary beater, beat until smooth (2 to 3 minutes). Pour batter into pie plate. Bake for 20 to 25 minutes or until golden brown. Meanwhile, in 10-inch skillet melt 2 tablespoons butter. Stir in dill and pepper. Add mushrooms, onion and red pepper. Cook over medium heat, stirring occasionally, until vegetables are tender (5 to 7 minutes). Stir in spinach. Continue cooking until heated through (3 to 4 minutes). Spoon filling into center of hot pancake; sprinkle with cheese. Cut into wedges; serve immediately.

*¼ teaspoon dried dill weed can be substituted for 1 teaspoon fresh dill.

Tip: Uneven or irregular edges are common when making a puff pancake.

Nutrition Information (1 serving)
• Calories 270 • Protein 12g • Carbohydrate 18g • Fat 17g
• Cholesterol 134mg • Sodium 449mg

Ham & Cheese Potato Pie

60 minutes

Chilies, ham and onion flavor this potato main dish.

1 (16 ounce) package (4 cups) frozen
    hash brown potato cubes, thawed
1 cup cubed ½-inch cooked ham
1 cup (4 ounces) shredded Monterey
    Jack cheese
¼ cup chopped green onions
1 (4 ounce) can chopped green chilies, drained

¾ cup milk
6 eggs
¼ teaspoon salt
⅛ teaspoon pepper
½ cup (2 ounces) shredded Cheddar cheese
                                        6 servings

Heat oven to 350°. In greased 13x9-inch baking pan spread potatoes. Top with ham, Monterey Jack cheese, green onions and chilies. In medium bowl combine milk, eggs, salt and pepper; beat with wire whisk or fork until frothy. Pour over potatoes. Bake for 30 minutes; sprinkle with Cheddar cheese. Continue baking for 5 to 10 minutes or until eggs are set.

Nutrition Information (1 serving)
• Calories 310 • Protein 21g • Carbohydrate 18g • Fat 17g
• Cholesterol 317mg • Sodium 635mg

Spinach-Filled Puff Pancake (pictured)
Ham & Cheese Potato Pie

Piña Colada Fruit Dip (pictured)
Baked Ambrosia in a Cup

Piña Colada Fruit Dip

2 hours 15 minutes

Fresh fruit dipped in a "taste of the tropics."

½ cup flaked coconut, toasted, reserve
   1 tablespoon
1 (16 ounce) carton (2 cups) dairy sour
   cream
1 (8 ounce) can crushed pineapple, drained
2 tablespoons firmly packed brown sugar

1 to 2 tablespoons rum *or* reserved
   pineapple juice
   Assorted fresh fruit (red *or* green apple
   slices, pear slices, strawberries, pineapple
   wedges, grapes, etc.)

2 cups

In medium bowl stir together all ingredients *except* fresh fruit and reserved 1 tablespoon coconut. Cover; refrigerate at least 2 hours. Garnish with reserved coconut. Serve with assorted fresh fruit.

Nutrition Information (1 tablespoon dip)
• Calories 30 • Protein 1g • Carbohydrate 4g • Fat 1g
• Cholesterol 2mg • Sodium 17mg

Baked Ambrosia in a Cup

45 minutes

This fresh fruit is sweetened with honey and baked in an orange cup.

2 large oranges
1 cup fresh pineapple chunks*
2 tablespoons firmly packed brown sugar
1 tablespoon honey

2 tablespoons flaked coconut

Pomegranate seeds *or* maraschino cherries

4 servings

Heat oven to 350°. Cut oranges in half crosswise. With small serrated knife remove fruit. Separate orange sections. In medium bowl toss together orange sections, pineapple, brown sugar and honey. Spoon into orange cups. Place filled cups in 9-inch square baking pan. Bake for 15 minutes. Sprinkle with coconut. Continue baking for 5 to 10 minutes or until fruit is heated through and coconut is lightly browned. Sprinkle with pomegranate seeds or top each with a maraschino cherry.

*1 (8 ounce) can pineapple chunks can be substituted for 1 cup fresh pineapple chunks.

Microwave Directions: Place coconut in 9-inch square baking dish. Microwave on HIGH, stirring every minute, until toasted (2½ to 4 minutes); set aside. Prepare cups as directed above. Place filled cups in 9-inch square baking dish. Microwave on HIGH until heated through (4 to 6 minutes). Sprinkle with toasted coconut. Sprinkle with pomegranate seeds or top each with a maraschino cherry.

Nutrition Information (1 serving)
• Calories 120 • Protein 1g • Carbohydrate 29g • Fat 1g
• Cholesterol 0mg • Sodium 3mg

On the frontier, Americans drank all sorts of "coffees" including those made from dry brown bread crusts, roasted horse beans, yellow beet root, acorns, dandelion roots and chicory. When Abe Lincoln was served one of these strange "coffees," he is supposed to have said, "If this is coffee, please bring me some tea."

Devonshire-Style Fruit

30 minutes

Layered fresh fruit, sour cream and brown sugar make a delightful salad or dessert.

½ cup dairy sour cream
2 teaspoons favorite liqueur, optional

3 cups cut-up fruit (seedless grapes, mandarin orange segments, pineapple, kiwi, strawberries, blueberries, etc.)
3 tablespoons firmly packed brown sugar

4 servings

In small bowl stir together sour cream and liqueur. Up to 1 hour before serving, place about ⅓ cup fruit in bottom of four tall dessert or parfait glasses; top each with 1 tablespoon sour cream mixture and about 1 teaspoon brown sugar. Repeat layering one more time, finishing with sour cream mixture and brown sugar. Refrigerate until ready to serve.

Nutrition Information (1 serving)
• Calories 170 • Protein 2g • Carbohydrate 27g • Fat 7g
• Cholesterol 13mg • Sodium 21mg

Ginger Glazed Fruit

60 minutes

Gingerroot adds a special flavor to this fresh fruit salad.

3 tablespoons sugar
2 teaspoons cornstarch
　Dash salt
½ cup apple juice
¼ teaspoon grated fresh gingerroot
½ teaspoon lemon juice

6 cups cut-up fresh fruit (cantaloupe, strawberries, pineapple, bananas, apples, etc.)

6 servings

In 1-quart saucepan combine sugar, cornstarch and salt. Stir in apple juice, gingerroot and lemon juice. Cook over medium heat, stirring constantly, until mixture comes to a full boil (7 to 8 minutes). Boil 1 minute. Cool completely. In large serving bowl combine fruit. Add dressing; stir gently to coat.

Tip: Cantaloupe or pineapple shells can be used as serving bowls.

Microwave Directions: In 2-cup measure combine sugar, cornstarch and salt. Stir in apple juice, gingerroot and lemon juice. Microwave on HIGH, stirring every minute, until mixture comes to a full boil (2½ to 3½ minutes). Cool completely. In large serving bowl combine fruit. Add dressing; stir gently to coat.

Nutrition Information (1 serving)
• Calories 120 • Protein 1g • Carbohydrate 29g • Fat 1g
• Cholesterol 0mg • Sodium 29mg

Devonshire-Style Fruit (top)
Ginger Glazed Fruit (bottom)

Orange Laced Fruit Compote

9 hours

Serve this dried fruit compote, glazed with orange marmalade, warm or cold.

2 (8 ounce) packages mixed dried fruit
½ cup orange marmalade

½ cup dry white wine *or* orange juice
½ cup water

8 servings

In 9-inch square baking pan place fruit. In small bowl stir together all remaining ingredients. Pour over fruit; stir gently to mix. Cover; refrigerate, stirring occasionally, 8 hours or overnight. *Heat oven to 350°.* Uncover; bake for 30 to 45 minutes or until syrup is bubbly and slightly thickened. Serve warm or cold. Store refrigerated.

Microwave Directions: *Reduce ½ cup water to ¼ cup.* In 9-inch square baking dish place fruit. In small bowl stir together all remaining ingredients. Pour over fruit; stir gently to mix. Cover with plastic wrap; refrigerate, stirring occasionally, 8 hours or overnight. Microwave on HIGH, stirring after half the time, until syrup is bubbly and slightly thickened (8 to 11 minutes). Serve warm or cold. Store refrigerated.

Nutrition Information (1 serving)
• Calories 200 • Protein 2g • Carbohydrate 51g • Fat 0g
• Cholesterol 0mg • Sodium 14mg

Orange Poppy Seed Fruit Salad

20 minutes

This refreshing dressing adds spark to fresh fruit.

2 tablespoons orange juice
½ cup dairy sour cream
1½ teaspoons sugar
½ teaspoon poppy seed
¼ teaspoon grated orange peel

4 cups fresh fruit, cut up

6 servings

In medium bowl stir together all ingredients *except* fresh fruit. Refrigerate until ready to serve. Serve over fresh fruit.

Tip: Dressing can be served poured over fresh melon slices.

Nutrition Information (1 serving)
• Calories 120 • Protein 1g • Carbohydrate 19g • Fat 5g
• Cholesterol 9mg • Sodium 12mg

In the 1920s a young wife described breakfast: "A farmer's breakfast was a big meal, as big as dinner or supper. Along with 4 to 6 six-inch pancakes, dripping with butter and drizzled with syrup, a man might eat several strips of home-cured bacon, a slice of ham or pork sausage patties, and hash browned potatoes and fried eggs. He also drank milk, along with cup after cup of hot coffee."

Orange Laced Fruit Compote (pictured)
Orange Poppy Seed Fruit Salad

Fresh Green Beans With Mushrooms & Celery (top)
Layered Artichoke & Tomato Bake (bottom)

Fresh Green Beans With Mushrooms & Celery   35 minutes

Mushrooms, celery and almonds make these green beans special.

1½ cups water
1 pound fresh green beans, trimmed
¼ cup butter *or* margarine
1 cup (2 stalks) diagonally sliced ¼-inch celery

2 cups (8 ounces) sliced ¼-inch fresh
  mushrooms
¼ cup sliced almonds
  Salt and pepper

6 servings

In 10-inch skillet place water. Bring to full boil; add beans. Cook over medium heat, stirring occasionally, until beans begin to cook (7 to 8 minutes). Drain; return beans to pan. Add butter and celery. Continue cooking, stirring occasionally, 4 minutes. Add mushrooms; continue cooking, stirring occasionally, until vegetables are crisply tender (4 to 5 minutes). Stir in almonds. Season to taste with salt and pepper.

Microwave Directions: *Reduce 1½ cups water to ¼ cup.* In 9-inch pie plate melt 1 tablespoon butter on HIGH (30 to 40 seconds). Add mushrooms. Cover; microwave on HIGH, stirring after half the time, until mushrooms are tender (1½ to 3 minutes). Set aside. In 2-quart casserole place ¼ cup water and beans. Cover; microwave on HIGH, stirring after half the time, until beans begin to cook (7 to 9 minutes). Stir in celery. Cover; microwave on HIGH, stirring after half the time, until vegetables are crisply tender (2 to 5 minutes). Drain. Stir in mushrooms, almonds and remaining 3 tablespoons butter. Season to taste with salt and pepper.

Nutrition Information (1 serving)
• Calories 130 • Protein 3g • Carbohydrate 9g • Fat 10g
• Cholesterol 21mg • Sodium 85mg

Layered Artichoke & Tomato Bake   45 minutes

Parmesan crumbs top artichoke hearts and tomatoes.

3 tablespoons butter *or* margarine
1 (9 ounce) package frozen artichoke hearts,
  thawed, drained
2 ripe tomatoes, each cut into 8 wedges

Crumb Topping
½ cup dried crumbly style herb seasoned
  stuffing
¼ cup freshly grated Parmesan cheese
2 tablespoons butter *or* margarine
¼ teaspoon salt

6 servings

Heat oven to 350°. In 9-inch square baking pan melt 3 tablespoons butter in oven (5 to 6 minutes). Stir in artichokes and tomatoes. In small bowl stir together all crumb topping ingredients. Sprinkle crumb topping over vegetables. Bake for 25 to 30 minutes or until heated through.

Microwave Directions: In 2-cup measure melt 2 tablespoons butter on HIGH (30 to 40 seconds). Stir in all remaining crumb topping ingredients; set aside. In 9-inch square baking dish melt 3 tablespoons butter on HIGH (40 to 50 seconds). Stir in artichokes. Cover with plastic wrap; microwave on HIGH, stirring after half the time, until artichokes are crisply tender (3 to 5 minutes). Stir in tomatoes; sprinkle with crumb topping. Cover with plastic wrap; microwave on HIGH until heated through (3 to 5 minutes).

Nutrition Information (1 serving)
• Calories 170 • Protein 5g • Carbohydrate 13g • Fat 12g
• Cholesterol 30mg • Sodium 442mg

Wild Rice Breakfast Cakes

30 minutes

Serve these rice cakes with breakfast meats and country scrambled eggs.

1 cup cooked converted rice*
1 cup cooked wild rice
½ cup chopped red pepper
½ cup dried bread crumbs
2 eggs, slightly beaten
½ teaspoon salt

¼ teaspoon coarsely ground pepper
2 tablespoons chopped fresh parsley
½ teaspoon finely chopped fresh garlic
3 tablespoons butter *or* margarine

9 servings

In medium bowl stir together all ingredients *except* butter. In 10-inch skillet heat *1 tablespoon* butter until sizzling. Cooking 3 rice cakes at a time, drop ¼ cup rice mixture into butter; flatten with spatula. Cook over medium heat, turning once, until lightly browned (1 to 2 minutes on each side). Place rice cakes on platter; keep warm. Repeat with remaining rice cakes adding *1 tablespoon* butter to skillet for each 3 rice cakes.

   *1 cup cooked long grain rice can be substituted for 1 cup cooked converted rice.

Nutrition Information (1 serving)
• Calories 120 • Protein 4g • Carbohydrate 15g • Fat 6g
• Cholesterol 72mg • Sodium 215mg

Easy Southwestern Potatoes

1 hour 30 minutes

These potatoes, a perfect accompaniment to eggs, feature the spicy flavors of the Southwest.

⅓ cup butter *or* margarine, melted
½ teaspoon salt
¼ teaspoon chili powder
⅛ teaspoon cayenne pepper
⅛ teaspoon pepper
8 cups (6 medium) sliced ¼-inch baking
   potatoes
1 medium onion, sliced ¼-inch, separated
   into rings

1½ cups (6 ounces) shredded hot pepper
   Monterey Jack cheese

Chopped fresh parsley
Salsa

8 servings

Heat oven to 400°. In 13x9-inch baking pan stir together butter, salt, chili powder, cayenne pepper and pepper. Add potatoes and onion; stir to coat. Bake, turning occasionally, for 60 to 70 minutes or until potatoes are fork tender. Sprinkle with cheese. Continue baking for 1 to 2 minutes or until cheese is melted. Garnish with parsley; serve with salsa.

Microwave Directions: In 13x9-inch baking dish melt butter on HIGH (1 to 1½ minutes). Stir in salt, chili powder, cayenne pepper and pepper. Add potatoes and onion; stir to coat. Cover with plastic wrap. Microwave on HIGH, stirring every 10 minutes, until potatoes are fork tender (20 to 25 minutes). Sprinkle with cheese; let stand 5 minutes. Garnish with parsley; serve with salsa.

Nutrition Information (1 serving)
• Calories 240 • Protein 8g • Carbohydrate 21g • Fat 14g
• Cholesterol 40mg • Sodium 333mg

Wild Rice Breakfast Cakes (pictured)
Easy Southwestern Potatoes

Strawberry n' Cream Tart

2 hours

Crust
½ cup butter *or* margarine, softened
⅓ cup sugar
1¼ cups all-purpose flour
2 tablespoons milk
½ teaspoon almond extract

Filling
1 (3 ounce) package cream cheese, softened
½ cup powdered sugar

½ teaspoon almond extract
1 cup whipping cream

Topping
1 pint fresh strawberries, sliced, *or*
fresh raspberries
2 to 4 tablespoons strawberry *or*
raspberry jelly, melted

10 servings

Heat oven to 400°. In small mixer bowl beat butter and sugar at medium speed, scraping bowl often, until light and fluffy (1 to 2 minutes). Add flour, milk and ½ teaspoon almond extract. Reduce speed to low; continue beating, scraping bowl often, until mixture leaves sides of bowl and forms a ball. Press dough onto bottom and up sides of greased 10-inch tart pan or 12-inch pizza pan; prick with fork. Bake for 10 to 15 minutes or until light golden brown. Cool. In small mixer bowl combine cream cheese, powdered sugar and ½ teaspoon almond extract. Beat at medium speed, scraping bowl often, until light and fluffy (1 to 2 minutes). Gradually add whipping cream; continue beating until mixture is thick and fluffy (2 to 3 minutes). Spread over top of cooled crust. Refrigerate at least 1 hour. Just before serving, arrange fruit on filling. Brush or drizzle melted jelly over fruit.

Nutrition Information (1 serving)
• Calories 320 • Protein 3g • Carbohydrate 29g • Fat 22g
• Cholesterol 68mg • Sodium 133mg

Glazed Fruit Cups

60 minutes

Cups
2 cups all-purpose flour
¼ teaspoon salt
⅔ cup butter *or* margarine
4 to 5 tablespoons cold water
1 teaspoon grated orange peel

Filling
¼ cup sugar
2 teaspoons cornstarch
½ cup orange juice
2 tablespoons butter *or* margarine
1½ cups cut-up fresh fruit (bananas, grapes, raspberries, strawberries, peaches, etc.)
Red raspberry preserves, melted

10 servings

Heat oven to 400°. In large bowl stir together flour and salt. Cut in ⅔ cup butter until crumbly; with fork mix in water and orange peel until dough leaves sides of bowl and forms a ball. Roll out dough on well-floured surface to ⅛-inch thickness. Cut into ten 4½-inch circles. Fit pastry into muffin cups; flute edges. With fork, prick bottom and sides of each cup. Bake for 14 to 18 minutes or until lightly browned. Cool; remove from pan. In 2-quart saucepan stir together sugar and cornstarch. Add orange juice. Cook over medium heat, stirring occasionally, until mixture comes to a full boil (5 to 8 minutes). Boil 2 minutes. Remove from heat. Stir in 2 tablespoons butter until melted. Gently stir in fruit. Spoon fruit mixture into each cup. If desired, top each cup with about 1 teaspoon melted raspberry preserves.

Nutrition Information (1 serving)
• Calories 280 • Protein 3g • Carbohydrate 34g • Fat 15g
• Cholesterol 39mg • Sodium 203mg

Strawberry n' Cream Tart (top)
Glazed Fruit Cups (bottom)

Old-Fashioned Poppy Seed Tea Bread · 1 hour 30 minutes

1½ cups sugar
 1 cup butter *or* margarine, softened
 3 eggs
1½ teaspoons almond extract
1½ teaspoons vanilla
 3 cups all-purpose flour
1½ cups milk

 1 tablespoon poppy seed
1½ teaspoons baking powder
1½ teaspoons salt

 Powdered sugar

16 servings

Heat oven to 350°. In large mixer bowl combine sugar, butter, eggs, almond extract and vanilla. Beat at medium speed, scraping bowl often, until light and fluffy (2 to 3 minutes). Add all remaining ingredients *except* powdered sugar. Continue beating until well mixed (1 to 2 minutes). Pour into greased and floured 12-cup Bundt pan or 10-inch tube pan. Bake for 50 to 65 minutes or until wooden pick inserted in center comes out clean. Cool 10 minutes; remove from pan. Cool completely; sprinkle with powdered sugar.

Nutrition Information (1 serving)
• Calories 290 • Protein 5g • Carbohydrate 38g • Fat 14g
• Cholesterol 85mg • Sodium 372mg

Delicate Cookie Cones With Orange Cream · 1 hour 30 minutes

Cookies
½ cup butter, softened
½ cup sugar
½ cup all-purpose flour
 2 egg whites, slightly beaten
½ teaspoon almond extract

Orange Cream
 1 cup whipping cream
 1 tablespoon orange flavored liqueur *or* orange juice
½ teaspoon grated orange peel
 2 tablespoons sugar

 Powdered sugar
 Assorted berries

8 servings

Heat oven to 400°. In small mixer bowl combine butter and ½ cup sugar. Beat at medium speed, scraping bowl often, until light and fluffy (1 to 2 minutes). Add flour, egg whites and almond extract. Reduce speed to low. Continue beating, scraping bowl often, until well mixed (1 to 2 minutes). Drop by tablespoonfuls 4 inches apart onto well-greased cookie sheets (bake only 4 cookies per cookie sheet). Spread dough with small spatula dipped in water to 3-inch diameter. Bake, 1 cookie sheet at a time, for 5 to 6 minutes or until edges are golden brown. (Do not overbake or cookies will be too crisp to shape.) Remove from oven; let stand on cookie sheet *1 minute*. With thin spatula quickly loosen each cookie from cookie sheet. Shape into cones; cool to set. (If cookies become too firm to shape, return to oven for a few seconds to soften.) Just before serving, in chilled small mixer bowl beat chilled whipping cream, liqueur and orange peel at high speed, scraping bowl often, until soft peaks form (1 to 2 minutes). Continue beating, gradually adding 2 tablespoons sugar, until stiff peaks form (30 to 60 seconds). To serve, sprinkle cookies with powdered sugar; serve filled with orange cream and with berries on the side.

Nutrition Information (1 serving)
• Calories 310 • Protein 2g • Carbohydrate 24g • Fat 23g
• Cholesterol 73mg • Sodium 146mg

Old-Fashioned Poppy Seed Tea Bread (pictured)
Delicate Cookie Cones With Orange Cream

How To: Flavor Cream Cheese & Butter

Pictured: Orange-spice Flavored Cream Cheese, left; Honey-Pecan Flavored Butter, right.

To Flavor Cream Cheese:

Flavor	Stir Into 1 (8 oz.) Package Softened Cream Cheese	Serving Suggestions
Fruit Preserve	¼ cup choice of fruit preserves (apricot, raspberry, peach, etc.) 2 tablespoons powdered sugar	Dip for fruit; spread for muffins, bagels, croissants, quick breads.
Honey-Pecan	¼ cup chopped pecans 2 tablespoons honey ¼ teaspoon cinnamon	Dip for fruit; spread for muffins, bagels, croissants, quick breads.
Orange-Spice	2 tablespoons sugar 2 tablespoons orange juice 1 teaspoon grated orange peel ⅛ teaspoon ground allspice	Dip for fruit; spread for muffins, bagels, croissants, quick breads.
Peanut Butter	¼ cup peanut butter 2 tablespoons powdered sugar 1 tablespoon milk	Dip for fruit; spread for graham crackers.
Strawberry	½ cup sliced strawberries 2 tablespoons sugar 1 teaspoon vanilla	Dip for fruit; spread for pound cake, bagels, croissants, quick breads.
Cheddar & Chive	½ cup finely shredded Cheddar cheese 1 tablespoon sliced green onion 2 teaspoons chopped fresh chives	Dip for vegetables; topping for hot cooked vegetables; spread for crackers, breads.
Italian Herb	2 tablespoons chopped fresh parsley 1 teaspoon Italian herb seasoning ⅛ teaspoon garlic salt	Spread for sandwiches or crackers; topping for hot cooked vegetables.
Lemon-Basil	2 teaspoons lemon juice ½ teaspoon dried basil leaves ⅛ teaspoon garlic powder	Dip for vegetables; spread for sandwiches, bagels, French bread, croissants.

Yield: Each flavored cream cheese yields 1 to 1¼ cups.

Tip: For softer consistency, add 1 to 2 tablespoons milk.

To Flavor Butter:

Flavor	Stir Into ½ Cup Softened Butter	Serving Suggestions
Almond-Peach	2 tablespoons peach preserves 1 tablespoon almond flavored liqueur *or* ¼ teaspoon almond extract	Toast, pastries, quick breads.
Fruit Preserve	⅓ cup powdered sugar 1 tablespoon choice of fruit preserves (strawberry, blackberry, pineapple, raspberry, etc.)	Toast, pancakes, waffles, French toast, croissants, quick breads.
Honey-Pecan	¼ cup honey 2 tablespoons chopped pecans ⅛ teaspoon ground nutmeg	Toast, pancakes, waffles, French toast, quick breads.
Maple	2 tablespoons pure maple syrup	Toast, pancakes, waffles, French toast.
Orange-Cinnamon	1 tablespoon firmly packed brown sugar 1 teaspoon grated orange peel ¼ teaspoon ground cinnamon	Toast, pancakes, waffles, French toast, quick breads.
Blue Cheese-Walnut	2 ounces crumbled blue cheese 2 tablespoons chopped walnuts ¼ teaspoon Worchestershire sauce Dash pepper	Crackers, breads.
Lemon-Chive	2 teaspoons chopped fresh chives ½ teaspoon grated lemon peel 6 drops hot pepper sauce	Fish, seafood, hot cooked vegetables.
Lemon-Pepper	½ teaspoon grated lemon peel ½ teaspoon cracked black pepper	Fish, seafood, hot cooked vegetables, warm bread.
Parsley-Herb	1 tablespoon chopped fresh parsley 1 tablespoon chopped green onion ¼ teaspoon dried marjoram leaves ⅛ teaspoon dried thyme leaves ⅛ teaspoon garlic powder	Crackers, breads, hot cooked pasta, hot cooked vegetables.

Yield: Each flavored butter yields ½ to ¾ cup.

Tip: Flavored butters can be shaped into stars. Spoon softened butter mixture into pastry bag fitted with star tip. Pipe butter stars onto waxed paper. Refrigerate until firm.

Tip: Herb flavored butters can also be shaped into rolls and sliced. Refrigerate butter mixture until slightly firm. Form butter mixture into a roll. Wrap in waxed paper. Refrigerate until firm. Remove waxed paper. Slice into pats.

SIMPLE SUPPERS

We Americans have always been busy. In the 1830s an Iowa pioneer boy wrote:

"Mother bore and cared for the babies, saw that the floor was white and clean, that the beds were made and cared for, the garden tended, the turkeys dressed, the deer flesh cured and fat prepared for candles or culinary use, that the wild fruits were garnered and preserved or dried, that the spinning and knitting was done and the clothing made. She did her part in all these tasks...and did the thousand things for us a mother only finds to do."

A pioneer woman also collected eggs, cleaned the hen house and often milked the cow. And at the end of a day like this, she had to think of a supper to feed her family, one she could make in a hurry and that called for simple ingredients. Working women are really nothing new in America.

Today we all arrive home tired and hungry, and often want to make supper quickly and then relax together in front of the TV while we eat. Frontier families probably ate by the fireplace to enjoy suppers like these, while in the 1930s families gathered around the radio. No matter. The feeling is still the same.

On the next pages, we've gathered some SIMPLE SUPPERS that are quick to prepare and sure to become family favorites the first time you serve them. They're proof that a lack of time in the kitchen doesn't mean a lack of loving care and great taste.

Chicken Express Dinner (30 min.)

A colorful, skillet supper with Oriental tastes.
Nutty sesame chicken, lemon rice and gingery pea pods and peppers
that you can serve in just 30 minutes!

Skillet Sesame Chicken p.98
Gingered Pea Pods & Red Pepper p.138
Lemon Zest Rice p.133

Country Spaghetti Supper (60 min.)

*A new way to say Italian! Smoky bacon gives this pasta
its unique country taste. With basil lemon garlic bread and
pears in almond cream sauce.*

Smoked Bacon Red Sauce Over Spaghetti p.134
Basil Lemon Garlic Bread p.81   Tossed Salad
Tender Pears in Almond Cream Sauce p.146

SIMPLE SUPPERS
MENU

Quick Family Dinner

This lemon-dipped, panfried pork picatta takes just minutes to make.
Serve with buttery bread-crumbed noodles and a tossed salad with spicy
tomato dressing. A fast finish? Orange-banana custard cream dessert.

Lemon Pork Picatta p.108
Butter Crumb Noodles p.133   Tossed Salad With Spicy Tomato Dressing p.124
Custard Cream With Oranges & Bananas p.146

SIMPLE SUPPERS
MENU

Lakeside Supper

Fresh-caught walleye pike rolled in a flavorful cracker crumb coating and cooked right in the skillet with new red potatoes. A summertime treat with herbed green beans, and strawberries, pineapple and kiwi topped with a light lemonade dressing.

Cracker Coated Walleye Pike p.114
Herbed Green Beans p.138
Lemon Zest Dressing Over Fresh Fruit p.124

SIMPLE SUPPERS
MENU

Down Home Cooking

This is the meal they'll ask for again and again – peppered minute steak and mashed potatoes mixed with cream cheese, green onions and sour cream. Add a tossed salad and fresh strawberries with orange chocolate sauce.

Peppered Minute Steak p.102
Mashed Potatoes With Sour Cream p.144   Tossed Salad
Strawberries With Orange Chocolate p.149

Simmering Supper

An easy way to visit Italy for supper tonight: Italian sausage and pasta stew topped with Parmesan cheese and served with fresh, hot rosemary breadstick twists. Dessert's very easy too – fresh fruit with no-bake chocolate cookies.

Sausage n' Pasta Stew p.88
Rosemary Breadstick Twists p.81   Fresh Fruit
No-Bake Chocolate Cookies p.150

Basil Lemon Garlic Bread (top)
Rosemary Breadstick Twists (bottom)

Basil Lemon Garlic Bread

30 minutes

Toasty French bread brushed with a garlic basil olive oil.

1 (1 pound) loaf French bread

⅓ cup olive oil *or* butter, melted
1 tablespoon dried basil leaves
   Dash cayenne pepper

1 tablespoon lemon juice
2 teaspoons grated lemon peel
½ teaspoon finely chopped fresh garlic

8 servings

   Slice French bread diagonally into 1½-inch slices, cutting two-thirds through loaf. *Heat oven to 400°.* In small bowl stir together all ingredients *except* French bread. Brush cut sides of French bread with olive oil mixture. Wrap in aluminum foil; place on cookie sheet. Bake for 15 to 20 minutes or until heated through.

Nutrition Information (1 serving)
• Calories 250 • Protein 5g • Carbohydrate 32g • Fat 11g
• Cholesterol 2mg • Sodium 329mg

Rosemary Breadstick Twists

45 minutes

Twist these breadsticks and dip in a rosemary garlic butter.

⅓ cup butter *or* margarine
2¼ cups all-purpose flour
2 tablespoons freshly grated Parmesan
   cheese
1 tablespoon sugar

3½ teaspoons baking powder
1 cup milk
1 teaspoon dried rosemary leaves, crushed
½ teaspoon finely chopped fresh garlic

1 dozen

   Heat oven to 400°. In 13x9-inch baking pan melt butter in oven (3 to 5 minutes). Meanwhile, in medium bowl stir together all remaining ingredients *except* milk, rosemary and garlic. Stir in milk just until moistened. Turn dough onto lightly floured surface; knead 10 times or until smooth. Roll dough into 12x6-inch rectangle. Cut into 12 (1-inch) strips. Stir rosemary and garlic into melted butter. Twist each strip of dough 6 times; dip in herbed butter mixture. Place in same pan. Bake for 20 to 25 minutes or until lightly browned.

Nutrition Information (1 serving)
• Calories 150 • Protein 4g • Carbohydrate 20g • Fat 6g
• Cholesterol 16mg • Sodium 167mg

Variations:

Basil Breadstick Twists: Omit 1 teaspoon dried rosemary leaves. Add 1 teaspoon dried basil leaves. Prepare as directed above.

Dill Breadstick Twists: Omit 1 teaspoon rosemary leaves. Add 2 teaspoons dried dill weed. Prepare as directed above.

Parmesan Basil Puffs (pictured)
Cinnamon Topped Rhubarb Muffins

Parmesan Basil Puffs
45 minutes

These rolls have a moist interior texture and a crisp crust that tastes great with soup.

¼ cup milk
¼ cup butter *or* margarine
½ cup all-purpose flour
1 teaspoon dried basil leaves

⅛ teaspoon coarsely ground pepper
2 eggs
½ cup freshly grated Parmesan cheese

6 servings

Heat oven to 400°. In 2-quart saucepan bring milk and butter to a full boil (2 to 3 minutes). Stir in flour, basil and pepper. Cook over low heat, stirring vigorously, until mixture forms a ball. Remove from heat. Add eggs, one at a time, stirring vigorously until smooth. Stir in Parmesan cheese. Drop about ¼ cup dough 2 inches apart onto 15x10x1-inch jelly roll pan. Bake for 18 to 22 minutes or until golden brown. Serve warm.

Nutrition Information (1 serving)
• Calories 180 • Protein 7g • Carbohydrate 9g • Fat 12g
• Cholesterol 99mg • Sodium 260mg

Cinnamon Topped Rhubarb Muffins
50 minutes

Cinnamon and sugar complement rhubarb's tartness in these delicious muffins.

½ cup firmly packed brown sugar
¼ cup butter *or* margarine, softened
1 (8 ounce) carton (1 cup) dairy sour cream
2 eggs
1½ cups all-purpose flour
¾ teaspoon baking soda
½ teaspoon cinnamon

1½ cups chopped fresh *or* frozen rhubarb (unthawed)

1 tablespoon sugar
½ teaspoon cinnamon

1½ dozen

Heat oven to 375°. In large mixer bowl combine brown sugar and butter. Beat at medium speed, scraping bowl often, until well mixed (1 to 2 minutes). Add sour cream and eggs; continue beating, scraping bowl often, until well mixed (1 to 2 minutes). In medium bowl stir together flour, baking soda and ½ teaspoon cinnamon. By hand, stir flour mixture into sour cream mixture just until moistened. Fold in rhubarb. Spoon into greased muffin pans. In small bowl stir together 1 tablespoon sugar and ½ teaspoon cinnamon. Sprinkle about ¼ teaspoon mixture on top of each muffin. Bake for 25 to 30 minutes or until lightly browned. Cool 10 minutes; remove from pans.

Nutrition Information (1 muffin)
• Calories 130 • Protein 2g • Carbohydrate 16g • Fat 6g
• Cholesterol 43mg • Sodium 91mg

An interesting fact about cheese is that people in the eastern states like white cheese while those elsewhere prefer it orange-yellow. So Land O'Lakes makes it both ways.

Onion Crusted Whole Grain Bread

20 minutes

Whole wheat bread is pan-toasted and coated with onions and Parmesan cheese.

¼ cup butter *or* margarine
¼ cup chopped onion

6 (½-inch) slices whole grain bread
2 tablespoons freshly grated Parmesan cheese

6 servings

Heat oven to 375°. In 13x9-inch baking pan melt butter in oven (3 to 5 minutes). Stir in onion; continue baking for 2 to 3 minutes or until onion is crisply tender. Meanwhile, cut each bread slice in half diagonally. Dip one side of each half of bread into melted butter; turn buttered side up, leaving bread in pan.

Spoon onions in pan on top of each bread half; sprinkle with Parmesan cheese. Bake for 10 to 12 minutes or until bread is toasted.

Nutrition Information (1 serving)
• Calories 140 • Protein 4g • Carbohydrate 13g • Fat 9g
• Cholesterol 23mg • Sodium 249mg

Jalapeño Corn Scones

30 minutes

Kernels of corn and jalapeño peppers peek from slightly sweet, tender cornmeal scones.

1¾ cups all-purpose flour
½ cup yellow cornmeal
¼ cup sugar
1 tablespoon baking powder
¼ teaspoon salt
½ cup butter *or* margarine

¼ cup shortening
1 (10 ounce) package frozen whole kernel corn, thawed, well drained
2 jalapeño peppers, seeded, chopped
½ cup whipping cream

1 dozen

Heat oven to 400°. In large bowl combine flour, cornmeal, sugar, baking powder and salt. Cut in butter and shortening until crumbly. Stir in corn and jalapeño peppers. Stir in whipping cream just until moistened. Turn dough onto lightly floured surface; knead until smooth (1 minute). Roll out dough to ¾-inch thickness.

With 2 to 3-inch cutter, cut out 12 scones. Place 1 inch apart on cookie sheet. Bake for 12 to 16 minutes or until lightly browned.

Nutrition Information (1 scone)
• Calories 260 • Protein 3g • Carbohydrate 27g • Fat 16g
• Cholesterol 34mg • Sodium 203mg

In 1871, Mary Carpenter wrote her sister at threshing time: "Got up before four, got breakfast, skimmed milk, churned, worked over the churning already on hand, did a large washing, baked 6 loaves of bread and 7 pumpkin pies. While I was baking, put on the irons and did the ironing, got supper, besides washing all the dishes, sweeping, etc."

Onion Crusted Whole Grain Bread (top)
Jalapeño Corn Scones (bottom)

Hearty Potato & Sausage Chowder

50 minutes

Onions, potatoes, sausage and cheese combine to make this hearty soup;
great for a cold winter night.

¼ cup butter *or* margarine
1½ cups (1 large) thinly sliced onion
3 tablespoons all-purpose flour
3 cups (3 medium) cubed ¾-inch potatoes
4 cups milk
1 teaspoon salt

¼ teaspoon pepper
2 cups (8 ounces) shredded Cheddar *or* pasteurized process American cheese
8 ounces (2 medium) cooked Polish sausages, cut into ¼-inch slices

8 servings

In 3-quart saucepan melt butter. Stir in onion; cook over medium heat until tender (4 to 5 minutes). Stir in flour until smooth and bubbly (1 minute). Stir in potatoes, milk, salt and pepper. Cover; continue cooking, stirring occasionally, until potatoes are fork tender (25 to 30 minutes). Stir in cheese and sausage. Continue cooking, stirring occasionally, until cheese is melted and sausage is heated through (2 to 3 minutes).

Microwave Directions: In 3-quart casserole combine butter, onion and potatoes. Cover; microwave on HIGH, stirring after half the time, until potatoes are fork tender (12 to 14 minutes). Meanwhile, in small bowl stir together flour and milk. Add milk mixture, salt and pepper to potatoes. Microwave on HIGH, stirring after half the time, until thickened (12 to 14 minutes). Stir in cheese and sausage. Microwave on HIGH, stirring after half the time, until cheese is melted and sausage is heated through (30 to 60 seconds).

Nutrition Information (1 serving)
• Calories 380 • Protein 17g • Carbohydrate 21g • Fat 26g
• Cholesterol 74mg • Sodium 815mg

Easy Turkey Soup

45 minutes

This easy soup features orzo – a rice-shaped pasta.

2 cups cubed ½-inch cooked turkey
½ cup (1 stalk) sliced ¼-inch celery
1 (10 ounce) package frozen mixed vegetables
1 (14½ ounce) can chicken broth
2 cups water

¼ teaspoon dried thyme leaves
⅛ teaspoon pepper
½ cup uncooked dried orzo *or* ring macaroni

6 servings

In 4-quart saucepan combine all ingredients *except* orzo. Cook over high heat, stirring occasionally, until mixture comes to a full boil (10 to 15 minutes). Add orzo; reduce heat to low. Cover; continue cooking, stirring occasionally, until orzo is tender (12 to 15 minutes).

Microwave Directions: In 3-quart casserole combine all ingredients *except* orzo. Cover; microwave on HIGH, stirring after half the time, until mixture comes to a full boil (18 to 22 minutes). Stir in orzo. Cover; microwave on HIGH, stirring after half the time, until orzo is tender (12 to 15 minutes).

Nutrition Information (1 serving)
• Calories 150 • Protein 18g • Carbohydrate 12g • Fat 3g
• Cholesterol 36mg • Sodium 282mg

Hearty Potato & Sausage Chowder (top)
Easy Turkey Soup (bottom)

Chunky Chicken n' Corn Chowder

60 minutes

Sage adds extra flavor to this robust chicken chowder.

6 slices bacon, cut into 1-inch pieces
1 medium onion, chopped
3 tablespoons all-purpose flour
3 cups chicken broth
4 new red potatoes, each cut into sixths
1 teaspoon dried sage leaves

¼ teaspoon pepper
2 cups cubed 1-inch cooked chicken
2 cups milk
1 (10 ounce) package frozen whole kernel corn

6 servings

In Dutch oven cook bacon over medium high heat until browned and crisp (6 to 8 minutes). With slotted spoon remove bacon; set aside. Add onion to bacon drippings; cook over medium heat, stirring occasionally, until tender (3 to 4 minutes). Stir in flour until smooth and bubbly (1 minute). Stir in chicken broth, potatoes, sage and pepper. Cover; continue cooking until potatoes are fork tender (15 to 20 minutes). Add all remaining ingredients *except* bacon. Continue cooking, stirring occasionally, until heated through (7 to 8 minutes). Top each serving with bacon.

Nutrition Information (1 serving)
• Calories 280 • Protein 23g • Carbohydrate 25g • Fat 9g
• Cholesterol 53mg • Sodium 573mg

Sausage n' Pasta Stew

60 minutes

Tomatoes, pasta, sausage and beans combine in this heartwarming stew.

¼ cup chopped onion
¾ pound sliced ½-inch Italian sausage links
½ teaspoon finely chopped fresh garlic
1 cup water
2 (28 ounce) cans whole tomatoes, cut up
2 teaspoons sugar
½ teaspoon Italian herb seasoning*

1 cup uncooked dried corkscrew *or* twist pasta
2 cups frozen cut broccoli
1 (16 ounce) can Great Northern beans, drained

Freshly grated Parmesan cheese

6 servings

In Dutch oven cook onion, sausage and garlic over medium high heat until sausage is browned (8 to 10 minutes); drain off fat. Add water, tomatoes, sugar and Italian seasoning. Continue cooking until mixture comes to a full boil (6 to 8 minutes); stir in pasta. Reduce heat to medium. Continue cooking, stirring occasionally, until pasta is tender (8 to 11 minutes). Stir in broccoli and beans. Continue cooking, stirring occasionally, until broccoli is crisply tender (5 to 7 minutes). Serve with Parmesan cheese.

*⅛ teaspoon *each* dried oregano leaves, dried marjoram leaves and dried basil leaves and ¹⁄₁₆ teaspoon rubbed dried sage can be substituted for ½ teaspoon Italian herb seasoning.

Microwave Directions: In 3-quart casserole place onion, sausage and garlic. Cover; microwave on HIGH, stirring after half the time, until sausage is no longer pink (8 to 10 minutes). Drain off fat. Stir in water, tomatoes, sugar and Italian seasoning. Cover; microwave on HIGH stirring after half the time, until mixture comes to a full boil (14 to 18 minutes). Stir in pasta. Cover; microwave on HIGH, stirring after half the time, until pasta is tender (14 to 18 minutes). Stir in broccoli and beans. Cover; microwave on HIGH until broccoli is crisply tender (7 to 9 minutes). Serve with Parmesan cheese.

Nutrition Information (1 serving)
• Calories 230 • Protein 13g • Carbohydrate 28g • Fat 8g
• Cholesterol 21mg • Sodium 472mg

Chunky Chicken n' Corn Chowder (pictured)
Sausage n' Pasta Stew

Cajun Gumbo Soup (pictured)
Vegetable Ground Beef Soup

Cajun Gumbo Soup

60 minutes

The favorite flavors of gumbo are found in this hearty soup.

12 ounces Italian sausage links, cut into
½-inch pieces
1 (28 ounce) can whole tomatoes, quartered
3 cups water
2 whole boneless chicken breasts, skinned,
halved, cut into quarters
1 (14½ ounce) can chicken broth
1 cup (1 medium) thinly sliced onion
½ cup uncooked long grain rice

1 bay leaf
½ teaspoon dried thyme leaves
½ teaspoon finely chopped fresh garlic
¼ teaspoon coarsely ground pepper
⅛ teaspoon cayenne pepper
2 cups (2 medium) sliced ¼-inch zucchini

6 servings

In 4-quart Dutch oven cook sausage over medium high heat until browned (6 to 8 minutes); drain off fat. Stir in all remaining ingredients *except* zucchini. Continue cooking, stirring occasionally, until soup comes to a full boil (6 to 8 minutes). Reduce heat to medium. Continue cooking, stirring occasionally, until rice is tender and soup is slightly thickened (30 to 35 minutes). Add zucchini; continue cooking until zucchini is crisply tender (4 to 6 minutes). Remove bay leaf.

Microwave Directions: *Reduce 3 cups water to 2 cups.* In 3-quart casserole place sausage. Cover; microwave on HIGH, stirring after half the time, until sausage is no longer pink. Drain off fat. Stir in all remaining ingredients *except* zucchini. Cover; microwave on HIGH, stirring after half the time, until rice is tender (30 to 40 minutes). Stir in zucchini. Cover; microwave on HIGH, stirring after half the time, until zucchini is crisply tender (4 to 7 minutes). Remove bay leaf.

Nutrition Information (1 serving)
• Calories 290 • Protein 27g • Carbohydrate 22g • Fat 10g
• Cholesterol 69mg • Sodium 724mg

Vegetable Ground Beef Soup

60 minutes

Simmering for 40 minutes brings extra flavor to this vegetable beef soup.

1 pound ground beef
3 cups shredded cabbage
2 cups (2 medium) sliced ¼-inch carrots
2 cups (6 medium) sliced ¼-inch new red
potatoes
1 cup (1 medium) thinly sliced onion
¼ cup chopped fresh parsley

4 cups water
1 (28 ounce) can whole tomatoes
2 bay leaves
½ teaspoon salt
½ teaspoon coarsely ground pepper

6 servings

In Dutch oven cook ground beef on medium high heat, stirring occasionally, until browned (8 to 12 minutes). Drain off fat; stir in all remaining ingredients. Reduce heat to medium; continue cooking, stirring occasionally, until vegetables are tender (30 to 40 minutes). Remove bay leaves.

Microwave Directions: *Reduce 4 cups water to 3 cups.* In 3-quart casserole crumble ground beef. Cover; microwave on HIGH, stirring after half the time, until no longer pink (4 to 7 minutes). Drain off fat; stir in all remaining ingredients. Cover; microwave on HIGH, stirring after half the time, until vegetables are tender (25 to 35 minutes). Remove bay leaves.

Nutrition Information (1 serving)
• Calories 330 • Protein 18g • Carbohydrate 40g • Fat 11g
• Cholesterol 46mg • Sodium 466mg

Chicken & Vegetables Over Fettuccine

45 minutes

6 ounces uncooked dried fettuccine
¼ cup butter *or* margarine
2 teaspoons finely chopped fresh garlic
2 whole boneless chicken breasts, skinned, cut into ½-inch lengthwise strips
2 cups (8 ounces) fresh mushrooms, cut into quarters
1 large onion, cut into rings
1 small red pepper, cut into strips

1 small green pepper, cut into strips
1 tablespoon all-purpose flour
1 cup whipping cream
¼ cup dry white wine *or* chicken broth
½ teaspoon salt

Coarsely ground pepper
Freshly grated Parmesan cheese

6 servings

Prepare fettuccine according to package directions; drain. Return to saucepan; set aside. Meanwhile, in 10-inch skillet melt butter until sizzling; stir in garlic. Add chicken. Cook over medium high heat, stirring constantly, 4 minutes. Stir in mushrooms, onion and pepper strips. Continue cooking, stirring constantly, until chicken is fork tender and vegetables are crisply tender (3½ to 4 minutes). Using slotted spoon, remove chicken and vegetables; keep warm. Whisk flour into butter mixture until smooth and bubbly (1 minute). Stir in whipping cream, wine and salt. Continue cooking, whisking constantly, until mixture comes to a full boil (6 to 8 minutes). Boil until mixture is slightly thickened (1 minute). Add chicken and vegetables to cream mixture. Continue cooking, stirring constantly, until heated through (1 to 2 minutes). Pour mixture over fettuccine; toss well to combine. Serve with pepper and Parmesan cheese.

Nutrition Information (1 serving)
• Calories 440 • Protein 24g • Carbohydrate 29g • Fat 25g
• Cholesterol 123mg • Sodium 317mg

Cheese & Tomato Turkey Cutlets

30 minutes

A tomato herb sauce is served over turkey cutlets, then topped with Provolone cheese.

Sauce
3 tablespoons finely chopped onion
2 teaspoons olive *or* vegetable oil
1 (16 ounce) can whole tomatoes, drained, chopped
¾ teaspoon dried basil leaves
½ teaspoon dried parsley flakes
⅛ teaspoon dried crushed red pepper

Cutlets
1 egg, slightly beaten
1 tablespoon milk
½ cup seasoned dry bread crumbs
⅛ teaspoon garlic powder
4 (4 ounces each) ¼-inch thick turkey cutlets
3 tablespoons olive *or* vegetable oil
8 slices Provolone *or* mozzarella cheese

4 servings

In 2-quart saucepan combine onion and 2 teaspoons oil. Cook over medium heat, stirring occasionally, until tender (3 to 5 minutes). Stir in all remaining sauce ingredients. Continue cooking, stirring occasionally, until heated through (2 to 3 minutes); set aside. Meanwhile, in 9-inch pie pan combine egg and milk. In medium bowl combine bread crumbs and garlic powder. Dip cutlets into egg mixture; then into crumb mixture, turning to coat. In 10-inch skillet heat 3 tablespoons oil over medium high heat. Add cutlets. Cook over medium heat, turning once, until golden brown (4 to 6 minutes per side). Spoon hot sauce over cutlets; place 2 pieces of cheese over sauce on each cutlet. Cover; reduce heat to low. Continue cooking until cheese begins to melt (2 to 4 minutes).

Nutrition Information (1 serving)
• Calories 520 • Protein 44g • Carbohydrate 16g • Fat 30g
• Cholesterol 179mg • Sodium 661mg

Chicken & Vegetables Over Fettucine (top)
Cheese & Tomato Turkey Cutlets (bottom)

Chicken Vegetable Sauté

45 minutes

Serve this chicken and vegetable skillet dinner over fluffy rice.

2 tablespoons butter *or* margarine
1 teaspoon finely chopped fresh garlic
2 whole boneless chicken breasts, skinned, halved
3 cups broccoli flowerets
2 cups (8 ounces) fresh mushrooms, halved
1 medium onion, cut into eighths
¼ cup sherry *or* chicken broth
1 tablespoon soy sauce

¼ teaspoon salt
¼ teaspoon pepper
1 tablespoon cornstarch
2 tablespoons water
2 medium cubed 1-inch ripe tomatoes

Cooked rice

4 servings

In 10-inch skillet melt butter until sizzling; stir in garlic. Add chicken. Cook over medium high heat, turning once, until chicken is lightly browned (5 to 6 minutes per side). Remove chicken; keep warm. Reduce heat to medium. Stir in broccoli, mushrooms, onion, sherry, soy sauce, salt and pepper. Continue cooking, stirring occasionally, until vegetables are crisply tender (5 to 7 minutes). Meanwhile, in small bowl stir together cornstarch and water. Stir cornstarch mixture into liquid in skillet. Continue cooking, stirring constantly, until liquid is thickened (1 to 2 minutes). Add tomatoes and chicken. Cover; reduce heat to low. Cook until tomatoes are heated through (2 to 3 minutes). Serve over hot cooked rice.

Nutrition Information (1 serving)
• Calories 270 • Protein 30g • Carbohydrate 13g • Fat 9g
• Cholesterol 88mg • Sodium 536mg

Garden Skillet Chicken

45 minutes

Carrots and pea pods add color and crunch to a tasty quick meal.

3 whole boneless chicken breasts, skinned, cut in half
3 tablespoons all-purpose flour
2 tablespoons butter *or* margarine
⅓ cup teriyaki sauce
3 tablespoons lemon juice
½ teaspoon sugar

1 teaspoon finely chopped fresh garlic
1 cup carrots, cut into 2x⅛x⅛-inch strips
4 ounces pea pods, trimmed*

Cooked rice

6 servings

Coat chicken with flour. In 10-inch skillet melt butter until sizzling; add chicken. Cook over medium heat until chicken is lightly browned (5 to 7 minutes). Turn chicken over; continue cooking until lightly browned (5 to 7 minutes). Stir in teriyaki sauce, lemon juice, sugar and garlic. Add carrots. Continue cooking, stirring occasionally, until mixture comes to a full boil (3 to 4 minutes). Cover; continue cooking 7 minutes. Remove cover; stir in pea pods. Continue cooking 3 minutes. Turn chicken over; continue cooking until chicken is fork tender (2 to 3 minutes). Serve over rice.

*1 (6 ounce) package frozen pea pods can be substituted for 4 ounces pea pods.

Nutrition Information (1 serving)
• Calories 220 • Protein 29g • Carbohydrate 10g • Fat 7g
• Cholesterol 83mg • Sodium 724mg

Chicken Vegetable Sauté (top)
Garden Skillet Chicken (bottom)

Skillet Chicken & Potato Dinner (pictured)
Tomato Patch Chicken

Skillet Chicken & Potato Dinner   50 minutes

Tender chicken breasts prepared with hearty vegetables.

3 tablespoons butter *or* margarine
1 teaspoon finely chopped fresh garlic
6 new red potatoes, quartered
1 medium onion, cut into 6 wedges
3 whole boneless chicken breasts, skinned, halved

1 (10 ounce) package frozen whole green beans*
½ teaspoon salt
¼ teaspoon pepper
¼ cup chopped fresh parsley

6 servings

In 10-inch skillet melt butter until sizzling; stir in garlic. Add potatoes and onion; cook over medium high heat, stirring occasionally, until browned (12 to 14 minutes). Remove from skillet; keep warm. Place chicken in same skillet. Cook over medium high heat, turning once, until fork tender and browned (5 to 6 minutes on each side). Remove chicken from skillet; keep warm. Place green beans, potato mixture, salt and pepper in same skillet. Cover; cook over medium high heat, stirring occasionally, until beans are crisply tender (6 to 9 minutes). Add chicken and parsley. Continue cooking, stirring occasionally, until heated through (1 to 3 minutes).

*1 (10 ounce) package frozen cut green beans can be substituted for 1 (10 ounce) package frozen whole green beans.

Microwave Directions: In 2½-quart casserole melt butter on HIGH (30 to 40 seconds). Stir in garlic and potatoes. Cover; microwave on HIGH 6 minutes. Stir in all remaining ingredients *except* green beans and parsley. Cover; microwave on HIGH, stirring after half the time, until chicken is fork tender and no longer pink (10 to 15 minutes). Stir in green beans. Cover; microwave on HIGH, stirring after half the time, until green beans are crisply tender (5 to 7 minutes). Sprinkle with parsley.

Nutrition Information (1 serving)
• Calories 260 • Protein 29g • Carbohydrate 15g • Fat 9g
• Cholesterol 88mg • Sodium 305mg

Tomato Patch Chicken   1 hour 15 minutes

Tomatoes and herbs enhance this chicken served over rice.

3 tablespoons butter *or* margarine
1 teaspoon finely chopped fresh garlic
2½ to 3½ pound frying chicken, cut into 8 pieces
2 cups (8 ounces) fresh mushrooms, cut in half
1 (28 ounce) can whole tomatoes, cut up
1 (6 ounce) can tomato paste
2 medium onions, cut into eighths

1 medium green pepper, cut into 1-inch pieces
1 teaspoon salt
1 teaspoon dried basil leaves
¼ teaspoon pepper
1 bay leaf

Cooked rice

6 servings

In Dutch oven melt butter until sizzling; stir in garlic. Add chicken; cook over medium high heat, turning occasionally, until golden brown (8 to 10 minutes). Stir in all remaining ingredients *except* rice. Cover; cook over medium heat, stirring occasionally, 25 minutes. Remove cover; continue cooking 10 to 20 minutes or until chicken is fork tender. Serve over cooked rice.

Nutrition Information (1 serving)
• Calories 240 • Protein 21g • Carbohydrate 16g • Fat 11g
• Cholesterol 70mg • Sodium 909mg

Garden Vegetable Skillet Dinner

60 minutes

Thyme's aromatic flavor blends well with garden-fresh vegetables in this skillet dinner.

2½ to 3½ pounds frying chicken, cut into
    8 pieces
⅓ cup all-purpose flour
3 tablespoons butter *or* margarine
¼ cup water
4 medium carrots, cut into 1-inch pieces

1 medium onion, cut into eighths
1 teaspoon salt
1 teaspoon dried thyme leaves
¼ teaspoon pepper
2 cups broccoli flowerets

6 servings

Coat chicken with flour. In 10-inch skillet melt butter until sizzling; add chicken. Cook over high heat, turning once, until golden brown (8 to 10 minutes). Reduce heat to medium. Add all remaining ingredients *except* broccoli. Cover; continue cooking until chicken is fork tender (20 to 30 minutes). Add broccoli. Cover; continue cooking 5 to 8 minutes or until broccoli is crisply tender.

Microwave Directions: Omit flour and water. In 2½-quart casserole melt butter on HIGH (40 to 50 seconds). Arrange chicken in dish, placing thickest part to outside edge, turning to coat with butter. Add remaining ingredients *except* broccoli. Cover; microwave on HIGH, rearranging chicken pieces after half the time, until chicken is fork tender and no longer pink (20 to 22 minutes). Add broccoli. Cover; microwave on HIGH until broccoli is crisply tender (4 to 4½ minutes). Let stand 3 minutes.

Nutrition Information (1 serving)
• Calories 230 • Protein 20g • Carbohydrate 13g • Fat 11g
• Cholesterol 70mg • Sodium 491mg

Skillet Sesame Chicken

20 minutes

Sesame oil and toasted sesame seed add a nutty taste to sautéed chicken breasts.

3 tablespoons sesame *or* vegetable oil
1 teaspoon finely chopped fresh garlic
2 whole boneless chicken breasts, skinned,
    cut in half
1 tablespoon sesame seed, toasted

¼ teaspoon coarsely ground pepper
⅛ teaspoon red pepper flakes
2 tablespoons chopped fresh parsley

4 servings

In 10-inch skillet heat oil over medium high heat; stir in garlic. Place chicken breasts in hot oil. Cook, turning occasionally, until golden brown (8 to 10 minutes). Sprinkle with sesame seed, pepper and red pepper flakes.

Continue cooking until chicken is fork tender (1 to 2 minutes). Sprinkle with parsley.

Nutrition Information (1 serving)
• Calories 240 • Protein 27g • Carbohydrate 1g • Fat 14g
• Cholesterol 72mg • Sodium 65mg

When the threshers came, a farm woman made breakfast, dinner, lunch and supper for 15-20 men for two or three days. Her chicken recipes started . . . "first catch and clean ten chickens."

Garden Vegetable Skillet Dinner (top)
Skillet Sesame Chicken (bottom)

Beef With Mushrooms & Pea Pods (pictured)
Skillet Pizza Casserole

Beef With Mushrooms & Pea Pods
30 minutes

This quick skillet dinner is ready to serve in thirty minutes.

¼ cup vegetable oil
1 pound beef sirloin steak, cut in
   2x½x¼-inch strips
2 cups (8 ounces) fresh mushrooms, quartered
1 medium onion, cut in 8 wedges
2 tablespoons cornstarch
2 tablespoons water
¾ cup water
¼ cup sherry *or* water

¾ teaspoon instant beef bouillon granules
1 (8 ounce) can sliced water chestnuts, drained
6 ounces fresh pea pods, trimmed*
½ teaspoon salt
¼ teaspoon pepper
¼ teaspoon ginger

Cooked rice

6 servings

In 10-inch skillet heat *2 tablespoons* oil over medium high heat (1 to 2 minutes). Stir in sirloin strips. Continue cooking, stirring occasionally, until meat is browned (6 to 8 minutes). Remove meat; set aside. In same skillet heat remaining 2 tablespoons oil over medium heat (1 to 2 minutes). Stir in mushrooms and onion. Continue cooking, stirring occasionally, until tender (3 to 4 minutes). In small bowl stir together cornstarch and 2 tablespoons water. Add ¾ cup water, sherry and beef bouillon granules to mushrooms and onion; stir in cornstarch mixture. Continue cooking, stirring constantly, until mixture comes

to a full boil (4 to 6 minutes); boil 1 minute. Add all remaining ingredients *except* rice. Continue cooking, stirring occasionally, until pea pods are crisply tender (3 to 5 minutes). Serve over rice.

*1 (6 ounce) package frozen pea pods can be substituted for 6 ounces fresh pea pods.

Tip: 1½ cups peas, strips of green *or* red pepper *or* sliced celery can be substituted for 6 ounces fresh pea pods.

Nutrition Information (1 serving)
• Calories 260 • Protein 17g • Carbohydrate 14g • Fat 14g
• Cholesterol 44mg • Sodium 260mg

Skillet Pizza Casserole
45 minutes

Your family will love this skillet dinner with all-time favorite pizza flavors.

2 cups uncooked dried egg noodles
½ pound bulk mild Italian sausage
½ cup (1 medium) chopped onion
¼ cup chopped green pepper
½ cup coarsely chopped pepperoni

¼ cup sliced ¼-inch ripe olives
1 (15 ounce) can pizza sauce
1 cup (4 ounces) shredded Mozzarella cheese

4 servings

Cook noodles according to package directions; drain. Meanwhile, in 10-inch skillet combine sausage, onion and green pepper. Cook over medium high heat, stirring occasionally, until sausage is browned (8 to 10 minutes). Drain off fat. Stir in noodles and all remaining ingredients *except* cheese. Continue cooking, stirring occasionally, until mixture is heated through (10 to 15 minutes). Sprinkle with cheese. Cover; let stand 3 minutes or until cheese is melted.

Tip: To do ahead, prepare as directed above; place in greased 1½-quart casserole. Cover; refrigerate. Heat oven to 350°. Bake for 40 to 45 minutes or until heated through. Sprinkle with cheese. Cover; let stand 3 minutes or until cheese is melted.

Nutrition Information (1 serving)
• Calories 420 • Protein 21g • Carbohydrate 28g • Fat 24g
• Cholesterol 69mg • Sodium 1442mg

Skillet Beef n' Vegetables

30 minutes

*Beef strips are marinated in a brown sugar sweetened herb mixture
and sautéed with summer squash and zucchini.*

Marinade

2 tablespoons olive *or* vegetable oil
2 tablespoons firmly packed brown sugar
½ teaspoon dried oregano leaves
¼ teaspoon salt
¼ teaspoon coarsely ground pepper
2 tablespoons red wine vinegar
1 teaspoon finely chopped fresh garlic
1 bay leaf

Meat & Vegetables

1 pound beef top round steak, cut into
  3x½x⅛-inch strips
1 tablespoon olive *or* vegetable oil
1 cup (1 medium) sliced ¼-inch yellow
  summer squash
1 cup (1 medium) sliced ¼-inch zucchini
1 cup (1 medium) thinly sliced onion,
  separated into rings
¼ cup chopped fresh parsley

Cooked egg noodles

4 servings

In medium bowl stir together all marinade
ingredients. Add beef sirloin strips; let stand
10 minutes. Meanwhile, in 10-inch skillet heat
1 tablespoon oil; add squash, zucchini and
onion. Cook over medium high heat, stirring
occasionally, until crisply tender (3 to 5 minutes). Remove from skillet; set aside. In same
skillet place beef strips; *reserve marinade.*
Continue cooking, stirring occasionally, until
meat is browned (3 to 5 minutes). Stir in squash
mixture and reserved marinade. Reduce heat
to medium; continue cooking, stirring occasionally, until heated through (2 to 3 minutes).
Remove bay leaf. Sprinkle with parsley; serve
over noodles.

Nutrition Information (1 serving)
• Calories 290 • Protein 27g • Carbohydrate 12g • Fat 15g
• Cholesterol 67mg • Sodium 188mg

Peppered Minute Steak

30 minutes

Cubed steaks are dipped in Italian dressing and then cooked with peppers and onions in a skillet.

¼ cup prepared Italian dressing
3 tablespoons vegetable oil
1 medium green pepper, cut into
  julienne strips
1 medium thinly sliced onion, separated
  into rings

⅓ cup all-purpose flour
½ teaspoon coarsely ground pepper
¼ teaspoon salt
4 beef cubed steaks

4 servings

In 10-inch skillet heat *1 tablespoon* Italian
dressing and *1 tablespoon* oil until sizzling. Add
green pepper and onion. Cook over medium
high heat, stirring occasionally, until vegetables
are crisply tender (3 to 4 minutes). Place vegetables on platter; keep warm. Meanwhile, in
9-inch pie pan stir together flour, pepper and
salt. Dip steaks in remaining Italian dressing,
then coat with flour mixture. Add remaining
2 tablespoons oil to skillet. Place 2 steaks in
skillet. Cook over medium high heat, turning
once, until brown and crispy (3 to 5 minutes
on each side). Remove steaks to platter with
vegetables; keep warm. Repeat with remaining steaks.

Nutrition Information (1 serving)
• Calories 360 • Protein 26g • Carbohydrate 13g • Fat 22g
• Cholesterol 64mg • Sodium 300mg

Skillet Beef n' Vegetables (pictured)
Peppered Minute Steak

Santa Fe Supper

40 minutes

Salsa-spiced ground beef is served over chili-seasoned rice and topped with Cheddar cheese.

1 cup uncooked long grain rice
1 pound ground beef
2 cups (2 medium) sliced ¼-inch zucchini
1 cup (1 medium) thinly sliced onion, separated into rings
1½ cups salsa *or* picante sauce
¼ teaspoon salt

¼ teaspoon coarsely ground pepper
1 cup (4 ounces) shredded hot pepper Monterey Jack *or* Monterey Jack cheese
1 (4 ounce) can diced green chilies, drained
1 cup (4 ounces) shredded Cheddar cheese

6 servings

Cook rice according to package directions. Meanwhile, in 10-inch skillet cook ground beef over medium high heat, stirring occasionally, until ground beef is browned (6 to 8 minutes). Drain off fat. Stir in zucchini, onion, *1 cup* salsa, salt and pepper. Continue cooking, stirring occasionally, until vegetables are crisply tender (2 to 3 minutes). Stir hot pepper cheese and green chilies into cooked rice. To serve, on individual plates place about ½ cup rice; top with about ½ cup ground beef mixture. Sprinkle with about 2 tablespoons Cheddar cheese. Drizzle remaining salsa over cheese.

Nutrition Information (1 serving)
• Calories 500 • Protein 25g • Carbohydrate 34g • Fat 23g
• Cholesterol 82mg • Sodium 814mg

Onion Stuffed Hamburgers With Sloppy Joe Sauce

45 minutes

This juicy hamburger has grilled onions for the filling and a sloppy joe sauce on top.

Hamburgers

1 tablespoon vegetable oil
½ cup thinly sliced onion, separated into rings
1½ pounds ground beef
¼ teaspoon salt
¼ teaspoon coarsely ground pepper
1 tablespoon Worcestershire sauce

Sauce

⅓ cup coarsely chopped celery
¼ cup ketchup

¼ cup water
1 (6 ounce) can tomato paste
1 tablespoon firmly packed brown sugar
¼ teaspoon salt
¼ teaspoon coarsely ground pepper
2 tablespoons red wine vinegar
1 tablespoon Worcestershire sauce
1 tablespoon country-style Dijon mustard

4 onion hamburger buns

4 servings

In 10-inch skillet heat oil over medium heat (1 to 2 minutes); add onion. Continue cooking, stirring occasionally, until tender (3 to 4 minutes). Remove from skillet; set aside. In medium bowl stir together all remaining hamburger ingredients. Form into 8 large ¼ inch thick patties. Place ¼ of onion on top of each of 4 patties. Top each with remaining meat patty; press around edges to seal. Place hamburgers in skillet. Cook over medium heat, turning once, until desired doneness (12 to 15 minutes for medium). Meanwhile, in 2-quart saucepan stir together all sauce ingredients *except* buns. Cook over medium heat, stirring occasionally, until heated through (7 to 10 minutes). Place hamburgers on bottom bun halves; spoon about 2 tablespoons sauce on hamburgers. Top with remaining bun halves. Serve with remaining sauce.

Nutrition Information (1 serving)
• Calories 560 • Protein 33g • Carbohydrate 40g • Fat 30g
• Cholesterol 105mg • Sodium 1281mg

Santa Fe Supper (pictured)
Onion Stuffed Hamburgers With Sloppy Joe Sauce

Pronto Pasta Dinner (pictured)
Mustard Cream Pork Chops

Pronto Pasta Dinner   30 minutes

Flavorful vegetables and ham served over a bed of Parmesan noodles.

8 ounces (4 cups) uncooked dried egg noodles
2 tablespoons butter *or* margarine
2 tablespoons freshly grated Parmesan cheese
2 tablespoons butter *or* margarine
2 cups (2 medium) sliced ¼-inch zucchini
¼ cup sliced ¼-inch green onions
1 teaspoon finely chopped fresh garlic
6 ounces cooked ham, cut into
    1½x¼-inch strips*

1 cup frozen whole kernel corn
¼ teaspoon salt
¼ teaspoon pepper

Freshly grated Parmesan cheese

6 servings

Cook noodles according to package directions; drain. Toss with 2 tablespoons butter and 2 tablespoons Parmesan cheese; keep warm. Meanwhile, in 10-inch skillet melt 2 tablespoons butter; add zucchini, onions and garlic. Cook over medium heat, stirring occasionally, 4 minutes. Stir in ham, corn, salt and pepper. Continue cooking, stirring occasionally, until zucchini is crisply tender and mixture is heated through

(3 to 5 minutes). Serve over noodles; sprinkle with Parmesan cheese.

*6 ounces cooked link sausage, cut into ½-inch slices, can be substituted for 6 ounces cooked ham, cut into 1½x¼-inch strips.

Nutrition Information (1 serving)
• Calories 300 • Protein 13g • Carbohydrate 35g • Fat 12g
• Cholesterol 74mg • Sodium 552mg

Mustard Cream Pork Chops   60 minutes

*Whipping cream is added to the pan drippings of pork chops
to make a rich sauce that tastes great over country-style egg noodles.*

Noodles
1 (12 ounce) package frozen egg noodles*
1 cup (2 medium) chopped onions
1 cup (2 medium) sliced ¼-inch carrots
¼ teaspoon coarsely ground pepper
½ cup chopped fresh parsley

Pork Chops
2 tablespoons butter *or* margarine
2 tablespoons country-style Dijon mustard
4 (½-inch thick) boneless pork chops
¼ teaspoon coarsely ground pepper
⅛ teaspoon salt
½ cup whipping cream

4 servings

Cook noodles according to package directions with all noodle ingredients *except* parsley. Meanwhile, in 10-inch skillet melt butter until sizzling; stir in mustard. Place pork chops in skillet; sprinkle with ¼ teaspoon pepper and salt. Cook over medium heat, turning occasionally, until pork chops are fork tender (15 to 20 minutes). Stir whipping cream into pan juices; spoon over pork chops. Stir parsley

into noodles. Serve pork chops and cream sauce over noodles.

*2 cups uncooked dried wide egg noodles can be substituted for 1 (12 ounce) package frozen egg noodles.

Nutrition Information (1 serving)
• Calories 690 • Protein 32g • Carbohydrate 69g • Fat 31g
• Cholesterol 201mg • Sodium 425mg

Sausage & Vegetable Pasta Supper
30 minutes

Smoked sausage, vegetables and pasta are combined in a skillet meal tossed with cheese.

8 ounces uncooked dried rigatoni *or* twist pasta
2 tablespoons butter *or* margarine
1 pound cooked smoked sausage, cut into ½-inch slices
1 green pepper, cut into 1-inch pieces
1 medium onion, cut into ½-inch slices

½ teaspoon finely chopped fresh garlic
1 (28 ounce) can whole tomatoes, drained, cut into pieces
2 cups (8 ounces) shredded Monterey Jack cheese

6 servings

Cook pasta according to package directions; drain. Meanwhile, in Dutch oven melt butter. Add sausage, green pepper, onion and garlic. Cook over medium heat, stirring occasionally, until green pepper is crisply tender (8 to 10 minutes). Stir in rigatoni, tomatoes and cheese. Continue cooking, stirring occasionally, until heated through (3 to 5 minutes).

Microwave Directions: Cook pasta according to package directions; drain. In 3-quart casserole melt butter on HIGH (30 to 40 seconds). Stir in sausage, green pepper, onion and garlic. Microwave on HIGH, stirring after half the time, until green pepper is crisply tender (10 to 14 minutes). Stir in pasta, tomatoes and cheese. Microwave on HIGH, stirring after half the time, until heated through (4 to 5 minutes).

Nutrition Information (1 serving)
• Calories 600 • Protein 26g • Carbohydrate 37g • Fat 39g
• Cholesterol 98mg • Sodium 969mg

Lemon Pork Picatta
15 minutes

For a quick main dish dip pork cutlets in lemon and a light flour mixture, then pan fry.

½ cup all-purpose flour
½ teaspoon salt
½ teaspoon coarsely ground pepper
¼ cup lemon juice
1 pound pork cutlets*

¼ cup butter *or* margarine

4 servings

In 9-inch pie pan stir together flour, salt and pepper. In medium bowl place lemon juice. Dip pork cutlets in lemon juice; lightly coat both sides of pork cutlets with flour mixture. In 10-inch skillet melt *2 tablespoons* butter over medium heat until sizzling. Place 4 to 6 pork cutlets in melted butter; cook until browned (2 to 4 minutes on each side). Remove pork cutlets to serving platter; keep warm. Repeat with remaining butter and pork cutlets.

*1 pound boneless pork loin roast, sliced ¼-inch, can be substituted for 1 pound pork cutlets. Meat cutter can slice pork loin roast at meat counter or freeze roast for 2 to 3 hours for easier slicing.

Nutrition Information (1 serving)
• Calories 300 • Protein 26g • Carbohydrate 13g • Fat 16g
• Cholesterol 110mg • Sodium 441mg

Sausage & Vegetable Pasta Supper (pictured)
Lemon Pork Picatta

Baked Fish With Herbed Vegetables
60 minutes

Fresh fish is baked to perfection, with fresh vegetables and succulent herbs.

1 pound fresh fish fillets
2 medium zucchini, cut in 2-inch julienne strips
1 cup sliced fresh mushrooms
3 tablespoons butter *or* margarine, melted
1 tablespoon lemon juice

1 teaspoon chopped fresh basil leaves*
¼ teaspoon salt
⅛ teaspoon pepper

4 servings

Heat oven to 350°. Place fish in 9-inch square baking pan. Place zucchini and mushrooms around and over fish. In small bowl stir together butter, lemon juice, basil, salt and pepper; pour over fish. Bake for 30 to 40 minutes or until fish flakes with a fork.

*¼ teaspoon dried basil leaves can be substituted for 1 teaspoon chopped fresh basil leaves.

Microwave Directions: Place all ingredients in 9-inch square baking dish as directed above. Cover; microwave on HIGH, turning dish ½ turn after half the time, until fish flakes with a fork (7 to 8 minutes).

Nutrition Information (1 serving)
• Calories 210 • Protein 27g • Carbohydrate 3g • Fat 10g
• Cholesterol 86mg • Sodium 313mg

Fresh Citrus Fish Sauté
20 minutes

This quick, light fish entrée is accented with lemon and lime.

2 tablespoons butter *or* margarine
1 tablespoon chopped fresh chives*
1 teaspoon sugar
½ teaspoon grated lemon peel
½ teaspoon grated lime peel

1 tablespoon lemon juice
1 tablespoon lime juice
1 pound fresh *or* frozen white fish fillets, thawed, cut into 4 equal pieces

4 servings

In 10-inch skillet melt butter over medium heat. Stir in all remaining ingredients *except* fish fillets. Add fish fillets; cover. Continue cooking, turning fish fillets over occasionally, until fish flakes with a fork (5 to 6 minutes). Serve with pan juices.

*1 teaspoon dried chives can be substituted for 1 tablespoon chopped fresh chives.

Microwave Directions: In 9-inch square baking dish melt butter on HIGH (30 to 40 seconds). Stir in all remaining ingredients *except* fish fillets. Arrange fish fillets in dish, turning to coat with butter mixture. Cover with plastic wrap; microwave on HIGH, turning dish ¼ turn after half the time, until fish flakes with a fork (5 to 8 minutes).

Nutrition Information (1 serving)
• Calories 150 • Protein 20g • Carbohydrate 2g • Fat 7g
• Cholesterol 64mg • Sodium 482mg

Baked Fish With Herbed Vegetables (pictured)
Fresh Citrus Fish Sauté

Orange Roughy With Caramelized Onions (pictured)
Broiled Sole Parmesan

Orange Roughy With Caramelized Onions   20 minutes

Honey provides a hint of sweetness to onions and orange roughy.

3 tablespoons butter *or* margarine
2 medium sliced ⅛-inch onions
1 tablespoon honey
⅛ teaspoon salt
⅛ teaspoon coarsely ground pepper

2 tablespoons red wine vinegar
1½ pounds fresh *or* frozen orange roughy
    fillets, thawed, drained

6 servings

In 10-inch skillet melt butter until sizzling; stir in onions and honey. Cook over high heat, stirring occasionally, until golden brown (5 to 7 minutes). Stir in salt, pepper and vinegar. Reduce heat to medium. Place fish in same skillet; place onions on top of fish. Continue cooking until fish flakes with a fork (6 to 8 minutes).

Microwave Directions: In 9-inch pie plate melt butter on HIGH (40 to 50 seconds). Stir in onions and honey. Microwave on HIGH, stirring every 4 minutes, until onions are golden brown (14 to 16 minutes). Stir in salt, pepper and vinegar. In 13x9-inch baking dish place fish; place onions on top of fish. Cover with plastic wrap; microwave on HIGH, turning dish ½ turn after half the time, until fish flakes with a fork (4 to 8 minutes).

Nutrition Information (1 serving)
• Calories 220 • Protein 17g • Carbohydrate 5g • Fat 14g
• Cholesterol 38mg • Sodium 176mg

Broiled Sole Parmesan   20 minutes

The Parmesan topping adds extra flavor to broiled sole.

½ cup freshly grated Parmesan cheese
3 tablespoons butter *or* margarine, softened
⅛ teaspoon cayenne pepper
2 tablespoons sliced ⅛-inch green onions
3 tablespoons mayonnaise

1 teaspoon grated lemon peel
1½ pounds fresh *or* frozen sole fillets, thawed,
    drained
2 tablespoons lemon juice

6 servings

Heat broiler. In medium bowl stir together all ingredients *except* sole fillets and lemon juice. Place sole fillets on broiler pan; sprinkle with lemon juice. Broil 3 to 4 inches from heat until fish flakes with a fork (3 to 5 minutes).

Spread Parmesan mixture on sole fillets; broil until bubbly and golden brown (3 to 5 minutes).

Nutrition Information (1 serving)
• Calories 240 • Protein 25g • Carbohydrate 1g • Fat 15g
• Cholesterol 81mg • Sodium 346mg

Country Rice With Shrimp

40 minutes

Thinly sliced onion, peas and lettuce add color and crunch to this main dish rice.

1 tablespoon vegetable oil
1 cup uncooked long grain rice
1 (14½ ounce) can chicken broth
1 tablespoon grated fresh gingerroot*
3 cups shredded lettuce
1 cup (1 medium) thinly sliced onion
¼ cup soy sauce

1 (12 ounce) package frozen deveined medium shrimp, thawed, drained
1 (10 ounce) package frozen tender, tiny peas, thawed, drained
1 (8 ounce) can sliced water chestnuts, drained
¼ cup sliced ¼-inch green onions

6 servings

In Dutch oven heat oil over medium heat (1 to 2 minutes); stir in rice. Continue cooking until rice is golden (2 to 3 minutes). Stir in chicken broth and gingerroot. Continue cooking until mixture comes to a full boil (3 to 5 minutes). Reduce heat to low. Cover; continue cooking until rice is tender and liquid is absorbed (12 to 17 minutes). Stir in all remaining ingredients *except* green onions. Continue cooking, stirring occasionally, until shrimp turn pink (5 to 8 minutes). Stir in green onions.

*1 teaspoon ground ginger can be substituted for 1 tablespoon grated fresh gingerroot.

Nutrition Information (1 serving)
• Calories 280 • Protein 19g • Carbohydrate 41g • Fat 4g
• Cholesterol 86mg • Sodium 1053mg

Cracker Coated Walleye Pike

45 minutes

Cook freshly caught fish fillets with potatoes for a delightful fish supper.

Potatoes
3 tablespoons butter *or* margarine
3 cups (9 medium) thinly sliced new red potatoes
¼ teaspoon salt
¼ teaspoon coarsely ground pepper

Fish Fillets
1 cup finely crushed saltine crackers
1 teaspoon dried dill weed

½ teaspoon coarsely ground pepper
¼ teaspoon salt
¼ teaspoon dry mustard
1 egg, slightly beaten
2 tablespoons lemon juice
2 tablespoons butter *or* margarine
2 tablespoons vegetable oil
1½ pounds fresh *or* frozen walleye pike *or* sole fillets, thawed

6 servings

In 10-inch skillet heat 3 tablespoons butter until sizzling. Add potatoes; sprinkle with ¼ teaspoon salt and ¼ teaspoon pepper. Cook over medium high heat, turning occasionally, until crisply tender and lightly browned (10 to 15 minutes). Meanwhile, in 9-inch pie pan stir together crackers, dill weed, ½ teaspoon pepper, ¼ teaspoon salt and mustard. Remove potatoes from skillet; keep warm. In another 9-inch pie pan stir together egg and lemon juice. In same 10-inch skillet heat *1 tablespoon* butter and *1 tablespoon* oil until sizzling. Meanwhile, dip fish fillets in egg mixture; coat with crumb mixture. Place 4 fish fillets in skillet; cook over medium heat until browned (2 to 3 minutes). Turn; continue cooking until browned and fish flakes with a fork (1 to 2 minutes). Place fish fillets on platter with potatoes; keep warm. Repeat with remaining butter, oil and fish fillets.

Nutrition Information (1 serving)
• Calories 360 • Protein 26g • Carbohydrate 24g • Fat 17g
• Cholesterol 106mg • Sodium 465mg

Country Rice With Shrimp (pictured)
Cracker Coated Walleye Pike

Zucchini, Tomato & Cheese Frittata (pictured)
Country Provence Eggs

Zucchini, Tomato & Cheese Frittata
45 minutes

Zucchini and tomato slices garnish the top of this baked frittata.

½ cup (1 medium) chopped onion
¼ cup milk
6 eggs, slightly beaten
½ teaspoon dried basil leaves
¼ teaspoon salt
¼ teaspoon coarsely ground pepper
3 tablespoons butter *or* margarine

½ teaspoon finely chopped fresh garlic
1 cup (1 medium) diagonally sliced ¼-inch zucchini
1 medium ripe tomato, cut into 6 slices
½ cup (2 ounces) shredded Mozzarella cheese
2 tablespoons freshly grated Parmesan cheese

6 servings

Heat oven to 350°. In medium bowl stir together onion, milk, eggs, basil, salt and pepper. In ovenproof 10-inch skillet melt butter over medium heat (2 to 3 minutes); stir in garlic. Pour egg mixture into skillet. Bake for 8 to 10 minutes or until egg is partially set. Remove from oven. Arrange zucchini slices in circle on top of egg mixture; place tomato slices on top of zucchini. Sprinkle with mozzarella and Parmesan cheese. Continue baking for 10 to 14 minutes or until eggs are set in center and cheese is melted.

Nutrition Information (1 serving)
• Calories 180 • Protein 11g • Carbohydrate 4g • Fat 13g
• Cholesterol 237mg • Sodium 307mg

Country Provence Eggs
30 minutes

*Sausage, potatoes and spinach are sautéed with scrambled eggs
to create a hearty provincial supper.*

8 ounces bulk pork sausage
2 cups (8 small) cubed ½-inch new red potatoes
1 cup (1 medium) thinly sliced onion, separated into rings
¼ cup milk
8 eggs, slightly beaten
½ teaspoon coarsely ground pepper

¼ teaspoon salt
2 cups (5 ounces) torn spinach leaves
1 cup (4 ounces) grated Provolone *or* Mozzarella cheese
2 tablespoons freshly grated Parmesan cheese

6 servings

In 10-inch skillet place sausage; cook over medium high heat until browned. Remove sausage with slotted spoon; set aside. Add potatoes and onion to same skillet; cook over medium heat, stirring occasionally, until browned and fork tender (10 to 14 minutes). Stir in sausage. In small bowl stir together milk, eggs, pepper and salt. Pour egg mixture over sausage mixture. Continue cooking, gently lifting portions and stirring with spatula so uncooked portion flows to bottom of pan, until eggs are partially set and scrambled (5 to 6 minutes). Gradually stir in spinach; sprinkle with Provolone cheese. Continue cooking, stirring occasionally, until spinach is wilted and eggs are set (2 to 3 minutes). Sprinkle with Parmesan cheese.

Nutrition Information (1 serving)
• Calories 310 • Protein 18g • Carbohydrate 13g • Fat 20g
• Cholesterol 313mg • Sodium 523mg

Canadian Bacon n' Egg Stack   30 minutes

1½ cups water
½ pound (12) asparagus spears, broken into thirds
6 (¼-inch) slices Canadian bacon *or* ham
6 eggs, slightly beaten
¼ cup milk
⅛ teaspoon salt

⅛ teaspoon coarsely ground pepper
3 tablespoons butter *or* margarine
⅓ cup mayonnaise
2 teaspoons grated lemon peel
1 to 2 tablespoons lemon juice
3 English muffins, split

6 servings

In 10-inch skillet bring water to a full boil; add asparagus. Cook over medium high heat until asparagus is crisply tender (3 to 4 minutes). Drain; set aside. In same 10-inch skillet cook Canadian bacon over medium heat, turning once, until heated through (2 minutes on each side). Meanwhile, in medium bowl stir together eggs, milk, salt, pepper and asparagus. Remove Canadian bacon from skillet; keep warm. In same 10-inch skillet melt *1 tablespoon* butter until sizzling. Cook egg mixture over medium heat, gently lifting and stirring portions with spatula so uncooked portion flows to bottom of pan, until eggs are set and scrambled (4 to 5 minutes). Meanwhile, in small bowl stir together mayonnaise, *1 teaspoon* lemon peel and lemon juice. Toast English muffins; spread with remaining 2 tablespoons butter. To serve, on individual plates place toasted English muffin half; top with 1 slice Canadian bacon. Divide egg mixture between English muffins. Spoon about 1 tablespoon lemon mayonnaise over each egg stack; sprinkle with remaining lemon peel.

Nutrition Information (1 serving)
• Calories 340 • Protein 17g • Carbohydrate 19g • Fat 23g
• Cholesterol 250mg • Sodium 568mg

Enchilada-Style Scrambled Eggs   30 minutes

6 (7-inch) flour tortillas
1 tablespoon butter *or* margarine
½ cup thinly sliced onion, separated into rings
¼ cup milk
8 eggs, slightly beaten
¼ teaspoon salt
¼ teaspoon coarsely ground pepper

1 cup (4 ounces) shredded Monterey Jack cheese
1 cup (1 medium) ½-inch pieces ripe tomato

¾ cup salsa *or* picante sauce
½ cup frozen whole kernel corn, thawed, drained

Dairy sour cream

6 servings

Heat oven to 350°. Wrap tortillas in aluminum foil. Bake for 8 to 10 minutes or until warm. Meanwhile, in 10-inch skillet melt butter until sizzling; add onion. Cook over medium heat, stirring occasionally, until onion is tender (2 to 3 minutes). Meanwhile, in medium bowl stir together milk, eggs, salt and pepper. Pour egg mixture over onion; stir to blend. Continue cooking, lifting and stirring portions with spatula so uncooked portion flows to bottom of pan, until eggs are set and scrambled (4 to 5 minutes). Sprinkle cheese and tomato over eggs; let stand until cheese is melted and tomatoes are heated through (2 to 4 minutes). Meanwhile, in small bowl stir together salsa and corn. Place about ½ cup egg mixture on one side of each tortilla; roll up jelly roll style. Spoon about 1 tablespoon salsa mixture over each tortilla. Serve with sour cream.

Nutrition Information (1 serving)
• Calories 310 • Protein 16g • Carbohydrate 24g • Fat 17g
• Cholesterol 308mg • Sodium 654mg

Canadian Bacon n' Egg Stack (top)
Enchilada-Style Scrambled Eggs (bottom)

Garden Chicken Salad

30 minutes

Chicken

2 whole, boneless chicken breasts, skinned, halved
1 tablespoon olive *or* vegetable oil
½ teaspoon finely chopped fresh garlic
1 teaspoon chopped fresh basil leaves
¼ teaspoon coarsely ground pepper
⅛ teaspoon salt

Salad

1 (10 ounce) package frozen whole kernel corn, thawed, drained
¼ teaspoon coarsely ground pepper
⅛ teaspoon salt
2 tablespoons red wine vinegar
1 tablespoon olive *or* vegetable oil
3 medium ripe tomatoes, sliced ¼-inch
½ cup torn fresh basil leaves
¼ cup freshly grated Parmesan cheese

6 servings

Cut each halved chicken breast lengthwise into thirds. In 10-inch skillet cook oil and garlic over medium high heat until garlic is tender (1 to 2 minutes). Add chicken breast pieces and all remaining chicken ingredients. Continue cooking, turning occasionally, until chicken is browned and fork tender (8 to 10 minutes). Meanwhile, in medium bowl stir together all salad ingredients *except* tomatoes, basil and

Parmesan cheese. On platter or individual salad plates place tomato slices; sprinkle with half of corn mixture, *¼ cup* basil leaves and *2 tablespoons* Parmesan cheese. Top with chicken and remaining corn, basil leaves and Parmesan cheese.

Nutrition Information (1 serving)
• Calories 210 • Protein 21g • Carbohydrate 13g • Fat 8g
• Cholesterol 51mg • Sodium 216mg

Chicken Caesar Salad

30 minutes

All the good flavors of Caesar salad with the added flavor of garlic sautéed chicken.

Chicken

2 whole boneless chicken breasts, skinned, halved
2 tablespoons butter *or* margarine
½ teaspoon finely chopped fresh garlic
¼ teaspoon salt
¼ teaspoon coarsely ground pepper

Dressing

2 tablespoons freshly grated Parmesan cheese
¼ teaspoon coarsely ground pepper

2 tablespoons vegetable oil
1 tablespoon cider vinegar
1 tablespoon lemon juice
2 tablespoons dairy sour cream
1 tablespoon country-style Dijon mustard

Salad

4 cups torn Romaine lettuce
1 medium ripe tomato, sliced
  Garlic melba rounds

4 servings

Cut each halved chicken breast lengthwise into thirds. In 10-inch skillet melt butter until sizzling. Add chicken, garlic, salt and ¼ teaspoon pepper. Cook over medium high heat, turning once, until chicken is browned and fork tender (7 to 10 minutes). Meanwhile, in small bowl stir together all dressing ingredients. In large

bowl place lettuce. Pour dressing over lettuce; toss to coat. On platter or individual salad plates place lettuce. Place tomato slices and chicken on lettuce. Arrange garlic rounds on salad.

Nutrition Information (1 serving)
• Calories 330 • Protein 31g • Carbohydrate 11g • Fat 18g
• Cholesterol 92mg • Sodium 448mg

Garden Chicken Salad (top)
Chicken Caesar Salad (bottom)

Tuna Salad With Corn Crisps (top)
Turkey Wild Rice Salad (bottom)

Tuna Salad With Corn Crisps 20 minutes

Tuna salad is served over crispy tortilla chips, or make your own corn chips by frying tortillas.

Salad
3 cups shredded lettuce
½ cup sliced ¼-inch ripe olives
¼ cup coarsely chopped sweet pickles
¾ cup mayonnaise
2 (6½ ounce) cans tuna in water, drained
¼ teaspoon coarsely ground pepper

Corn Crisps*
¼ cup vegetable oil
4 (6-inch) corn tortillas

4 servings

In large bowl stir together all salad ingredients. Cover; refrigerate. In 10-inch skillet heat oil over medium high heat (1 to 2 minutes). Fry each tortilla in hot oil for 1 minute; turn. Continue frying until crispy and lightly browned (1 minute); drain on paper towels. Cut tortillas into quarters. On individual plates arrange salad with corn crisps tucked in and under salad.

*2 cups tortilla chips can be substituted for corn crisps.

Nutrition Information (1 serving)
• Calories 670 • Protein 28g • Carbohydrate 24g • Fat 52g
• Cholesterol 40mg • Sodium 884mg

Turkey Wild Rice Salad 2 hours 30 minutes

Make the night before or early in the day for a quick supper.

Salad
2 cups cubed ½-inch cooked turkey
2 cups cooked wild rice
1½ cups (3 stalks) sliced ¼-inch celery
1 cup red *or* green grapes, halved
1 (20 ounce) can pineapple chunks in
  unsweetened juice, drained

Dressing
¾ cup mayonnaise
¾ cup dairy sour cream
2 tablespoons Dijon-style mustard
¼ teaspoon salt

Lettuce leaves

4 servings

In large bowl toss together all salad ingredients. In medium bowl stir together all dressing ingredients *except* lettuce leaves. Stir dressing into salad to coat well. Refrigerate at least 2 hours. Serve salad on lettuce leaves.

Nutrition Information (1 serving)
• Calories 680 • Protein 26g • Carbohydrate 39g • Fat 47g
• Cholesterol 98mg • Sodium 709mg

A Missouri woman in the 1840s said she could tell whether a covered wagon was going East or West when it passed her house just by the sound it made, empty or full. "I missed the company of other women, but I couldn't even look up and wave. I was too busy."

Lemon Zest Dressing Over Fresh Fruit   20 minutes

A light lemonade dressing is drizzled over sliced pineapple, strawberries and kiwi.

¼ cup lemon juice
2 teaspoons sugar
1 teaspoon grated lemon peel
6 (¼-inch) slices fresh pineapple, peeled, cored

1 pint strawberries, hulled, sliced ¼-inch
1 kiwi, peeled, sliced ⅛-inch, cut in half

6 servings

In small bowl stir together lemon juice, sugar and lemon peel. On individual salad plates place 1 slice pineapple; divide strawberries and kiwi evenly between salad plates. Spoon about 2 teaspoons dressing over each serving.

Tip: Dressing can be used on your favorite combination of fruits.

Nutrition Information (1 serving)
• Calories 70 • Protein 1g • Carbohydrate 18g • Fat 1g
• Cholesterol 0mg • Sodium 4mg

Tossed Salad With Spicy Tomato Dressing   30 minutes

When tomatoes aren't in season, make this dressing for a flavorful tomato taste.

Dressing
1 (6 ounce) can spicy hot vegetable juice
2 tablespoons red wine vinegar
2 tablespoons vegetable oil
2 tablespoons tomato paste
1 tablespoon lemon juice
2 tablespoons chopped fresh parsley

Salad
4 cups torn lettuce
1 cup (1 medium) sliced ⅛-inch cucumber
1 cup sliced ⅛-inch red onion, separated into rings
1 cup pitted ripe olives
½ cup sweet pickled cherry peppers, quartered

8 servings

In medium bowl whisk together all dressing ingredients *except* parsley. Stir in parsley. In large bowl toss together all salad ingredients. Serve dressing over salad.

Nutrition Information (1 serving)
• Calories 80 • Protein 1g • Carbohydrate 8g • Fat 5g
• Cholesterol 0mg • Sodium 284mg

 In the 1930s, a new bride asked her husband if his farm had running water. "Yes," he replied, "you run to the pump with a pail and then you run back to the house."

Lemon Zest Dressing Over Fresh Fruit (top)
Tossed Salad With Spicy Tomato Dressing (bottom)

Apple Cheese n' Turkey Grill

15 minutes

Children can help make this oh-so-easy sandwich.

8 slices cinnamon swirl raisin bread
½ pound (8) ¼-inch slices smoked turkey
2 medium apples, cored, each cut into
    4 (¼-inch) rings

4 (4x4x¼-inch) slices Colby cheese
¼ cup butter *or* margarine

4 servings

On cookie sheet place 4 slices raisin bread; top each with 2 slices turkey. Lay 2 apple rings on each sandwich; top with slice of cheese and remaining slice of bread. In 10-inch skillet melt *2 tablespoons* butter until sizzling. Place 2 sandwiches in skillet; cook over medium heat, turning once, until grilled and cheese is melted (3 to 5 minutes on each side). Place sandwiches on platter; keep warm. Repeat with remaining butter and sandwiches. Cut sandwiches in half diagonally.

Nutrition Information (1 serving)
• Calories 510 • Protein 28g • Carbohydrate 43g • Fat 25g
• Cholesterol 103mg • Sodium 548mg

Grilled Chicken Sandwich With Spinach

25 minutes

*A grilled sandwich with the unique filling of a sautéed chicken breast,
spinach leaves and a lemon mustard spread.*

2 tablespoons butter *or* margarine
½ teaspoon finely chopped fresh garlic
2 whole boneless chicken breasts,
    skinned, halved
¼ teaspoon salt
¼ teaspoon coarsely ground pepper

1 tablespoon lemon juice
1 tablespoon country-style Dijon mustard
4 slices round sourdough bread*
16 spinach leaves, trimmed**
2 tablespoons butter *or* margarine

4 servings

In 10-inch skillet melt 2 tablespoons butter until sizzling; add garlic and chicken breasts. Sprinkle with salt and pepper. Cook over medium high heat, turning once, until chicken is browned and fork tender (5 to 8 minutes per side). Meanwhile, in small bowl stir together lemon juice and mustard. Cut each slice bread in half; spread one side of four halves with mustard mixture. Place 4 spinach leaves on each bread half spread with mustard. Place chicken on spinach leaves; top with remaining bread half. In clean 10-inch skillet melt 2 tablespoons butter until sizzling. Cook over medium heat, turning once, until bread is lightly browned (2 to 3 minutes on each side).

*8 slices English muffin bread can be substituted for 4 slices sourdough bread. Do not cut each bread slice in half.

**1 medium cucumber, thinly sliced, can be substituted for spinach leaves. Place about 5 slices cucumber on each bread half spread with mustard. Continue as directed above.

Nutrition Information (1 serving)
• Calories 350 • Protein 30g • Carbohydrate 20g • Fat 16g
• Cholesterol 104mg • Sodium 633mg

In the 1940s, when the King and Queen of England visited the United States, Eleanor Roosevelt had a cookout for them on the White House lawn. She served the royal pair hot dogs, and the newspaper reports of the day said they loved them.

Apple Cheese n' Turkey Grill (pictured)
Grilled Chicken Sandwich With Spinach

Open-Faced Salami n' Relish Sandwich

30 minutes

Crisp vegetables top slices of salami on caraway rye bread.

Relish

⅔ cup chopped ripe tomato
⅓ cup thinly sliced radishes
1 medium zucchini, cut into
　1½x⅛x⅛-inch thin strips
1 tablespoon chopped fresh chives*
¼ teaspoon coarsely ground pepper
⅛ teaspoon salt
1 tablespoon lime juice

1 tablespoon olive *or* vegetable oil
1 tablespoon red wine vinegar
1 teaspoon grated lime peel

Sandwich

6 slices caraway rye bread
½ pound (2-inch diameter) thinly sliced salami
1½ cups (6 ounces) shredded Mozzarella cheese

6 sandwiches

　In medium bowl stir together relish ingredients. *Heat broiler.* Place bread slices on cookie sheet. Divide salami among bread slices; top each sandwich with about ⅓ cup relish mixture. Sprinkle about ¼ cup shredded cheese on each sandwich. Broil 3 to 4 inches from heat until cheese is melted (2 to 3 minutes).

　*1 teaspoon dried chives can be substituted for 1 tablespoon chopped fresh chives.

Nutrition Information (1 sandwich)
• Calories 270 • Protein 16g • Carbohydrate 17g • Fat 15g
• Cholesterol 40mg • Sodium 782mg

Stroganoff Beef Sandwich

20 minutes

Deli roast beef is served on toasted caraway rye bread with a creamy mushroom and onion sauce.

1 (3 ounce) package cream cheese, softened
½ teaspoon dried marjoram leaves
¼ teaspoon salt
¼ teaspoon coarsely ground pepper
2 tablespoons dairy sour cream
3 to 4 tablespoons milk
2 cups (8 ounces) sliced ¼-inch fresh mushrooms

1 cup (1 medium) thinly sliced onion, separated into rings
2 tablespoons chopped fresh parsley
8 slices caraway rye bread
½ pound thinly sliced roast beef

4 servings

　In 10-inch skillet stir together cream cheese, marjoram, salt, pepper, sour cream and milk. Cook over medium heat, stirring occasionally, until smooth and creamy (3 to 4 minutes). Add mushrooms and onion; continue cooking, stirring occasionally, until vegetables are tender (6 to 7 minutes). Stir in parsley. Meanwhile, in toaster or broiler, toast bread. Place on serving platter. Divide roast beef between 4 slices toasted bread. Spoon mushroom sauce over roast beef; top with remaining toasted bread slices.

Microwave Directions: In 1-quart casserole stir together cream cheese, marjoram,

salt, pepper, sour cream and milk. Microwave on HIGH until smooth and creamy (45 to 60 seconds). Stir in mushrooms and onion. Microwave on HIGH, stirring after half the time, until vegetables are tender (4 to 7 minutes). Stir in parsley. Meanwhile, in toaster or broiler, toast bread. Place on serving platter. Divide roast beef between 4 slices toasted bread. Spoon mushroom sauce over roast beef; top with remaining toasted bread slices.

Nutrition Information (1 serving)
• Calories 310 • Protein 18g • Carbohydrate 32g • Fat 13g
• Cholesterol 59mg • Sodium 504mg

Open-Faced Salami n' Relish Sandwich (pictured)
Stroganoff Beef Sandwich

Cheese n' Vegetable Linguine (pictured)
Quick Tortellini Supper

Cheese n' Vegetable Linguine

30 minutes

A quick pasta dinner even the kids will love.

8 cups water
1 cup (2 medium) sliced ¼-inch carrots
7 ounces uncooked dried linguine
2 tablespoons butter *or* margarine
1 cup (1 medium) sliced ½-inch zucchini, quartered
¼ cup half-and-half
3 eggs

¼ teaspoon salt
1 cup (4 ounces) shredded mozzarella cheese
½ cup (2 ounces) freshly grated Parmesan cheese

Coarsely ground pepper

4 servings

In 3-quart saucepan bring water to a full boil (8 to 12 minutes). Add carrots. Cook over medium heat 3 minutes. Add linguine; continue cooking until carrots are crisply tender and linguine is done (8 to 10 minutes). Drain. Meanwhile, in 10-inch skillet melt butter; add zucchini. Cook over medium heat, stirring occasionally, until zucchini is crisply tender (3 to 4 minutes). In small bowl, with wire whisk, beat together half-and-half, eggs and salt. Add egg mixture, linguine, carrots and cheeses to zucchini; toss gently. Reduce heat to low; continue cooking, stirring constantly, until thickened and cheese is melted (1 to 2 minutes). Serve with pepper.

Microwave Directions: Prepare carrots and linguine as directed above. In 2-quart casserole combine butter and zucchini. Microwave on HIGH until zucchini is crisply tender (3 to 5 minutes). In small bowl, with wire whisk, beat together half-and-half, eggs and salt. Add egg mixture, linguine, carrots and cheese to zucchini; toss gently. Microwave on HIGH, stirring every 2 minutes, until thickened and cheese is melted (6 to 8 minutes). Serve with pepper.

Nutrition Information (1 serving)
• Calories 470 • Protein 25g • Carbohydrate 45g • Fat 21g
• Cholesterol 252mg • Sodium 660mg

Quick Tortellini Supper

30 minutes

Fresh pasta combines with mushrooms, peas and cheese for an easy meal.

2 (9 ounce) packages fresh tortellini*
¼ cup butter *or* margarine
1 cup sliced fresh mushrooms
1 (10 ounce) package frozen peas, thawed

1½ cups (6 ounces) shredded Cheddar cheese
Salt and pepper

4 servings

Cook tortellini according to package directions; drain. In 10-inch skillet melt butter; add mushrooms. Cook over medium heat, stirring occasionally, until tender (3 to 5 minutes). Stir in tortellini and peas; continue cooking until heated through (3 to 5 minutes). Stir in *1 cup* cheese; salt and pepper to taste. Sprinkle with remaining cheese.

*1 (7 ounce) package dried tortellini *or* 2½ cups dried medium macaroni shells can be substituted for fresh tortellini. Cook according to package directions; drain.

Microwave Directions: Cook tortellini according to package directions; drain. In 2-quart casserole combine butter and mushrooms. Cover; microwave on HIGH until tender (2 to 2½ minutes). Stir in tortellini and peas. Cover; microwave on HIGH until heated through (4 to 5 minutes). Stir in *1 cup* cheese; salt and pepper to taste. Sprinkle with remaining cheese.

Nutrition Information (1 serving)
• Calories 650 • Protein 34g • Carbohydrate 47g • Fat 36g
• Cholesterol 229mg • Sodium 937mg

Lemon Zest Rice (top)
Butter Crumb Noodles (bottom)

Lemon Zest Rice

30 minutes

Rice is seasoned with chicken broth, bay leaves and lemon juice.

1   tablespoon butter *or* margarine
1   cup uncooked long grain rice
¼   cup lemon juice
2   (10½ ounce) cans chicken broth
2   bay leaves

½   teaspoon coarsely ground pepper
1   teaspoon grated lemon peel
2   tablespoons sliced ⅛-inch green onions

4 servings

In 2-quart saucepan melt butter; add rice. Cook over medium high heat, stirring constantly, until rice is a golden brown color (2 to 3 minutes). Add all remaining ingredients *except* green onions. Continue cooking until mixture comes to a full boil (8 to 10 minutes); reduce heat to low. Cover; continue cooking until all liquid is absorbed. Stir in green onions.

Microwave Directions: In 3-quart casserole melt butter on HIGH (30 to 40 seconds). Stir in rice. Microwave on HIGH until rice is a golden color (3 to 5 minutes). Add all remaining ingredients *except* green onions. Cover with plastic wrap; microwave on HIGH until mixture comes to a full boil (6 to 9 minutes). Reduce power to MEDIUM (50% power); microwave, stirring after half the time and adding additional water if needed, until rice is tender and all liquid is absorbed (15 to 20 minutes). Stir in green onions.

Nutrition Information (1 serving)
• Calories 220 • Protein 6g • Carbohydrate 39g • Fat 4g
• Cholesterol 8mg • Sodium 517mg

Butter Crumb Noodles

20 minutes

Fresh, buttery bread crumbs tossed with egg noodles make an easy family side dish.

8   ounces uncooked dried egg noodles
⅓   cup butter *or* margarine
3   slices whole wheat *or* white bread
¼   cup chopped fresh parsley

¼   to ½ teaspoon coarsely ground pepper
¼   teaspoon salt

6 servings

Cook egg noodles according to package directions. Meanwhile, place bread in food processor or blender. Process with pulses until coarse crumbs are formed. In 10-inch skillet melt butter until sizzling. Add bread crumbs. Cook over medium heat, stirring constantly, until golden brown (5 to 7 minutes).

Drain noodles. Toss with bread crumbs, parsley, pepper and salt. Serve immediately.

Tip: If using a blender, process 1 slice of bread at a time.

Nutrition Information (1 serving)
• Calories 270 • Protein 6g • Carbohydrate 34g • Fat 12g
• Cholesterol 64mg • Sodium 263mg

Ham & Broccoli Fettuccine
40 minutes

Two colors of fettuccine are tossed with ham and broccoli for a one-dish supper.

4 ounces uncooked dried fettuccine
4 ounces uncooked dried spinach fettuccine
½ cup butter *or* margarine
2 cups broccoli flowerets*
½ teaspoon finely chopped fresh garlic
¼ cup chopped fresh parsley
1 cup whipping cream

¼ teaspoon pepper
¾ cup freshly grated Parmesan cheese
4 ounces cubed ½-inch cooked ham

Freshly grated Parmesan cheese

4 servings

In Dutch oven cook fettuccine according to package directions; drain. Set aside. In same pan melt butter. Add broccoli and garlic; cook over medium heat, stirring occasionally, until broccoli is crisply tender (4 to 5 minutes). Stir in parsley, cream and pepper. Continue cooking, stirring occasionally, until heated through (4 to 5 minutes). Stir in fettuccine, ¾ cup Parmesan cheese and ham. Continue cooking, stirring occasionally, until heated through and cheese is melted (4 to 6 minutes). Serve with additional Parmesan cheese.

*2 cups frozen cut broccoli can be substituted for 2 cups broccoli flowerets.

Microwave Directions: Prepare fettuccine according to package directions; drain. Set aside. In 3-quart casserole melt butter on HIGH (1 to 1½ minutes). Stir in garlic. Microwave on HIGH 1 minute. Stir in broccoli. Cover; microwave on HIGH, stirring after half the time, until broccoli is crisply tender (3 to 4 minutes). Stir in cream. Microwave on HIGH, stirring after half the time, until cream is heated through (2 to 3 minutes). Stir in fettuccine, ¾ cup Parmesan cheese and ham. Microwave on HIGH, stirring after half the time, until heated through and cheese is melted (3 to 4 minutes). Serve with additional Parmesan cheese.

Nutrition Information (1 serving)
• Calories 760 • Protein 24g • Carbohydrate 48g • Fat 53g
• Cholesterol 173mg • Sodium 961mg

Smoked Bacon Red Sauce Over Spaghetti
60 minutes

Smoked bacon and lots of onions give a delicious, rich flavor to this red sauce.

1 pound bacon, cut into ½-inch pieces
3 cups (3 medium) thinly sliced onions
2 teaspoons finely chopped fresh garlic
¾ cup dry red wine *or* water
2 (28 ounce) cans plum-style tomatoes
1 (12 ounce) can tomato paste
1 tablespoon dried basil leaves

1 teaspoon dried oregano leaves
1 teaspoon coarsely ground pepper
2 bay leaves

8 ounces uncooked dried spaghetti

6 servings

In Dutch oven cook bacon, onions and garlic over medium high heat, stirring occasionally, until bacon is cooked (8 to 10 minutes). Drain off fat. Add all remaining ingredients *except* spaghetti. Reduce heat to medium; cook, stirring occasionally, until sauce is thickened (40 to

45 minutes). Remove bay leaves. Meanwhile, cook spaghetti according to package directions; drain. Serve red sauce over spaghetti.

Nutrition Information (1 serving)
• Calories 410 • Protein 17g • Carbohydrate 57g • Fat 12g
• Cholesterol 18mg • Sodium 1221mg

Ham & Broccoli Fettuccine (pictured)
Smoked Bacon Red Sauce Over Spaghetti

Rigatoni With Eggplant & Parmesan Cheese   45 minutes

This pasta is tossed with eggplant and garden-ripened tomatoes.

8 ounces uncooked dried rigatoni
8 slices bacon, cut into 1-inch pieces
1 medium eggplant, sliced ¼-inch, cut in half
½ teaspoon finely chopped fresh garlic
2 cups (8 ounces) fresh mushrooms, halved
2 medium (2 cups) ripe tomatoes, cut into 1-inch pieces
½ teaspoon coarsely ground pepper

¼ teaspoon salt
⅛ teaspoon cayenne pepper, if desired
1 tablespoon olive *or* vegetable oil
½ cup chopped fresh parsley

2 ounces freshly shaved *or* grated Parmesan cheese

6 servings

Cook rigatoni according to package directions; drain. Meanwhile, in Dutch oven cook bacon, eggplant and garlic over medium high heat, stirring occasionally, until bacon is browned (6 to 8 minutes). Reduce heat to medium. Stir in all remaining ingredients *except* rigatoni, parsley and Parmesan cheese. Cook, stirring occasionally, until mushrooms are tender (3 to 4 minutes). Add rigatoni and parsley. Continue cooking, stirring occasionally, until rigatoni is heated through (3 to 5 minutes). Top with shavings of Parmesan cheese.

Nutrition Information (1 serving)
• Calories 500 • Protein 20g • Carbohydrate 79g • Fat 11g
• Cholesterol 15mg • Sodium 410mg

Chicken Divan Pasta   40 minutes

*Fettuccine is topped with a cream sauce subtly seasoned with
mozzarella and Parmesan cheeses, then tossed with chicken, broccoli and red onion.*

8 ounces uncooked dried fettuccine
¼ cup butter *or* margarine
3 cups broccoli flowerets
3 whole boneless chicken breasts, skinned, cut into 3x½-inch strips
1 cup sliced ⅛-inch red onion, separated into rings
¼ teaspoon salt

¼ teaspoon coarsely ground pepper
1 tablespoon all-purpose flour
1 cup (4 ounces) shredded mozzarella cheese
1 cup half-and-half
¼ cup freshly grated Parmesan cheese

Freshly grated Parmesan cheese

6 servings

Cook fettuccine according to package directions; drain. Meanwhile, in 10-inch skillet melt butter until sizzling. Stir in broccoli and chicken strips. Cook over medium high heat, stirring occasionally, until chicken is fork tender (6 to 8 minutes). Stir in onion, salt and pepper. Continue cooking, stirring occasionally, until onion is crisply tender (2 to 3 minutes). Reduce heat to medium. Push chicken and vegetables to one side of pan; stir flour into pan juices until smooth, then stir into chicken and vegetables. Stir in all remaining ingredients *except* ¼ cup Parmesan cheese. Continue cooking, stirring occasionally, until cheese is melted and sauce is slightly thickened (4 to 5 minutes). Serve over fettuccine; sprinkle with Parmesan cheese.

Tip: 1 (16 ounce) package frozen cut broccoli can be substituted for 3 cups broccoli flowerets. Add to cooked chicken with onion, salt and pepper.

Nutrition Information (1 serving)
• Calories 500 • Protein 41g • Carbohydrate 36g • Fat 21g
• Cholesterol 121mg • Sodium 436mg

Rigatoni With Eggplant & Parmesan Cheese (pictured)
Chicken Divan Pasta

Herbed Green Beans

25 minutes

These seasoned green beans are tossed with ripe olives and Parmesan cheese.

3 tablespoons butter *or* margarine
1 (16 ounce) package frozen cut green beans
1 (4 ounce) can sliced ripe olives, drained

1 teaspoon Italian herb seasoning*
¼ cup freshly grated Parmesan cheese

6 servings

In 3-quart saucepan melt butter. Stir in all remaining ingredients *except* Parmesan cheese. Cover; cook over medium heat, stirring occasionally, until beans are crisply tender (13 to 18 minutes). Sprinkle with Parmesan cheese.

*¼ teaspoon *each* dried oregano leaves, dried marjoram leaves and dried basil leaves and ⅛ teaspoon rubbed dried sage can be substituted for 1 teaspoon Italian herb seasoning.

Microwave Directions: In 1½-quart casserole melt butter on HIGH (40 to 50 seconds). Stir in all remaining ingredients *except* Parmesan cheese. Cover; microwave on HIGH 7 minutes. Stir well; microwave on HIGH until beans are crisply tender (6 to 8 minutes). Sprinkle with Parmesan cheese.

Nutrition Information (1 serving)
• Calories 100 • Protein 3g • Carbohydrate 6g • Fat 8g
• Cholesterol 19mg • Sodium 194mg

Gingered Pea Pods & Red Pepper

20 minutes

Fresh grated gingerroot adds a spark of flavor to sweet red pepper and crisp pea pods.

2 tablespoons butter *or* margarine
4 ounces fresh pea pods, remove tips and strings*
2 small onions, each cut into 8 wedges

1 medium red pepper, cut into strips
1 tablespoon grated fresh gingerroot**
¼ teaspoon salt

4 servings

In 2-quart saucepan melt butter until sizzling; stir in all remaining ingredients. Cook over medium heat, stirring occasionally, until vegetables are crisply tender (7 to 11 minutes).

*1 (6 ounce) package frozen pea pods, thawed, can be substituted for 4 ounces fresh pea pods.

**½ teaspoon ground ginger can be substituted for 1 tablespoon grated fresh gingerroot.

Microwave Directions: In 2-quart casserole melt butter on HIGH (30 to 40 seconds). Stir in onions and gingerroot. Cover; microwave on HIGH 2 minutes. Stir in pea pods, red pepper and salt. Cover; microwave on HIGH, stirring after half the time, until vegetables are crisply tender (2 to 4 minutes).

Nutrition Information (1 serving)
• Calories 80 • Protein 1g • Carbohydrate 6g • Fat 6g
• Cholesterol 16mg • Sodium 196mg

In 1924, Land O'Lakes offered $500 in GOLD for a name for our new butter. Over 100,000 entries poured in and the winners were Mrs. E. B. Foss and George Swift who both came up with our name, LAND O LAKES® Butter.

Herbed Green Beans (top)
Gingered Pea Pods & Red Pepper (bottom)

Skillet Zucchini Sauté (top)
Creamed Dilly Peas (bottom)

Skillet Zucchini Sauté

30 minutes

Bountiful zucchini prepared in a skillet.

3 tablespoons butter *or* margarine
½ cup (1 medium) chopped onion
½ teaspoon salt
1 teaspoon chopped fresh basil leaves*
½ teaspoon finely chopped fresh garlic
3 cups (4 medium) coarsely chopped zucchini

1 cup (1 medium) cubed ½-inch ripe tomato
2 tablespoons sliced ripe olives

½ cup (2 ounces) shredded Cheddar cheese, if desired

6 servings

In 10-inch skillet melt butter over medium heat. Stir in onion, salt, basil and garlic. Cook over medium heat, stirring occasionally, until onion is crisply tender (4 to 5 minutes). Stir in zucchini. Continue cooking, stirring constantly, until zucchini is crisply tender (3 to 4 minutes). Stir in tomatoes and olives. Continue cooking until heated through (1 to 2 minutes). If desired, sprinkle with cheese.

* ½ teaspoon dried basil leaves can be substituted for 1 teaspoon chopped fresh basil leaves.

Microwave Directions: In 2-quart casserole melt butter on HIGH (40 to 50 seconds). Stir in onion, salt, basil and garlic. Cover; microwave on HIGH, stirring after half the time, until onion is crisply tender (2½ to 3½ minutes). Stir in zucchini. Microwave on HIGH, stirring after half the time, until zucchini is crisply tender (2½ to 4½ minutes). Stir in tomatoes and olives. Microwave on HIGH until heated through (1 to 2 minutes). If desired, sprinkle with cheese.

Nutrition Information (1 serving)
• Calories 110 • Protein 4g • Carbohydrate 4g • Fat 9g
• Cholesterol 25mg • Sodium 322mg

Creamed Dilly Peas

30 minutes

Colorful carrots and peas, served in an old-fashioned dill-flavored cream sauce.

¾ cup water
1 cup (2 medium) sliced ¼-inch carrots
¼ cup butter *or* margarine
1 tablespoon cornstarch
1 cup half-and-half
1 (10 ounce) package frozen tiny peas, thawed, drained

2 tablespoons sliced ⅛-inch green onions
½ teaspoon salt
½ teaspoon dried dill weed
⅛ teaspoon pepper

5 servings

In 2-quart saucepan bring water to a full boil. Add carrots. Cover; cook over medium heat until carrots are crisply tender (8 to 10 minutes). Drain; set aside. In same saucepan melt butter. Stir in cornstarch until smooth. Stir in carrots and all remaining ingredients.

Cook over medium heat, stirring constantly, until mixture comes to a full boil (8 to 10 minutes). Boil, stirring constantly, 1 minute.

Nutrition Information (1 serving)
• Calories 210 • Protein 5g • Carbohydrate 14g • Fat 15g
• Cholesterol 43mg • Sodium 399mg

Garlic Spinach With Red Onion

20 minutes

Tender leaves of spinach are cooked in garlic seasoned olive oil.

2 tablespoons olive *or* vegetable oil
1 cup thinly sliced red onion
½ teaspoon finely chopped fresh garlic
10 ounces spinach leaves, washed, trimmed

¼ teaspoon salt
¼ teaspoon coarsely ground pepper

4 servings

In Dutch oven heat oil over medium high heat; stir in onion and garlic. Cook, stirring occasionally, until onion is crisply tender (2 to 3 minutes). Add spinach, salt and pepper. Continue cooking, stirring occasionally, until spinach is wilted (3 to 5 minutes).

Microwave Directions: In 2-quart casserole stir together oil, onion and garlic. Microwave on HIGH, stirring after half the time, until onion is crisply tender (4 to 6 minutes). Add spinach, salt and pepper. Cover with plastic wrap; microwave on HIGH, stirring every 2 minutes, until spinach is wilted (4 to 6 minutes).

Nutrition Information (1 serving)
• Calories 85 • Protein 2g • Carbohydrate 5g • Fat 7g
• Cholesterol 0mg • Sodium 190mg

Potato Ratatouille

30 minutes

Potatoes, eggplant, zucchini and tomatoes simmer in an herbed garlic butter.

¼ cup butter *or* margarine
6 new red potatoes, quartered
½ teaspoon finely chopped fresh garlic
2 cups (1 small) ½-inch pieces eggplant
2 cups (2 medium) sliced ¼-inch zucchini

1 cup (1 medium) ½-inch pieces ripe tomato
1 teaspoon dried basil leaves
½ teaspoon salt
½ teaspoon coarsely ground pepper

6 servings

In 10-inch skillet melt butter until sizzling; add potatoes and garlic. Cover; cook over medium high heat, stirring occasionally, until potatoes are browned and fork tender (12 to 15 minutes). Reduce heat to medium; add all remaining ingredients. Cook, stirring occasionally, until vegetables are crisply tender (6 to 8 minutes).

Microwave Directions: In 2½-quart casserole melt butter on HIGH (50 to 60 seconds). Stir in potatoes and garlic. Cover; microwave on HIGH, stirring after half the time, until potatoes are fork tender (7 to 9 minutes). Add all remaining ingredients. Cover; microwave on HIGH, stirring after half the time, until vegetables are crisply tender (6 to 8 minutes).

Nutrition Information (1 serving)
• Calories 140 • Protein 3g • Carbohydrate 17g • Fat 8g
• Cholesterol 21mg • Sodium 266mg

Pioneer women were expected to offer hospitality to anyone and everyone who dropped by. This included meals and lodging, because inns and hotels were few and far between. One account tells us of a family's 16x18-foot cabin that provided lodging for over 30 people in one night. It didn't mention breakfast.

Garlic Spinach With Red Onion (top)
Potato Ratatouille (bottom)

Rosemary Garlic Potatoes

45 minutes

These skillet potatoes are simple to prepare and deliciously seasoned with rosemary and garlic.

3 tablespoons olive *or* vegetable oil
10 small red potatoes, quartered
1 tablespoon chopped fresh rosemary leaves*
½ teaspoon salt

¼ teaspoon coarsely ground pepper
½ teaspoon finely chopped fresh garlic

4 servings

In 10-inch skillet heat oil; stir in all remaining ingredients. Cook over medium heat, stirring occasionally, until crisply tender (30 to 35 minutes).

*1 teaspoon dried rosemary leaves, crushed, can be substituted for 1 tablespoon fresh rosemary leaves.

Nutrition Information (1 serving)
• Calories 170 • Protein 2g • Carbohydrate 18g • Fat 10g
• Cholesterol 0mg • Sodium 275mg

Mashed Potatoes With Sour Cream

60 minutes

Cream cheese, sour cream and green onions turn ordinary mashed potatoes into extra-special mashed potatoes.

1½ pounds potatoes, peeled, cut into 2-inch chunks
¼ cup dairy sour cream
⅓ cup milk
1 (3 ounce) package cream cheese, softened

2 tablespoons chopped green onions
⅛ teaspoon pepper
⅛ teaspoon salt

4 servings

In Dutch oven place potatoes and enough water to cover. Cook over medium heat until fork tender (25 to 35 minutes); drain. In large mixer bowl combine potatoes and all remaining ingredients. Beat at medium speed, scraping bowl often, until potatoes are smooth and creamy (3 to 4 minutes).

Microwave Directions: In 2-quart casserole place potatoes and ½ *cup water.* Cover; microwave on HIGH, stirring after half the time, until potatoes are fork tender (12 to 16 minutes). Let stand 5 minutes; drain. In large mixer bowl combine potatoes and all remaining ingredients. Beat at medium speed, scraping bowl often, until potatoes are smooth and creamy (3 to 4 minutes).

Nutrition Information (1 serving)
• Calories 252 • Protein 6g • Carbohydrate 33g • Fat 11g
• Cholesterol 32mg • Sodium 158mg

According to a farm wife, in 1922, "Making butter was hard work. You'd fill a one-gallon jar with thick cream and turn the crank for thirty or forty minutes until the crank got hard to turn. When it held together in large chunks, you'd work the soft butter to get the water out and salt in. Then it was pressed into a butter mold. You'd do this 2-3 times a week."

Rosemary Garlic Potatoes (pictured)
Mashed Potatoes With Sour Cream

Tender Pears in Almond Cream Sauce

30 minutes

These juicy, tender pears are served in a delicate sauce.

¼ cup butter *or* margarine
6 cups (4 medium) firm ripe pears, cored, sliced ½-inch
⅓ cup firmly packed brown sugar
1 teaspoon almond extract

½ cup whipping cream
Sweetened whipped cream
Toasted sliced almonds

6 servings

In 10-inch skillet melt butter; add pear slices. Cook over medium heat, stirring occasionally, 3 minutes. Stir in brown sugar and almond extract. Continue cooking, stirring occasionally, until pears are fork tender* (3 to 5 minutes). Remove pears with slotted spoon to individual dessert dishes. Gradually stir ½ cup whipping cream into liquid in skillet. Cook over medium high heat, stirring constantly, until mixture comes to a full boil. Boil, stirring constantly, 3 to 5 minutes or until sauce is reduced to desired consistency. Pour sauce over pear slices. If desired, serve with sweetened whipped cream and toasted sliced almonds.

*Bartlett pears will require less cooking time than Bosc or Anjou.

Microwave Directions: In 2-quart casserole melt butter on HIGH (50 to 60 seconds). Stir in pears. Cover; microwave on HIGH until pears begin to cook (2½ to 3½ minutes). Stir in brown sugar and almond extract. Cover; microwave on HIGH, stirring after half the time, until pears are fork tender (3 to 5 minutes). Remove pears with slotted spoon to individual dessert dishes. Combine 2 teaspoons cornstarch with ½ cup whipping cream. Stir into liquid in casserole. Microwave on HIGH, stirring every minute, until sauce is thickened (3 to 5 minutes). Pour sauce over pear slices. If desired, serve with additional sweetened whipped cream and toasted sliced almonds.

Nutrition Information (1 serving)
• Calories 250 • Protein 1g • Carbohydrate 29g • Fat 16g
• Cholesterol 48mg • Sodium 90mg

Custard Cream With Oranges & Bananas

30 minutes

A rich custard pudding is garnished with orange slices, bananas and toasted coconut.

½ cup sugar
2 tablespoons cornstarch
2 cups half-and-half
3 egg yolks, slightly beaten
2 teaspoons vanilla

2 oranges, peeled, sliced ¼-inch, quartered
1 banana, sliced ¼-inch
¼ cup flaked coconut, toasted

4 servings

In 2-quart saucepan combine sugar and cornstarch. Gradually stir in half-and-half. Cook over medium heat, stirring constantly, until mixture thickens and comes to a full boil (9 to 12 minutes); boil 1 minute. In small bowl place egg yolks. Stir ½ of half-and-half mixture into egg yolks, then stir egg yolk mixture into remaining half-and-half mixture. Cook over medium heat, stirring constantly, until mixture just comes to a boil (2 to 3 minutes). Stir in vanilla. Pour into individual dessert dishes. Serve warm or cover; store refrigerated. To serve, arrange slices of oranges and bananas on custard cream. Sprinkle with toasted coconut.

Nutrition Information (1 serving)
• Calories 400 • Protein 7g • Carbohydrate 50g • Fat 20g
• Cholesterol 249mg • Sodium 57mg

Tender Pears in Almond Cream Sauce (top)
Custard Cream With Oranges & Bananas (bottom)

Peach & Berry Shake (pictured)
Strawberries With Orange Chocolate

Peach & Berry Shake

15 minutes

Two favorite fruits combine in a quick, tasty shake; great for a snack or dessert.

2 cups (3 medium) peaches, peeled, sliced
¼ cup milk
1 pint strawberries, hulled, *reserve 4 strawberries*

1 to 3 tablespoons sugar
2 cups vanilla ice cream

4 servings

In 5-cup blender container combine peaches, milk, strawberries and sugar. Cover; blend at High speed until well blended (30 to 60 seconds). Add ice cream. Continue blending at High speed until well blended (30 to 40 seconds).

Pour into glasses; garnish with reserved strawberries. Serve immediately.

Nutrition Information (1 serving)
• Calories 220 • Protein 4g • Carbohydrate 35g • Fat 8g
• Cholesterol 31mg • Sodium 67mg

Strawberries With Orange Chocolate

20 minutes

This rich, chocolate sauce tastes good served over berries, ice cream or pound cake.

1 cup semi-sweet real chocolate chips
1 cup whipping cream
2 tablespoons orange juice
2 teaspoons grated orange peel
1 quart strawberries, hulled, halved

1 tablespoon powdered sugar, if desired
1 teaspoon grated orange peel, if desired

8 servings

In 1-quart saucepan place chocolate chips and whipping cream. Cook over low heat, stirring constantly, until chocolate is melted (5 to 7 minutes). Stir in orange juice and 2 teaspoons orange peel; set aside. Spoon strawberries into individual dessert dishes; spoon chocolate

sauce over strawberries. If desired, garnish with powdered sugar and orange peel.

Nutrition Information (1 serving)
• Calories 240 • Protein 2g • Carbohydrate 20g • Fat 19g
• Cholesterol 41mg • Sodium 13mg

On Long Island in the 1700s, during strawberry time, families would ride out to the fields, bringing with them wine, cream and sugar to enjoy the new berries as they picked them.

No-Bake Chocolate Cookies

20 minutes

An easy ending to a quick meal.

1½ cups quick-cooking oats
½ cup flaked coconut
¼ cup chopped walnuts
¾ cup sugar

¼ cup milk
¼ cup butter *or* margarine
3 tablespoons unsweetened cocoa

2 dozen

In medium bowl combine oats, coconut and walnuts; set aside. In 2-quart saucepan combine sugar, milk, butter and cocoa. Cook over medium heat, stirring occasionally, until mixture comes to a full boil (3 to 4 minutes). Remove from heat. Stir in oat mixture. Quickly drop mixture by rounded teaspoonfuls onto waxed paper. Cool completely. Store in refrigerator.

Microwave Directions: In medium bowl combine oats, coconut and walnuts; set aside. In medium bowl melt butter on HIGH (50 to 60 seconds). Stir in sugar, milk and cocoa. Microwave on HIGH, stirring every minute, until mixture comes to a full boil (2 to 3 minutes). Stir in oat mixture. Quickly drop mixture by rounded teaspoonfuls onto waxed paper. Cool completely. Store in refrigerator.

Nutrition Information (1 cookie)
• Calories 80 • Protein 1g • Carbohydrate 11g • Fat 4g
• Cholesterol 5mg • Sodium 26mg

Chewy Crunch Bars

60 minutes

These bars are packed full of your favorite treats.

6 cups bite-size crispy corn cereal squares
1 cup salted peanuts
1 (8 ounce) package candy coated milk
   chocolate pieces
½ cup butter *or* margarine

2 tablespoons all-purpose flour
1 cup firmly packed brown sugar
½ cup light corn syrup

2 dozen

In large bowl combine cereal, peanuts and candy; set aside. In 2-quart saucepan melt butter. Stir in flour until smooth; stir in brown sugar and corn syrup. Cook over medium heat, stirring occasionally, until mixture comes to a full boil (2 to 4 minutes). Boil 1 minute. Pour caramel mixture over cereal mixture; toss to coat well. Press into greased 13x9-inch pan. Cool completely; cut into bars.

Microwave Directions: In large bowl combine cereal, peanuts and candy; set aside. In 4-cup measure melt butter on HIGH (1 to 1½ minutes). Stir in flour until smooth; stir in brown sugar and corn syrup. Microwave on HIGH, stirring after half the time, until mixture comes to a full boil (2½ to 5 minutes). Boil 1 minute. Pour caramel mixture over cereal mixture; toss to coat well. Press on bottom of greased 13x9-inch pan. Cool completely; cut into bars.

Nutrition Information (1 bar)
• Calories 200 • Protein 3g • Carbohydrate 29g • Fat 9g
• Cholesterol 11mg • Sodium 145mg

No-Bake Chocolate Cookies (top)
Chewy Crunch Bars (bottom)

HEARTY DINNERS

In the early 1900s, the wave of immigrants to America became a flood as hundreds of thousands of new citizens arrived at Ellis Island from all parts of Europe. On the West Coast, many more new Americans were arriving from the Orient. Each group brought a recipe for their very own hearty dinner, a traditional meal that would comfort and sustain them in this strange new land.

Over the years in America, these meals may have changed in cooking methods and even ingredients, but they remained family favorites. An American hearty dinner is really more than a dinner, it's a statement of family solidarity and the continuing of well-loved traditions.

These are delicious, nourishing dinners and chances are your family has its favorite. It might be the one you had at Grandma's house every Sunday. Or it might be the special dinner your whole family gathered to celebrate just once a year. It was probably the first meal you had Mom teach you how to make when you started your own home.

We've gathered some of our favorite hearty dinners from all parts of America and updated them for today. They're all nourishing, homemade dinners...the kind of comfort food your family asks for again and again.

HEARTY DINNERS
MENU
Fisherman's Delight

You'll catch your limit of compliments when you serve delicate, pan-fried rosemary rainbow trout with delicious vegetable rice pilaf and your favorite tossed salad. Finish the meal with this pretty almond-accented mixed berry pie.

Rosemary Rainbow Trout p.188
Vegetable Rice Pilaf p.202   Tossed Salad
Mixed Berry Almond Pie p.210

HEARTY DINNERS
MENU

Fall Harvest Dinner

The perfect fall dinner, filled with autumn's bounty! Swiss steak in a rich blue cheese sauce, served with a grapefruit and pea salad, honey thyme squash and hot spinach bread made with frozen whole wheat dough for a head start!

Blue Cheese & Onion Baked Steak p.181
Grapefruit Salad Tossed With Peas p.196 Harvest Honey Thyme Squash p.208
Spinach Swirl Whole Wheat Bread p.164

HEARTY DINNERS
MENU

Homemade Pot Roast

This is a perfect pot roast, to simmer slowly with wonderful vegetables, filling the house with winter-warming aromas. Serve with spoon bread. Then treat them to a buttery coconut pecan cake with browned butter frosting.

Pot Roast With Winter Vegetables p.178
Old-Fashioned Spoon Bread With Maple Butter p.162
Apple & Pear Slices   Buttery Coconut Pecan Cake p.212

HEARTY DINNERS
MENU

Family Favorite

Crispy chicken that's easy to bake with a Parmesan cheese coating for a new flavor crunch! Serve with homemade wheat rolls, ginger chived green beans and fresh fruit. Dessert is old-fashioned chewy molasses cookies served with ice cream.

Oven-Baked Parmesan Chicken p.172
Ginger Chive Green Beans p.205   Honey n' Wheat Potato Rolls p.164
Fresh Fruit   Old-Fashioned Chewy Molasses Cookies p.217   Ice Cream

HEARTY DINNERS
MENU

Touch of the Southwest

A little chili picante sauce puts the spice in roast pork loin with vegetables.
On the side, tossed salad and hearty Parmesan soda bread. For dessert lovers,
our yummy choco-peanut butter ice cream pie satisfies the sweetest tooth!

Chili Picante Roasted Pork Loin p.184
Hearty Parmesan Soda Bread p.161
Tossed Salad   Choco-Peanut Butter Ice Cream Pie p.214

HEARTY DINNERS
MENU

Bubbling Kettle Dinner

The heartiest of bean soups made with a variety of beans. It simmers slowly on the stove while you make hot oatmeal pecan muffins to go with it. Finally, Aunt Emma's Rhubarb Custard Dessert in a buttery cookie crust.

Mixed-Up Bean Soup p.167
Oatmeal Pecan Muffins p.161   Carrot & Celery Sticks
Aunt Emma's Rhubarb Custard Dessert p.214

Hearty Parmesan Soda Bread (pictured)
Oatmeal Pecan Muffins

Hearty Parmesan Soda Bread

60 minutes

Fresh Parmesan cheese and onion add new flavor to soda bread.

2½ cups all-purpose flour
⅓ cup freshly grated Parmesan cheese
2 tablespoons sugar
1 teaspoon baking powder
1 teaspoon baking soda
¼ teaspoon salt
2 tablespoons chopped onion

3 tablespoons butter *or* margarine
1 (8 ounce) carton (1 cup) dairy sour cream
¼ cup milk

1 egg white, slightly beaten
2 tablespoons freshly grated Parmesan cheese

2 loaves (16 servings)

Heat oven to 350°. In large bowl combine flour, ⅓ cup Parmesan cheese, sugar, baking powder, baking soda, salt and onion. Cut in 3 tablespoons butter until crumbly. Stir in sour cream and milk just until moistened. Turn dough onto lightly floured surface; knead until smooth (1 minute). Divide dough into 2 portions; shape into 5-inch round loaves. Place on greased cookie sheet. Brush tops of loaves with egg white; sprinkle with 2 tablespoons

Parmesan cheese. Cut an X about ½ inch through top of each loaf. Bake for 45 to 50 minutes or until golden brown.

Tip: To reheat bread, wrap in aluminum foil. Bake at 325° for 15 to 20 minutes or until heated through.

Nutrition Information (1 serving)
• Calories 150 • Protein 4g • Carbohydrate 18g • Fat 6g
• Cholesterol 15mg • Sodium 211mg

Oatmeal Pecan Muffins

40 minutes

Pecans add crunch to these oatmeal muffins.

1⅓ cups quick-cooking oats
1¼ cups all-purpose flour
½ cup sugar
1 tablespoon baking powder
½ teaspoon salt

⅓ cup butter *or* margarine
1 cup milk
1 egg
½ cup chopped pecans

14 muffins

Heat oven to 400°. In large bowl combine oats, flour, sugar, baking powder and salt. Cut in butter until crumbly. Combine milk and egg; pour all at once into dry mixture. Stir just until moistened. Stir in pecans. Spoon into

greased muffin pans. Bake for 17 to 20 minutes or until golden brown. Cool 5 minutes; remove from pans.

Nutrition Information (1 muffin)
• Calories 180 • Protein 4g • Carbohydrate 23g • Fat 9g
• Cholesterol 33mg • Sodium 201mg

Every culture seems to have a stone soup recipe, the original hearty dinner! The legend is that a delicious dinner can be made with a stone. Simply take the stone, scrub it well and put it in a large pot. Now add water, carrots, onions, potatoes and other fresh vegetables from the garden, season with salt and pepper and serve.

Old-Fashioned Spoon Bread
With Maple Butter

1 hour 15 minutes

This soufflé-like spoonable bread is delicious served with ham.

Spoon Bread
2 cups milk
1 cup yellow cornmeal
2 tablespoons butter *or* margarine, softened
1 teaspoon baking powder
½ teaspoon salt
1 cup milk
3 eggs, separated

Maple Butter
½ cup butter *or* margarine, softened
2 tablespoons maple syrup *or* maple flavored syrup
⅛ teaspoon cinnamon

8 servings

Heat oven to 350°. In 2-quart saucepan combine 2 cups milk and cornmeal. Cook over medium heat, stirring constantly, until *all* milk is absorbed and mixture is of cooked cereal consistency (8 to 11 minutes). Remove from heat. Add 2 tablespoons butter, baking powder and salt; stir until well mixed and butter is melted. With wire whisk beat in milk and egg yolks until smooth. Transfer to large bowl; set aside. In small mixer bowl beat egg whites at high speed, scraping bowl often, until stiff peaks form (1 to 2 minutes). Fold into cornmeal mixture until uniform and no lumps are visible. Carefully pour into 2-quart greased casserole. Bake for 40 to 50 minutes or until golden brown and top springs back when touched lightly in center. In small bowl stir together all maple butter ingredients; serve with warm spoon bread.

Nutrition Information (1 serving)
• Calories 270 • Protein 7g • Carbohydrate 19g • Fat 19g
• Cholesterol 149mg • Sodium 392mg

To Prepare Old-Fashioned Spoon Bread With Maple Butter:

1. Cook over medium heat, stirring constantly, until *all* milk is absorbed and mixture is of cooked cereal consistency (8 to 11 minutes).

2. In small mixer bowl beat egg whites at high speed, scraping bowl often, until stiff peaks form (1 to 2 minutes).

3. Fold into cornmeal mixture until uniform and no lumps are visible.

Old-Fashioned Spoon Bread With Maple Butter

Honey n' Wheat Potato Rolls

3 hours 15 minutes

A touch of honey sweetens these hearty dinner rolls.

1 (¼ ounce) package active dry yeast
1½ cups warm water (105 to 115°F)
5 to 5½ cups all-purpose flour
2 cups whole wheat flour
⅔ cup butter *or* margarine, softened
1 cup lukewarm mashed potatoes

⅔ cup honey
2 eggs
1½ teaspoons salt

Butter *or* margarine

40 rolls

In large mixer bowl dissolve yeast in warm water. Add 2 cups all-purpose flour, whole wheat flour, ⅔ cup butter, potatoes, honey, eggs and salt. Beat at medium speed, scraping bowl often, until smooth (1 to 2 minutes). Stir in enough remaining flour to make dough easy to handle. Turn dough onto lightly floured surface; knead until smooth and elastic (about 5 minutes). Place in greased bowl, turn greased side up.* Cover; let rise in warm place until double in size (about 1½ hours). Dough is ready if indentation remains when touched. Punch down dough; divide in half.

With floured hands shape each half into 20 balls; place in 2 greased 13x9-inch baking pans. Cover; let rise until double in size (about 1 hour). *Heat oven to 375°.* Bake for 20 to 30 minutes or until golden brown. If desired, brush tops of rolls with butter.

*Dough can be covered tightly and refrigerated at least 8 hours but no longer than 5 days. Continue as directed above except let rise until double in size (about 2 hours).

Nutrition Information (1 roll)
• Calories 130 • Protein 3g • Carbohydrate 22g • Fat 4g
• Cholesterol 22mg • Sodium 132mg

Spinach Swirl Whole Wheat Bread

3 hours

Spinach peeks out from the slits in a whole wheat, horseshoe shaped bread.

2 (1 pound each) loaves frozen honey wheat
  bread, thawed (do not let dough rise)
1 (10 ounce) package frozen spinach,
  thawed, well drained

3 tablespoons butter *or* margarine, melted
½ cup freshly grated Parmesan cheese
  Butter *or* margarine, melted

2 loaves (24 servings)

On lightly floured surface roll 1 loaf of dough into 15x10-inch rectangle; spread with *1½ tablespoons* melted butter; sprinkle with *¼ cup* Parmesan cheese and ½ of spinach. Roll up jelly roll fashion beginning with 15-inch side. Pinch edge of dough into roll to seal well. On large greased cookie sheet form dough into horseshoe shape. With serrated knife, cut slits one-third through dough every 2 inches. Repeat to form second horseshoe fitting on same

cookie sheet with first horseshoe. Cover; let rise until double in size (about 45 minutes). *Heat oven to 375°.* Bake for 20 to 25 minutes or until golden brown. Remove from cookie sheet. Place on wire rack; brush with melted butter, if desired. Serve warm.

Nutrition Information (1 serving)
• Calories 140 • Protein 4g • Carbohydrate 19g • Fat 5g
• Cholesterol 10mg • Sodium 250mg

Honey n' Wheat Potato Rolls (top)
Spinach Swirl Whole Wheat Bread (bottom)

Smoked Turkey Lentil Soup (pictured)
Mixed-Up Bean Soup

Smoked Turkey Lentil Soup

1 hour 30 minutes

Smoked turkey and fresh lemon are the secret ingredients in this delicious homemade soup.

2 cups (8 ounces) sliced ¼-inch fresh
  mushrooms
1 cup (2 medium) chopped onions
¼ cup butter *or* margarine
1 teaspoon finely chopped fresh garlic
2 cups (4 medium) sliced ¼-inch carrots
2 cups (4 stalks) sliced ¼-inch celery
1 cup lentils, rinsed
2 cups water
2 (14½ ounce) cans chicken broth

12 ounces smoked turkey, cut into
  ½-inch cubes
1 teaspoon dried summer savory leaves
1 teaspoon dried thyme leaves
½ teaspoon salt
¼ teaspoon pepper
¼ cup chopped fresh parsley
1 tablespoon lemon juice
½ teaspoon grated lemon peel

8 servings

In Dutch oven combine mushrooms, onions, butter and garlic. Cook over medium heat, stirring occasionally, until vegetables are tender (10 to 12 minutes). Add all remaining ingredients *except* parsley, lemon juice and lemon peel. Cover; cook over medium high heat, stirring occasionally, until mixture comes to a full boil (12 to 15 minutes). Reduce heat to low; continue cooking until lentils are tender (35 to 45 minutes). Stir in parsley, lemon juice and lemon peel.

Nutrition Information (1 serving)
• Calories 260 • Protein 23g • Carbohydrate 22g • Fat 9g
• Cholesterol 48mg • Sodium 586mg

Mixed-Up Bean Soup

4 hours 30 minutes

Any assortment of dried beans or peas can be used in this hearty soup.

2 cups (1 pound) mixed dried beans *or* peas*
8 cups water
2 cups cubed ½-inch cooked ham
1½ cups (3 medium) chopped onions
1 teaspoon salt
¼ teaspoon pepper

1 (28 ounce) can whole tomatoes, undrained,
  cut up
2 teaspoons chili powder
2 tablespoons lemon juice

8 servings

In Dutch oven combine beans and water. Cook over high heat until water comes to a full boil (15 to 20 minutes). Boil 2 minutes; remove from heat. Cover; let stand 1 hour. Add ham, onions, salt and pepper to beans. Cover; cook over low heat until beans are tender (about 2 hours). Add all remaining ingredients. Cover; continue cooking until flavors are blended (about 1 hour). Season to taste.

*Suggested dried beans or peas include navy beans, lima beans, pinto beans, kidney beans, whole peas, split peas, black-eyed peas and yellow peas.

Nutrition Information (1 serving)
• Calories 250 • Protein 19g • Carbohydrate 37g • Fat 3g
• Cholesterol 19mg • Sodium 864mg

Cashew Rice & Chicken Casserole (top)
Hearty Turkey Divan Bake (bottom)

Cashew Rice & Chicken Casserole   1 hour 30 minutes

Crunchy, salty cashews contrast with tender chicken and rice in this wholesome casserole.

2½ cups cubed 1-inch cooked chicken
 2 cups cooked wild rice
 1 cup salted whole cashews
 1 cup (2 stalks) sliced 1-inch celery
 ½ cup uncooked long grain rice
 ¼ cup chopped fresh parsley
 3 tablespoons butter *or* margarine, melted
1½ cups chicken broth

½ cup white wine *or* chicken broth
 2 (2 ounce) jars chopped pimiento, drained
 1 (8 ounce) carton (1 cup) dairy sour cream
 1 teaspoon dried basil leaves
 ½ teaspoon salt
 2 teaspoons finely chopped fresh garlic

6 servings

Heat oven to 350°. In 3-quart casserole or 13x9-inch baking pan stir together all ingredients. Cover; bake, stirring occasionally, for 50 to 60 minutes or until rice is tender. Uncover; continue baking for 10 to 15 minutes or until rice has absorbed all liquid.

Microwave Directions: In 4-quart casserole stir together all ingredients. Cover; microwave on HIGH, stirring every 15 minutes, until rice is tender (40 to 50 minutes).

Nutrition Information (1 serving)
• Calories 510 • Protein 26g • Carbohydrate 34g • Fat 29g
• Cholesterol 84mg • Sodium 669mg

Hearty Turkey Divan Bake   60 minutes

Pasta, turkey and broccoli combine in this all-time favorite.

6 ounces uncooked dried spaghetti, broken into thirds
2 tablespoons butter *or* margarine
2 tablespoons all-purpose flour
1 cup chicken broth
2 cups (8 ounces) shredded Cheddar cheese

½ cup milk
2 cups cubed cooked turkey
2 cups frozen cut broccoli
1 (4 ounce) can sliced mushrooms

6 servings

Heat oven to 350°. Cook spaghetti according to package directions; drain. In 2-quart saucepan melt 2 tablespoons butter. Stir in flour until smooth and bubbly (1 minute). Add chicken broth. Cook over medium heat, stirring constantly, until mixture comes to a full boil (4 to 5 minutes). Boil 1 minute. Remove from heat. Stir in *1½ cups* cheese and milk until cheese is melted. In greased 2-quart casserole combine spaghetti, turkey, broccoli, mushrooms and cheese mixture. Top with remaining ½ cup cheese. Bake for 25 to 30 minutes or until bubbly around edges.

Microwave Directions: *Reduce ½ cup milk to ¼ cup.* Cook spaghetti according to package directions; drain. In 4-cup measure melt butter on HIGH (30 to 40 seconds). Stir in flour until smooth. Microwave on HIGH until bubbly (30 to 60 seconds). Stir in chicken broth. Microwave on HIGH 2 minutes. Stir well; microwave on HIGH until mixture comes to a full boil (1½ to 2½ minutes). Stir in *1½* cups cheese. Stir milk into cheese mixture. In greased 2-quart casserole combine spaghetti, turkey, broccoli and cheese mixture. Cover; microwave on HIGH, stirring after half the time, until heated through (9 to 13 minutes). Sprinkle with cheese. Let stand 2 minutes.

Nutrition Information (1 serving)
• Calories 410 • Protein 30g • Carbohydrate 28g • Fat 20g
• Cholesterol 88mg • Sodium 530mg

Lemon Honey Glazed Chicken

3 hours

Thyme leaves and lemon add special flavor to this roasted chicken.

Stuffing
4 cups dried bread cubes
1 cup (2 stalks) sliced ½-inch celery
½ cup butter *or* margarine, melted
1 cup (2 medium) chopped onions
¼ cup lemon juice
½ teaspoon salt
¼ teaspoon dried thyme leaves

¼ teaspoon pepper
4 to 5 pound whole roasting chicken

Glaze
¼ cup honey
2 tablespoons lemon juice

6 servings

Heat oven to 350°. In medium bowl stir together all stuffing ingredients *except* chicken. Stuff chicken with about ⅓ stuffing; secure wings to body of chicken. Place remaining stuffing in 1½-quart casserole; set aside. Place chicken on rack in roasting pan. Bake 1½ hours. In small bowl stir together glaze ingredients; spoon over chicken. Continue baking chicken, basting occasionally, for 30 to 60 minutes or

until chicken is fork tender. If necessary, add ¼ cup water to basting juices. Meanwhile, bake remaining stuffing, basting occasionally with chicken pan juices, for 30 to 60 minutes or until vegetables are crisply tender.

Nutrition Information (1 serving)
• Calories 540 • Protein 39g • Carbohydrate 37g • Fat 26g
• Cholesterol 151mg • Sodium 646mg

Honey Nut Baked Chicken

1 hour 30 minutes

Honey and pecans create a sweet, nutty coating for this moist, oven-baked chicken.

¼ cup butter *or* margarine
¾ cup chopped pecans
½ cup corn flake crumbs
¼ cup chopped fresh parsley
1 teaspoon salt
1 teaspoon ginger

2½ to 3½ pound frying chicken, cut into
   8 pieces
1 tablespoon butter *or* margarine
2 tablespoons honey
¼ cup chopped pecans

6 servings

Heat oven to 350°. In 13x9-inch baking pan melt ¼ cup butter in oven (5 to 7 minutes). Meanwhile, combine ¾ cup pecans, corn flake crumbs, parsley, salt and ginger. Dip chicken in melted butter, then coat with crumb mixture. In same pan place chicken; sprinkle with remaining crumbs. Bake for 60 to 70 minutes or until fork tender. Meanwhile, in 1-quart

saucepan melt 1 tablespoon butter over low heat. Stir in honey and ¼ cup pecans. Pour sauce over chicken. Continue baking for 5 to 7 minutes or until sauce is heated through.

Nutrition Information (1 serving)
• Calories 450 • Protein 30g • Carbohydrate 16g • Fat 30g
• Cholesterol 110mg • Sodium 609mg

Lemon Honey Glazed Chicken (pictured)
Honey Nut Baked Chicken

Roasted Chicken n' Vegetables

60 minutes

In an hour's time, a complete dinner is prepared and baked in a roasting pan or skillet.

6 small new red potatoes, halved
1 (12 ounce) package (2 cups) fresh
   baby carrots, cut in half lengthwise
2 medium onions, quartered
2 tablespoons butter *or* margarine
1 teaspoon dry mustard
1 teaspoon dried dill weed

½ teaspoon salt
½ teaspoon pepper
2 tablespoons lemon juice
2½ to 3½-pound frying chicken, cut into
   8 pieces

4 servings

Heat oven to 425°. In roasting pan or 10-inch ovenproof skillet place potatoes, carrots and onions. In 1-quart saucepan melt butter; stir in all remaining ingredients *except* chicken. Brush about 2 tablespoons butter mixture over vegetables. Place chicken, skin side up, in pan on top of and around vegetables. Brush chicken with remaining butter mixture. Bake for 45 to 50 minutes or until chicken is fork tender and golden brown.

Microwave Directions: In 4-quart casserole place potatoes, carrots and onions. In small bowl melt butter on HIGH (30 to 40 seconds).

Stir in all remaining ingredients *except* chicken. Brush 2 tablespoons butter mixture over vegetables. Arrange chicken in casserole on top of and around vegetables placing thickest part to outside edge. Brush with remaining butter mixture; sprinkle with paprika. Cover; microwave on HIGH, rearranging chicken and stirring vegetables after half the time, until chicken is fork tender and no longer pink (25 to 35 minutes). Let stand 5 minutes.

Nutrition Information (1 serving)
• Calories 350 • Protein 30g • Carbohydrate 28g • Fat 13g
• Cholesterol 97mg • Sodium 440mg

Oven-Baked Parmesan Chicken

60 minutes

Parmesan cheese forms a crunchy coating on this oven-baked chicken.

¼ cup butter *or* margarine
½ cup all-purpose flour
½ cup grated Parmesan cheese
2 teaspoons dried basil leaves
1 teaspoon dried oregano leaves

½ teaspoon salt
½ teaspoon pepper
6 split chicken breasts
⅓ cup milk

4 servings

Heat oven to 400°. In 13x9-inch baking pan melt butter in oven (5 to 7 minutes). Meanwhile, in 9-inch pie pan stir together all remaining ingredients *except* chicken breasts and milk. Dip chicken breasts in milk then coat with flour mixture. Dip chicken in butter; place skin side up in pan. Bake for 45 to 50 minutes or until chicken is fork tender and golden brown.

Tip: 3 to 3½-pound frying chicken can be substituted for chicken breasts.

Nutrition Information (1 serving)
• Calories 440 • Protein 47g • Carbohydrate 14g • Fat 21g
• Cholesterol 151mg • Sodium 722mg

Roasted Chicken n' Vegetables (pictured)
Oven-Baked Parmesan Chicken

Southern Fried Peanut Chicken (pictured)
Peppery Fried Chicken & Potatoes

Southern Fried Peanut Chicken
60 minutes

The family is sure to gather at the table for this fried chicken with a crunchy peanut gravy.

Chicken
½ cup all-purpose flour
½ teaspoon salt
¼ teaspoon pepper
½ cup shortening
2½ to 3½ pound frying chicken, cut into
    8 pieces

Gravy
½ cup sliced ¼-inch green onions
½ cup crunchy-style peanut butter
1¼ cups milk
¼ teaspoon pepper
¼ cup salted peanuts

6 servings

In 9-inch pie pan stir together flour, salt and pepper. Coat chicken pieces with flour mixture. In 10-inch skillet melt shortening. Place 4 chicken pieces in hot shortening. Cover; cook over medium high heat, turning occasionally, until chicken is golden brown and fork tender (20 to 25 minutes). Place fried chicken on platter; keep warm while frying remaining chicken. Place fried chicken on same platter. Pour off fat; *reserve brown particles.* In same skillet add all gravy ingredients *except* peanuts. Cook over medium heat, stirring occasionally, until gravy is thickened (4 to 5 minutes). Serve gravy over fried chicken; sprinkle with peanuts.

Microwave Directions: Prepare chicken as directed above. Place chicken on bacon/roast rack, large pieces to outside. *Sprinkle with paprika.* Microwave on HIGH, turning ½ turn after half the time, until chicken is fork tender and no longer pink (25 to 35 minutes); keep warm. In small bowl combine all gravy ingredients *except* peanuts. Cover; microwave on HIGH, stirring after half the time, until gravy is slightly thickened (5 to 7 minutes). Serve gravy over fried chicken; sprinkle with peanuts.

Nutrition Information (1 serving)
• Calories 490 • Protein 27g • Carbohydrate 17g • Fat 36g
• Cholesterol 58mg • Sodium 386mg

Peppery Fried Chicken & Potatoes
60 minutes

Old-fashioned, wholesome flavor comes through in this fried chicken with its rich, peppery gravy.

⅓ cup all-purpose flour
½ teaspoon salt
¼ teaspoon coarsely ground pepper
¼ cup butter *or* margarine
2½ to 3½ pound frying chicken, cut into
    8 pieces

6 to 8 new red potatoes, quartered
2 tablespoons all-purpose flour
1½ cups milk

6 servings

In 9-inch pie pan stir together ⅓ cup flour, salt and pepper. Coat chicken with flour mixture. In 12-inch skillet or 10-inch deep skillet melt butter until sizzling. Place chicken, skin side down, in hot butter. Add potatoes. Cover; cook over medium heat, turning occasionally, until chicken and potatoes are fork tender (20 to 30 minutes). Place chicken and potatoes on platter; keep warm. Stir 2 tablespoons flour into pan drippings. Cook over medium high heat, stirring constantly, 1 minute. Reduce heat to medium. Stir in milk. Continue cooking, stirring constantly, until thickened and heated through (5 to 7 minutes). Serve gravy with chicken and potatoes.

Tip: Leftover flour mixture used to coat chicken can be used to thicken gravy.

Nutrition Information (1 serving)
• Calories 290 • Protein 22g • Carbohydrate 20g • Fat 14g
• Cholesterol 80mg • Sodium 342mg

Roasted Beef With Horseradish   2 hours 15 minutes

Slices of carrot, leek and thin strips of fresh horseradish are roasted with beef.

3 to 4 pound boneless top round beef roast
1 tablespoon olive *or* vegetable oil
½ teaspoon salt
½ teaspoon coarsely ground pepper
3 cups (3 medium) sliced ½-inch carrots
1 cup (1 medium) sliced ½-inch leek

⅓ cup fresh horseradish, cut into very thin
   julienne strips
1 (10¾ ounce) can beef broth
2 tablespoons fresh chives, cut into
   ¼-inch pieces

8 servings

Heat oven to 400°. Place roast in 13x9-inch baking pan. Brush with oil; sprinkle with salt and pepper. Bake for 30 minutes. Place carrots, leek and horseradish around roast; pour broth over vegetables. *Reduce oven to 325°.* Cover; bake for 1 hour 15 minutes to 1 hour 30 minutes or until vegetables are fork tender and meat thermometer reaches 160°F (Medium). Stir chives into vegetables. Let stand 15 minutes; carve roast into ½-inch slices. If desired, arrange carrot and leek slices on each slice of roast; garnish with horseradish. Serve with broth spooned over roast.

Nutrition Information (1 serving)
• Calories 280 • Protein 40g • Carbohydrate 9g • Fat 9g
• Cholesterol 100mg • Sodium 351mg

Beef	Internal Cooking Temperature
Rare	140°F
Medium	160°F
Well	180°F

Barbecued Beef Brisket   3 hours 45 minutes

Brisket bakes slowly in a rich flavorful barbecue sauce until moist and tender.

Brisket
3 to 4 pound beef brisket
¾ cup red wine vinegar
¼ cup honey
2 (14½ ounce) cans beef broth
1 (6 ounce) can tomato paste
1 tablespoon paprika
2 teaspoons ginger
1 teaspoon salt
1 teaspoon cumin
¼ teaspoon cayenne pepper

Barbecue Sauce
1 cup (2 medium) chopped onions
1 cup chili sauce
1 cup ketchup
1 teaspoon dry mustard
2 tablespoons molasses
1 tablespoon Worcestershire sauce
1 tablespoon red wine vinegar
1 teaspoon finely chopped fresh garlic

8 servings

Heat oven to 350°. In Dutch oven place brisket; add all remaining brisket ingredients. Cover; bake for 3 to 3½ hours or until brisket is fork tender. Meanwhile, in 2-quart saucepan stir together all barbecue sauce ingredients. Cook over medium heat, stirring occasionally, until sauce is heated through (8 to 10 minutes). Remove brisket to cutting board; *reserve pan juices.* Stir 1 cup reserved pan juices into barbecue sauce. Slice brisket thinly; spoon barbecue sauce over sliced brisket.

Tip: Leftover brisket can be used for sandwiches.

Nutrition Information (1 serving)
• Calories 420 • Protein 35g • Carbohydrate 37g • Fat 15g
• Cholesterol 99mg • Sodium 1683mg

Roasted Beef With Horseradish (pictured)
Barbecued Beef Brisket

Family Swiss Steak
1 hour 15 minutes

Memories stir as the aroma of this hearty dinner fills the air.

1½ pounds (¾-inch thick) beef top
    round steak
3 tablespoons all-purpose flour
1 tablespoon chopped fresh parsley
¼ teaspoon dried thyme leaves
⅛ teaspoon pepper

2 tablespoons vegetable oil
½ cup sliced ¼-inch onion
2 medium carrots, cut into 1½ x ¼-inch strips
1 (10½ ounce) can condensed French
    onion soup

6 servings

With mallet, pound steak to ¼-inch thickness; cut into 6 pieces. In 9-inch pie pan stir together flour, parsley, thyme and pepper. Coat steak with flour mixture. In 10-inch skillet heat oil; add steak. Brown over medium high heat (3 to 4 minutes on each side). Add all remaining ingredients. Reduce heat to low. Cover; continue cooking until steak is tender (50 to 60 minutes).

Nutrition Information (1 serving)
• Calories 240 • Protein 28g • Carbohydrate 10g • Fat 10g
• Cholesterol 67mg • Sodium 485mg

Pot Roast With Winter Vegetables
3 hours 30 minutes

This wholesome family dinner is perfect on a cold winter day.

2 tablespoons vegetable oil
3 to 4 pounds beef chuck roast
4 medium carrots, cut into julienne strips
3 medium turnips, cut into julienne strips
2 medium onions, sliced ¼-inch
1 medium rutabaga, cut into
    julienne strips
1 (10¾ ounce) can beef broth
1 tablespoon chopped fresh parsley

2 teaspoons firmly packed brown sugar
½ teaspoon dried rosemary leaves,
    crushed
¼ teaspoon salt
¼ teaspoon pepper
¼ cup all-purpose flour
¼ cup water

8 servings

Heat oven to 350°. In ovenproof Dutch oven heat oil; add roast. Cook over medium high heat, turning once, until browned (3 to 5 minutes on each side). Add vegetables to roast. In medium bowl stir together beef broth, parsley, sugar, rosemary, salt and pepper. Pour over roast. Cover; bake for 2½ to 3 hours or until roast is fork tender. Remove roast and vegetables to serving platter; keep warm. In small bowl stir together flour and water until smooth; gradually whisk into hot pan juices. Cook over medium heat, stirring constantly, until gravy is thickened (4 to 5 minutes). Serve over carved roast and vegetables.

Tip: 2 cups (2 medium) cubed ½-inch potatoes can be substituted for 2 cups rutabaga or 2 cups turnips.

Nutrition Information (1 serving)
• Calories 270 • Protein 27g • Carbohydrate 14g • Fat 11g
• Cholesterol 77mg • Sodium 288mg

 In New England in the 1600s, dinners were usually thick stews eaten with a spoon and with bread to mop up the gravy. Forks weren't used until the 1700s.

Family Swiss Steak (pictured)
Pot Roast With Winter Vegetables

Rolled Burgundy Steak (pictured)
Blue Cheese & Onion Baked Steak

Rolled Burgundy Steak
5 hours 30 minutes

Rolled flank steak is filled with a moist stuffing.

Marinade
½ cup burgundy wine
2 tablespoons Worcestershire sauce
2 tablespoons vegetable oil
1 tablespoon chopped fresh tarragon leaves*
½ teaspoon coarsely ground pepper
1 teaspoon finely chopped fresh garlic

1½ to 2 pounds beef flank steak

Stuffing
3 tablespoons butter *or* margarine
1 cup chopped fresh mushrooms
½ cup (1 medium) shredded carrot
½ cup shredded zucchini
½ cup fresh bread crumbs
⅛ teaspoon salt

8 servings

In medium bowl stir together all marinade ingredients *except* steak. With mallet, pound steak to ¼-inch thickness. Place steak in plastic food bag. Pour marinade into bag; seal tightly. Place bag in 13x9-inch pan. Refrigerate, turning twice, for 4 hours or overnight. *Heat oven to 400°.* Remove steak from marinade; *reserve marinade.* In 10-inch skillet melt butter. Add mushrooms, carrot and zucchini. Cook over medium heat, stirring occasionally, until vegetables are crisply tender (3 to 4 minutes). In medium bowl stir together bread crumbs and salt. Using a slotted spoon, remove vegetables from skillet. Add vegetables to bread crumbs; toss gently to combine. Spoon mixture over entire surface of steak, pressing slightly. Tightly roll up steak, jelly roll fashion. Tie with string to secure filling inside roll. Place roasting rack in 13x9-inch baking pan. Place steak on rack; baste with reserved marinade. Bake, basting with marinade every 15 minutes, for 50 to 70 minutes or until desired doneness. Let stand 5 to 10 minutes before slicing. Just before serving baste with marinade.

*1 teaspoon dried tarragon leaves can be substituted for 1 tablespoon chopped fresh tarragon leaves.

Nutrition Information (1 serving)
• Calories 270 • Protein 17g • Carbohydrate 7g • Fat 17g
• Cholesterol 56mg • Sodium 220mg

Blue Cheese & Onion Baked Steak
1 hour 15 minutes

8 slices bacon, cut into ½-inch pieces
1 teaspoon finely chopped fresh garlic
¼ cup crumbled blue cheese
1 (3 ounce) package cream cheese, softened
¾ cup milk

1 medium red onion, sliced ⅛-inch
½ teaspoon pepper
1½ pounds (1-inch thick) beef top round steak
¼ cup chopped fresh parsley

6 servings

Heat oven to 350°. In 10-inch skillet cook bacon and garlic over medium high heat, stirring occasionally, until bacon is browned (8 to 10 minutes). Drain off fat *except* for 2 tablespoons. Reduce heat to medium; stir in blue cheese and cream cheese. Cook, stirring constantly, until cheeses are melted (2 to 3 minutes). Gradually stir in milk. Continue cooking, stirring occasionally, until sauce just comes to a boil (3 to 5 minutes). Stir in onion and pepper. In 13x9-inch baking pan place steak; pour sauce over steak. Bake for 40 to 45 minutes or until desired doneness. Sprinkle with parsley. Let stand 10 minutes. Slice steak thinly on the diagonal.

Nutrition Information (1 serving)
• Calories 330 • Protein 31g • Carbohydrate 4g • Fat 21g
• Cholesterol 101mg • Sodium 320mg

Fiesta Taco Bake (pictured)
Corn Bread Topped Casserole

Fiesta Taco Bake

60 minutes

The zesty flavors of Southwestern cooking in a one-dish meal.

2 cups (8 ounces) uncooked dried radiatore
   pasta*
1 pound ground beef
½ cup (1 medium) chopped onion
1 cup frozen whole kernel corn
½ cup mild taco sauce
1 (8 ounce) can tomato sauce
1 (4 ounce) can chopped green chilies, drained

¼ teaspoon cumin
¼ teaspoon salt
1 cup (4 ounces) shredded Cheddar cheese
½ cup (2 ounces) shredded Mozzarella cheese

Tomato wedges
Avocado slices

6 servings

Heat oven to 350°. Cook radiatore according to package directions; drain. Meanwhile, in 10-inch skillet cook ground beef and onion, stirring occasionally, until browned (5 to 7 minutes); drain off fat. Stir in corn, taco sauce, tomato sauce, chilies, cumin and salt. Stir in radiatore. Spoon into greased 2-quart casserole. Sprinkle cheeses over mixture in alternating rows to form 3 Cheddar and 2 Mozzarella stripes. Bake for 25 to 30 minutes or until heated through. Garnish with tomato wedges and avocado slices.

*2 cups (6 ounces) uncooked dried medium shell macaroni can be substituted for 2 cups (8 ounces) uncooked dried radiatore pasta.

Nutrition Information (1 serving)
• Calories 440 • Protein 26g • Carbohydrate 42g • Fat 19g
• Cholesterol 70mg • Sodium 683mg

Corn Bread Topped Casserole

45 minutes

Cheesy corn bread tops this hamburger mixture for a popular main dish.

Casserole
⅓ cup chopped onion
1 pound ground beef
1 teaspoon finely chopped fresh garlic
½ cup sliced ripe olives
1 (16 ounce) can kidney beans, undrained
1 (15 ounce) can tomato sauce
1 tablespoon sugar
2 teaspoons chili powder

Corn Bread
2 cups (8 ounces) shredded Cheddar *or*
   process American cheese
½ cup yellow cornmeal
½ cup all-purpose flour
⅔ cup milk
1 egg
2 tablespoons butter *or* margarine, softened
2 teaspoons baking powder
¼ teaspoon salt

6 servings

Heat oven to 425°. In 10-inch skillet combine onion, ground beef and garlic. Cook over medium heat, stirring occasionally, until browned (8 to 10 minutes). Drain off fat. Stir in all remaining casserole ingredients. Reduce heat to low; continue cooking 15 minutes. Meanwhile, in medium bowl stir together *1 cup* cheese and remaining corn bread ingredients. Spoon meat mixture into 9-inch square baking pan. Spread corn bread mixture over meat mixture. Bake for 18 to 22 minutes or until wooden pick inserted in center of corn bread comes out clean and corn bread is golden brown. Remove from oven; sprinkle with remaining 1 cup cheese.

Nutrition Information (1 serving)
• Calories 550 • Protein 31g • Carbohydrate 38g • Fat 31g
• Cholesterol 133mg • Sodium 1321mg

Market Meat Loaf

1 hour 15 minutes

1 tablespoon butter *or* margarine
1 cup (2 medium) chopped onions
1 cup (2 medium) chopped carrots
1 cup (2 stalks) chopped celery
1 cup (1 medium) chopped green pepper
1 teaspoon finely chopped fresh garlic
1 cup dried bread crumbs
½ cup ketchup
1 pound ground beef
1 pound ground pork*

2 eggs, slightly beaten
½ teaspoon salt
½ teaspoon coarsely ground pepper
½ teaspoon cumin
¼ teaspoon cayenne pepper

1 cup ketchup
½ cup water

8 servings

Heat oven to 350°. In 10-inch skillet melt butter until sizzling. Stir in *½ cup* onion, *½ cup* carrot, *½ cup* celery, *½ cup* green pepper and garlic. Cook over medium heat, stirring occasionally, until vegetables are crisply tender (3 to 4 minutes). In large bowl stir together bread crumbs, ½ cup ketchup, ground beef, pork, eggs, salt, pepper, cumin, cayenne pepper and cooked vegetables. Form into 2 loaves; place in 13x9-inch baking pan. Bake for 40 to 50 minutes or until browned. Meanwhile, in

2-quart saucepan stir together remaining onion, carrot, celery, green pepper, 1 cup ketchup and water. Cook over medium heat, stirring occasionally, until vegetables are crisply tender and sauce is slightly thickened (10 to 15 minutes). Serve with meatloaf.

*1 pound ground beef can be substituted for 1 pound ground pork.

Nutrition Information (1 serving)
• Calories 340 • Protein 26g • Carbohydrate 28g • Fat 14g
• Cholesterol 132mg • Sodium 870mg

Chili Picante Roasted Pork Loin

2 hours

2 cups (2 medium) thinly sliced onions
12 small new red potatoes, halved
4 carrots, each cut into 6 strips (entire length of carrot)
4 cloves garlic
1 (14½ ounce) can chicken broth
1 tablespoon chili powder
1 teaspoon cumin

½ teaspoon salt
½ teaspoon dried oregano leaves
½ teaspoon coarsely ground pepper
2 tablespoons cider vinegar
3 to 4 pound boneless center cut pork loin roast (2 loins tied)
2 bay leaves

8 servings

Heat oven to 325°. In 13x9-inch baking pan place onions, potatoes, carrots and garlic; pour chicken broth over vegetables. Cover; bake 30 minutes to partially roast vegetables. Meanwhile, in small bowl stir together all remaining ingredients *except* roast and bay leaves. Place roast in pan with vegetables. Pour herb mixture over roast; place bay leaves in broth. Bake, basting roast and vegetables with pan juices occasionally, for 1 hour 30 minutes to 1 hour 45 minutes or until meat thermometer reaches 160°F (Medium). Remove from oven; let stand

10 minutes. Place roast on serving platter; place vegetables around roast. Remove bay leaves; serve roast and vegetables with pan juices.

Nutrition Information (1 serving)
• Calories 520 • Protein 52g • Carbohydrate 23g • Fat 23g
• Cholesterol 155mg • Sodium 442mg

Pork	Internal Cooking Temperature
Medium	160°F
Well	170°F

Market Meat Loaf (pictured)
Chili Picante Roasted Pork Loin

Stuffed Eggplant (pictured)
Braised Pork Chops & Cabbage

Stuffed Eggplant

1 hour 15 minutes

Garden eggplant is delicious stuffed with hearty sausage and topped with Mozzarella cheese.

12 ounces bulk pork sausage
2 medium eggplants
¼ cup olive *or* vegetable oil
2 cups (8 ounces) sliced fresh mushrooms
1 cup (1 medium) chopped green pepper
½ cup (1 medium) chopped onion
1 teaspoon finely chopped fresh garlic

1 cup fresh bread crumbs
½ cup freshly grated Parmesan cheese
1 teaspoon dried basil leaves
⅛ teaspoon salt
⅛ teaspoon pepper
1 cup (4 ounces) shredded Mozzarella cheese

4 servings

Heat oven to 350°. In 10-inch skillet cook sausage over medium heat, stirring occasionally, until browned (4 to 6 minutes); drain off fat. Set aside. Cut eggplants in half lengthwise. Remove and cube pulp, leaving ¼-inch shell. In same skillet heat oil; add eggplant pulp, mushrooms, green pepper, onion and garlic. Cook over medium heat, stirring occasionally, until vegetables are crisply tender (4 to 5 minutes).

In medium bowl combine cooked vegetables, bread crumbs, Parmesan cheese, basil, salt and pepper. Place eggplant shells in 13x9-inch baking pan. Spoon vegetable mixture into shells; sprinkle with Mozzarella cheese. Bake for 40 to 45 minutes or until eggplant is fork tender.

Nutrition Information (1 serving)
• Calories 510 • Protein 26g • Carbohydrate 26g • Fat 36g
• Cholesterol 59mg • Sodium 1034mg

Braised Pork Chops & Cabbage

60 minutes

A hearty skillet dinner with traces of a rich German heritage.

2 tablespoons vegetable oil
4 (1-inch thick) pork chops
1 cup (1 medium) thinly sliced onion
1 medium head cabbage, cut into ½-inch slices
1 cup tomato juice
2 teaspoons instant beef bouillon granules

½ teaspoon caraway seed
¼ teaspoon pepper
2 tablespoons all-purpose flour
3 tablespoons water

4 servings

In 10-inch skillet heat oil. Add pork chops; cook over medium heat, turning once, until browned (3 to 4 minutes on each side). Top with onion and cabbage. In small bowl stir together tomato juice, bouillon granules, caraway seed and pepper. Pour over pork chops. Cover; reduce heat to low. Continue cooking until pork chops are fork tender and cabbage is crisply tender (30 to 35 minutes). Place pork chops and vegetables on serving platter; keep warm. In small bowl whisk together flour and water until smooth. Stir into pan juices. Cook over medium heat until mixture comes to a full boil (2 to 3 minutes). Boil 1 minute. Serve over pork chops and vegetables.

Nutrition Information (1 serving)
• Calories 510 • Protein 46g • Carbohydrate 17g • Fat 28g
• Cholesterol 119mg • Sodium 490mg

The famous Saturday night baked bean dinner of Boston has religious roots. To keep cooking to a minimum on the Sabbath, a Puritan woman put the bean pot on to bake on Friday night. It bubbled away with little care and was served as the Sabbath started, at sundown on Saturday.

Hearty Shrimp Jambalaya

1 hour 30 minutes

Serve this spicy Cajun stew for a hearty country taste.

2 tablespoons butter *or* margarine
½ cup (1 stalk) sliced celery
½ cup chopped green pepper
½ cup (1 medium) chopped onion
½ teaspoon finely chopped fresh garlic
½ cup uncooked long grain rice
1 cup cubed ¾-inch cooked chicken
1 cup water
1 (16 ounce) can tomatoes
½ pound cooked smoked sausage link, cut into ¼-inch slices
1½ teaspoons instant chicken bouillon granules

½ teaspoon paprika
⅛ teaspoon dried thyme leaves
⅛ teaspoon cayenne pepper
⅛ teaspoon pepper
1 small bay leaf
½ pound (10 to 12) fresh *or* frozen raw shrimp, shelled, deveined, rinsed*

Hot pepper sauce

4 servings

In 3-quart saucepan melt butter; add celery, green pepper, onion and garlic. Cook over medium heat, stirring occasionally, until vegetables are tender (4 to 6 minutes). Add all remaining ingredients *except* shrimp and hot pepper sauce. Cook over high heat until mixture comes to a full boil (3 to 4 minutes). Cover; reduce heat to low. Continue cooking, stirring occasionally, until rice is fork tender (20 to 25 minutes). Add shrimp; continue cooking until shrimp turn pink (4 to 5 minutes). Remove bay leaf. Serve with hot pepper sauce.

*12 ounces frozen cooked shrimp can be substituted for ½ pound fresh *or* frozen raw shrimp.

Nutrition Information (1 serving)
• Calories 490 • Protein 33g • Carbohydrate 28g • Fat 27g
• Cholesterol 173mg • Sodium 1049mg

Rosemary Rainbow Trout

30 minutes

Rainbow trout is pan-fried in butter seasoned with rosemary and horseradish.

¼ cup butter *or* margarine, softened
½ teaspoon coarsely ground pepper
¼ teaspoon salt
2 tablespoons chopped fresh rosemary leaves*

2 tablespoons prepared horseradish
½ teaspoon finely chopped fresh garlic
4 (½ to ¾ pound each) pan-dressed rainbow trout, head, tail, fins removed

4 servings

In small bowl stir together all ingredients *except* trout. Place about 1 teaspoon mixture in cavity of each trout. In 10-inch skillet melt remaining butter mixture until sizzling. Place 2 trout in skillet; cook over medium high heat, turning once, until fish flakes with a fork (4 to 5 minutes on each side). Remove to serving platter; keep warm. Repeat with remaining trout.

*2 teaspoons dried rosemary leaves, crushed, can be substituted for 2 tablespoons chopped fresh rosemary leaves.

Nutrition Information (1 serving)
• Calories 340 • Protein 32g • Carbohydrate 1g • Fat 22g
• Cholesterol 121mg • Sodium 339mg

Hearty Shrimp Jambalaya (pictured)
Rosemary Rainbow Trout

Red Snapper Baked With Asparagus

60 minutes

A bulb of fennel is sliced like celery and baked with asparagus and fillets of fish.

1½ pounds red snapper fillets
1 pound (24) asparagus spears, trimmed
1 cup (1 bulb) sliced ¼-inch fresh fennel, separated into pieces
2 tablespoons chopped fresh fennel weed
½ teaspoon salt

½ teaspoon coarsely ground pepper
½ teaspoon finely chopped fresh garlic
2 tablespoons grated orange peel
2 tablespoons orange juice
3 tablespoons olive *or* vegetable oil

6 servings

Heat oven to 350°. In 13x9-inch baking pan place fillets, skin side down. Place asparagus spears and fennel pieces on top and around fillets. In small bowl stir together all remaining ingredients; pour over fillets. Bake, basting occasionally, for 30 to 40 minutes or until fish flakes with a fork. Serve with pan juices.

Tip: If desired, recipe can be prepared without fennel bulb and fennel weed.

Microwave Directions: *Reduce 3 tablespoons oil to 1 tablespoon.* In 13x9-inch baking dish place fillets, skin side down. Place asparagus and fennel pieces on top of fillets. In small bowl stir together all remaining ingredients; pour over fillets. Cover with plastic wrap; microwave on HIGH, rearranging after half the time, until fish flakes with a fork (11 to 14 minutes). Serve with pan juices.

Nutrition Information (1 serving)
• Calories 200 • Protein 26g • Carbohydrate 5g • Fat 9g
• Cholesterol 42mg • Sodium 253mg

To Prepare Fennel:

1. Cut fresh fennel bulb into ¼-inch slices.

2. Separate fennel slices into pieces.

3. Chop fresh fennel weed.

Red Snapper Baked With Asparagus

Country Vegetable Lasagna

1 hour 45 minutes

You won't miss the meat in this flavorful cheese lasagna.

9 uncooked dried lasagna noodles

Sauce
3 tablespoons olive *or* vegetable oil
2 cups (8 ounces) coarsely chopped fresh mushrooms
1 cup (1 medium) chopped green pepper
½ cup (1 medium) chopped onion
1 teaspoon finely chopped fresh garlic
¼ cup chopped fresh parsley
1 (28 ounce) can whole tomatoes, cut up
1 (12 ounce) can tomato paste
2 teaspoons sugar
1 teaspoon dried basil leaves
1 teaspoon dried oregano leaves
2 bay leaves

Cheese Mixture
¼ cup freshly grated Parmesan cheese
1 (15 ounce) carton ricotta cheese*
2 eggs
¼ teaspoon pepper

3 cups (12 ounces) shredded mozzarella cheese
¼ cup freshly grated Parmesan cheese

8 servings

Heat oven to 350°. Cook lasagna noodles according to package directions; drain. Meanwhile, in 10-inch skillet heat oil; add mushrooms, green pepper, onion and garlic. Cook over medium heat, stirring occasionally, until vegetables are crisply tender (7 to 9 minutes). Stir in parsley, tomatoes, tomato paste, sugar, basil, oregano and bay leaves. Continue cooking, stirring occasionally, until mixture comes to a full boil (2 to 3 minutes). Reduce heat to low; continue cooking, stirring occasionally, 30 minutes. Remove bay leaves. Meanwhile, in medium bowl stir together ¼ cup Parmesan cheese, ricotta cheese, eggs and pepper. On bottom of 13x9-inch baking pan spread *1 cup* sauce. Top with *3* lasagna noodles, ⅓ cheese mixture, ⅓ sauce and *1 cup* mozzarella cheese. Repeat layers 2 more times, ending with mozzarella cheese. Sprinkle with ¼ cup Parmesan cheese. Bake for 30 to 35 minutes or until bubbly and heated through. Let stand 10 minutes.

*2 cups cottage cheese can be substituted for 1 (15 ounce) carton ricotta cheese.

Microwave Directions: Cook lasagna noodles according to package directions; drain. In 3-quart casserole combine oil, mushrooms, green pepper, onion and garlic. Cover; microwave on HIGH, stirring after half the time, until vegetables are crisply tender (6 to 8 minutes). Stir in parsley, tomatoes, tomato paste, sugar, basil, oregano and bay leaves. Microwave on HIGH 5 minutes; stir. Reduce to MEDIUM (50% power). Microwave, stirring every 10 minutes, until flavors are blended and sauce is thickened (25 to 30 minutes). Remove bay leaves. Meanwhile, in medium bowl stir together ¼ cup Parmesan cheese, ricotta cheese, eggs and pepper. On bottom of 13x9-inch baking dish spread *1 cup* sauce. Top with *3* lasagna noodles, ⅓ cheese mixture, ⅓ sauce and *1 cup* mozzarella cheese. Repeat layers 2 more times, ending with mozzarella cheese. Sprinkle with ¼ cup Parmesan cheese. Microwave on MEDIUM (50% power), turning dish ½ turn after half the time, until bubbly and heated through (18 to 20 minutes). Let stand 10 minutes.

Nutrition Information (1 serving)
• Calories 460 • Protein 29g • Carbohydrate 40g • Fat 21g
• Cholesterol 113mg • Sodium 1009mg

Country Vegetable Lasagna

Mixed Grill Whole Wheat Pizza   1 hour 30 minutes

Have your family choose the toppings to create a delicious and colorful pizza.

Crust
1 (¼ ounce) package active dry yeast
1 cup warm water (105 to 115°F)
1 teaspoon sugar
½ teaspoon salt
2 tablespoons olive *or* vegetable oil
1¼ to 1½ cups all-purpose flour
1 cup whole wheat flour

Sauce
1 (8 ounce) can tomato sauce
1 (6 ounce) can tomato paste
2 teaspoons dried basil leaves
½ teaspoon dried oregano leaves
¼ teaspoon coarsely ground pepper

Toppings
1 cup (1 medium) thinly sliced onion,
  separated into rings
2½ cups (10 ounces) shredded Mozzarella
  cheese
  Marinated artichokes, drained, quartered
  Pitted ripe *or* green olives
  Red *or* green pepper, cut into thin julienne
    strips
  Sautéed mushrooms
  Browned Italian sausage
  Sliced pepperoni
  Red pepper flakes
¼ cup freshly grated Parmesan cheese

6 servings

In large bowl dissolve yeast in warm water; stir in sugar, salt and oil. Gradually stir in all-purpose flour and whole wheat flour to make soft dough. Turn dough onto lightly floured surface; knead 10 to 15 times. Place in greased bowl; turn greased side up. Cover; let stand 20 minutes. Meanwhile, in medium bowl stir together all sauce ingredients. *Heat oven to 425°.* Roll dough into 15x10-inch rectangle; place on greased cookie sheet. Cover; let rise for 15 to 20 minutes. Bake for 8 to 12 minutes or until lightly browned. Spread sauce to within ½ inch of outside edge of crust. Top with onion rings and *2 cups* Mozzarella cheese. Sprinkle with choice of topping ingredients. Sprinkle with remaining ½ cup Mozzarella cheese and Parmesan cheese. Bake for 10 to 15 minutes or until cheese is lightly browned.

Nutrition Information (1 serving without toppings)
• Calories 400 • Protein 22g • Carbohydrate 46g • Fat 15g
• Cholesterol 29mg • Sodium 960mg

In Pilgrim days, there wasn't always meat or fish to be had, so settlers invented hearty dinners like corn oysters and poor man's stew, a vegetable chowder stew made with milk and a tiny amount of salt pork for flavor.

Mixed Grill Whole Wheat Pizza

Carrot n' Turnip Salad With Mustard Dressing 30 minutes

This salad made with carrots and turnips complements roasted meats.

Salad
1 cup water
1 (12 ounce) package baby carrots, peeled
2 cups (2 medium) quartered, thinly sliced turnips
¼ cup chopped fresh parsley

Dressing
1 teaspoon mustard seed
⅛ teaspoon salt
⅛ teaspoon coarsely ground pepper
2 tablespoons vegetable oil
2 tablespoons red wine vinegar
1 tablespoon country-style Dijon mustard
1 teaspoon honey

Lettuce leaves

4 servings

In 2-quart saucepan bring water to a full boil; add carrots. Cook over medium high heat until carrots are crisply tender (5 to 7 minutes). Drain; rinse with cold water. Meanwhile, in medium bowl stir together turnips and parsley. In small bowl stir together all dressing ingredients. Add carrots to turnip mixture. Pour dressing over salad; toss to coat. Line bowl with lettuce leaves or on individual salad plates place lettuce leaves; top with salad.

Microwave Directions: *Reduce 1 cup water to ¼ cup.* In 1-quart casserole place water and carrots. Cover; microwave on HIGH, stirring after half the time, until carrots are crisply tender (4 to 6 minutes). Drain; rinse with cold water. Meanwhile, in medium bowl stir together turnips and parsley. In small bowl stir together all dressing ingredients. Add carrots to turnip mixture. Pour dressing over salad; toss to coat. Line bowl with lettuce leaves or on individual salad plates place lettuce leaves; top with salad.

Nutrition Information (1 serving)
• Calories 130 • Protein 2g • Carbohydrate 15g • Fat 8g
• Cholesterol 0mg • Sodium 247mg

Grapefruit Salad Tossed With Peas 30 minutes

Serve this citrus salad as a refreshing accompaniment to roasted meats.

2 teaspoons sugar
2 tablespoons vegetable oil
2 tablespoons red wine vinegar
1 tablespoon chopped fresh chives
4 cups torn Romaine *or* red leaf lettuce

2 red grapefruit, pared, sectioned, drained
1 (10 ounce) package frozen tiny peas, thawed, drained

6 servings

In large bowl stir together all ingredients *except* lettuce, grapefruit and peas. Add all remaining ingredients; toss to coat.

Nutrition Information (1 serving)
• Calories 110 • Protein 4g • Carbohydrate 16g • Fat 5g
• Cholesterol 0mg • Sodium 294mg

Carrot n' Turnip Salad With Mustard Dressing (pictured)
Grapefruit Salad Tossed With Peas

Spinach Apple Toss (pictured)
Nutty Wild Rice Salad

Spinach Apple Toss

30 minutes

*Spinach and apples are tossed with bacon, eggs and
Colby cheese to make an easy salad.*

8 slices bacon, cut into ½-inch pieces
4 cups torn spinach leaves
2 hard-cooked eggs, cut into pieces
2 medium red tart cooking apples, cored,
    sliced ¼-inch

2 ounces Colby cheese, cut into very thin
    slices
¼ cup mayonnaise
2 tablespoons orange juice

4 servings

In 10-inch skillet cook bacon over medium high heat, stirring occasionally, until browned (5 to 7 minutes). Drain off fat. Meanwhile, in large bowl combine all remaining ingredients *except* mayonnaise and orange juice. In small bowl stir together mayonnaise and orange juice. Add bacon to salad mixture. Pour 2 tablespoons dressing over salad; toss to coat. Serve with remaining dressing.

Nutrition Information (1 serving)
• Calories 230 • Protein 12g • Carbohydrate 14g • Fat 25g
• Cholesterol 169mg • Sodium 444mg

Nutty Wild Rice Salad

1 hour 15 minutes

A tangy dressing lightly coats this salad of wild rice, tomatoes, almonds and green onions.

3 cups cooked wild rice
1 cup cherry tomatoes, halved
½ cup sliced almonds
⅓ cup sliced ½-inch green onions
1 (10 ounce) package frozen tiny peas,
    thawed, drained

¼ cup vegetable oil
1 teaspoon sugar
3 tablespoons red wine vinegar

8 Boston Bibb lettuce leaves

8 servings

In large bowl stir together wild rice, tomatoes, almonds, green onions and peas; set aside. In small bowl whisk together all remaining ingredients *except* lettuce leaves. Pour dressing over salad; toss to coat. On individual salad plates place lettuce leaves. Spoon salad on lettuce leaves.

Nutrition Information (1 serving)
• Calories 200 • Protein 6g • Carbohydrate 23g • Fat 10g
• Cholesterol 0mg • Sodium 44mg

*Johnny Appleseed was born John Chapman in Boston in 1775. He spent 40 years
in the American wilderness planting apple trees and preaching. He carried his
mission ... and apples ... as far as Iowa and is buried in Indiana.*

Pasta With Artichoke Hearts (pictured)
Spinach & Cheese Mostaccioli

Pasta With Artichoke Hearts

45 minutes

A rich, tangy pasta sauce with artichoke hearts and red pepper.

8 ounces uncooked dried spinach fettuccine
1 cup mayonnaise
1½ cups milk
1 tablespoon all-purpose flour
1 cup (4 ounces) shredded Mozzarella
  cheese
1 cup (1 medium) julienne strip red pepper
½ cup chopped fresh parsley

¼ cup freshly grated Parmesan cheese
1 (14 ounce) can artichoke hearts, drained,
  quartered
½ teaspoon coarsely ground pepper
⅛ teaspoon cayenne pepper
1 teaspoon finely chopped fresh garlic

6 servings

Cook fettuccine according to package directions; drain. Meanwhile, in 10-inch skillet whisk together mayonnaise, milk and flour. Cook over medium heat, stirring occasionally, until smooth (2 to 3 minutes). Add all remaining ingredients *except* fettuccine. Continue cooking, stirring occasionally, until mixture comes to a full boil (6 to 10 minutes). Serve over fettuccine.

Microwave Directions: Cook fettuccine according to package directions; drain. Meanwhile, in 2-quart casserole whisk together mayonnaise, milk and flour. Microwave on HIGH, whisking every minute, until smooth (4 to 7 minutes). Stir in all remaining ingredients *except* fettuccine. Microwave on HIGH, stirring after half the time, until mixture comes to a full boil (3 to 5 minutes). Serve over fettuccine.

Nutrition Information (1 serving)
• Calories 540 • Protein 16g • Carbohydrate 40g • Fat 36g
• Cholesterol 40mg • Sodium 450mg

Spinach & Cheese Mostaccioli

45 minutes

Serve this pasta dish with broiled hamburgers or steak.

9 ounces (3 cups) uncooked dried
  mostaccioli *or* rigatoni*
3 tablespoons butter *or* margarine
⅓ cup chopped onion
3 tablespoons all-purpose flour
¼ teaspoon salt
⅛ teaspoon nutmeg

⅛ teaspoon pepper
1½ cups half-and-half
½ cup freshly grated Parmesan cheese
1 (10 ounce) package frozen chopped
  spinach, thawed, well drained

6 servings

Cook mostaccioli according to package directions; drain. Meanwhile, in 3-quart saucepan melt butter; add onion. Cook over medium heat, stirring occasionally, until onions are tender (4 to 6 minutes). Stir in flour, salt, nutmeg and pepper. Continue cooking, stirring occasionally, until smooth and bubbly (1 minute). Add half-and-half; continue cooking until mixture comes to a full boil (3 to 4 minutes). Stir in Parmesan cheese and spinach. Stir in

mostaccioli; reduce heat to low. Continue cooking, stirring occasionally, until heated through (4 to 5 minutes).

*9 ounces (3 cups) uncooked dried medium pasta shells can be substituted for 9 ounces (3 cups) uncooked dried mostaccioli.

Nutrition Information (1 serving)
• Calories 360 • Protein 13g • Carbohydrate 41g • Fat 16g
• Cholesterol 44mg • Sodium 360mg

Angel Hair Pasta With Basil & Shrimp

30 minutes

Basil accents shrimp and tomatoes served over pasta.

1 (8 ounce) package uncooked dried angel hair pasta *or* vermicelli
¼ cup olive *or* vegetable oil
1 teaspoon finely chopped fresh garlic
1 pound (40-45) medium fresh *or* frozen raw shrimp, shelled, deveined, rinsed
2 (28 ounce) cans Italian-style tomatoes, drained, cut up

½ cup dry white wine *or* chicken broth
¼ cup chopped fresh parsley
3 tablespoons torn fresh basil leaves*

Freshly grated Parmesan cheese

6 servings

Prepare pasta according to package directions. Drain; toss with *1 tablespoon* oil. Keep warm. In 10-inch skillet add remaining oil and garlic. Cook over medium high heat, stirring constantly, until garlic is tender (30 to 60 seconds). Add shrimp; continue cooking, stirring constantly, until shrimp turn pink (1 to 2 minutes). Remove shrimp; set aside. Stir in all remaining ingredients *except* Parmesan cheese. Continue cooking, stirring occasionally, until

liquid is reduced by half (7 to 10 minutes). Add shrimp; continue cooking until shrimp are heated through (2 to 3 minutes). Serve over cooked pasta; sprinkle with Parmesan cheese.

*2 teaspoons dried basil leaves can be substituted for 3 tablespoons torn fresh basil leaves.

Nutrition Information (1 serving)
• Calories 300 • Protein 10g • Carbohydrate 41g • Fat 10g
• Cholesterol 28mg • Sodium 487mg

Vegetable Rice Pilaf

45 minutes

Rice simmers with chicken broth, mushrooms and peas for a delicious accompaniment to fish, pork or chicken.

2 tablespoons olive *or* vegetable oil
1½ cups uncooked long grain rice
1 teaspoon finely chopped fresh garlic
2 (10¾ ounce) cans chicken broth
Dry white wine *or* water
½ teaspoon dried thyme leaves
¼ teaspoon coarsely ground pepper

2 cups (8 ounces) fresh mushrooms, quartered
1 (10 ounce) package frozen tender, tiny peas, thawed, drained
¼ cup freshly grated Parmesan cheese
¼ cup chopped fresh parsley

8 servings

In Dutch oven heat oil; stir in rice and garlic. Cook over medium heat, stirring occasionally, until rice is golden (4 to 6 minutes). In 4-cup measure place chicken broth; add wine to total 3¼ cups liquid. Slowly stir into rice mixture; add thyme and pepper. Continue cooking until mixture comes to a full boil. Reduce heat to low. Cover; continue cooking 10 minutes.

Stir in mushrooms. Cover; continue cooking until rice is tender (5 to 7 minutes). Stir in peas, Parmesan cheese and parsley. Continue cooking until heated through (2 to 3 minutes).

Nutrition Information (1 serving)
• Calories 220 • Protein 8g • Carbohydrate 35g • Fat 5g
• Cholesterol 2mg • Sodium 344mg

Angel Hair Pasta With Basil & Shrimp (pictured)
Vegetable Rice Pilaf

Tangy Mustard Carrots (pictured)
Ginger Chive Green Beans

Tangy Mustard Carrots

30 minutes

A touch of mustard adds zest to cooked carrots.

1 cup water
3 cups (6 medium) peeled, sliced ¾-inch carrots
3 tablespoons butter *or* margarine

1 tablespoon firmly packed brown sugar
1 tablespoon country-style Dijon mustard

6 servings

In 2-quart saucepan bring water to a full boil; add carrots. Cover; cook over medium heat until crisply tender (12 to 15 minutes). Drain; stir in all remaining ingredients. Reduce heat to low. Continue cooking, stirring occasionally, until sauce is thickened (1 to 2 minutes).

Microwave Directions: *Reduce 1 cup water to 2 tablespoons.* In 1½-quart casserole combine water and carrots. Cover; microwave on HIGH, stirring after half the time, until carrots are crisply tender (8 to 11 minutes). Drain; stir in all remaining ingredients. Cover; microwave on HIGH until sauce is thickened (2 to 3 minutes).

Nutrition Information (1 serving)
• Calories 100 • Protein 1g • Carbohydrate 10g • Fat 6g
• Cholesterol 16mg • Sodium 184mg

Ginger Chive Green Beans

30 minutes

Fresh ginger and chives add special flavor to fresh green beans.

1½ cups water
1 pound green beans, trimmed
3 tablespoons butter *or* margarine
2 tablespoons chopped fresh chives
2 teaspoons grated lemon peel

½ teaspoon chopped fresh gingerroot*
⅛ teaspoon salt
¼ teaspoon pepper

6 servings

In 10-inch skillet place water; bring to a full boil (3 to 5 minutes). Add beans. Cook over medium heat until crisply tender (9 to 14 minutes); drain. Return to skillet; add all remaining ingredients. Cook over medium heat, stirring occasionally, until heated through (2 to 4 minutes).

*¼ teaspoon ground ginger can be substituted for ½ teaspoon chopped fresh gingerroot.

Microwave Directions: *Reduce 1½ cups water to ¼ cup.* In 2-quart casserole place beans and ¼ cup water. Cover; microwave on HIGH, stirring after half the time, until crisply tender (6 to 10 minutes). Drain; add all remaining ingredients. Cover; microwave on HIGH, stirring after half the time, until heated through (2 to 3 minutes).

Nutrition Information (1 serving)
• Calories 75 • Protein 2g • Carbohydrate 6g • Fat 6g
• Cholesterol 16mg • Sodium 108mg

Fried chicken was popular in the South during the 1700s but not in the North. The busy New England housewife often had no servants and preferred a boiled dinner cooked in a pot that didn't have to be constantly stirred or watched.

Hearty Twice-Baked Potatoes   1 hour 45 minutes

Twice-baked potatoes flavored with cheese and horseradish; great with roast beef!

4 large baking potatoes, washed, each
   pierced with a fork
¼ cup butter *or* margarine
¼ cup milk
½ teaspoon salt

⅛ teaspoon pepper
1 to 2 tablespoons prepared horseradish
2 tablespoons chopped fresh parsley
¼ cup (1 ounce) shredded Cheddar cheese

4 servings

Heat oven to 350°. Place potatoes on oven rack. Bake for 60 to 75 minutes or until potatoes are fork tender. Cut a thin lengthwise slice from each potato; scoop out inside, leaving a thin shell. In large mixer bowl combine potato insides and all remaining ingredients *except* cheese. Beat at medium speed, scraping bowl often, until light and fluffy (2 to 3 minutes). Fill shells with potato mixture. Sprinkle with cheese; place on cookie sheet. Continue baking for 10 to 15 minutes or until cheese is melted.

Microwave Directions: Place potatoes on a paper towel in microwave. Arrange potatoes in a circle, pointing toward the center. Microwave on HIGH 8 minutes. Turn over and rearrange potatoes. Microwave on HIGH until potatoes are fork tender (6 to 8 minutes). Let stand 5 to 10 minutes. Prepare potato shells and filling as directed above. Place filled potatoes on plate; microwave on HIGH until cheese is melted (2 to 3 minutes).

Nutrition Information (1 serving)
• Calories 320 • Protein 7g • Carbohydrate 42g • Fat 14g
• Cholesterol 40mg • Sodium 454mg

Mashed Potatoes With Buttered Peas 1 hour 30 minutes

These extra special mashed potatoes can be made ahead of time; just heat them up before serving.

Potatoes
1 tablespoon butter *or* margarine, melted
2 pounds (8 medium) russet potatoes, peeled,
   boiled, mashed
1 (8 ounce) package cream cheese, softened
2 tablespoons butter *or* margarine, softened
⅛ teaspoon salt
⅛ teaspoon pepper

Peas
2 tablespoons butter *or* margarine
1 (10 ounce) package frozen peas, thawed,
   drained
½ teaspoon marjoram leaves

6 servings

Heat oven to 325°. Using 1 tablespoon melted butter generously grease 6-cup ring mold. In large mixer bowl combine all potato ingredients. Beat at medium speed, scraping bowl often, until well mixed (1 to 2 minutes). Spread potatoes into prepared ring mold. Bake for 40 to 50 minutes or until heated through. Meanwhile, 15 minutes before serving time, in 2-quart saucepan melt 2 tablespoons butter over medium heat (3 to 4 minutes). Stir in peas and marjoram. Cover; cook over medium

heat, stirring occasionally, until peas are crisply tender (8 to 10 minutes). Unmold potatoes onto serving plate. Pour peas into center of molded potatoes.

Tip: Potatoes can be prepared ahead of time. Spread in ring mold; cover tightly. Refrigerate until ready to bake.

Nutrition Information (1 serving)
• Calories 370 • Protein 9g • Carbohydrate 35g • Fat 23g
• Cholesterol 67mg • Sodium 316mg

Hearty Twice-baked Potatoes (pictured)
Mashed Potatoes With Buttered Peas

Garden Harvest Stuffed Peppers

60 minutes

Green pepper shells hold a hearty vegetable and cheese filling.

10 cups water
3 large green peppers, cut in half lengthwise, remove stem and seeds

2 tablespoons butter *or* margarine
½ cup (1 medium) chopped onion
¾ cup chopped ripe tomato
1 (10 ounce) package frozen whole kernel corn, thawed

½ teaspoon salt
½ teaspoon dried basil leaves
1 cup (4 ounces) cubed ½-inch Cheddar cheese

1 cup fresh bread crumbs
2 tablespoons butter *or* margarine, melted

6 servings

Heat oven to 350°. In Dutch oven bring water to a full boil. Add peppers; return water to a full boil. Cook peppers in boiling water 5 minutes; drain. In 10-inch skillet melt 2 tablespoons butter; add onion. Cook over medium heat, stirring occasionally, until tender (3 to 4 minutes). Stir in tomato, corn, salt and basil. Cook, stirring occasionally, until heated through (3 to 5 minutes). Stir in cheese. Place peppers in 13x9-inch baking pan. Fill each pepper with about ½ cup vegetable mixture. In small bowl stir together bread crumbs and 2 tablespoons melted butter. Sprinkle over vegetable mixture. Bake for 30 to 35 minutes or until heated through.

Nutrition Information (1 serving)
• Calories 240 • Protein 8g • Carbohydrate 20g • Fat 15g
• Cholesterol 41mg • Sodium 417mg

Harvest Honey Thyme Squash

45 minutes

Autumn brings crisp, cool days and a bounty of squash from the garden.

2 cups water
1½ pound butternut squash, peeled, remove seeds, cut into 1½-inch chunks
¼ cup butter *or* margarine
2 tablespoons chopped fresh parsley

¼ teaspoon salt
⅛ teaspoon dried thyme leaves
⅛ teaspoon pepper
1 tablespoon honey

4 servings

In 3-quart saucepan bring 2 cups water to a full boil. Add squash. Cover; cook over medium heat until squash is fork tender (12 to 15 minutes). Drain. Mash; set aside. In same saucepan melt butter. Stir in squash and all remaining ingredients. Cover; cook over medium heat, stirring occasionally, until heated through (5 to 7 minutes).

Microwave Directions: *Decrease water to 1½ cups.* In 2-quart casserole combine water and squash. Cover; microwave on HIGH, stirring after half the time, until squash is fork tender (8 to 10 minutes). Let stand 1 minute. Drain. Mash; set aside. In same casserole melt butter on HIGH (60 to 70 seconds). Stir in squash and all remaining ingredients. Cover; microwave on HIGH, stirring after half the time, until squash is heated through (3 to 4 minutes). Let stand 1 minute.

Nutrition Information (1 serving)
• Calories 180 • Protein 2g • Carbohydrate 21g • Fat 12g
• Cholesterol 31mg • Sodium 258mg

Garden Harvest Stuffed Peppers (pictured)
Harvest Honey Thyme Squash

Mixed Berry Almond Pie

2 hours 30 minutes

Almond accents fresh berries in this incredibly delicious homemade berry pie.

Crust
2 cups all-purpose flour
¼ teaspoon salt
¼ cup finely chopped almonds
⅔ cup butter *or* margarine
5 to 7 tablespoons cold water

Filling
6 cups mixed fresh *or* frozen berries
    (blueberries, blackberries, raspberries,
    strawberries)
½ cup sugar
¼ cup cornstarch
¼ teaspoon almond extract

1 egg, slightly beaten

8 servings

Heat oven to 425°. In large bowl stir together flour, salt and almonds. Cut in butter until crumbly. With fork mix in water until flour is just moistened. Divide dough in half; shape into 2 balls and flatten. On lightly floured surface roll out one ball into 12-inch circle. Place in 9-inch pie pan. Trim pastry to ½ inch from rim of pan; set aside. In large bowl combine all filling ingredients *except* egg; toss lightly to coat berries. Spoon into prepared crust. Roll remaining pastry ball into 12-inch circle; cut 8 large slits in top crust. Place over pie; crimp or flute crust. Brush with egg. Bake for 40 to 50 minutes or until crust is lightly browned and juice begins to bubble through slits in crust. If crust edges begin to brown too quickly, cover with 2-inch strip of aluminum foil. Cool pie 1 hour before serving.

Tip: If using fresh strawberries, slice strawberries.

Tip: If desired, prepare lattice crust for top crust.

Nutrition Information (1 serving)
• Calories 400 • Protein 6g • Carbohydrate 53g • Fat 19g
• Cholesterol 68mg • Sodium 234mg

Blackberry Cobbler

60 minutes

A deep dish berry pie is topped with sweet biscuits.

Filling
¾ cup sugar
1 (16 ounce) package fresh *or* frozen
    blackberries *or* raspberries
2 tablespoons cornstarch
½ teaspoon cinnamon
1 teaspoon lemon juice

Topping
2 cups buttermilk baking mix
¼ cup butter *or* margarine, melted
⅔ cup milk
1 tablespoon sugar

Whipping cream *or* ice cream

6 servings

Heat oven to 400°. In 2-quart saucepan combine all filling ingredients. Cook over medium heat, stirring constantly, until mixture comes to a full boil (14 to 16 minutes). Boil 1 minute. Pour into 2-quart casserole. In medium bowl stir together all topping ingredients *except* whipping cream. Drop 6 equal portions of topping onto hot filling. Bake for 25 to 30 minutes or until topping is golden brown and filling is bubbly around edges. Serve warm with whipping cream, sweetened whipped cream or ice cream.

Nutrition Information (1 serving)
• Calories 400 • Protein 5g • Carbohydrate 65g • Fat 14g
• Cholesterol 23mg • Sodium 557mg

Mixed Berry Almond Pie (top)
Blackberry Cobbler (bottom)

Grandma's Apple Blueberry Cake   1 hour 30 minutes

This not too sweet fruit filled old-fashioned cake is full of flavor.

½ cup butter *or* margarine
¼ cup whipping cream
1¼ cups sugar
3 eggs
2⅓ cups all-purpose flour
2 teaspoons baking powder
½ teaspoon salt

2 cups (2 medium) peeled, cored, coarsely
   chopped tart cooking apples
2 cups fresh *or* frozen blueberries

Sweetened whipped cream

15 servings

Heat oven to 350°. In 1-quart saucepan combine butter and cream. Cook over low heat, stirring occasionally, until butter melts (7 to 8 minutes); set aside. In large mixer bowl combine sugar and eggs. Beat at medium speed, scraping bowl often, until well mixed (1 to 2 minutes). Add butter mixture, flour, baking powder and salt. Continue beating, scraping bowl often, until smooth (1 to 2 minutes). By hand, stir in apples and blueberries. Spread into greased and floured 13x9-inch baking pan. Bake for 45 to 55 minutes or until wooden pick inserted in center comes out clean. Serve warm with sweetened whipped cream.

Nutrition Information (1 serving)
• Calories 260 • Protein 4g • Carbohydrate 37g • Fat 11g
• Cholesterol 83mg • Sodium 194mg

Buttery Coconut Pecan Cake   3 hours

Rich, moist cake topped with an old-fashioned browned butter frosting.

Cake
2 cups all-purpose flour
2 cups sugar
1½ cups butter *or* margarine, softened
1 cup buttermilk*
4 eggs
1 teaspoon baking soda
½ teaspoon salt
1 tablespoon vanilla

2 cups flaked coconut
1 cup chopped pecans

Frosting
⅓ cup butter *or* margarine
3 cups powdered sugar
1½ teaspoons vanilla
1 to 3 tablespoons milk

15 servings

Heat oven to 350°. In large mixer bowl combine all cake ingredients *except* coconut and pecans. Beat at low speed, scraping bowl often, until all ingredients are moistened. Beat at high speed, scraping bowl often, until smooth (3 to 4 minutes). By hand, stir in coconut and pecans. Pour into greased and floured 13x9-inch baking pan. Bake for 45 to 50 minutes or until center of cake is firm to the touch and edges begin to pull away from sides of pan. Cool completely. In 1-quart saucepan heat ⅓ cup butter over medium heat, stirring constantly, until delicate brown (5 to 6 minutes). In small mixer bowl combine melted butter, powdered sugar and vanilla. Beat at medium speed, gradually adding milk and scraping bowl often, until frosting is smooth and spreadable. Frost cooled cake.

*1 tablespoon vinegar plus enough milk to equal 1 cup can be substituted for 1 cup buttermilk.

Nutrition Information (1 serving)
• Calories 570 • Protein 5g • Carbohydrate 66g • Fat 33g
• Cholesterol 135mg • Sodium 415mg

Grandma's Apple Blueberry Cake (pictured)
Buttery Coconut Pecan Cake

Choco-Peanut Butter Ice Cream Pie

6 hours

Crust
1½ cups graham cracker crumbs
3 tablespoons sugar
2 tablespoons chopped salted peanuts
¼ cup butter *or* margarine, melted

Filling
2 cups chocolate ice cream, softened slightly
4 cups vanilla ice cream, softened slightly
⅓ cup peanut butter
2 tablespoons chopped salted peanuts

Chocolate syrup

8 servings

Heat oven to 350°. In small bowl stir together all crust ingredients. Press on bottom and up sides of 9-inch or 10-inch pie pan. Bake for 6 to 8 minutes or until lightly browned. Cool completely. Spread softened chocolate ice cream over bottom of cooled pie crust. Freeze until firm (about 30 minutes). In large mixer bowl combine vanilla ice cream and peanut butter. Beat at low speed, scraping bowl often, until peanut butter is evenly distributed. Freeze until ice cream and peanut butter mixture holds soft mounds (30 to 45 minutes).

Spoon ice cream and peanut butter mixture over chocolate ice cream layer. Spread to edges of crust, mounding slightly higher in center. Sprinkle with 2 tablespoons chopped peanuts. Freeze 4 to 5 hours or until firm. Let stand at room temperature 5 minutes before serving; drizzle with chocolate syrup.

Tip: Do not use 8-inch pie pan.

Nutrition Information (1 serving)
• Calories 420 • Protein 9g • Carbohydrate 43g • Fat 26g
• Cholesterol 61mg • Sodium 325mg

Aunt Emma's Rhubarb Custard Dessert

1 hour 30 minutes

Crust
2 cups all-purpose flour
½ cup butter *or* margarine, softened
2 tablespoons sugar

Filling
2 cups sugar
¼ cup all-purpose flour
1 cup whipping cream
6 egg yolks, *reserve egg whites*

¼ teaspoon salt
5 cups chopped rhubarb

Meringue
6 reserved egg whites
¼ teaspoon salt
1 teaspoon vanilla
¾ cup sugar

12 servings

Heat oven to 350°. In small mixer bowl combine all crust ingredients. Beat at low speed, scraping bowl often, until crumbly (1 to 2 minutes). Press on bottom of 13x9-inch baking pan. Bake for 15 minutes. Meanwhile, in large mixer bowl combine all filling ingredients *except* rhubarb. Beat at medium speed, scraping bowl often, until smooth (1 to 2 minutes). By hand, stir in rhubarb; pour over hot crust. Continue baking for 45 to 55 minutes or until filling is firm to the touch. *Increase oven temperature to*

400°. Meanwhile, in clean large mixer bowl with clean beaters beat egg whites at high speed, scraping bowl often, until soft peaks form (1 to 2 minutes). Add salt and vanilla. Continue beating, gradually adding sugar, until stiff peaks form (2 to 4 minutes). Spread over hot filling, sealing around edges. Continue baking for 6 to 8 minutes or until meringue is lightly browned. Cool completely; store refrigerated.

Nutrition Information (1 serving)
• Calories 460 • Protein 7g • Carbohydrate 69g • Fat 18g
• Cholesterol 184mg • Sodium 207mg

Choco-Peanut Butter Ice Cream Pie (pictured)
Aunt Emma's Rhubarb Custard Dessert

Old-Fashioned Chewy Molasses Cookies (top)
Butterscotch Refrigerator Cookies (bottom)

216

Old-Fashioned Chewy Molasses Cookies

3 hours

These chewy, spiced molasses cookies are sure to stir up fond memories.

4½ cups all-purpose flour
2 cups sugar
1 cup butter *or* margarine, softened
1 cup light molasses
½ cup milk
2 eggs
1 teaspoon baking soda

1 teaspoon ginger
½ teaspoon cinnamon
¼ teaspoon salt

Sugar

4½ dozen

In large mixer bowl combine all ingredients *except* additional sugar. Beat at low speed, scraping bowl often, until well mixed (2 to 3 minutes). Cover; refrigerate until firm (at least 2 hours). *Heat oven to 350°.* Shape rounded tablespoonfuls of dough into balls; roll in sugar. Place 2 inches apart on cookie sheets. Bake for 14 to 16 minutes or until slightly firm to the touch.

Nutrition Information (1 cookie)
• Calories 120 • Protein 1g • Carbohydrate 20g • Fat 4g
• Cholesterol 20mg • Sodium 72mg

Butterscotch Refrigerator Cookies

3 hours

Sliced refrigerator cookies are made extra special with the addition of butterscotch and pecans.

1 (6 ounce) package (1 cup) butterscotch chips
2¾ cups all-purpose flour
½ cup sugar
½ cup firmly packed brown sugar

1 cup butter *or* margarine, softened
1 egg
½ teaspoon baking soda
½ cup chopped pecans

5½ dozen

In 1-quart saucepan melt butterscotch chips over low heat, stirring constantly, until melted (3 to 5 minutes). Pour into large mixer bowl; add all remaining ingredients *except* pecans. Beat at low speed, scraping bowl often, until well mixed (1 to 2 minutes). By hand, stir in pecans. Divide dough in half; shape each half into 8-inch roll (about 1½-inch diameter). Wrap in plastic wrap. Refrigerate at least 2 hours. *Heat oven to 400°.* Cut rolls into ⅛-inch slices. Place about 1 inch apart on cookie sheets. Bake for 5 to 7 minutes or until set. Cool 1 minute; remove from cookie sheets.

Tip: For chewier cookies, slice dough into ¼-inch slices.

Tip: Dough can be refrigerated up to 1 month.

Nutrition Information (1 cookie)
• Calories 75 • Protein 1g • Carbohydrate 9g • Fat 4g
• Cholesterol 12mg • Sodium 39mg

PICNICS & BARBECUES

In the 1950s America moved to the suburbs, the outdoor eating craze began and for the first time men were doing the cooking! Although Dad at the barbecue was a new sight in the land, outdoor cooking had been with us always. Indians cooked over an open fire and Southern Indians grilled or smoked their meats and fish on a grid of green sticks which they called a *barbacoa*, today's barbecue. As the settlers moved West, they added the spicy sauces of the Spaniards with lots of garlic and red, hot chili peppers.

Any large social gathering in America by the 1700s was likely to be an outdoor cookout, a bring-a-basket picnic, or a clambake or fish fry if you lived near the oceans. Big outdoor parties were a great way to get far-flung neighbors together, and are still the most popular way to gather a crowd on holidays and summer Sundays.

We've updated some of these old favorite recipes to take advantage of today's new foods and easier preparation. And we've got dozens of delightful hot-weather recipes that can be made ahead and taken along on picnics or camping trips. So whether you're in your backyard or enjoying the great big outdoors, the food never tasted better!

Southwestern BBQ

A spicy, colorful fiesta for your backyard . . . pork tenderloin in a honey lime marinade, hot red beans over rice and chilled vegetables served with chili mayonnaise. Dessert cools things down with a great lemon ribbon ice cream pie.

Honey Lime Marinated Pork Tenderloin p.246
Spicy Red Beans Over Rice p.264   Vegetables With Chili Mayonnaise p.270
Lemon Ribbon Ice Cream Pie p.276

PICNICS & BARBECUES
MENU
Grilled Hamburger Special

Here's something new for your favorite grilled burgers . . . a great cucumber, tomato and red onion relish. Add homemade onion buns and brown sugar baked beans. Dessert is a new twist on your favorite fruit shortcake.

Hamburgers With Cucumber Relish p.244
Onion Hamburger Buns p.235   Brown Sugar Baked Beans p.264
Chocolate Chip Biscuits With Strawberries n' Bananas p.274

Summertime Steak Grill

A perfect picnic starts with a great grilled steak and a garden tomato basil sauce. Serve with creamy potato salad and green beans. Save room for ice cream with a choice of hot fudge or toasted pecan caramel sauce.

Citrus Iced Tea p.232   Grilled Steaks With Garden Tomato Basil Sauce p.243
Crisp Green Beans With Red Pepper p.270   Potato Salad With Mustard Mayonnaise p.259
Ice Cream   Special Hot Fudge Sauce p.273

Company's Coming BBQ

A meal pretty and fresh as summer…chicken breasts stuffed with spinach and ricotta, on the grill with sweet corn and garlic-basil sourdough bread topped with ripe tomatoes. To finish…summer berries in an orange cream sauce.

Minted Lemon Ginger Ale p.232   Spinach Ricotta Chicken Breasts p.240
Grilled Sourdough Bread With Garden Tomatoes p.236
Grilled Corn With Herb Butter p.267   Berries With Orange Cream p.274

Catch of the Day

Lure them into your backyard with this supper of lemon peppered fish steaks and vegetable kabobs sizzling on the grill and your freshly baked onion dill picnic bread. While they wait, pass cooked tortellini pasta to dip into sour cream pesto sauce.

Sour Cream Pesto Dip p.229
Lemon Pepper Grilled Fish Steaks p.251   Onion Dill Picnic Bread p.235
Grilled Vegetable Kabobs p.268   Fruit Sorbet or Sherbet

Picnic Basket Time

Your basket will be the best one, filled with a peppered cheese and meat hoagie on French bread, sweet n' tangy coleslaw, fresh fruit and dessert bars, rich with chopped, salted peanuts and chocolate chips.

Picnic Peppered Hoagie p.260
Sweet n' Tangy Slaw p.257   Fresh Fruit
Peanut Chocolate Swirl Bars p.278

Pineapple Pepper Dip (pictured)
Peanut Butter n' Honey Fruit Dip

Pineapple Pepper Dip

1 hour 30 minutes

Assorted bell peppers, pineapple and fresh lime add color to this refreshing dip.

1 cup chopped assorted bell peppers (green, red and yellow)
1 (8 ounce) carton (1 cup) dairy sour cream
1 (8 ounce) package cream cheese, softened
1 (8 ounce) can crushed pineapple, well drained
⅛ teaspoon salt
2 tablespoons coarsely chopped fresh cilantro *or* parsley
2 tablespoons chopped green onion

2 teaspoons finely chopped seeded jalapeño pepper
1 teaspoon grated lime peel
1 teaspoon lime juice

Fresh vegetable sticks (pepper, celery, carrot, cucumber, etc.)
Tortilla chips

3¼ cups

In small mixer bowl combine all ingredients *except* vegetable sticks and tortilla chips. Beat at medium speed, scraping bowl often, until well mixed (1 to 2 minutes). Cover; refrigerate at least 1 hour. Serve with fresh vegetable sticks or tortilla chips.

Nutrition Information (1 tablespoon)
• Calories 22 • Protein 1g • Carbohydrate 1g • Fat 2g
• Cholesterol 6mg • Sodium 23mg

Peanut Butter n' Honey Fruit Dip

10 minutes

Creamy peanut butter combines with sour cream, honey and cinnamon for a fun fruit dip.

½ cup creamy peanut butter
¼ cup milk
1 (8 ounce) carton (1 cup) dairy sour cream
1 teaspoon cinnamon
2 tablespoons honey

Apple slices, pear slices, banana chunks, strawberries, etc.

1½ cups

In medium bowl stir together all ingredients *except* fruit until smooth. Use as dip for fruit. Store refrigerated.

Tip: Peanut Butter n' Honey Fruit Dip can be used as a spread for crackers, bagels, toast or bread.

Nutrition Information (1 tablespoon)
• Calories 60 • Protein 2g • Carbohydrate 3g • Fat 5g
• Cholesterol 4mg • Sodium 32mg

In the 1830s, the future Napoleon III came to the United States and had a picnic with his American uncle, of partridge, duck, oysters and caviar, all served on gold plates.

Garlic Pepper Toast (pictured)
Sour Cream Pesto Dip

Garlic Pepper Toast

20 minutes

A simple colorful appetizer — French bread topped with peppers and Mozzarella cheese.

2 tablespoons olive *or* vegetable oil
1 teaspoon finely chopped fresh garlic
1 cup (1 medium) thinly sliced onion, separated into rings
1 medium red pepper, cut into thin julienne strips
1 medium yellow pepper, cut into thin julienne strips

½ teaspoon dried basil leaves
12 (1-inch) diagonal slices French bread
3 tablespoons olive *or* vegetable oil
1 cup (4 ounces) shredded Mozzarella cheese

6 servings

Prepare grill; heat until coals are ash white. Meanwhile, in 10-inch skillet heat oil over medium high heat (1 to 2 minutes); stir in garlic. Add onion, peppers and basil. Continue cooking, stirring occasionally, until crisply tender (3 to 5 minutes). Place bread slices on grill. Grill until toasted (2 to 3 minutes). Turn; brush each lightly with oil. Divide pepper mixture evenly between grilled bread; sprinkle each with 1 tablespoon cheese. Grill until toasted and cheese is bubbly (2 to 4 minutes).

Broiling Directions: Prepare onion and peppers as directed above. Heat broiler; toast bread. Brush one side of each slice of bread lightly with oil. Divide pepper mixture evenly between toasted bread; sprinkle each with 1 tablespoon cheese. Broil 3 to 5 inches from heat until toasted and cheese is bubbly (3 to 5 minutes).

Nutrition Information (1 serving)
• Calories 370 • Protein 12g • Carbohydrate 43g • Fat 17g
• Cholesterol 12mg • Sodium 507mg

Sour Cream Pesto Dip

1 hour 20 minutes

The flavor of pesto comes alive in this sour cream dip served with colorful kabobs.

Dip
1 (8 ounce) carton (1 cup) dairy sour cream
½ cup freshly grated Parmesan cheese
1 clove garlic
¼ teaspoon salt
¼ teaspoon pepper
⅓ cup firmly packed chopped fresh basil leaves

Kabobs
Tortellini pasta, cooked, drained
Fresh vegetables (cherry tomatoes, mushrooms, pea pods, etc.)
Wooden picks

1 cup

In 5 cup blender container or food processor bowl with steel blade combine ⅓ *cup* sour cream, Parmesan cheese and garlic. Blend on High until smooth (1 to 2 minutes). Add basil leaves; continue blending until mixture is creamy and smooth. Pour into medium bowl; stir in remaining sour cream until smooth.

Cover; refrigerate at least 1 hour. Meanwhile, skewer 1 tortellini and 1 vegetable piece on each wooden pick. Serve kabobs with dip.

Nutrition Information (1 tablespoon dip)
• Calories 45 • Protein 2g • Carbohydrate 1g • Fat 4g
• Cholesterol 9mg • Sodium 100mg

Grilled Lemonade Drummies

8 hours

Picnic chicken wings grilled with a savory lemonade marinade.

Marinade
⅓ cup Worcestershire sauce
1 (6 ounce) can frozen lemonade
   concentrate, thawed
1 teaspoon celery salt
1 teaspoon seasoned salt

½ teaspoon coarsely ground pepper
½ teaspoon finely chopped fresh garlic

Drummies
3 pounds chicken wing drummettes*

8 servings

In medium bowl stir together all marinade ingredients. Place chicken drummettes in plastic food bag. Pour marinade into bag; seal tightly. Place bag in 13x9-inch pan. Refrigerate, turning occasionally, 8 hours or overnight. Prepare grill; heat until coals are ash white. Place chicken drummettes on grill; brush with marinade. Grill, basting and turning occasionally, until chicken drummettes are fork tender (20 to 25 minutes).

Oven Directions: Prepare chicken drummettes as directed above. *Heat oven to 400°.* Line 15x10x1-inch jelly roll pan with aluminum foil. Place chicken drummettes in prepared pan. Bake, basting occasionally and turning after half the time, until chicken drummettes are fork tender (40 to 45 minutes).

*Chicken wing drummettes are the drumstick-like portion of the chicken wing.

Nutrition Information (1 serving)
• Calories 170 • Protein 15g • Carbohydrate 4g • Fat 11g
• Cholesterol 46mg • Sodium 176mg

Spicy Cajun Shrimp

30 minutes

A spicy Cajun sauce complements fresh shrimp.

Sauce
¼ cup butter *or* margarine
1 teaspoon chopped fresh thyme leaves*
½ teaspoon pepper
⅛ to ¼ teaspoon cayenne pepper
2 tablespoons ketchup
1 teaspoon Worcestershire sauce
½ teaspoon finely chopped fresh garlic

Kabobs
1 pound (20 to 25) fresh raw shrimp, cleaned,
   shelled, deveined
8 green onions, each cut into 3 (2-inch) pieces
2 lemons, each cut into 6 slices, then cut in half

12 (6-inch) wooden skewers, soaked in water

8 servings

Prepare grill; heat until coals are ash white. Meanwhile, in 1-quart saucepan combine all sauce ingredients. Cook over medium heat, stirring occasionally, until butter is melted (4 to 5 minutes). On each wooden skewer place 1 shrimp, 1 green onion piece, 1 lemon, 1 shrimp and 1 green onion piece; brush with sauce. Place kabobs on grill. Grill, brushing

with sauce and turning frequently, until shrimp turn pink (6 to 10 minutes).

*¼ teaspoon dried thyme leaves can be substituted for 1 teaspoon chopped fresh thyme leaves.

Nutrition Information (1 serving)
• Calories 120 • Protein 10g • Carbohydrate 6g • Fat 7g
• Cholesterol 80mg • Sodium 174mg

Grilled Lemonade Drummies (top)
Spicy Cajun Shrimp (bottom)

Minted Lemon Ginger Ale

20 minutes

*Before going on a picnic stir together fresh squeezed lemon juice and mint,
then just before serving add ginger ale.*

¼ cup lemon juice
1 tablespoon chopped fresh mint leaves

4 cups ginger ale
8 sprigs fresh mint leaves

8 (½ cup) servings

In small bowl stir together lemon juice
and chopped mint; let stand 10 to 15 minutes.
Strain. In pitcher place strained lemon juice;
pour in ginger ale. Serve over ice; garnish
each serving with a sprig of mint.

Nutrition Information (1 serving)
• Calories 42 • Protein 0g • Carbohydrate 11g • Fat 0g
• Cholesterol 0mg • Sodium 7mg

Citrus Iced Tea

20 minutes

Steeped tea is sweetened with sugar and blended with citrus juices for a refreshing beverage.

4 tea bags
2 cups boiling water
¼ cup sugar
4 cups cold water
¼ cup grapefruit juice

¼ cup lemon juice
¼ cup orange juice

Orange slices

6 (1 cup) servings

Place tea bags in teapot or medium bowl.
Pour in boiling water. Let stand 8 to 10 minutes.
Remove tea bags. Add sugar; stir until dissolved.
In 2-quart pitcher stir together all remaining
ingredients *except* orange slices. Stir in tea.
Serve over ice; garnish each serving with
orange slices. Sweeten to taste.

Tip: If desired, omit ¼ cup grapefruit juice,
increase orange juice to ½ cup.

Nutrition Information (1 serving)
• Calories 16 • Protein 0g • Carbohydrate 4g • Fat 0g
• Cholesterol 0mg • Sodium 1mg

*On Southern plantations in the 1700s, barbecue was a favored way
to entertain. George Washington was reported to be a guest at many
such outdoor parties.*

Minted Lemon Ginger Ale (left)
Citrus Iced Tea (right)

Onion Dill Picnic Bread (pictured)
Onion Hamburger Buns

Onion Dill Picnic Bread

3 hours 30 minutes

½ cup sugar
½ cup milk
¾ cup butter *or* margarine, slightly softened
1 teaspoon salt
2 (¼ ounce) packages active dry yeast
½ cup warm water (105 to 115°F)
2 tablespoons instant minced onion

4½ teaspoons dill seed
2 eggs, slightly beaten
3¾ to 4¼ cups all-purpose flour

1 egg yolk
1 tablespoon water

2 loaves (16 servings)

In 1-quart saucepan cook sugar, milk, *½ cup* butter and salt over medium heat, stirring occasionally, until butter is melted (4 to 6 minutes). Cool to warm (105 to 115°F). Meanwhile, in large bowl dissolve yeast in ½ cup warm water; stir in minced onion and *4 teaspoons* dill seed. Stir in milk mixture, 2 eggs and enough flour to make dough easy to handle. Turn dough onto lightly floured surface. Knead until smooth (8 to 10 minutes). Place in greased bowl; turn greased side up. Cover; let rise in warm place until double in size (about 1½ hours). Dough is ready if indentation remains when touched. Punch down dough; divide dough in half. Roll half of dough into 24x8-inch rectangle. Spread

with *2 tablespoons* butter. Cut 24-inch side into 6 equal pieces; stack on top of each other, buttered side up. Cut stack into 5 equal pieces. Place, cut edge down, in greased 9x5-inch loaf pan. Repeat with remaining half of dough and *2 tablespoons* butter. Cover; let rise until double in size (about 1 hour). *Heat oven to 350°.* Bake for 25 to 30 minutes or until lightly browned. Meanwhile, in small bowl stir together egg yolk and 1 tablespoon water. Brush each loaf with egg mixture; sprinkle each loaf with ¼ *teaspoon* dill seed. Continue baking for 4 to 5 minutes or until golden brown. Remove from pan immediately.

Nutrition Information (1 serving)
• Calories 230 • Protein 5g • Carbohydrate 30g • Fat 10g
• Cholesterol 76mg • Sodium 237mg

Onion Hamburger Buns

3 hours

½ cup milk
3 tablespoons butter *or* margarine
3 tablespoons sugar
1 tablespoon instant minced onion
2 teaspoons salt
1 (¼ ounce) package active dry yeast

1½ cups warm water (105 to 115°F)
5 to 5½ cups all-purpose flour

Coarse salt
Coarsely ground pepper

1 dozen

In 1-quart saucepan heat milk until just comes to a boil (3 to 4 minutes); stir in butter, sugar, onion and 2 teaspoons salt. Cool to warm (105 to 115°F). In large mixer bowl dissolve yeast in warm water. Add cooled milk mixture and *3 cups* flour. Beat at medium speed, scraping bowl often, until smooth (1 to 2 minutes). By hand, stir in enough remaining flour to make dough easy to handle. Turn dough onto lightly floured surface; knead until smooth and elastic (about 10 minutes). Place in greased bowl, turn greased side up. Cover; let rise in warm place until double in size

(about 1 hour). Dough is ready if indentation remains when touched. Punch down dough; divide in half. With floured hands shape each half into 6 rounds. Place each round on greased cookie sheets; flatten to 3½-inch circle. Sprinkle with coarse salt and pepper. Cover; let rise until double in size (about 30 minutes). *Heat oven to 400°.* Bake for 15 to 20 minutes or until golden brown. Cool completely on wire rack. To serve, cut buns in half.

Nutrition Information (1 bun)
• Calories 240 • Protein 6g • Carbohydrate 44g • Fat 4g
• Cholesterol 9mg • Sodium 395mg

Grilled Cheese Bread

45 minutes

This tasty bread complements grilled fish, pork or beef.

¾ cup (3 ounces) finely shredded
   Cheddar cheese
⅓ cup butter *or* margarine, softened
¼ cup chopped fresh parsley
1 teaspoon paprika
1 teaspoon finely chopped fresh garlic

1 (16 ounce) loaf (16x4-inch) crusty French
   or Italian bread, sliced diagonally ¾-inch

Heavy-duty aluminum foil

1 loaf (18 servings)

Prepare grill placing coals to one side; heat until coals are ash white. In small bowl stir together cheese, butter, parsley, paprika and garlic. Spread between bread slices. Wrap bread in aluminum foil, tightly sealing tops and sides. Place bread on grill opposite coals. Grill covered, turning over after half the time, for 15 to 20 minutes or until cheese is melted.

Oven Directions: Heat oven to 400°. Prepare bread as directed above. Wrap bread in aluminum foil, tightly sealing tops and sides. Bake for 15 to 20 minutes or until cheese is melted.

Nutrition Information (1 serving)
• Calories 120 • Protein 4g • Carbohydrate 14g • Fat 6g
• Cholesterol 15mg • Sodium 211mg

Grilled Sourdough Bread With Garden Tomatoes

40 minutes

¼ cup butter *or* margarine
2 tablespoons chopped shallots *or* onion
½ teaspoon finely chopped fresh garlic
4 (½-inch) slices round sourdough bread
¼ cup torn fresh basil leaves

2 medium ripe tomatoes, each cut into 6 slices
2 teaspoons red wine vinegar
   Salt and coarsely ground pepper

4 servings

Prepare grill; heat until coals are ash white. Meanwhile, in 1-quart saucepan melt butter until sizzling; stir in shallots and garlic. Cook over medium heat, stirring occasionally, until shallots are tender (1 to 2 minutes). Place bread slices on grill. Grill until toasted (2 to 3 minutes). Turn; brush each bread slice with butter mixture. Sprinkle with basil; top each bread slice

with 3 tomato slices. Sprinkle each with ½ *teaspoon* vinegar; season with salt and pepper. Continue grilling until bread is lightly browned (1 to 2 minutes).

Nutrition Information (1 serving)
• Calories 220 • Protein 4g • Carbohydrate 22g • Fat 13g
• Cholesterol 32mg • Sodium 326mg

One of the most interesting kitchens in America was the chuckwagon, a kitchen on wheels that went on long cattle drives with cowboys in the 1860s. Colonel Charles Goodnight, a Texan, is said to be the inventor of the chuckwagon.

Grilled Cheese Bread (pictured)
Grilled Sourdough Bread With Garden Tomatoes

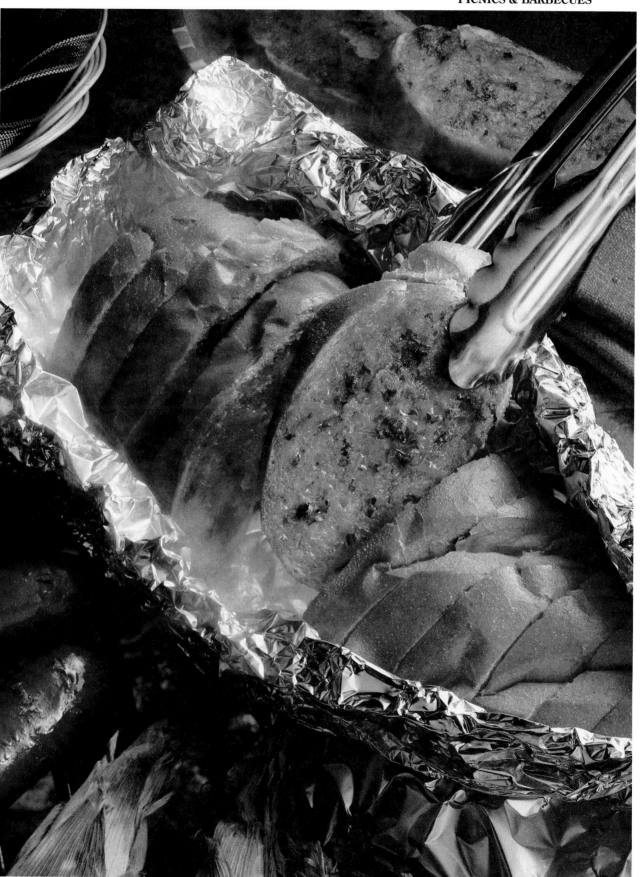

Barbecued Chicken Bundles (pictured)
Light Barbecue Chicken

Barbecued Chicken Bundles   1 hour 30 minutes

These tasty bundles may be assembled ahead of time, covered and refrigerated before grilling.

4 whole boneless chicken breasts, skinned, cut in half
8 (4 ounce) 1x1x½-inch chunks Cheddar cheese

16 (about ¾ pound) slices bacon
¼ cup barbecue sauce

8 servings

Prepare grill placing coals to one side; heat until coals are ash white. Make aluminum foil drip pan; place opposite coals. Make slit in each chicken breast half to form pocket. Place 1 chunk cheese in each pocket. Roll each chicken breast into bundle and wrap criss-cross with 2 slices bacon. Secure bacon with wooden picks. Place bundles on grill over drip pan. Grill, turning every 15 minutes, for 30 to 40 minutes or until chicken is fork tender. If crisp bacon is desired, place bundle over direct heat, turning 2 to 3 times, during last 10 minutes. Brush with barbecue sauce during last 10 minutes of cooking.

Nutrition Information (1 serving)
• Calories 280 • Protein 34g • Carbohydrate 1g • Fat 15g
• Cholesterol 99mg • Sodium 432mg

Light Barbecue Chicken

A light refreshing oil, wine and herb marinade enhances grilled chicken.

Marinade
⅔ cup vegetable oil
½ cup dry white wine
1 tablespoon finely chopped fresh garlic
2 teaspoons dried basil leaves

1 teaspoon salt
½ teaspoon pepper

2½ to 3½ pound frying chicken, cut into 8 pieces

6 servings

In large bowl stir together all marinade ingredients. Place chicken in plastic food bag. Add marinade; turn to coat all sides. Place in 13x9-inch pan. Refrigerate, turning bag 2 to 3 times, 4 hours or overnight. *Prepare grill placing coals to one side;* heat until coals are ash white. Make aluminum foil drip pan; place opposite coals. Place chicken on grill over drip pan. Brush with marinade. Grill, turning and basting occasionally with marinade, for 40 to 50 minutes or until fork tender. In 1-quart saucepan cook remaining marinade over medium heat, stirring occasionally, until marinade comes to a full boil (2 to 3 minutes). Just before serving, brush marinade over chicken.

Microwave Directions: *Reduce ⅔ cup oil to 2 tablespoons.* In 13x9-inch baking dish stir together all marinade ingredients. Dip chicken in marinade; turn to coat all sides. Cover with plastic wrap; refrigerate, turning chicken 2 to 3 times, 4 hours or overnight. Pour off and *reserve marinade.* In same pan, arrange chicken with thickest part to outside edge. *Sprinkle chicken with paprika.* Cover with waxed paper. Microwave on HIGH, rearranging chicken after half the time, until fork tender and no longer pink (20 to 25 minutes). In 2-cup measure microwave reserved marinade until mixture comes to a full boil (2 to 3 minutes). Just before serving, brush marinade over chicken.

Nutrition Information (1 serving)
• Calories 220 • Protein 25g • Carbohydrate 0g • Fat 12g
• Cholesterol 76mg • Sodium 163mg

Spiced Orange Chicken

1 hour 15 minutes

Cinnamon and nutmeg spice up this orange-flavored chicken.

2½ to 3½ pound frying chicken, cut into
    8 pieces

Basting Sauce
½ cup butter *or* margarine
1 (6 ounce) can frozen orange juice
    concentrate, thawed

1 teaspoon paprika
½ teaspoon cinnamon
½ teaspoon nutmeg

6 servings

Prepare grill placing coals to one side; heat until coals are ash white. Make aluminum foil drip pan; place opposite coals. Place chicken on grill over drip pan. Grill, turning occasionally, for 45 to 60 minutes or until fork tender. Meanwhile, in 1-quart saucepan combine all basting sauce ingredients. Cook over low heat, stirring occasionally, until heated through (2 to 3 minutes). During last 15 minutes of grilling, brush chicken with basting sauce. Serve with remaining warm sauce.

Microwave Directions: *Reduce butter to ⅓ cup.* In 12x8-inch baking dish melt butter on HIGH (60 to 70 seconds). Stir in all remaining ingredients *except* chicken. Arrange chicken in dish, with thickest part to outside edge, turning to coat with butter. Cover; microwave on HIGH, rearranging chicken after half the time, until fork tender and no longer pink (16 to 18 minutes).

Nutrition Information (1 serving)
• Calories 300 • Protein 19g • Carbohydrate 11g • Fat 20g
• Cholesterol 96mg • Sodium 210mg

Spinach Ricotta Chicken Breasts

60 minutes

Grilled chicken breasts are stuffed with a delicate seasoned spinach ricotta filling.

1 cup ricotta cheese
1 (10 ounce) package frozen chopped
    spinach, thawed, drained
1 teaspoon seasoned salt
1 teaspoon coarsely ground pepper

¼ teaspoon nutmeg
4 to 6 split chicken breasts
2 tablespoons vegetable oil

6 servings

Prepare grill placing coals to one side; heat until coals are ash white. Make aluminum foil drip pan; place opposite coals. Meanwhile, in medium bowl stir together all ingredients *except* chicken breasts and oil. Gently loosen skin of each chicken breast, stuff with equal amounts of spinach ricotta mixture; tighten skin. Brush oil on chicken breasts. Place chicken breasts on grill over drip pan. Grill,

turning occasionally, for 25 to 35 minutes or until chicken breasts are fork tender and no longer pink. If more browning is desired, place chicken breasts over direct heat last 5 minutes of cooking time.

Nutrition Information (1 serving)
• Calories 250 • Protein 33g • Carbohydrate 5g • Fat 11g
• Cholesterol 85mg • Sodium 411mg

Spiced Orange Chicken (pictured)
Spinach Ricotta Chicken Breasts

Spinach & Artichoke Rolled Flank Steak (pictured)
Grilled Steaks With Garden Tomato Basil Sauce

Spinach & Artichoke Rolled Flank Steak   1 day

Marinade
¼ cup vegetable oil
¼ cup red wine vinegar
1 teaspoon salt
½ teaspoon coarsely ground pepper
2 tablespoons lemon juice
2 tablespoons Worcestershire sauce

1½ to 2 pounds beef flank steak

Filling
¼ cup mayonnaise
1 (6 ounce) jar marinated artichokes, drained, chopped
¼ teaspoon salt
¼ teaspoon coarsely ground pepper
1 tablespoon lemon juice
1 teaspoon grated lemon peel
1 teaspoon finely chopped fresh garlic
2 cups spinach leaves

8 servings

In medium bowl stir together all marinade ingredients *except* steak. With mallet, pound steak to ¼-inch thickness. Place steak in plastic food bag. Pour marinade into bag; seal tightly. Place bag in 13x9-inch pan. Refrigerate, turning twice, 24 hours. Prepare grill; heat until coals are ash white. Remove steak from marinade; *reserve marinade*. In medium bowl combine all filling ingredients *except* spinach.

Spoon filling mixture over entire surface of steak; lay spinach over top. Tightly roll up steak jelly roll fashion. Tie with string to secure filling inside roll. Place steak on grill. Grill, basting with marinade and turning occasionally, for 15 to 25 minutes or until desired doneness.

Nutrition Information (1 serving)
• Calories 350 • Protein 25g • Carbohydrate 5g • Fat 26g
• Cholesterol 65mg • Sodium 528mg

Grilled Steaks With Garden Tomato Basil Sauce 60 minutes

Marinade
¼ cup vegetable oil
2 teaspoons dried oregano leaves
½ teaspoon coarsely ground pepper
⅛ teaspoon salt
2 tablespoons lemon juice

4 to 6 ribeye *or* porterhouse beef steaks

Sauce
¼ cup chopped red onion
2 cups (2 medium) cubed ½-inch ripe tomatoes
1 (6 ounce) can tomato paste
1 tablespoon chopped fresh basil leaves
⅛ teaspoon salt
⅛ teaspoon cayenne pepper
2 tablespoons red wine vinegar
1 tablespoon lemon juice
½ teaspoon finely chopped fresh garlic

6 servings

Prepare grill; heat until coals are ash white. Meanwhile, in medium bowl stir together all marinade ingredients *except* steaks. Place steaks in plastic food bag. Pour marinade into bag; seal tightly. Place in 13x9-inch pan; let stand 20 minutes. Meanwhile, in medium bowl stir together all sauce ingredients. In 5-cup blender container place about 1 cup sauce mixture. Blend on High speed until saucy (30 to 45 seconds).

Stir back into sauce mixture. Set aside. Remove steaks from marinade; *reserve marinade*. Place steaks on grill. Grill, basting with marinade and turning once, until desired doneness (10 to 15 minutes for medium). Serve sauce over steaks.

Nutrition Information (1 serving)
• Calories 330 • Protein 33g • Carbohydrate 9g • Fat 18g
• Cholesterol 92mg • Sodium 367mg

Western Barbecued Rib Sampler

60 minutes

Ribs are simmered in beer, then coated with a flavorful, hot and spicy barbecue sauce.

Ribs
½ cup firmly packed brown sugar
¼ cup country-style Dijon mustard
2 (12 ounce) cans beer*
1 teaspoon hot pepper sauce
3 pounds beef, pork loin *or* country-style ribs

Barbecue Sauce
¼ cup firmly packed brown sugar
¼ cup chopped onion
1 cup ketchup
½ cup Worcestershire sauce
¼ cup lemon juice
½ teaspoon coarsely ground pepper
¼ teaspoon salt
¼ teaspoon cayenne pepper

4 servings

In Dutch oven stir together all rib ingredients *except* ribs; add ribs. Cook over high heat until mixture comes to a full boil (5 to 10 minutes). Cover; reduce heat to low. Continue cooking, turning ribs occasionally, until ribs are fork tender (40 to 50 minutes). Meanwhile, prepare grill; heat until coals are ash white. In 1-quart saucepan stir together all barbecue sauce ingredients. Place ribs on grill. Brush ribs with barbecue sauce. Grill, brushing with barbecue sauce and turning occasionally, until ribs are done (12 to 15 minutes). Cook remaining barbecue sauce over medium heat, stirring occasionally, until just comes to a boil (3 to 5 minutes). Serve with ribs.

*3 cups apple juice can be substituted for 2 (12 ounce) cans beer.

Nutrition Information (1 serving)
• Calories 680 • Protein 40g • Carbohydrate 70g • Fat 21g
• Cholesterol 114mg • Sodium 1749mg

Hamburgers With Cucumber Relish

60 minutes

Hamburgers
1½ pounds ground beef
¼ cup chopped onion
¼ teaspoon salt
¼ teaspoon pepper
2 tablespoons country-style Dijon mustard

Relish
1 teaspoon dill seed
1 teaspoon mustard seed
2 tablespoons cider vinegar
1 tablespoon vegetable oil
1 tablespoon country-style Dijon mustard
1 cup (1 medium) thinly sliced cucumber
1 cup (2 medium) thinly sliced ripe tomatoes
1 cup thinly sliced red onion, separated into rings

6 servings

Prepare grill; heat until coals are ash white. In medium bowl stir together ground beef, onion, salt, pepper and 2 tablespoons mustard. Form into 6 large ¼-inch thick patties; set aside. In medium bowl combine all relish ingredients *except* cucumbers, tomatoes and onion. Add vegetables; toss to coat. Place hamburgers on grill. Grill, turning once, until desired doneness (10 to 15 minutes for medium). Spoon relish on hamburgers.

Nutrition Information (1 serving)
• Calories 270 • Protein 19g • Carbohydrate 5g • Fat 19g
• Cholesterol 68mg • Sodium 376mg

Western Barbecued Rib Sampler (pictured)
Hamburgers With Cucumber Relish

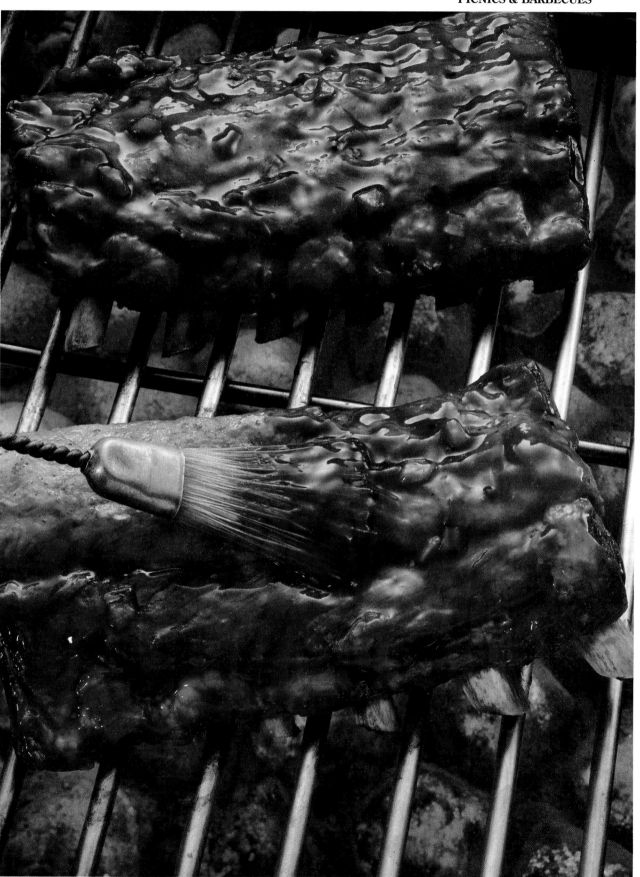

Pork Chops Stuffed With Corn Relish   45 minutes

A colorful, flavorful corn relish is stuffed inside and served over pork chops.

1 cup (1 medium) coarsely chopped red pepper
½ cup thinly sliced red onion, separated into rings
¼ cup chopped fresh cilantro *or* parsley
1 (10 ounce) package frozen whole kernel corn, thawed, drained
½ teaspoon cumin

¼ teaspoon salt
¼ teaspoon coarsely ground pepper
2 tablespoons cider vinegar
2 tablespoons vegetable oil
6 (1-inch thick) pork chops

6 servings

Prepare grill; heat until coals are ash white. Meanwhile, in medium bowl stir together all ingredients *except* pork chops; set aside. To prepare pork chops, split each pork chop from outer edges toward bone, making a pocket. Place about 2 tablespoons corn relish in each pocket. Place pork chops on grill. Grill, turning occasionally, for 20 to 30 minutes or until desired doneness. Serve remaining corn relish over pork chops.

Nutrition Information (1 serving)
• Calories 260 • Protein 20g • Carbohydrate 12g • Fat 14g
• Cholesterol 52mg • Sodium 123mg

Honey Lime Marinated Pork Tenderloin   60 minutes

Lime marinade provides a delicious flavor and extra tenderness for pork tenderloin.

⅓ cup lime juice
¼ cup olive *or* vegetable oil
1 teaspoon coarsely ground pepper
½ teaspoon salt
½ teaspoon cumin
⅛ teaspoon cayenne pepper
2 tablespoons honey

1 tablespoon country-style Dijon mustard
1 teaspoon finely chopped fresh garlic
1 teaspoon grated lime peel

2 (¾ pound) pork tenderloins

6 servings

Prepare grill; heat until coals are ash white. Meanwhile, in medium bowl stir together all ingredients *except* tenderloins. Pierce tenderloins all over with fork; place tenderloins in plastic food bag. Pour in marinade; seal tightly. Place in 13x9-inch pan; let stand 20 minutes. Remove tenderloins from marinade; *reserve marinade.* Place tenderloins on grill. Grill, basting with marinade and turning occasionally, for 15 to 20 minutes or until meat thermometer reaches 160°F. Let stand 10 minutes. Meanwhile, in 1-quart saucepan cook remaining marinade over medium heat until mixture comes to a full boil (2 to 3 minutes). To serve, slice tenderloins on the diagonal. Serve with marinade.

Nutrition Information (1 serving)
• Calories 260 • Protein 26g • Carbohydrate 8g • Fat 14g
• Cholesterol 83mg • Sodium 312mg

Pork	Internal Cooking Temperature
Medium	160°F
Well	170°F

Pork Chops Stuffed With Corn Relish (pictured)
Honey Lime Marinated Pork Tenderloin

Shrimp & Artichoke Kabobs

45 minutes

Shrimp and marinated artichoke kabobs are served over a lemon-zested pasta.

1 (9 ounce) package uncooked fresh linguini*
1 pound (about 24 medium) fresh *or* frozen raw shrimp
1 medium red onion, cut into 12 wedges
2 (6 ounce) jars marinated artichokes, *reserve marinade*

6 (12-inch) metal skewers

Basting Sauce
2 teaspoons dried basil leaves
½ teaspoon salt
½ teaspoon coarsely ground pepper
  Dash cayenne pepper
½ teaspoon finely chopped fresh garlic
2 tablespoons olive *or* vegetable oil

2 teaspoons grated lemon peel

6 servings

Prepare grill; heat until coals are ash white. Cook linguini according to package directions; drain. Place in large bowl; set aside. Meanwhile, peel and devein shrimp, leaving tail intact. (If shrimp are frozen, do not thaw; peel under running cold water.) Alternate shrimp, onion and artichokes on skewers. In small bowl stir together 2 tablespoons reserved marinade and all basting sauce ingredients *except* lemon peel; brush over kabobs. Place kabobs on grill. Grill, basting and turning occasionally, for 7 to 10 minutes or until shrimp turn pink. Meanwhile, add remaining artichoke marinade and lemon peel to linguini; toss to coat. Serve pasta with kabobs.

*9 ounces uncooked dried linguini can be substituted for 1 (9 ounce) package uncooked fresh linguini.

Nutrition Information (1 serving)
• Calories 300 • Protein 18g • Carbohydrate 40g • Fat 8g
• Cholesterol 86mg • Sodium 239mg

Minted Pesto Lamb Chops

45 minutes

Pesto is made with fresh mint and walnuts, then served with lamb chops and grilled tomatoes.

Pesto
½ cup chopped walnuts
½ cup chopped fresh mint leaves
⅓ cup olive *or* vegetable oil
2 tablespoons freshly grated Parmesan cheese
¼ teaspoon coarsely ground pepper
1 teaspoon finely chopped fresh garlic

Lamb Chops
⅛ teaspoon salt
⅛ teaspoon coarsely ground pepper
2 tablespoons olive *or* vegetable oil
6 (1-inch thick) lamb loin chops
3 ripe tomatoes, halved
2 tablespoons freshly grated Parmesan cheese

6 servings

Prepare grill; heat until coals are ash white. In medium bowl stir together all pesto ingredients; set aside. In small bowl stir together salt, ⅛ teaspoon pepper and 2 tablespoons oil. Brush lamb chops with oil mixture; place on grill. Grill, basting and turning occasionally, for 10 to 15 minutes or until fork tender. Spoon about 1 tablespoon pesto on each lamb chop. Place tomato halves on grill; spoon about *1 teaspoon* Parmesan cheese on each tomato half. Continue grilling for 2 to 4 minutes or until heated through. Serve tomato half alongside each lamb chop; serve with remaining pesto.

Nutrition Information (1 serving)
• Calories 260 • Protein 22g • Carbohydrate 5g • Fat 29g
• Cholesterol 68mg • Sodium 174mg

Shrimp & Artichoke Kabobs (pictured)
Minted Pesto Lamb Chops

Grilled Halibut With Pineapple Salsa (pictured)
Lemon Pepper Grilled Fish Steaks

Grilled Halibut With Pineapple Salsa   45 minutes

Ginger and cilantro season pineapple salsa for a flavorful accompaniment to grilled fish.

Salsa
1 large pineapple, pared
1 tablespoon sugar
1 tablespoon chopped fresh cilantro *or* parsley
2 teaspoons grated fresh gingerroot*
2 teaspoons grated lime peel
1 tablespoon lime juice

Halibut
⅛ teaspoon salt
⅛ teaspoon coarsely ground pepper
2 tablespoons olive *or* vegetable oil
6 (6 ounces each) 1-inch thick halibut *or* swordfish steaks
6 (⅛-inch) lime slices

6 servings

Prepare grill; heat until coals are ash white. Meanwhile, slice 3 (¼-inch) slices of pineapple. Cut each slice in half; set aside. Coarsely chop remaining pineapple (about 1½ cups). Place in medium bowl; stir in all remaining salsa ingredients. Set aside. In small bowl stir together salt, pepper and oil. Brush halibut steaks with oil mixture; place on grill. Grill, basting and turning occasionally, until fish flakes with a fork (12 to 15 minutes). Place pineapple slices on grill; grill, turning once, until lightly browned (1 to 2 minutes). Serve halibut on grilled pineapple slices; serve with salsa. Garnish with lime slices.

Broiling Directions: Prepare pineapple slices and salsa as directed. *Heat broiler.* Brush halibut with oil mixture; place on broiler pan. Broil 3 to 5 inches from heat, basting and turning occasionally, until fish flakes with a fork (10 to 12 minutes). Place pineapple halves on pan; broil, turning once, until lightly browned (1 to 2 minutes). Serve halibut on broiled pineapple slices; serve with salsa. Garnish with lime slices.

*¾ teaspoon ground ginger can be substituted for 2 teaspoons fresh gingerroot.

Nutrition Information (1 serving)
• Calories 270 • Protein 31g • Carbohydrate 18g • Fat 8g
• Cholesterol 46mg • Sodium 124mg

Lemon Pepper Grilled Fish Steaks   45 minutes

These grilled fresh fish steaks are flavored with lemon and allspice.

¼ cup butter *or* margarine, softened
1 teaspoon allspice
1 teaspoon coarsely ground pepper
½ teaspoon salt
2 teaspoons grated lemon peel
1 teaspoon finely chopped fresh garlic

4 (1-inch thick) fish steaks (swordfish, halibut *or* salmon)

4 servings

Prepare grill placing coals to one side; heat until coals are ash white. Make aluminum foil drip pan; place opposite coals. In small bowl stir together all ingredients *except* fish steaks. Spread each side of fish steaks with about 1 teaspoon butter mixture. Grill, turning after half the time, until fish flakes with a fork (8 to 12 minutes). Dollop remaining butter on fish steaks; serve immediately.

Nutrition Information (1 serving)
• Calories 230 • Protein 24g • Carbohydrate 1g • Fat 14g
• Cholesterol 67mg • Sodium 446mg

Grilled Garden Vegetables & Sole

45 minutes

Garden vegetables add color and flavor to this grilled fish.

1 pound (4 fillets) fresh *or* frozen sole, thawed, drained
2 medium zucchini, cut into julienne strips
½ cup shredded carrot
½ small onion, cut into rings
¼ cup sliced ripe olives

½ teaspoon Italian herb seasoning*
¼ teaspoon garlic salt
½ cup (2 ounces) shredded Monterey Jack cheese

4 servings

Prepare grill; heat until coals are ash white. Place each fish fillet in center of 18-inch square heavy duty aluminum foil. Top fillets with zucchini, carrot, onion and olives. Sprinkle with Italian seasoning and garlic salt; sprinkle with cheese. Bring edges of aluminum foil up to center; tightly seal tops and sides. Place bundles on grill. Grill until fish flakes with a fork (10 to 14 minutes). Open bundles carefully.

*⅛ teaspoon *each* dried oregano leaves, dried marjoram leaves and dried basil leaves

and ¹⁄₁₆ teaspoon rubbed dried sage can be substituted for ½ teaspoon Italian herb seasoning.

Microwave Directions: In 9-inch square baking dish place fish fillets; top with all remaining ingredients. Cover; microwave on HIGH, turning dish ½ turn after half the time, until fish flakes with a fork (7 to 8 minutes).

Nutrition Information (1 serving)
• Calories 190 • Protein 26g • Carbohydrate 4g • Fat 7g
• Cholesterol 67mg • Sodium 358mg

To Prepare Grilled Garden Vegetables & Sole:

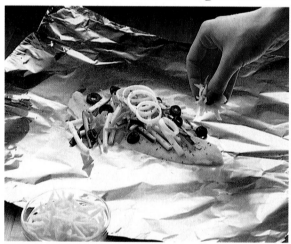

1. Place each fish fillet in center of 18-inch square heavy duty aluminum foil. Top fillets with zucchini, carrot, onion and olives. Sprinkle with Italian seasoning and garlic salt; sprinkle with cheese.

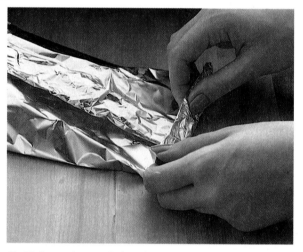

2. Bring edges of aluminum foil up to center; tightly seal tops and sides.

Grilled Garden Vegetables & Sole

Summer Fruit With Lime Ginger Dressing   30 minutes

This refreshing lime, ginger and honey dressing lightly coats fresh fruit.

Fruit
½ medium cantaloupe, seeded, peeled, thinly sliced
½ medium honeydew, seeded, peeled, thinly sliced
½ medium fresh pineapple, peeled, cored, thinly sliced
½ pint (1 cup) strawberries, hulled, halved

Dressing
¼ teaspoon ginger
2 tablespoons lime juice
2 tablespoons honey
2 teaspoons grated lime peel

8 servings

Cut cantaloupe and honeydew slices into thirds and pineapple slices in half. In large bowl combine all fruit. In small bowl stir together all dressing ingredients. Cover fruit and dressing; refrigerate until ready to serve.

Just before serving pour dressing over fruit; toss to coat.

Nutrition Information (1 serving)
• Calories 80 • Protein 1g • Carbohydrate 20g • Fat 0g
• Cholesterol 0mg • Sodium 12mg

Vegetable n' Cracked Wheat Salad   1 hour 30 minutes

Colorful tomatoes and pea pods liven up this easy-to-tote tabbouleh salad.

1 cup cracked wheat (bulgur)
4 ounces fresh pea pods, trimmed, cut in half*
1 medium ripe tomato, cubed ½-inch
¼ cup lemon juice
2 tablespoons chopped onion

1 tablespoon chopped fresh parsley
¼ teaspoon salt
3 tablespoons olive *or* vegetable oil

6 servings

Prepare cracked wheat according to package directions; drain (cracked wheat should be soft yet chewy). In large bowl toss together cracked wheat and all remaining ingredients. Cover; refrigerate 30 minutes.

*1 (6 ounce) package frozen pea pods, thawed, can be substituted for 4 ounces fresh pea pods.

Nutrition Information (1 serving)
• Calories 170 • Protein 3g • Carbohydrate 24g • Fat 7g
• Cholesterol 0mg • Sodium 93mg

Sunday was a day of rest for pioneer women. "Community picnics were spent mingling with friends and meeting the newcomers, and Sunday suppers were a time for exchanging news and viewpoints. In the quiet of the evening, the family gathered alone to read from the Scriptures, play music or enjoy long talks by the fireside."

Summer Fruit With Lime Ginger Dressing (top)
Vegetable n' Cracked Wheat Salad (bottom)

Sweet n' Tangy Slaw (top)
Creamy Marinated Vegetable Salad (bottom)

Sweet n' Tangy Slaw

1 hour 15 minutes

Shredded cabbage, zucchini and carrots tossed with a cooked dressing make a delicious slaw.

Dressing
⅓ cup sugar
½ teaspoon salt
½ teaspoon dry mustard
2 tablespoons cider vinegar
¼ cup half-and-half
1 egg yolk

Salad
1 large head cabbage
1 cup (1 medium) shredded zucchini
½ cup (1 medium) shredded carrot
2 tablespoons finely chopped onion

8 servings

In 1-quart saucepan combine sugar, salt, dry mustard and vinegar. Whisk in half-and-half and egg yolk. Cook over low heat, whisking constantly, until mixture is hot and slightly thickened (5 to 9 minutes). Cover; refrigerate at least 1 hour. Meanwhile, cut ¾-inch slice from top of cabbage head. With sharp knife, hollow out inside of cabbage leaving ¾-inch shell; set aside. Finely chop or shred removed cabbage. Place chopped cabbage in medium bowl. Add remaining salad ingredients; toss to combine. Add dressing; toss well to coat. Spoon salad into cabbage shell. Serve immediately or cover; refrigerate. Refill shell with additional slaw as needed.

Nutrition Information (1 serving)
• Calories 90 • Protein 3g • Carbohydrate 17g • Fat 2g
• Cholesterol 37mg • Sodium 167mg

Creamy Marinated Vegetable Salad

6 hours 30 minutes

*Allowing this salad to marinate blends the flavors;
it's the perfect accompaniment for barbecued ribs.*

Dressing
⅓ cup mayonnaise
⅓ cup dairy sour cream
3 tablespoons French dressing
1 tablespoon sugar
2 tablespoons sliced green onion
2 teaspoons tarragon vinegar *or* cider vinegar
½ teaspoon salt

Salad
1 cup bite-size cauliflower flowerets
1 cup bite-size broccoli flowerets
1 cup (2 stalks) sliced ¼-inch celery
1 cup (1 medium) sliced ¼-inch carrot
1 cup (1 medium) ½-inch pieces green pepper
1 cup (1 medium) peeled, seeded, ½-inch pieces cucumber

8 servings

In large bowl stir together all dressing ingredients. Add all salad ingredients; toss to coat well. Cover; refrigerate 6 hours or overnight. Just before serving toss to coat well. Serve with slotted spoon.

Nutrition Information (1 serving)
• Calories 50 • Protein 1g • Carbohydrate 6g • Fat 3g
• Cholesterol 3mg • Sodium 94mg

Fresh Herb Tomato-Jack Salad (pictured)
Potato Salad With Mustard Mayonnaise

Fresh Herb Tomato-Jack Salad

60 minutes

Fresh basil and oregano tantalize tomato and Monterey Jack cheese in this easy salad.

Salad
2 cups (2 medium) cubed 1-inch ripe tomatoes
1 cup (4 ounces) cubed ½-inch Monterey Jack
   or Mozzarella cheese
2 cups (2 medium) sliced ⅛-inch zucchini

Dressing
2 teaspoons chopped fresh oregano leaves*
2 teaspoons torn fresh basil leaves**
½ teaspoon sugar
¼ teaspoon garlic salt
¼ teaspoon coarsely ground pepper
2 tablespoons olive *or* vegetable oil
2 teaspoons vinegar

6 servings

In medium bowl combine all salad ingredients; set aside. In tightly covered jar combine all dressing ingredients; shake well to mix. Pour over tomato mixture; toss to coat. Cover; refrigerate at least 30 minutes.

*½ teaspoon dried oregano leaves can be substituted for 2 teaspoons chopped fresh oregano leaves.

**½ teaspoon dried basil leaves can be substituted for 2 teaspoons torn fresh basil leaves.

Nutrition Information (1 serving)
• Calories 120 • Protein 5g • Carbohydrate 3g • Fat 10g
• Cholesterol 17mg • Sodium 183mg

Potato Salad With Mustard Mayonnaise

3 hours

A creamy potato salad with the accents of mustard seed and refreshing cucumber.

4 cups water
1 teaspoon salt
4 cups quartered small new red potatoes
½ cup sliced ¼-inch celery
¼ cup chopped red onion
½ cup mayonnaise
2 hard cooked eggs, chopped
1 tablespoon mustard seed

½ teaspoon salt
½ teaspoon coarsely ground pepper
2 tablespoons country-style Dijon mustard
1 cup (1 medium) sliced ⅛-inch cucumber,
   cut in half
⅓ cup chopped fresh parsley

8 servings

In 3-quart saucepan bring water and 1 teaspoon salt to a full boil; add potatoes. Cook over high heat until potatoes are fork tender (12 to 15 minutes). Rinse under cold water. In large bowl stir together all remaining ingredients *except* cucumber and parsley. Add potatoes, cucumber and parsley; toss to coat. Refrigerate at least 2 hours to blend flavors.

Nutrition Information (1 serving)
• Calories 200 • Protein 4g • Carbohydrate 16g • Fat 13g
• Cholesterol 77mg • Sodium 353mg

Grilled German Dip Sandwich

30 minutes

Serve this hearty sandwich with potato salad and crisp relishes.

Dip
½ cup mayonnaise
¼ cup Dijon-style mustard

Sandwiches
4 cooked bratwurst, split lengthwise
 Butter *or* margarine, softened

4 hoagie rolls, split
1 cup sauerkraut, drained
½ teaspoon caraway seed
12 (3x1½x¼-inch) slices Swiss cheese

4 sandwiches

Prepare grill; heat until coals are ash white. In small bowl stir together mayonnaise and mustard; set aside. Place bratwurst on grill. Grill, turning once, until browned and heated through (2 to 3 minutes on each side). Spread butter on cut surfaces of rolls; place, cut side down, on grill. Grill until rolls are toasted (2 to 3 minutes). Meanwhile, in ovenproof 1-quart saucepan stir together sauerkraut and caraway seed. Place saucepan on grill while cooking bratwurst. Cook, stirring occasionally, until heated through (4 to 6 minutes). Layer each bottom half of roll with ¼ cup sauerkraut mixture, 1 bratwurst, 3 slices cheese and top half of roll. Serve warm sandwiches with dip.

Broiling Directions: In small bowl stir together mayonnaise and mustard; set aside. *Heat broiler.* Place bratwurst on broiler pan. Broil 4 to 5 inches from heat, turning once, until browned and heated through (2 to 3 minutes on each side). Spread butter on cut surfaces of rolls; place on broiler pan with bratwurst. Broil until rolls are toasted (2 to 3 minutes). Meanwhile, in 1-quart saucepan stir together sauerkraut and caraway seed. Cook over medium heat, stirring occasionally, until heated through (4 to 6 minutes). Layer each bottom half of roll with ¼ cup sauerkraut mixture, 1 bratwurst, 3 slices cheese and top half of roll. Serve warm sandwiches with dip.

Nutrition Information (1 serving)
• Calories 950 • Protein 40g • Carbohydrate 28g • Fat 75g
• Cholesterol 158mg • Sodium 1801mg

Picnic Peppered Hoagie

30 minutes

1 pound (12 to 18-inch) loaf French bread
½ cup butter *or* margarine, softened
½ teaspoon coarsely ground pepper
1 cup shredded lettuce
6 slices bologna, folded in half
12 slices process American cheese, cut in half
24 slices salami, folded in half

6 slices ripe tomato
5 green pepper rings
4 slices Provolone cheese, cut in half

 Pitted ripe olives
6 (6-inch) wooden skewers

8 servings

Cut bread in half lengthwise. In small bowl stir together butter and pepper. Spread over cut surfaces of bread. Sprinkle ½ *cup* shredded lettuce over bottom of loaf. Layer with 6 slices bologna, 6 slices American cheese, 12 slices salami, tomato, green pepper, Provolone cheese, 12 slices salami, 6 slices American cheese and

remaining shredded lettuce. Place top half of loaf over lettuce. Thread olives onto skewers. Secure hoagie with skewers.

Nutrition Information (1 serving)
• Calories 710 • Protein 31g • Carbohydrate 36g • Fat 49g
• Cholesterol 135mg • Sodium 2124mg

Grilled German Dip Sandwich (top)
Picnic Peppered Hoagie (bottom)

Grilled Salami & Onion Sandwich

45 minutes

1 cup thinly sliced red onion
1 cup thinly sliced onion
2 tablespoons honey
1 tablespoon country-style Dijon mustard
1 tablespoon cider vinegar
2 tablespoons butter *or* margarine

4 (¼-inch) slices round loaf sourdough bread, halved
½ pound (2-inch diameter) sliced ⅛-inch hard salami
8 (4 ounces) 3x1¼x¼-inch slices Mozzarella cheese

4 servings

Prepare grill; heat until coals are ash white. Meanwhile, in 2-quart saucepan place red onion, onion, honey, mustard and vinegar. Cook over medium heat, stirring occasionally, until onions are crisply tender (2 to 3 minutes). Butter 1 side of each half slice bread; place, buttered side up, on cookie sheet. Top buttered side of each of 4 half slices bread with ¼ of salami. Criss-cross *2 slices* cheese over salami. Divide onion mixture evenly between 4 sandwiches. Top with remaining bread slices, buttered sides down. Place on grill. Grill, turning occasionally, for 10 to 15 minutes or until cheese is melted and bread is toasted.

Nutrition Information (1 serving)
• Calories 440 • Protein 20g • Carbohydrate 35g • Fat 24g
• Cholesterol 69mg • Sodium 1191mg

Lemon Chili Chicken Breasts in Tortillas

60 minutes

Chicken
⅓ cup lemon juice
1 teaspoon chili powder
½ teaspoon finely chopped fresh garlic
2 whole boneless chicken breasts, skinned, halved

Guacamole
2 medium avocados, peeled
1 teaspoon chili powder
½ teaspoon salt
2 tablespoons lemon juice
½ cup chopped ripe tomato
¼ cup sliced ⅛-inch green onions
1 red jalapeño pepper, seeded, finely chopped
2 tablespoons chopped fresh cilantro *or* parsley
4 green onions, trimmed
4 (6-inch) flour *or* corn tortillas

4 servings

Prepare grill; heat until coals are ash white. In small bowl stir together all chicken ingredients *except* chicken breasts. Place chicken breasts in plastic food bag. Pour marinade into bag; seal tightly. Place in 13x9-inch pan; refrigerate 30 minutes. Meanwhile, in medium bowl place avocados; mash with fork. Stir in 1 teaspoon chili powder, salt and 2 tablespoons lemon juice until well blended. Stir in all remaining guacamole ingredients *except* 4 green onions and tortillas. Remove chicken from marinade; *reserve marinade*. Place chicken breasts on grill. Grill, basting with marinade and turning occasionally, for 12 to 15 minutes or until chicken is fork tender. Remove chicken from grill; place green onions and tortillas on grill. Grill for 4 to 5 minutes or until green onions and tortillas are heated through. Spread guacamole on tortillas; place one chicken breast and one green onion in center of each tortilla. Fold over tortilla; serve as a sandwich.

Nutrition Information (1 serving)
• Calories 410 • Protein 31g • Carbohydrate 28g • Fat 21g
• Cholesterol 72mg • Sodium 466mg

Grilled Salami & Onion Sandwich (top)
Lemon Chili Chicken Breasts in Tortillas (bottom)

Brown Sugar Baked Beans

2 hours

These baked beans are all-American and will become a family favorite.

4 slices bacon, cut into ½-inch pieces
½ cup firmly packed brown sugar
½ cup chili sauce
½ cup chopped onion
2 (21 ounce) cans pork and beans

2 tablespoons country-style Dijon mustard
1 tablespoon Worcestershire sauce
¼ teaspoon hot pepper sauce

8 servings

Heat oven to 325°. In 10-inch skillet cook bacon over medium high heat, stirring occasionally, until bacon is browned (4 to 6 minutes). Place bacon on paper towel. In large bowl stir together bacon and all remaining ingredients. Pour into 2-quart casserole. Bake, stirring occasionally, for 1½ to 2 hours or until slightly thickened.

Microwave Directions: In 2-quart casserole microwave bacon on HIGH, stirring after half the time, until browned (3½ to 4½ minutes). Place bacon on paper towel. Drain off fat from casserole. In same casserole stir together bacon and all remaining ingredients. Cover with waxed paper; microwave on HIGH, stirring after half the time, until mixture comes to a full boil (7 to 10 minutes). Reduce power to MEDIUM (50% power); microwave, stirring after half the time, until flavors are blended and mixture is slightly thickened (20 to 25 minutes).

Nutrition Information (1 serving)
• Calories 250 • Protein 9g • Carbohydrate 48g • Fat 4g
• Cholesterol 13mg • Sodium 1031mg

Spicy Red Beans Over Rice

1 day

As these spicy beans bake, a wonderful, mouth-watering aroma fills the air.

2 cups dried red beans
1 cup (2 medium) sliced onions
1 (14½ ounce) can whole tomatoes
1 (10¾ ounce) can chicken broth
2 slices bacon, cut into ½-inch pieces
2 bay leaves
1 teaspoon dried thyme leaves

½ teaspoon salt
¼ to ½ teaspoon cayenne pepper
1 tablespoon Worcestershire sauce
½ teaspoon finely chopped fresh garlic

4 cups cooked long grain rice

8 servings

In Dutch oven place beans and enough water to cover; soak overnight. If needed, add more water to cover beans. Cook over high heat until water comes to a full boil. Reduce heat to medium; continue cooking until beans are tender (30 to 45 minutes). Drain beans. *Heat oven to 350°.* In 2-quart casserole combine beans and all remaining ingredients *except* cooked rice. Bake, stirring occasionally, for 2 to 3 hours or until sauce is slightly thickened. Remove bay leaves. Serve over cooked rice.

Nutrition Information (1 serving)
• Calories 300 • Protein 15g • Carbohydrate 57g • Fat 2g
• Cholesterol 1mg • Sodium 396mg

Brown Sugar Baked Beans (pictured)
Spicy Red Beans Over Rice

Parmesan Potato & Carrot Bundles (top)
Grilled Corn With Herb Butter (bottom)

Parmesan Potato & Carrot Bundles 1 hour 30 minutes

Prepare bundles ahead of time, then grill at mealtime.

4 (14x12-inch) pieces heavy-duty aluminum foil
4 medium sliced ⅛-inch baking potatoes
2 cups (4 medium) julienne carrots
1 cup (1 medium) 1-inch pieces green pepper
1 small onion, sliced
¼ cup freshly grated Parmesan cheese

1 teaspoon salt
1 teaspoon garlic powder
½ teaspoon pepper
½ cup butter *or* margarine

4 servings

Prepare grill; heat until coals are ash white. On each piece of aluminum foil place *1* sliced potato, *½ cup* carrots, *¼ cup* green pepper and several slices of onion. Sprinkle each potato bundle with *1 tablespoon* Parmesan cheese, *¼ teaspoon* salt, *¼ teaspoon* garlic powder and *⅛ teaspoon* pepper; place *2 tablespoons* butter on top of vegetables. Bring edges of aluminum foil up to center; tightly seal tops and sides. Place bundles on grill; cover. Grill, turning over after half the time, for 45 to 55 minutes or until potatoes are fork tender. Open bundles carefully.

Oven Directions: Heat oven to 400°. Prepare bundles as directed above. Place bundles in 13x9-inch baking pan. Bake, turning bundles over after 30 minutes, for 45 to 60 minutes or until potatoes are fork tender. Open bundles carefully.

Nutrition Information (1 serving)
• Calories 390 • Protein 7g • Carbohydrate 37g • Fat 25g
• Cholesterol 67mg • Sodium 916mg

Grilled Corn With Herb Butter 2 hours

Grilled corn on the cob is served with a flavorful spread.

6 ears fresh corn, in husks
   Water

Herb Butter
¾ cup butter *or* margarine, softened
2 tablespoons finely chopped red pepper

½ teaspoon Italian herb seasoning*
½ teaspoon salt
¼ teaspoon garlic powder

6 servings

Loosen husks on ears of corn enough to remove silk. Fill Dutch oven with water. Dip corn in water; shake well. Rewrap husks around corn. Plunge corn in water; let stand until husks are soaked (about 1 hour). Meanwhile, prepare grill; heat until coals are ash white. In small bowl stir together all herb butter ingredients until well mixed; set aside. Place corn on grill. Grill, turning frequently, until corn is crisply tender (15 to 20 minutes). Immediately husk corn; serve with herb butter.

*⅛ teaspoon *each* dried oregano leaves, dried marjoram leaves and dried basil leaves and ¹⁄₁₆ teaspoon rubbed dried sage can be substituted for ½ teaspoon Italian herb seasoning.

Nutrition Information (1 serving)
• Calories 270 • Protein 3g • Carbohydrate 15g • Fat 24g
• Cholesterol 62mg • Sodium 423mg

Blue Cheese Grilled Potatoes

2 hours

Blue cheese and onions smother grilled potatoes.

¼ cup butter *or* margarine
1 (4 ounce) package crumbled blue cheese
1 tablespoon chopped fresh parsley
1 teaspoon salt
½ teaspoon coarsely ground pepper

4 medium baking potatoes, cut in half lengthwise
4 small onions, sliced ¼-inch (about 24 slices)
4 (14x12-inch) pieces heavy duty aluminum foil

4 servings

Prepare grill; heat until coals are ash white. Meanwhile, in small bowl stir together butter, blue cheese, parsley, salt and pepper. Spread one-fourth of butter mixture on cut sides of both halves of each potato. Top one half of each potato with about 6 onion slices. Put each potato back together. Wrap each potato in aluminum foil; tightly seal top and sides. Place on grill. Grill, turning potatoes every 15 minutes, until potatoes are fork tender (50 to 60 minutes).

Oven Directions: Heat oven to 400°. Prepare potatoes as directed above. Wrap each potato in aluminum foil; tightly seal top and sides. Place prepared potatoes in 13x9-inch baking pan. Bake, turning potatoes after half the time, for 55 to 65 minutes or until potatoes are fork tender.

Nutrition Information (1 serving)
• Calories 340 • Protein 10g • Carbohydrate 31g • Fat 20g
• Cholesterol 52mg • Sodium 1056mg

Grilled Vegetable Kabobs

45 minutes

Colorful and flavorful, these crisp vegetables are grilled to perfection.

3 medium zucchini, each cut into 4 pieces
2 medium onions, each cut into 6 wedges
12 large mushroom caps
2 red *or* green peppers, cut into 2-inch pieces
6 large cherry tomatoes

6 (12-inch) metal skewers

Butter Baste
½ cup butter *or* margarine
1 teaspoon chopped fresh dill weed*
1 teaspoon chopped fresh chives**
1 teaspoon lemon juice

6 servings

Prepare grill placing coals to one side; heat until coals are ash white. Make aluminum foil drip pan; place opposite coals. To assemble kabobs on metal skewers, alternate zucchini, onion, mushrooms and green pepper. In small bowl stir together all butter baste ingredients. Place kabobs on grill over drip pan. Cover; grill, turning occasionally and basting during last 10 minutes, until vegetables are crisply tender (20 to 25 minutes). Using oven mitts

add tomato to each skewer during last 3 minutes of grilling.

*½ teaspoon dried dill weed can be substituted for 1 teaspoon chopped fresh dill weed.

**½ teaspoon dried chives can be substituted for 1 teaspoon chopped fresh chives.

Nutrition Information (1 serving)
• Calories 70 • Protein 2g • Carbohydrate 7g • Fat 4g
• Cholesterol 10mg • Sodium 44mg

Blue Cheese Grilled Potatoes (top)
Grilled Vegetable Kabobs (bottom)

Crisp Green Beans With Red Pepper

30 minutes

Red pepper and black olives are tossed with crisply tender green beans.

1 pound fresh green beans, trimmed
¼ cup red wine vinegar
2 tablespoons olive *or* vegetable oil
¼ teaspoon coarsely ground pepper
1 teaspoon Dijon-style mustard

½ teaspoon finely chopped fresh garlic
½ cup sliced ¼-inch ripe olives
1 medium red pepper, cut into strips

4 servings

In 3-quart saucepan place beans; add enough water to cover. Bring to a full boil. Cook over medium heat until beans are crisply tender (10 to 12 minutes). Drain; rinse with cold water. Meanwhile, in small bowl stir together all remaining ingredients *except* olives and red pepper. In large bowl toss together beans, olives and red pepper. Pour vinegar mixture over bean mixture; toss to coat.

Microwave Directions: In 3-quart saucepan combine beans and ½ cup water. Cover; microwave on HIGH, stirring after half the time, until beans are crisply tender (8 to 10 minutes). Drain; rinse with cold water. Meanwhile, in small bowl stir together all remaining ingredients *except* olives and red pepper. In large bowl toss together beans, olives and red pepper. Pour vinegar mixture over bean mixture; toss to coat.

Nutrition Information (1 serving)
• Calories 130 • Protein 3g • Carbohydrate 11g • Fat 9g
• Cholesterol 0mg • Sodium 182mg

Vegetables With Chili Mayonnaise

30 minutes

*Serve these crisp, blanched vegetables with jalapeño-seasoned mayonnaise
at your next picnic or barbecue.*

5 cups water

Vegetables
12 asparagus spears, trimmed
6 carrots, diagonally sliced 2-inch
2 medium zucchini, diagonally sliced ½-inch
½ pound fresh green beans, trimmed
½ head broccoli, cut into flowerets

Mayonnaise
1 cup mayonnaise
1 to 2 red *or* green jalapeño peppers, seeded, finely chopped
1 tablespoon chopped fresh chives *or* parsley
1 teaspoon red pepper flakes
¼ teaspoon cumin
2 tablespoons lemon juice

8 servings

In 3-quart saucepan bring water to a full boil. To blanch vegetables immerse each vegetable in water; cook 1 minute for all vegetables *except* 7 minutes for green beans. Place blanched vegetables in ice water to chill. In medium

bowl stir together all mayonnaise ingredients. Drain vegetables; serve with mayonnaise.

Nutrition Information (1 serving)
• Calories 250 • Protein 3g • Carbohydrate 12g • Fat 23g
• Cholesterol 17mg • Sodium 189mg

Crisp Green Beans With Red Pepper (top)
Vegetables With Chili Mayonnaise (bottom)

Special Hot Fudge Sauce (top)
Toasted Pecan Ice Cream Sauce (bottom)

Special Hot Fudge Sauce
20 minutes

Create your own special flavor with this delicious ice cream topper.

1 cup sugar
1 (12 ounce) package (2 cups) semi-sweet real chocolate chips
1 (12 ounce) can evaporated milk
1 tablespoon butter *or* margarine

1 teaspoon vanilla
¼ cup your favorite liqueur (almond, mint, orange, cherry, coffee, etc.)

3 cups

In 2-quart saucepan combine sugar, chocolate chips and evaporated milk. Cook over medium heat, stirring constantly, until chocolate chips are melted and mixture just comes to a boil (8 to 12 minutes). Remove from heat; stir in butter, vanilla and liqueur. Serve warm. Store refrigerated.

Microwave Directions: In 2½-quart casserole combine sugar, chocolate chips and evaporated milk. Microwave on HIGH until chocolate chips are melted (4 to 6 minutes). Stir until smooth. Microwave on HIGH, stirring after half the time, until mixture just comes to a boil (2½ to 4 minutes). Stir in butter, vanilla and liqueur. Serve warm. Store refrigerated.

Nutrition Information (1 tablespoon)
• Calories 70 • Protein 1g • Carbohydrate 10g • Fat 3g
• Cholesterol 3mg • Sodium 11mg

Toasted Pecan Ice Cream Sauce
15 minutes

Toasted pecans in a rich caramel sauce; great over homemade ice cream.

½ cup sugar
⅓ cup butter *or* margarine
1 cup light corn syrup
1 egg, slightly beaten

1 tablespoon vanilla
1 cup pecan halves, toasted

2 cups

In 2-quart saucepan combine all ingredients *except* pecans. Cook over medium heat, stirring constantly, until mixture comes to a full boil (6 to 8 minutes). Just before serving, stir in pecans. Serve warm or cool over ice cream, cake, pancakes or waffles.

Microwave Directions: In 2-quart casserole combine sugar, butter and corn syrup. Microwave on HIGH 2 minutes; stir to mix well. Stir 1 tablespoon hot sugar mixture into beaten egg. Slowly stir egg mixture and vanilla into hot sugar mixture. Microwave on HIGH, stirring every minute, until mixture comes to a full boil (3 to 4 minutes). Just before serving, stir in pecans. Serve warm or cool over ice cream, cake, pancakes or waffles.

Nutrition Information (1 tablespoon)
• Calories 85 • Protein 1g • Carbohydrate 12g • Fat 4g
• Cholesterol 14mg • Sodium 29mg

Chocolate Chip Biscuits
With Strawberries n' Bananas

60 minutes

A tender biscuit is split and filled with whipped cream and sliced bananas.

Biscuits
2 cups all-purpose flour
½ cup sugar
1 tablespoon baking powder
½ teaspoon salt
½ cup butter *or* margarine
¼ cup shortening
⅔ cup whipping cream
½ cup coarsely chopped semi-sweet
   chocolate chips*

Whipped Cream
1⅓ cups whipping cream
3 tablespoons powdered sugar
1 teaspoon vanilla

1 pint strawberries, hulled, sliced
2 tablespoons sugar
2 bananas

8 servings

Heat oven to 400°. In large bowl combine flour, ½ cup sugar, baking powder and salt. Cut in butter and shortening until crumbly. With fork stir in ⅔ cup whipping cream just until moistened. Stir in chopped chocolate chips. Turn dough onto lightly floured surface; knead until smooth (1 minute). Roll out dough to ¾-inch thickness. With 2½-inch scalloped round cutter cut out 8 biscuits. Place 1 inch apart on cookie sheet. Bake for 10 to 14 minutes or until lightly browned. Meanwhile, in chilled small mixer bowl beat 1⅓ cups chilled whipping cream at high speed, scraping bowl often, until soft peaks form. Continue beating, gradually adding powdered sugar and vanilla until stiff

peaks form (1 to 2 minutes). In medium bowl place sliced strawberries; toss with 2 tablespoons sugar. To serve, split biscuits; place on individual dessert plates. Spoon whipped cream on bottom half of biscuits; place banana slices on whipped cream. Top with remaining half of biscuits; spoon strawberries over biscuits.

*3 (1 ounce) squares coarsely chopped semi-sweet chocolate or ½ cup miniature chocolate chips can be substituted for ½ cup coarsely chopped chocolate chips.

Nutrition Information (1 serving)
• Calories 640 • Protein 6g • Carbohydrate 60g • Fat 44g
• Cholesterol 111mg • Sodium 387mg

Berries With Orange Cream

15 minutes

Orange Cream
¼ cup powdered sugar
1 (8 ounce) package cream cheese, softened
⅓ cup orange juice
2 teaspoons grated orange peel
1 tablespoon orange-flavored liqueur, optional

Berries
1 pint strawberries, hulled, halved
½ pint (1 cup) blackberries
½ pint (1 cup) blueberries
½ pint (1 cup) raspberries

8 servings

In small mixer bowl combine powdered sugar and cream cheese. Beat at medium speed, scraping bowl often, until smooth (1 to 2 minutes). Add all remaining orange cream ingredients; continue beating until well mixed (1 to 2 minutes). In medium bowl gently toss

together all berries. Serve orange cream over berries.

Nutrition Information (1 serving)
• Calories 160 • Protein 3g • Carbohydrate 15g • Fat 10g
• Cholesterol 31mg • Sodium 85mg

Chocolate Chip Biscuits With Strawberries n' Bananas (top)
Berries With Orange Cream (bottom)

Choco-Scotch Bars

1 hour 30 minutes

The topping is baked right on the bars in this easy and toteable picnic dessert.

1½ cups all-purpose flour
1 cup sugar
½ teaspoon salt
½ teaspoon baking soda
1 teaspoon vanilla
½ cup butter *or* margarine, softened
⅔ cup cold water
2 (1 ounce) squares unsweetened chocolate, melted
2 eggs

1 (12 ounce) package (2 cups) butterscotch chips
1 cup chopped walnuts

2 dozen

Heat oven to 350°. In large mixer bowl combine all ingredients *except* butterscotch chips and nuts. Beat at medium speed, scraping bowl often, until well mixed (2 to 3 minutes). Spread into greased 15x10x1-inch jelly roll pan. Sprinkle with butterscotch chips and nuts. Bake for 15 to 20 minutes or until top springs back when touched lightly in center. Cool completely; cut into bars.

Nutrition Information (1 bar)
• Calories 220 • Protein 2g • Carbohydrate 24g • Fat 13g
• Cholesterol 33mg • Sodium 114mg

Lemon Ribbon Ice Cream Pie

9 hours

Ribbons of lemon are layered between vanilla ice cream and topped with meringue in this refreshing pie.

½ cup butter *or* margarine
¾ cup sugar
5 egg yolks, slightly beaten, *reserve whites*
⅓ cup lemon juice
2 teaspoons grated lemon peel

9-inch baked pie shell

4 cups (1 quart) vanilla ice cream, slightly softened

5 reserved egg whites
⅓ cup sugar
⅛ teaspoon cream of tartar

8 servings

In 2-quart saucepan melt butter. In medium bowl stir together sugar and egg yolks. Gradually stir sugar mixture into melted butter. Cook over medium heat, stirring constantly, until slightly thickened (5 to 7 minutes). Stir in lemon juice and lemon peel. Refrigerate 1 hour. Meanwhile, in bottom of baked pie shell spread *2 cups* ice cream. Freeze 1 hour. Spread half of lemon mixture on ice cream; spread remaining ice cream on top of lemon mixture. Top with remaining lemon mixture. Freeze 1 hour. *Heat oven to 425°.* Meanwhile, in large mixer bowl beat egg whites on high speed, scraping bowl often, until soft peaks form (1 to 2 minutes). Reduce speed to medium. Continue beating, gradually adding sugar and cream of tartar, scraping bowl often, until stiff peaks form (3 to 4 minutes). Spread carefully onto frozen pie, sealing edges of crust. Bake for 3 to 5 minutes or until lightly browned. Freeze until firm (6 hours or overnight).

Nutrition Information (1 serving)
• Calories 510 • Protein 8g • Carbohydrate 54g • Fat 30g
• Cholesterol 231mg • Sodium 350mg

Choco-Scotch Bars (pictured)
Lemon Ribbon Ice Cream Pie

Peanut Chocolate Swirl Bars
1 hour 30 minutes

These blonde brownies are swirled with chocolate chips and peanuts.

½ cup butter *or* margarine
2 cups firmly packed brown sugar
2 teaspoons vanilla
2 eggs
1½ cups all-purpose flour

2 teaspoons baking powder
½ teaspoon salt
1 cup chopped salted peanuts
1 cup semi-sweet chocolate chips

3 dozen

Heat oven to 350°. In 3-quart saucepan melt butter over medium heat (3 to 5 minutes). Remove from heat. Stir in brown sugar, vanilla and eggs. Stir in flour, baking powder and salt. Stir in peanuts and chocolate chips. Spread into greased 13x9-inch baking pan. (Chips will melt slightly and give a swirled effect.)

Bake for 18 to 25 minutes or until firm to the touch. (Do not overbake.) Cool completely; cut into bars.

Nutrition Information (1 bar)
• Calories 140 • Protein 2g • Carbohydrate 19g • Fat 7g
• Cholesterol 22mg • Sodium 98mg

Crazy-Topped Brownies
1 hour 30 minutes

An all-time favorite jazzed up with peanut butter frosting and toppings of your choice.

Brownie
½ cup butter *or* margarine
2 (1 ounce) squares unsweetened chocolate
1 cup sugar
¾ cup all-purpose flour
2 eggs

Frosting
1 cup powdered sugar
⅓ cup peanut butter
1½ teaspoons vanilla
2 to 3 tablespoons milk

Toppings
Semi-sweet chocolate chips, raisins, salted peanuts, etc.

2 dozen

Heat oven to 350°. In 2-quart saucepan combine butter and unsweetened chocolate. Cook over medium heat, stirring constantly, until melted (4 to 6 minutes). Stir in all remaining brownie ingredients until well mixed. Spread into greased 9-inch square baking pan. Bake for 20 to 25 minutes or until brownie begins to pull away from sides of pan. (Do not overbake.) Cool completely. In small mixer bowl combine

all frosting ingredients *except* milk. Beat at medium speed, adding milk slowly, until frosting is smooth and creamy (1 to 2 minutes). Spread over brownie. Sprinkle with any combination of desired toppings (about 1 cup total); press lightly. Cut into bars.

Nutrition Information (1 brownie)
• Calories 170 • Protein 2g • Carbohydrate 21g • Fat 10g
• Cholesterol 28mg • Sodium 63mg

The famous Virginia pound cake was so named because it was made with a pound each of butter, sugar and eggs. It was made before baking powder, so air had to be beaten into the batter by hand for at least an hour. One recipe called for beating the eggs for 5 hours.

Peanut Chocolate Swirl Bars (top)
Crazy-Topped Brownies (bottom)

CASUAL ENTERTAINING

In the 1930s, America was in the depths of the Great Depression but social life had never been busier. The entertaining was just a lot more casual and featured home fun and simpler meals. One was the potluck dinner, where every guest was invited to bring something to share. This had always been popular in America, but during the Depression it became a necessity and was the mainstay of gatherings from family feasts to church suppers.

Americans have always looked for reasons to get together for casual fun and good eating. On the frontier we gathered for cornhusking, barn raising, quilting, logrolling, apple paring, and harvesting, first to work and then to eat together.

Today we gather our nearest and dearest for our favorite informal meals. It's a kick-off-your-shoes and bring-the-kids kind of party with people we're the most at ease with. We've gathered food ideas to go with this fun, from easy meals to special treats you might bring as a guest. All of them are great eating and easy to make, and they fit into the kind of casual, comfortable entertaining we all love.

CASUAL ENTERTAINING
MENU

Summertime Outdoor BBQ

*The secret? Marinating steak overnight in horseradish and sour cream sauce.
As you grill, steam the broccoli and bake colorful Cheddar cheese pan biscuits.
A company-special, yet easy, dessert . . . new mocha brownie sundae.*

Horseradish Steak With Cream Sauce p.315
Cheddar Cheese Pan Biscuits p.305   Steamed Broccoli
Mocha Brownie Sundae p.342

Sunday Evening Entertaining

*For starters, nibblers and a crunchy blue cheese ball. Then summer squash,
asparagus and peppers in a wine sauce add color and summer sunshine to a
new-generation pasta primavera. Serve with garlic pull-apart bread.*

Crunchy Blue Cheese Ball p.294   Garlic Pull-Apart Bread p.308
Pasta & Vegetables in Wine Sauce p.332
Fruit Sorbet or Sherbet

CASUAL ENTERTAINING
MENU

3-Alarm Chili Dinner

*Our recipe for spiced-just-right chili feeds 10 hungry friends. Add skillet corn bread,
made a delicious new country custard way, and crisp marinated vegetables.
A sweet finish – peanut squares topped with ice cream, nuts and caramel sauce.*

Chili For a Crowd p.317
Country Custard Skillet Corn Bread p.305   Crisp Marinated Vegetables p.334
Salted Peanut Ice Cream Squares p.342

CASUAL ENTERTAINING
MENU

Appetizer Buffet

Delicious do-ahead appetizers are an easy way to feed a crowd. Serve a hearty marinated antipasto platter, baked chicken wings with BBQ sauce and garlic eggplant dip, then add your favorite breads and beverages for an almost instant party!

Cranberry Citrus Sparkler p.291
Marinated Antipasto Platter p.292   Garlic Eggplant Dip p.294
Oven-Baked Chicken Wings p.298   Breadsticks

CASUAL ENTERTAINING
MENU
Southwestern Fare

Welcome to this sunny, easy-doing supper. Start with salsa and chips,
then serve a do-ahead chicken, cheese, chili and tortilla hot dish.
Dessert is fun too – fresh fruit with a rich chocolate sauce for dipping.

Homemade Salsa & Chips p.301
Layered Mexicana Casserole p.317
Rich Chocolate Fruit Dip p.345

Light Summer Supper

When the weather is hot, stay cool with this light summer supper. Chilled vinaigrette chicken and spinach salad is perfect with herbed breadsticks and a pretty corn and red pepper chowder. Next pass the spicy oatmeal raisin bars and relax.

Corn Chowder With Red Pepper p.310

Buttery Herbed Breadsticks p.306   Vinaigrette Chicken & Spinach Salad p.323

Spicy Oatmeal Raisin Bars p.346

CASUAL ENTERTAINING
MENU

Casual Winter Get-Together

Paella, a classic one-dish meal, is made with fresh seafood, chicken and vegetables baked with a saffron rice. A crusty hearth bread with thin sliced onions and rosemary rounds out the meal. Dessert is sautéed apples served warm with ice cream.

Paella p.312
Tossed Salad   Country Flat Bread p.308
Sautéed Apple Wedges p.339

CASUAL ENTERTAINING
MENU

When Good Friends Gather

When good friends gather, make them a new lasagna with seafood in a luscious sauce. Add garlic green beans and crusty French bread. End supper sweetly with colorful sherbets garnished with crisp, buttery lemon fingers.

Seafood Lasagna p.332
French Bread   Garlic Green Beans p.336
Lemon Fingers With Sherbet p.345

Cranberry Citrus Sparkler (top)
Sweet & Sour Meatballs (bottom)

Cranberry Citrus Sparkler

15 minutes

*Sparkling water and lime juice are added to cranberry juice
for a refreshing nonalcoholic beverage.*

½ cup (2 medium) fresh lime juice
1 (12 ounce) can frozen cranberry juice
   cocktail concentrate
4 cups ice cubes
1½ cups water

2 (12 ounce) cans lemon *or* lime flavored
   sparkling mineral water

Lime slices

8 servings

Place *1 tablespoon* lime juice into each of 8 (10 to 12 ounce) beverage glasses. In 5-cup blender container combine cranberry cocktail concentrate, ice cubes and water. Blend at High speed until ice cubes are finely chopped (20 to 30 seconds). Add about ⅔ *cup* cranberry mixture and ⅓ *cup* sparkling water to each glass. Garnish with lime slices.

Nutrition Information (1 serving)
• Calories 110 • Protein 0g • Carbohydrate 28g • Fat 0g
• Cholesterol 0mg • Sodium 2mg

Sweet & Sour Meatballs

1 hour 30 minutes

These spicy meatballs are served in a sweet and sour ginger sauce.

Meatballs
½ cup dry bread crumbs
1 pound lean ground beef
1 (12 ounce) package spicy bulk pork sausage
1 egg
½ teaspoon dry mustard
1 tablespoon soy sauce

Sauce
1 (20 ounce) can pineapple chunks in
   unsweetened juice, drained, *reserve juice*
2 tablespoons firmly packed brown sugar
1 tablespoon cornstarch
½ teaspoon ginger
2 tablespoons cider vinegar
1 tablespoon soy sauce
2 medium green peppers, cut into 1-inch pieces

5 dozen

Heat oven to 350°. In large bowl stir together all meatball ingredients. Shape into 1-inch balls. Place meatballs on 15x10x1-inch jelly roll pan. Bake for 15 to 20 minutes or until meatballs are browned. Meanwhile, in 1-quart saucepan combine reserved pineapple juice, brown sugar, cornstarch, ginger, vinegar and 1 tablespoon soy sauce. Cook over medium heat, stirring occasionally, until mixture is thickened and bubbly (4 to 6 minutes). Boil, stirring constantly, 1 minute. In 2-quart casserole place meatballs, pineapple chunks, green pepper and sauce; stir gently to coat. Cover; bake for 10 to 15 minutes or until green peppers are crisply tender. Serve in chafing dish with wooden picks.

Nutrition Information (1 meatball)
• Calories 38 • Protein 2g • Carbohydrate 3g • Fat 2g
• Cholesterol 11mg • Sodium 80mg

Hot Pepper Cheese Party Dip

2 hours 15 minutes

Hot pepper cheese brings pizazz to this great party dip.

1 (8 ounce) package cream cheese, softened
1 (8 ounce) carton (1 cup) dairy sour cream
2 cups (8 ounces) shredded hot pepper
   Monterey Jack cheese
¼ cup chopped ripe olives

1 (2 ounce) jar diced pimiento, drained
1 tablespoon sliced green onion

Tortilla chips

3 cups

In small mixer bowl combine cream cheese and sour cream. Beat at medium speed, scraping bowl often, until smooth (1 to 2 minutes). By hand, stir in all remaining ingredients *except* tortilla chips. Cover; refrigerate at least 2 hours. Serve with tortilla chips.

Nutrition Information (1 tablespoon)
• Calories 50 • Protein 2g • Carbohydrate 0g • Fat 4g
• Cholesterol 11mg • Sodium 49mg

Marinated Antipasto Platter

5 hours

A variety of vegetables and meats are marinated and served with cheese for a delightful appetizer.

Marinade
½ cup olive *or* vegetable oil
½ cup white wine vinegar
2 tablespoons country-style Dijon mustard
1 tablespoon honey
⅛ teaspoon salt
½ teaspoon coarsely ground pepper
1 tablespoon chopped fresh basil leaves*
1 teaspoon chopped fresh oregano leaves**
1 teaspoon chopped fresh parsley
1 teaspoon finely chopped fresh garlic

Antipasto
2 cups (8 ounces) fresh whole mushrooms
1 pint cherry tomatoes
1 medium green pepper, cut into ¼-inch strips
1 (5¾ ounce) can ripe colossal olives, drained
⅓ pound thinly sliced roast beef, each slice
   cut into 1-inch strips, rolled up and
   fastened with a wooden pick
2 (6 ounce) jars marinated artichoke hearts,
   drained
1 (11½ ounce) jar peperoncini (pickled
   peppers), drained
½ pound Provolone *or* Mozzarella cheese,
   cut into ½-inch cubes
¼ pound thinly sliced salami, rolled up and
   fastened with a wooden pick

Lettuce

16 servings

In medium bowl stir together all marinade ingredients. Place each of the following ingredients in their own separate container: mushrooms, tomatoes, green peppers, olives and roast beef. Pour about ¼ *cup* marinade into each container; stir to coat. Cover; refrigerate, stirring occasionally, 4 hours or overnight. Drain vegetables, olives and roast beef; arrange on lettuce-lined platter with artichokes, peperoncini, cheese and salami.

*1 teaspoon dried basil leaves can be substituted for 1 tablespoon chopped fresh basil leaves.

**¼ teaspoon dried oregano leaves can be substituted for 1 teaspoon chopped fresh oregano leaves.

Nutrition Information (1 serving)
• Calories 120 • Protein 7g • Carbohydrate 5g • Fat 9g
• Cholesterol 20mg • Sodium 435mg

Hot Pepper Cheese Party Dip (top)
Marinated Antipasto Platter (bottom)

Crunchy Blue Cheese Ball

4 hours 30 minutes

Blue cheese adds extra-special flavor to this easy cheese ball.

1 (8 ounce) package cream cheese, softened
1 (4 ounce) package crumbled blue cheese
2 tablespoons chopped fresh parsley
2 tablespoons chopped red pepper
⅛ teaspoon white pepper
4 to 5 tablespoons chopped walnuts

Crackers *or* vegetable sticks

1 ball (20 servings)

In medium bowl stir together all ingredients *except* walnuts and crackers. Form into ball or 5-inch log. Roll in chopped walnuts. Wrap in plastic wrap; refrigerate 4 hours or overnight. Serve with crackers or vegetable sticks.

Nutrition Information (1 serving)
• Calories 70 • Protein 2g • Carbohydrate 1g • Fat 7g
• Cholesterol 17mg • Sodium 113mg

Garlic Eggplant Dip

3 hours 15 minutes

Eggplant brings a unique flavor and texture to this garlic dip.

1 medium eggplant, cut in half lengthwise
1 (8 ounce) carton (1 cup) dairy sour cream
2 tablespoons chopped fresh parsley
1½ teaspoons sesame seed
¼ teaspoon salt
½ teaspoon finely chopped fresh garlic

Chopped fresh parsley

Pita bread, cut into wedges, split, toasted, if desired

2 cups

Heat oven to 325°. In 13x9-inch baking pan place eggplant halves. Bake for 55 to 65 minutes or until fork tender. Let cool 20 minutes. Scoop out pulp; discard skin. Place pulp in 5-cup blender container. Blend at High speed until smooth (30 to 60 seconds). In medium bowl stir together eggplant, sour cream, 2 tablespoons parsley, sesame seed, salt and garlic. Cover; refrigerate until flavors are well blended (about 2 hours). Garnish with chopped parsley; serve with pita bread.

Microwave Directions: In 13x9-inch baking dish place eggplant halves, cut side down, and *¼ cup water.* Cover with plastic wrap; microwave on HIGH 6 minutes. Turn cut side up. Cover with plastic wrap; microwave on HIGH until fork tender (6 to 9 minutes). Let cool 20 minutes. Scoop out pulp; discard skin. Place pulp in 5-cup blender container. Blend at High speed until smooth (30 to 60 seconds). In medium bowl stir together eggplant, sour cream, 2 tablespoons parsley, sesame seed, salt and garlic. Cover; refrigerate until flavors are well blended (about 2 hours). Garnish with chopped parsley; serve with pita bread.

Nutrition Information (1 serving)
• Calories 20 • Protein 0g • Carbohydrate 1g • Fat 2g
• Cholesterol 3mg • Sodium 21mg

Crunchy Blue Cheese Ball (top)
Garlic Eggplant Dip (bottom)

Cheese n' Spinach Pinwheels (top)
Tortilla Wedges (bottom)

Cheese n' Spinach Pinwheels   2 hours 30 minutes

Tortillas are topped with cheese and spinach, then rolled for a pinwheel appetizer.

1½ cups dairy sour cream
 1 cup (4 ounces) shredded Cheddar cheese
 ½ cup chopped pitted ripe olives
 1 (10 ounce) package frozen chopped
    spinach, thawed, well drained
 1 (8 ounce) can water chestnuts, drained,
    chopped

 ⅛ teaspoon salt
 1 tablespoon finely chopped onion
 ½ teaspoon finely chopped fresh garlic
 ½ teaspoon hot pepper sauce

 6 (10-inch) flour tortillas

                                    5 dozen

In medium bowl stir together all ingredients *except* tortillas. On each tortilla spread about ½ cup spinach mixture. Roll up tortillas tightly; wrap in plastic wrap. Refrigerate at least 2 hours or until firm. To serve, remove plastic wrap; cut each rolled tortilla into 10 slices.

Nutrition Information (1 pinwheel)
• Calories 40 • Protein 1g • Carbohydrate 4g • Fat 2g
• Cholesterol 5mg • Sodium 53mg

Tortilla Wedges   30 minutes

Salsa and sour cream top these warm tortilla appetizers.

 2 (8-inch) flour tortillas
1½ cups (6 ounces) shredded Cheddar *or*
    Monterey Jack cheese*
 ½ cup cooked ground pork sausage, well
    drained
 ¼ cup cubed ½-inch ripe tomato
 2 tablespoons sliced green onions

Salsa
Dairy sour cream

                                    1 dozen

Heat oven to 425°. Place tortillas on cookie sheet; top each with ½ *cup* shredded cheese and ¼ *cup* sausage to within ½ inch from edge. Bake for 6 to 8 minutes or until tortillas are beginning to crisp and cheese is melted and bubbly. Top with tomato, green onions and remaining cheese. Cut each tortilla into 6 wedges; serve hot with salsa and sour cream.

*A combination of Cheddar and Monterey Jack cheese can be used.

Nutrition Information (1 wedge)
• Calories 110 • Protein 5g • Carbohydrate 4g • Fat 8g
• Cholesterol 22mg • Sodium 227mg

Armenian etiquette says that there must always be twice as much food on the table as can be eaten when you have guests. Today, church bazaars in Massachusetts, where Armenians bring their traditional foods, are among the greatest feasts in America.

Oven-Baked Chicken Wings

1 hour 15 minutes

Baked chicken wings are dipped in a spicy sauce.

Chicken Wings
- ⅔ cup buttermilk baking mix, pancake mix *or* all-purpose flour
- 1 tablespoon paprika
- 2 teaspoons garlic salt
- 1 teaspoon coarsely ground pepper
- 2 tablespoons butter *or* margarine, melted
- 3 pounds chicken wings, each wing cut into 3 parts (discard tips)

Sauce
- 2 tablespoons finely chopped onion
- 2 teaspoons vegetable oil
- ½ teaspoon finely chopped fresh garlic
- 1 (8 ounce) can tomato sauce
- 1 tablespoon firmly packed brown sugar
- 1 teaspoon paprika
- ¼ teaspoon coarsely ground pepper
- ⅛ teaspoon cayenne pepper
- 2 teaspoons cider vinegar

2½ to 3 dozen

Heat oven to 425°. In small bowl stir together buttermilk baking mix, paprika, garlic salt and 1 teaspoon pepper. Coat chicken wings with mixture. In 15x10x1-inch jelly roll pan melt butter in oven (3 to 5 minutes). Place chicken wings in pan, turning to coat with butter. Bake, turning chicken wings after 20 minutes, for 40 to 45 minutes or until browned and fork tender. In 2-quart saucepan combine onion, oil and garlic. Cook over low heat, stirring occasionally, until onion is tender (4 to 6 minutes). Stir in all remaining sauce ingredients. Cook over low heat, stirring occasionally, until flavors are blended and sauce thickens slightly (3 to 5 minutes). Serve warm sauce with chicken wings.

Nutrition Information (1 chicken wing)
- Calories 55 • Protein 4g • Carbohydrate 3g • Fat 4g
- Cholesterol 12mg • Sodium 183mg

Pizza Breadsticks

45 minutes

The flavors and textures of pizza are found in this easy appetizer.

- ½ cup chopped ripe tomato
- ½ cup finely chopped pepperoni *or* Canadian bacon
- ½ cup pizza sauce
- 2 tablespoons finely chopped green pepper
- 2 teaspoons chopped fresh parsley
- 1 cup (4 ounces) shredded mozzarella cheese
- 4 soft breadsticks *or* bagel sticks, cut in half lengthwise

8 servings

Heat oven to 375°. In medium bowl stir together all ingredients *except* cheese and breadsticks. Stir in ¾ *cup* cheese. Place breadsticks, cut side up, on cookie sheet. Divide meat mixture evenly among breadsticks; sprinkle with remaining cheese. Bake for 11 to 14 minutes or until heated through and cheese is melted.

Microwave Directions: In medium bowl stir together all ingredients *except* cheese and breadsticks. Stir in ¾ *cup* cheese. Place breadsticks, cut side up, in paper towel lined 13x9-inch baking dish. Divide meat mixture evenly among breadsticks; sprinkle with remaining cheese. Microwave on HIGH, turning dish ½ turn after half the time, until heated through and cheese is melted (3½ to 5½ minutes).

Nutrition Information (1 serving)
- Calories 130 • Protein 7g • Carbohydrate 8g • Fat 8g
- Cholesterol 15mg • Sodium 429mg

Oven-Baked Chicken Wings (top)
Pizza Breadsticks (bottom)

Honey-Glazed Snack Mix (pictured)
Homemade Salsa & Chips

Honey-Glazed Snack Mix

60 minutes

The honey-glazed crunchy coating makes this an irresistible snack.

5 cups bite-size crispy corn cereal squares
3 cups miniature pretzels
2 cups pecan halves

½ cup butter *or* margarine, melted
½ cup honey

32 (¼ cup) servings

Heat oven to 300°. In 15x10x1-inch jelly roll pan combine cereal, pretzels and pecans; set aside. In small bowl stir together butter and honey until well mixed. Pour honey mixture over cereal mixture; stir until well coated. Bake 10 minutes; stir. Continue baking for 10 to 15 minutes or until cereal is glazed and honey mixture is absorbed. Immediately place snack mix on waxed paper; cool completely. Store in tightly covered container.

Microwave Directions: In 13x9-inch baking dish combine cereal, pretzels and pecans; set aside. In 2-cup measure melt butter on HIGH (1 to 1½ minutes). Stir in honey until well mixed. Pour honey mixture over cereal mixture; stir until well coated. Microwave on HIGH, stirring every 3 minutes, until cereal is glazed and honey mixture is absorbed (10 to 13 minutes). Immediately place snack mix on waxed paper; cool completely. Store in tightly covered container.

Nutrition Information (1 serving)
• Calories 130 • Protein 2g • Carbohydrate 15g • Fat 8g
• Cholesterol 8mg • Sodium 188mg

Homemade Salsa & Chips

60 minutes

Homemade salsa and tortilla chips make a terrific appetizer for a casual gathering.

Salsa
2½ cups (3 medium) cubed ½-inch ripe tomatoes
¾ cup chopped onion
¼ cup (3 medium) seeded, chopped jalapeño peppers
¾ teaspoon salt
¼ teaspoon pepper
2 tablespoons vinegar

Chips
12 (6-inch) corn tortillas
3 cups vegetable oil
Salt

2½ cups salsa
6 dozen chips (18 servings)

In 2-quart saucepan combine all salsa ingredients. Cook over medium heat, stirring occasionally, until mixture is slightly thickened (20 to 30 minutes). Cool to room temperature (about 30 minutes). Meanwhile, to prepare chips, cut each tortilla into 6 wedges. In deep 10-inch skillet heat oil to 400° F. Place 12 tortilla wedges in hot oil. Fry, turning occasionally, until chips are very lightly browned (35 to 45 seconds). Remove chips from oil; drain on paper towels. Sprinkle with salt, if desired. Repeat with remaining tortilla wedges. Serve warm with salsa. Store salsa refrigerated.

Variation:

Cinnamon Sugar Crispies: Omit salsa. Substitute 10 flour tortillas for corn tortillas; cut each into 8 wedges. In large plastic food bag combine ¼ cup sugar and 2 teaspoons cinnamon. Fry tortillas according to directions above; do not sprinkle with salt. While tortillas are still warm, place in bag with cinnamon and sugar mixture; shake until chips are well coated.

Nutrition Information (1 serving)
• Calories 120 • Protein 2g • Carbohydrate 13g • Fat 7g
• Cholesterol 0mg • Sodium 181mg

Cheesy Snack Bread

45 minutes

Frozen bread dough makes this cheese topped snack bread easy to prepare.

1 cup (4 ounces) shredded Cheddar cheese
1 cup (4 ounces) shredded mozzarella cheese
1 (1 pound) loaf frozen bread dough, thawed
2 tablespoons butter *or* margarine, melted
½ teaspoon chili powder

½ cup sliced ripe olives
1 (4 ounce) can chopped green chilies, drained
1 (2 ounce) jar chopped pimiento, drained

3 dozen

Heat oven to 375°. Press bread dough on bottom of greased 15x10x1-inch jelly roll pan. Brush with melted butter. Sprinkle with chili powder, *½ cup* Cheddar cheese, *½ cup* mozzarella cheese, olives, chilies and pimiento. Bake for 18 to 24 minutes or until bread is lightly browned. Sprinkle with remaining cheeses. Continue baking for 1 to 2 minutes or until cheeses are melted. Cut into 2-inch square, triangle or diamond shapes; serve warm.

Nutrition Information (1 piece)
• Calories 60 • Protein 3g • Carbohydrate 6g • Fat 3g
• Cholesterol 7mg • Sodium 122mg

Parmesan Twists

30 minutes

These Italian-seasoned breadsticks are dipped in pizza sauce for a tasty appetizer.

1 cup freshly grated Parmesan cheese
1½ teaspoons Italian herb seasoning*
1 loaf frozen bread dough, thawed
⅓ cup butter *or* margarine, melted

Pizza sauce

32 twists

Heat oven to 450°. In 9-inch pie pan combine Parmesan cheese and Italian seasoning. Divide bread dough into 8 sections; divide each section into 4 pieces (total of 32 pieces of dough). Roll each piece into 4-inch rope. Dip each rope in butter; roll in Parmesan mixture. Twist rope 3 times. Place on greased cookie sheets. Bake for 7 to 9 minutes or until golden brown. Meanwhile, in 1-quart saucepan heat pizza sauce. Serve warm twists with pizza sauce.

**¼ teaspoon *each* dried oregano leaves, dried marjoram leaves and dried basil leaves and ⅛ teaspoon rubbed dried sage can be substituted for 1½ teaspoons Italian herb seasoning.*

Nutrition Information (1 twist)
• Calories 70 • Protein 2g • Carbohydrate 7g • Fat 4g
• Cholesterol 9mg • Sodium 147mg

In the 1950s, TV was still a novelty. If you had a set, and your friends didn't, you invited them over to see "Toast of the Town" on Sunday night or "Your Show of Shows" on Saturday night, usually preceded or followed by a casual meal.

Cheesy Snack Bread (top)
Parmesan Twists (bottom)

Cheddar Cheese Pan Biscuits (pictured)
Country Custard Skillet Corn Bread

Cheddar Cheese Pan Biscuits

45 minutes

Cheddar cheese adds flavor and color to these flaky old-time biscuits.

⅓ cup butter *or* margarine
2¼ cups all-purpose flour
1½ cups (6 ounces) shredded Cheddar cheese
1 tablespoon sugar

1 tablespoon baking powder
¼ teaspoon salt
1 cup milk

1 dozen

Heat oven to 400°. In 9-inch square baking pan melt butter in oven (3 to 5 minutes). Meanwhile, in medium bowl combine all ingredients *except* milk. Stir in milk just until moistened. Turn dough onto lightly floured surface; knead 10 times or until smooth. Pat or roll dough into a 12x6-inch rectangle. Cut into 12 (1-inch) strips. Dip each strip into melted butter in pan. Fold strip in half. Place folded strips in 2 rows in same pan. Bake for 20 to 25 minutes or until lightly browned.

Tip: For extra flavor use sharp Cheddar cheese.

Nutrition Information (1 biscuit)
• Calories 200 • Protein 7g • Carbohydrate 20g • Fat 10g
• Cholesterol 30mg • Sodium 270mg

Country Custard Skillet Corn Bread

60 minutes

This extra moist corn bread forms its own custard layer during baking.

1½ cups yellow cornmeal
½ cup all-purpose flour
½ cup sugar
1 cup milk
1 cup buttermilk*
2 eggs

1 teaspoon baking soda
1 teaspoon salt
2 tablespoons butter *or* margarine
1 cup milk

8 servings

Heat oven to 350°. In large mixer bowl combine all ingredients *except* butter and *1 cup* milk. Beat at low speed, scraping bowl often, until smooth (1 to 2 minutes). In heavy ovenproof 10-inch skillet melt butter over low heat; pour batter into skillet. Pour remaining 1 cup milk over batter; do not stir. Bake for 35 to 45 minutes or until center is firm to the touch. Let stand 10 minutes; serve warm.

*1 tablespoon vinegar plus enough milk to equal 1 cup can be substituted for 1 cup buttermilk.

Tip: 9-inch square baking pan can be used in place of skillet. Melt butter in pan in oven (3 to 5 minutes). Bake for 35 to 40 minutes or until center is firm to the touch.

Nutrition Information (1 serving)
• Calories 250 • Protein 8g • Carbohydrate 40g • Fat 7g
• Cholesterol 82mg • Sodium 516mg

On the frontier, fall corn-husking parties were popular. Neighbors would gather to help strip the dried leaves off the corn and if you found an ear of red corn you were allowed to kiss each member of the opposite sex.

Hearty Caraway Rye Bread

4 hours

These hearty round loaves of rye bread are topped with savory onion.

Bread
⅓ cup firmly packed brown sugar
¼ cup butter *or* margarine
1 cup water
¼ cup molasses
1 tablespoon salt
1 teaspoon caraway seed
1 tablespoon grated orange peel
1 cup buttermilk*
¼ teaspoon baking soda
2 (¼ ounce) packages active dry yeast

¼ cup warm water (105 to 115° F)
2 cups rye flour
4¼ to 4¾ cups all-purpose flour

Topping
2 tablespoons butter *or* margarine
¾ cup (1 large) chopped onion
1 teaspoon caraway seed

2 loaves (16 servings)

In 1-quart saucepan combine brown sugar, ¼ cup butter, 1 cup water, molasses, salt, 1 teaspoon caraway seed and orange peel. Cook over medium heat until mixture comes to a full boil (4 to 7 minutes). In large bowl combine buttermilk and baking soda. Stir in molasses mixture; cool to warm (105 to 115° F). In small bowl dissolve yeast in ¼ cup warm water. Add yeast mixture to buttermilk mixture. Stir in rye flour until smooth. Stir in enough flour to make dough easy to handle. Cover; let stand 10 minutes. Turn dough onto lightly floured surface; knead until smooth and elastic (about 10 minutes). Place in greased bowl; turn greased side up. Cover; let rise in warm place until double in size (1 to 1½ hours). Dough is ready if indentation

remains when touched. Punch down dough; divide in half. Shape each half into round loaf. Place on greased cookie sheets; flatten slightly. In 10-inch skillet melt 2 tablespoons butter. Add onion and 1 teaspoon caraway seed; cook over medium heat until onion is tender (3 to 5 minutes). Spoon over loaves. Cover; let rise until double in size (35 to 45 minutes). *Heat oven to 350°.* Bake for 35 to 40 minutes or until loaves sound hollow when tapped.

*1 tablespoon vinegar plus enough milk to equal 1 cup can be substituted for 1 cup buttermilk.

Nutrition Information (1 serving)
• Calories 240 • Protein 6g • Carbohydrate 43g • Fat 5g
• Cholesterol 13mg • Sodium 484mg

Buttery Herbed Breadsticks

20 minutes

Great with soup or chili, these breadsticks are easy to prepare.

½ (10x4-inch) loaf French *or* Italian bread
¾ cup butter *or* margarine
½ teaspoon paprika
½ teaspoon dried rosemary leaves

¼ teaspoon dried marjoram leaves
¼ teaspoon ground thyme

1 dozen

Heat oven to 400°. Cut half loaf in half horizontally, then cut each half in thirds lengthwise to make 6 sticks. Cut each stick in half to make 12 (5x1-inch) sticks. In 15x10x1-inch jelly roll pan or 13x9-inch baking pan melt butter in oven (3 to 4 minutes). Stir in paprika, rosemary, marjoram and thyme. Dip breadsticks

in butter; arrange in pan. Bake for 7 to 8 minutes or until bread is crisp and golden brown. Serve warm.

Nutrition Information (1 breadstick)
• Calories 160 • Protein 2g • Carbohydrate 11g • Fat 12g
• Cholesterol 32mg • Sodium 227mg

Hearty Caraway Rye Bread (pictured)
Buttery Herbed Breadsticks

Country Flat Bread

1 hour 30 minutes

Thinly sliced onion and rosemary roast in olive oil on top of crisp flat bread.

1 (¼ ounce) package active dry yeast
1¼ cups warm water (105 to 115°F)
¼ cup olive oil *or* butter, melted
1 teaspoon salt
¼ teaspoon sugar
3¼ to 3¾ cups bread *or* all-purpose flour
3 tablespoons olive oil *or* butter, melted

1 medium onion, thinly sliced, separated
   into rings
1 tablespoon chopped fresh rosemary leaves*
1 teaspoon coarse salt
½ teaspoon coarsely ground pepper

12 servings

In large bowl dissolve yeast in warm water. Stir in ¼ cup oil, salt and sugar. Stir in enough flour to make dough easy to handle. Turn dough onto lightly floured surface; knead until smooth and elastic (about 10 minutes). Place in greased bowl, turn greased side up. Cover; let rise in warm place until double in size (about 40 minutes). Dough is ready if indentation remains when touched. Punch down dough; divide in half. *Heat oven to 400°.* Roll each half into 10-inch circle. Place on greased cookie sheets. Brush each round with about *1½ teaspoons* oil. Divide onion rings between rounds; sprinkle

each with *1½ teaspoons* rosemary, *½ teaspoon* coarse salt and *¼ teaspoon* pepper. Bake 10 minutes; brush each with about *1½ teaspoons* oil. Continue baking for 7 to 13 minutes or until lightly browned. Remove to wire rack; brush each with about *1½ teaspoons* oil.

*1 teaspoon dried rosemary leaves, crushed, can be substituted for 1 tablespoon chopped fresh rosemary leaves.

Nutrition Information (1 serving)
• Calories 210 • Protein 5g • Carbohydrate 29g • Fat 9g
• Cholesterol 0mg • Sodium 359mg

Garlic Pull-Apart Bread

3 hours

This pull-apart bread is a garlic lover's delight

1 (1 pound) loaf frozen whole wheat *or* white
   bread dough, thawed, cut into 32 pieces
⅓ cup butter *or* margarine, melted
2 tablespoons chopped fresh parsley

2 tablespoons finely chopped onion
1 teaspoon finely chopped fresh garlic

8 servings

In large bowl place bread dough pieces. In small bowl combine all remaining ingredients. Pour over bread dough; toss to coat well. Arrange bread dough in greased 12-cup Bundt pan or tube pan. Cover; let rise in warm place until double in size (1½ to 2 hours). *Heat oven to 350°.* Bake for 25 to 30 minutes or until golden

brown. If bread begins to brown too quickly, shield with aluminum foil. Cool 10 minutes; invert pan to remove bread. Serve warm.

Nutrition Information (1 serving)
• Calories 220 • Protein 4g • Carbohydrate 27g • Fat 11g
• Cholesterol 24mg • Sodium 352mg

Barn dances were held in the 1900s all over the Midwest. They were usually held in the spring and fall when the barns were emptier and the wooden floors polished to a shine by straw and hay.

Country Flat Bread (pictured)
Garlic Pull-Apart Bread

Broccoli Beer Cheese Soup

45 minutes

Creamy beer cheese soup has the extra addition of broccoli.

4 cups (16 ounces) shredded process
   American cheese
3 cups milk, *reserve ¼ cup*
1 (12 ounce) can beer
¼ teaspoon coarsely ground pepper

⅛ teaspoon garlic powder
3 tablespoons cornstarch
2 (9 ounce) packages frozen cut broccoli,
   thawed

8 servings

In Dutch oven combine all ingredients *except* ¼ cup reserved milk, cornstarch and broccoli. Cook over medium heat, stirring occasionally, until cheese is completely melted (14 to 18 minutes). In small bowl stir together reserved ¼ cup milk and cornstarch; stir into hot soup. Continue cooking, stirring occasionally, until soup just comes to a boil (3 to 4 minutes). Stir in broccoli. Continue cooking until heated through (2 to 3 minutes).

Microwave Directions: In 3-quart casserole combine all ingredients *except* ¼ cup reserved milk, cornstarch and broccoli. Cover; microwave on HIGH, stirring after half the time, until cheese is melted (7 to 10 minutes). In small bowl stir together reserved ¼ cup milk and cornstarch; stir into hot soup. Microwave on HIGH, stirring after half the time, until soup just comes to a boil (3 to 5 minutes). Stir in broccoli. Microwave on HIGH until heated through (3 to 5 minutes).

Nutrition Information (1 serving)
• Calories 300 • Protein 18g • Carbohydrate 12g • Fat 20g
• Cholesterol 60mg • Sodium 875mg

Corn Chowder With Red Pepper

45 minutes

Flavorful red pepper adds a zesty flavor to corn chowder.

¼ cup butter *or* margarine
½ cup (1 medium) chopped onion
½ teaspoon finely chopped fresh garlic
2 tablespoons all-purpose flour
1 (14½ ounce) can chicken broth
1 (16 ounce) package frozen whole
   kernel corn*

⅛ teaspoon white pepper
   Dash cayenne pepper
1 cup milk
½ cup chopped red pepper

4 servings

In 2-quart saucepan melt butter; add onion and garlic. Cook over medium heat, stirring occasionally, until tender (4 to 5 minutes). Stir in flour until smooth and bubbly (1 minute). Stir in chicken broth, *2 cups* corn, white pepper and cayenne pepper. Continue cooking, stirring constantly, until mixture comes to a full boil (8 to 10 minutes). Continue boiling until corn is crisply tender (5 to 8 minutes). Stir in milk. In 5-cup blender container blend corn mixture on High, one half at a time, until pureed (30 to 60 seconds). Strain soup through sieve to remove corn hulls. Return strained soup to saucepan; add remaining corn and red pepper. Cook over medium heat until corn is tender and chowder is heated through (6 to 8 minutes).

*5 to 6 ears of corn on the cob (3 cups) can be substituted for frozen corn. Cut and scrape the kernels from the cobs with a sharp knife.

Nutrition Information (1 serving)
• Calories 280 • Protein 9g • Carbohydrate 33g • Fat 14g
• Cholesterol 36mg • Sodium 479mg

Broccoli Beer Cheese Soup (top)
Corn Chowder With Red Pepper (bottom)

Chicken Coq Au Vin

2 hours 15 minutes

This rich country chicken stew tastes great on a cold winter's night.

8 slices bacon, cut into ½-inch pieces
4 (2 pounds) whole boneless chicken
   breasts, skinned, cut into 2-inch pieces
1 teaspoon finely chopped fresh garlic
¼ cup all-purpose flour
1 (10¾ ounce) can chicken broth
2 cups (8 ounces) whole fresh mushrooms
¼ cup chopped fresh parsley

1 cup red wine *or* chicken broth
8 small new red potatoes, cut in half
8 medium carrots, cut into 1-inch pieces
3 medium onions, quartered
1 teaspoon coarsely ground pepper
1 teaspoon dried thyme leaves

8 servings

Heat oven to 375°. In Dutch oven cook bacon over medium high heat 5 minutes. Add chicken and garlic. Continue cooking, stirring occasionally, until chicken is browned (8 to 10 minutes). Meanwhile, in medium bowl whisk together flour and chicken broth. Add to browned chicken mixture. Stir in all remaining ingredients.

Cover; bake for 1 hour 15 minutes to 1 hour 45 minutes or until carrots and potatoes are fork tender.

Nutrition Information (1 serving)
• Calories 300 • Protein 30g • Carbohydrate 25g • Fat 7g
• Cholesterol 72mg • Sodium 313mg

Paella

1 hour 30 minutes

Fresh seafood, chicken and vegetables are baked with saffron rice in this flavorful one dish meal.

2 tablespoons vegetable oil
4 (2 pounds) whole boneless chicken breasts,
   skinned, cut into 2½ to 3-inch pieces
1 pound chorizo *or* smoked pork link
   sausage, cut into ½-inch slices
1½ cups uncooked long grain rice
1 medium onion, sliced ¼-inch
2 (14½ ounce) cans chicken broth
½ teaspoon salt
½ teaspoon coarsely ground pepper

½ teaspoon dried oregano leaves
1/16 teaspoon powdered saffron*
1 teaspoon finely chopped fresh garlic
1 cup frozen peas
2 ripe tomatoes, cut into 1-inch cubes
8 ounces large fresh *or* frozen raw shrimp,
   shelled, deveined, rinsed
8 fresh whole clams, in shells, scrubbed

8 servings

Heat oven to 350°. In 10-inch skillet heat 2 tablespoons oil over medium high heat (1 to 2 minutes). Add chicken and sausage; cook until chicken is lightly browned and sausage is no longer pink (15 to 20 minutes). Remove chicken and sausage; set aside. Drain off fat; reserve *2 tablespoons.* Stir rice and onion into reserved fat. Cook over medium heat, stirring occasionally, until rice is golden (3 to 5 minutes). Gradually stir in chicken broth, salt, pepper, oregano, saffron and garlic. Continue cooking until mixture comes to a full boil (10 to

12 minutes); place mixture in roasting pan. Top with chicken and sausage. Bake for 30 to 35 minutes or until rice is tender. Stir in peas and tomatoes; top with shrimp and clams. Cover; continue baking, stirring occasionally, until shrimp turn pink and clams open. Discard any clams that do not open.

*Saffron threads, ground to a powder, can be substituted for powdered saffron.

Nutrition Information (1 serving)
• Calories 640 • Protein 49g • Carbohydrate 34g • Fat 33g
• Cholesterol 155mg • Sodium 1279mg

Chicken Coq Au Vin (pictured)
Paella

Double Crust Pizza Pie (pictured)
Horseradish Steak With Cream Sauce

Double Crust Pizza Pie
3 hours

2 (1 pound) loaves frozen white bread dough, thawed

Filling
1 pound ground beef
½ pound bulk Italian sausage
1 cup (2 medium) chopped onions
1 cup (2 medium) chopped green peppers
1 (14 ounce) jar extra-thick spaghetti sauce
1 (4 ounce) can mushroom stems and pieces, drained

1 teaspoon dried thyme leaves
½ teaspoon dried oregano leaves

2 tablespoons cornmeal
3 cups (12 ounces) shredded Mozzarella cheese
2 teaspoons milk

10 servings

Shape each loaf of thawed dough into a ball; place both balls on greased 12-inch pizza pan or cookie sheet. Grease surface of dough. Cover; let rise in warm place until double in size (1½ to 2 hours). On floured surface punch down dough. Cover; let rest 10 to 15 minutes. Meanwhile, in 10-inch skillet brown ground beef, sausage, onions and green peppers; drain well. Stir in all remaining filling ingredients *except* cornmeal, cheese and milk. Cook over medium heat, stirring occasionally, until heated through (3 to 5 minutes). *Heat oven to 350°.* Sprinkle *1 tablespoon* cornmeal on greased 12-inch pizza pan or into a 12-inch circle on

greased cookie sheet. On lightly floured surface roll one ball of dough into 13-inch circle. Place on prepared pan. Layer, to within ½ inch from edge, *1½ cups* cheese, filling mixture and remaining 1½ cups cheese. Roll remaining dough into 13-inch circle; place over layered filling. Fold edges of dough under bottom crust; pinch to seal well. Brush top of dough with milk; sprinkle with remaining 1 tablespoon cornmeal. Cut 8 (1-inch) slits in top of dough. Bake for 40 to 45 minutes or until golden brown.

Nutrition Information (1 serving)
• Calories 520 • Protein 27g • Carbohydrate 54g • Fat 21g
• Cholesterol 60mg • Sodium 1057mg

Horseradish Steak With Cream Sauce
9 hours

5 tablespoons prepared horseradish
1 teaspoon Worcestershire sauce
1 teaspoon finely chopped fresh garlic
½ teaspoon salt
½ teaspoon coarsely ground pepper

¼ cup tarragon vinegar *or* white wine vinegar
3 tablespoons vegetable oil
2 pounds (1-inch thick) beef sirloin steak
1 (8 ounce) carton (1 cup) dairy sour cream

4 servings

In small bowl combine horseradish, Worcestershire sauce, garlic, salt and pepper. *Reserve 2 tablespoons horseradish mixture;* refrigerate. Add vinegar and oil to remaining horseradish mixture. Place steak in plastic food bag. Pour horseradish and oil mixture into bag; seal tightly. Turn to coat both sides of steak. Place in 13x9-inch pan; refrigerate, turning occasionally, 8 hours or overnight. Prepare grill; heat

until coals are ash white. Remove steak from marinade; reserve marinade. Place steak on grill. Grill, basting with marinade and turning occasionally, until desired doneness (10 to 15 minutes for medium). Meanwhile, in small bowl stir together sour cream and reserved 2 tablespoons horseradish mixture. Serve with steak.

Nutrition Information (1 serving)
• Calories 470 • Protein 39g • Carbohydrate 6g • Fat 33g
• Cholesterol 132mg • Sodium 408mg

Layered Mexicana Casserole (pictured)
Chili For a Crowd

Layered Mexicana Casserole

60 minutes

Layers of tortillas, chicken, salsa and cheese star in this Southwestern main dish.

- 3 cups shredded cooked chicken*
- 1 cup (4 ounces) shredded Cheddar cheese
- ½ cup sliced green onions
- 1 (16 ounce) carton (2 cups) dairy sour cream
- 1 (4 ounce) can diced green chilies, drained
- ¾ teaspoon cumin
- 1 (12 ounce) jar mild *or* medium salsa
- 8 (8-inch) flour tortillas
- ½ cup (2 ounces) shredded Cheddar cheese

Salsa

8 servings

Heat oven to 400°. In large bowl stir together chicken, 1 cup cheese, green onions, sour cream, chilies and cumin. Pour 1 cup salsa into 10-inch pie pan. Lay one tortilla in salsa, coating one side lightly. Place tortilla, salsa side down, in 2-quart greased soufflé dish or straight sided round deep casserole. Spread *½ cup* chicken mixture on top of tortilla. Repeat with three tortillas and chicken mixture. Spread with *½ cup* salsa. Continue layering tortillas and chicken mixture ending with tortilla. Top with any remaining salsa and ½ cup shredded Cheddar cheese. Cover; bake for 35 to 40 minutes or until heated through. Let stand 10 minutes; cut into wedges. Serve with additional salsa.

Microwave Directions: Prepare casserole as directed above. Cover; microwave on HIGH, turning ¼ turn every 8 minutes, until heated through (23 to 28 minutes). Let stand 10 minutes; cut into wedges.

*3 split chicken breasts, cooked, shredded equal about 3 cups.

Nutrition Information (1 serving)
• Calories 430 • Protein 25g • Carbohydrate 24g • Fat 25g
• Cholesterol 94mg • Sodium 630mg

Chili For a Crowd

1 hour 30 minutes

An interesting blend of herbs and spices creates this popular chili.

- 1 cup (2 medium) chopped onions
- ½ cup chopped green pepper
- ½ cup (1 stalk) chopped celery
- 1½ pounds ground beef
- 1 teaspoon finely chopped fresh garlic
- 3 (16 ounce) cans whole tomatoes
- 2 (16 ounce) cans kidney beans
- 1 to 2 tablespoons chili powder
- 1½ teaspoons dried oregano leaves
- 1½ teaspoons cumin
- 1 teaspoon sugar
- 1 teaspoon seasoned salt
- ¼ teaspoon pepper
- ¼ teaspoon cayenne pepper
- 1 tablespoon Worcestershire sauce

10 servings

In Dutch oven cook onions, green pepper, celery, ground beef and garlic over medium heat, stirring occasionally, until meat is browned (10 to 12 minutes); drain off fat. Stir in all remaining ingredients. Continue cooking until mixture comes to a full boil (5 to 8 minutes); reduce heat to low. Simmer for 30 to 40 minutes or until flavors are blended.

Nutrition Information (1 serving)
• Calories 250 • Protein 18g • Carbohydrate 23g • Fat 10g
• Cholesterol 41mg • Sodium 770mg

Grilled Ham With Apple Chutney

2 hours 15 minutes

Apple and raisin chutney served over ham steak.

½ lemon, pared, chopped
½ teaspoon finely chopped fresh garlic
2½ cups (2 medium) tart apples, cored, chopped
1 cup firmly packed brown sugar
1 cup raisins
1 teaspoon grated fresh gingerroot*

½ teaspoon salt
⅛ teaspoon cayenne pepper
¾ cup cider vinegar

1½ pounds (½-inch thick) ham steak

6 servings

In 2-quart saucepan combine all ingredients *except* ham steak. Cook over low heat, stirring occasionally, until tender and thickened (1½ to 2 hours). Place ham steak on broiler pan. Broil 3 to 5 inches from heat until edges are lightly browned (3 to 4 minutes). Turn ham steak over; spread with ¼ cup chutney. Continue broiling until heated through (3 to 4 minutes). Serve with additional warm chutney.

*¼ teaspoon ground ginger can be substituted for 1 teaspoon grated fresh gingerroot.

Nutrition Information (1 serving)
• Calories 410 • Protein 25g • Carbohydrate 66g • Fat 6g
• Cholesterol 60mg • Sodium 1557mg

Florentine-Style Fish

45 minutes

Spinach, Cheddar cheese and bread crumbs add color and flavor to fresh fish.

3 tablespoons butter *or* margarine
10 ounces spinach leaves, torn into pieces*
¼ cup chopped onion
½ cup (2 ounces) shredded Cheddar cheese
¾ cup dried unseasoned bread cubes
1 (2 ounce) jar diced pimiento, drained

¼ teaspoon salt
⅛ teaspoon pepper

1½ pounds (6) fresh *or* frozen fish fillets, thawed, drained

6 servings

Heat oven to 350°. In Dutch oven melt butter; add spinach and onion. Cook over medium heat, stirring occasionally, until tender (4 to 5 minutes); remove from heat. Stir in all remaining ingredients *except* fish fillets. Place fish fillets in 13x9-inch baking pan. Place ⅓ cup spinach mixture on top of each fish fillet. Cover pan tightly with aluminum foil; bake for 20 to 25 minutes or until fish flakes with a fork.

*1 (10 ounce) package frozen chopped spinach, thawed, drained, can be substituted for 10 ounces spinach leaves.

Grilling Directions: Prepare grill; heat until coals are ash white. Prepare spinach mixture as directed above. Place each fish fillet in center of 18-inch square heavy duty aluminum foil. Place ⅓ cup spinach mixture on top of each fish fillet. Bring edges of aluminum foil up to center; tightly seal tops and sides. Place on grill. Grill until fish flakes with a fork (10 to 14 minutes).

Nutrition Information (1 serving)
• Calories 220 • Protein 25g • Carbohydrate 6g • Fat 10g
• Cholesterol 75mg • Sodium 341mg

Grilled Ham With Apple Chutney (pictured)
Florentine-Style Fish

Molded Raspberry Peach Salad

7 hours

*Just a touch of sugar lets the natural sweetness
from orange juice and fruit flavor this gelatin salad.*

2 (¼ ounce) envelopes unflavored gelatin
1½ cups water
1 (6 ounce) can frozen orange juice
  concentrate, slightly thawed
2 teaspoons sugar
3 tablespoons lemon juice
1 (16 ounce) package frozen peaches,
  thawed, cut into ½-inch pieces, drained,
  reserve juice

1 (10 ounce) package frozen raspberries in
  syrup, thawed, drained, *reserve juice*
½ cup (1 medium) sliced ¼-inch banana

Sweetened whipped cream

10 servings

In 1-quart saucepan soften gelatin in water
(1 minute). Cook over low heat, stirring occasionally, until gelatin is dissolved (3 to 5 minutes); set aside. In large bowl combine orange juice concentrate, sugar, lemon juice, reserved fruit juices and gelatin mixture. Refrigerate until slightly thickened (about 45 minutes). Carefully fold in peaches, raspberries and

banana. Pour into greased 8-cup mold. Refrigerate until firm (6 hours or overnight). Unmold onto serving plate; serve with sweetened whipped cream.

Nutrition Information (1 serving)
• Calories 120 • Protein 2g • Carbohydrate 28g • Fat 0g
• Cholesterol 0mg • Sodium 5mg

Crunchy Cabbage Salad

20 minutes

Colorful vegetables mixed with crunchy noodles and a tangy dressing make a delightful salad.

Dressing
¼ cup vegetable oil
2 tablespoons sugar
¼ teaspoon salt
¼ teaspoon pepper
3 tablespoons red wine vinegar

Salad
3 cups shredded green cabbage
3 cups shredded red cabbage
1 cup (2 medium) shredded carrots
3 tablespoons sliced green onions
¾ cup salted peanuts
1 (3 ounce) package chicken flavored
  Oriental dry noodle soup mix with
  seasoning packet

8 servings

In small bowl stir together all dressing ingredients. In large bowl toss together green cabbage, red cabbage, carrots, green onions and ½ *cup* peanuts. Sprinkle dry soup seasoning packet over salad. Break noodles into small pieces and stir into salad. Pour dressing over salad; toss to coat. Sprinkle with remaining peanuts.

Tip: If softer noodles are preferred, salad can be prepared up to 4 hours ahead. Cover; refrigerate until ready to serve.

Nutrition Information (1 serving)
• Calories 220 • Protein 6g • Carbohydrate 18g • Fat 15g
• Cholesterol 0mg • Sodium 441mg

Molded Raspberry Peach Salad (pictured)
Crunchy Cabbage Salad

Vinaigrette Chicken & Spinach Salad (pictured)
Curried Chicken Rice Salad

Vinaigrette Chicken & Spinach Salad

3 hours

Honey and mustard flavor this chicken and spinach salad — perfect for a light lunch.

2 whole boneless chicken breasts, skinned, cooked

Dressing
½ cup sesame *or* vegetable oil
½ cup white wine vinegar
3 tablespoons country-style Dijon mustard
2 tablespoons honey
⅛ teaspoon salt

Salad
10 ounces torn spinach leaves
 8 to 10 radishes, thinly sliced
 1 medium cucumber, cut into ½-inch slices, quartered
 2 tablespoons chopped pecans *or* walnuts, if desired

4 servings

Slice cooked chicken breasts into thin diagonal strips; set aside. In medium bowl stir together all dressing ingredients. Add sliced chicken. Cover; refrigerate at least 2 hours to marinate. With slotted spoon remove chicken from dressing; set aside. In large bowl toss together all salad ingredients. Drizzle about

½ cup dressing over salad; toss to coat. On individual plates place salad; top with slices of chicken.

Nutrition Information (1 serving)
• Calories 480 • Protein 29g • Carbohydrate 16g • Fat 34g
• Cholesterol 72mg • Sodium 521mg

Curried Chicken Rice Salad

3 hours

Curry and artichoke hearts make chicken salad extra special.

Salad
1 cup uncooked long grain white rice
2 cups water
1 tablespoon butter *or* margarine
4 teaspoons instant chicken bouillon granules
3 cups shredded cooked chicken
¼ cup sliced ¼-inch green onions
2 (6 ounce) jars marinated artichoke hearts, drained, *reserve marinade*
 Red leaf lettuce

Dressing
 Reserved artichoke marinade
½ cup mayonnaise
1½ teaspoons curry powder
½ cup chopped salted peanuts

6 servings

In 2-quart saucepan combine rice, water, butter and bouillon granules. Cook over medium high heat until mixture comes to a full boil (3 to 4 minutes). Reduce heat to medium low. Cover; simmer until rice is tender and liquid is absorbed (15 to 20 minutes). Cool rice completely. In large bowl stir together rice and all remaining salad ingredients *except* lettuce. Refrigerate until chilled (about 1 hour). In small bowl stir together all dressing ingredients.

Pour over salad; toss to coat well. On platter or individual salad plates place lettuce; top with chicken salad. Sprinkle with chopped peanuts.

Tip: 3 split chicken breasts, cooked, shredded, equals about 3 cups.

Nutrition Information (1 serving)
• Calories 590 • Protein 28g • Carbohydrate 35g • Fat 38g
• Cholesterol 79mg • Sodium 730mg

Garlic n' Lime Chicken Fajitas

4 hours

These chicken fajitas have a mild garlic flavor with just a hint of lime.

Fajitas
¼ cup beer *or* chicken broth
½ teaspoon dried basil leaves
2 tablespoons lime juice
2 tablespoons vegetable oil
½ teaspoon Worcestershire sauce
½ teaspoon finely chopped fresh garlic
⅛ teaspoon hot pepper sauce
2 whole boneless chicken breasts, skinned, cut into ¼-inch strips
1 green pepper, cut into 2x¼-inch strips
1 medium onion, cut into ¼-inch slices

8 (8-inch) flour tortillas *or* 4 pita breads cut in half, warmed

Toppings
Shredded Cheddar cheese
Chopped ripe tomato
Dairy sour cream
Guacamole
Salsa

4 servings

In small bowl combine beer, basil, lime juice, oil, Worcestershire sauce, garlic and hot pepper sauce. Place chicken strips in plastic food bag. Pour beer mixture into bag; seal tightly. Place bag in 13x9-inch pan. Refrigerate, turning occasionally, for 3 to 4 hours. Drain. In 10-inch skillet cook chicken, green pepper and onion over medium high heat, stirring occasionally, until chicken is fork tender (8 to 10 minutes). Serve in warm tortillas or pita bread. Serve with cheese, tomato, sour cream, guacamole and salsa.

Nutrition Information (1 serving)
• Calories 400 • Protein 31g • Carbohydrate 36g • Fat 14g
• Cholesterol 72mg • Sodium 316mg

Whole Wheat Chicken Sandwich

30 minutes

Sautéed chicken breasts, with a honey mustard dressing, are served on hoagie buns.

Dressing
½ cup mayonnaise
3 tablespoons honey
2 tablespoons country-style Dijon mustard

Sandwich
2 whole boneless chicken breasts, skinned, halved
2 tablespoons butter *or* margarine

¼ teaspoon salt
⅛ teaspoon pepper

4 whole wheat hoagie buns, French rolls *or* sourdough rolls, split
4 lettuce leaves*
8 slices ripe tomato

4 servings

In small bowl stir together all dressing ingredients; set aside. Flatten each chicken breast to about ¼-inch thickness by pounding between sheets of waxed paper. In 10-inch skillet melt butter until sizzling. Stir in salt and pepper; add chicken. Cook over medium heat, turning once, until chicken is lightly browned and fork tender (3 to 4 minutes). To assemble each sandwich spread dressing on bottom and top roll halves. Top each bottom half with 1 lettuce leaf, 2 slices tomato and 1 cooked chicken breast; top with remaining roll half. Serve with remaining dressing on side.

*1 cup alfalfa sprouts can be substituted for 4 lettuce leaves.

Tip: If desired, avocado slices can be added to sandwich.

Nutrition Information (1 serving)
• Calories 570 • Protein 30g • Carbohydrate 36g • Fat 34g
• Cholesterol 107mg • Sodium 840mg

Garlic n' Lime Chicken Fajitas (top)
Whole Wheat Chicken Sandwich (bottom)

Stuffed Hamburger-Cabbage Buns   1 hour 15 minutes

This meal-in-a-bun is fun family fare.

2 (1 pound) loaves frozen white bread dough, thawed
1 pound ground beef
2 cups shredded cabbage
1 cup (2 medium) chopped onions
¼ cup chopped fresh parsley
½ teaspoon salt
½ teaspoon pepper
1 teaspoon finely chopped fresh garlic
1 cup (4 ounces) shredded Cheddar cheese
¼ cup ketchup

1 egg, slightly beaten
1 tablespoon milk
   Coarse salt and cracked pepper, if desired

   Ketchup, mustard, barbecue sauce and relish

8 servings

Have thawed bread dough ready. *Heat oven to 350°.* In 10-inch skillet cook ground beef over medium heat, stirring occasionally, until browned (8 to 10 minutes). Drain off fat. Stir in cabbage, onions, parsley, ½ teaspoon salt, ½ teaspoon pepper and garlic. Continue cooking, stirring occasionally, until cabbage is crisply tender (5 to 6 minutes). Stir in cheese and ketchup. Divide each bread loaf into four equal pieces. On lightly floured surface roll each piece into 6-inch circle; place about ½ cup ground beef mixture in center of each circle. Carefully pinch together edges to enclose ground beef mixture and form a bun. Place

seam side down on greased cookie sheet. In small bowl stir together egg and milk; brush each bun with egg mixture. Sprinkle each bun with a pinch of salt and pepper. Bake for 25 to 30 minutes or until browned. Serve with ketchup, mustard, barbecue sauce and relish.

Tip: Buns can be stored frozen. To reheat, wrap in aluminum foil; place on cookie sheet. Bake at 350° for 55 to 60 minutes or until heated through.

Nutrition Information (1 serving)
• Calories 500 • Protein 23g • Carbohydrate 59g • Fat 19g
• Cholesterol 82mg • Sodium 902mg

To Prepare Stuffed Hamburger-Cabbage Buns:

1. On lightly floured surface roll each piece into 6-inch circle; place about ½ cup ground beef mixture in center of each circle.

2. Carefully pinch together edges to enclose ground beef mixture and form a bun.

326

Stuffed Hamburger-Cabbage Buns

Super Sloppy Subs

45 minutes

Seasoned Italian sausage is topped with shredded Mozzarella cheese and served on French rolls.

½ cup (1 medium) chopped onion
½ cup chopped green pepper
1 pound bulk Italian sausage
¼ cup ketchup
1 (16 ounce) can whole tomatoes, drained, cut up
1 teaspoon Italian herb seasoning*

¼ cup butter *or* margarine, melted
¼ teaspoon garlic powder
4 French rolls *or* hoagie buns, split lengthwise
1 cup (4 ounces) shredded Mozzarella cheese

4 servings

In 10-inch skillet combine onion, green pepper and sausage. Cook over medium heat, stirring occasionally, until sausage is browned (10 to 15 minutes); drain off fat. Stir in ketchup, tomatoes and Italian seasoning. Cook over medium high heat, stirring occasionally, until mixture thickens (5 to 7 minutes). *Heat broiler.* In small bowl stir together butter and garlic powder; brush on split rolls. Place rolls, cut side up, on cookie sheet. Place ¼ sausage mixture on bottom half of each roll; top with cheese.

Broil 2 to 5 inches from heat for 2 to 3 minutes or until cheese is melted. Place top half of each roll over bottom half.

*¼ teaspoon *each* dried oregano leaves, dried marjoram leaves and dried basil leaves and ⅛ teaspoon rubbed dried sage can be substituted for 1 teaspoon Italian herb seasoning.

Nutrition Information (1 serving)
• Calories 610 • Protein 27g • Carbohydrate 52g • Fat 33g
• Cholesterol 90mg • Sodium 1350mg

Barbecued Beef Sandwiches

4 hours

This barbecued beef can be made the day before and warmed up just before serving or prepared in your crockery cooker.

3 to 4-pound beef chuck roast

1½ cups ketchup
1 (1¼ ounce) package onion soup mix
1 tablespoon chili powder
3 tablespoons vinegar

2 tablespoons Worcestershire sauce
2 teaspoons prepared mustard
1 teaspoon finely chopped fresh garlic

18 small sandwich buns

1½ dozen

Heat oven to 350°. Trim fat from meat; place meat in Dutch oven or roasting pan. In medium bowl stir together all remaining ingredients *except* buns; pour over meat. Cover; bake, turning meat once or twice, for 2½ to 3½ hours or until fork tender. Remove meat from sauce; skim off fat. Shred meat; return to sauce. Serve on buns.

Tip: A crockery cooker can be used. Cut meat to fit cooker; pour sauce over meat. Cook on HIGH for 4 to 5 hours or until fork tender. Continue as directed above.

Tip: Top each sandwich with one slice of your favorite cheese.

Nutrition Information (1 serving)
• Calories 270 • Protein 21g • Carbohydrate 29g • Fat 8g
• Cholesterol 54mg • Sodium 677mg

Super Sloppy Subs (top)
Barbecued Beef Sandwiches (bottom)

Giant Corned Beef & Swiss Hero (pictured)
Sausage & Vegetable Melt

Giant Corned Beef & Swiss Hero

30 minutes

Serve this spectacular hero at your next get-together.

Butter Mixture
½ cup butter *or* margarine, softened
1 teaspoon caraway seed
2 tablespoons country-style Dijon mustard
2 teaspoons prepared horseradish

Sandwich
1 pound unsliced loaf *or* round pumpernickel bread
Leaf lettuce
¾ to 1 pound thinly sliced corned beef
6 slices Swiss cheese
1 small red onion, sliced ¼-inch, separated into rings
1 green pepper, cut into ¼-inch rings

6 (8-inch) wooden skewers

6 servings

In small bowl stir together butter, caraway seed, mustard and horseradish. Cut loaf horizontally into 3 slices; spread all cut surfaces with butter mixture. Place bottom slice of loaf on platter; top with half of lettuce, corned beef, cheese, onion and green pepper. Repeat layering with second bread slice. Top with remaining bread slice. Skewer loaf with 6 skewers from top to bottom. Cut into slices or wedges.

Nutrition Information (1 serving)
• Calories 590 • Protein 26g • Carbohydrate 43g • Fat 35g
• Cholesterol 124mg • Sodium 1446mg

Sausage & Vegetable Melt

45 minutes

This hearty sandwich combines sausage and vegetables and is smothered in cheese.

1 pound plain *or* spicy bulk sausage
2 cups chopped ½-inch broccoli
1 cup (2 medium) thinly sliced carrots
1 small onion, coarsely chopped
1 small red pepper, cut into ½-inch pieces
2 cups (8 ounces) shredded Mozzarella cheese

½ cup butter *or* margarine, softened
½ teaspoon Italian herb seasoning*
¼ teaspoon garlic powder
2 (8 ounce) about 12-inch loaves French bread, cut in half lengthwise

8 servings

In 10-inch skillet cook sausage over medium heat, stirring occasionally, until browned (6 to 8 minutes); drain off fat. Stir in broccoli and carrots. Continue cooking, stirring constantly, until vegetables are crisply tender (4 to 6 minutes). Stir in onion and red pepper. Continue cooking, stirring constantly, until vegetables are crisply tender (2 to 3 minutes). Stir in *1 cup* shredded cheese. Set aside; keep warm. In small bowl stir together butter, Italian herb seasoning and garlic powder. Spread each half of bread with butter mixture. *Heat broiler.* Place bread halves, buttered side up, on broiler rack 2 to 5 inches from heat. Broil until lightly toasted (1 to 2 minutes). Divide sausage mixture evenly over each half; top with remaining cheese. Broil until cheese is melted and sandwich is heated through (1 to 2 minutes).

*⅛ teaspoon *each* dried oregano leaves, dried marjoram leaves and dried basil leaves and ¹⁄₁₆ teaspoon rubbed sage can be substituted for ½ teaspoon Italian herb seasoning.

Nutrition Information (1 serving)
• Calories 460 • Protein 19g • Carbohydrate 36g • Fat 27g
• Cholesterol 70mg • Sodium 952mg

Pasta & Vegetables in Wine Sauce

30 minutes

1 (9 ounce) package uncooked fresh linguine
3 tablespoons olive *or* vegetable oil
1 medium thinly sliced red onion
½ teaspoon finely chopped fresh garlic
2 cups (2 medium) halved lengthwise, sliced ⅛-inch yellow summer squash
1 cup (1 medium) cubed ½-inch ripe tomato
1 pound (24) asparagus spears, trimmed, cut into thirds

1 medium red *or* green pepper, cut into ¼-inch strips
½ cup dry white wine *or* chicken broth
2 tablespoons chopped fresh dill weed
¼ teaspoon salt
¼ teaspoon coarsely ground pepper
¼ cup freshly grated Parmesan cheese
Freshly grated Parmesan cheese

6 servings

Cook linguine according to package directions; drain. Meanwhile, in 10-inch skillet heat oil over medium heat (1 to 2 minutes); add onion and garlic. Continue cooking, stirring occasionally, until onion is crisply tender (3 to 4 minutes). Add squash, tomato, asparagus and red pepper. Continue cooking, stirring occasionally, until vegetables are crisply tender (8 to 10 minutes). Stir in wine, dill weed, salt and pepper. Continue cooking, stirring occasionally, until heated through (4 to 5 minutes). Serve over linguine; sprinkle with ¼ cup Parmesan cheese. Serve with additional Parmesan cheese.

Nutrition Information (1 serving)
• Calories 290 • Protein 11g • Carbohydrate 41g • Fat 9g
• Cholesterol 2mg • Sodium 176mg

Seafood Lasagna

1 hour 45 minutes

9 uncooked dried lasagna noodles

Sauce
3 tablespoons butter *or* margarine
¼ cup all-purpose flour
2 teaspoons finely chopped fresh garlic
1½ cups milk
½ cup dry white wine *or* milk
1 teaspoon nutmeg
½ teaspoon salt
¼ teaspoon pepper
⅛ teaspoon hot pepper sauce

Ricotta Filling
2 eggs
¾ cup freshly grated Parmesan cheese
½ cup chopped fresh parsley
1 (15 ounce) carton (2 cups) ricotta cheese
1 (4 ounce) jar sliced pimiento, drained

Layers
1 (12 ounce) package small frozen cooked shrimp, thawed, drained, *reserve 12 for garnish*
1 (8 ounce) package frozen salad chunks imitation sea stixs, thawed, drained
3 cups (12 ounces) shredded Swiss cheese
12 fresh parsley sprigs

12 servings

Heat oven to 375°. Cook noodles according to package directions; rinse. Drain; set aside. In 2-quart saucepan melt butter over medium heat. Stir in flour and garlic until bubbly (1 minute). Stir in 1½ cups milk. Continue cooking, stirring occasionally, until mixture comes to a full boil (4 to 5 minutes); boil 1 minute. Stir in all remaining sauce ingredients; set aside. In small bowl slightly beat eggs; stir in remaining ricotta filling ingredients. In greased 13x9-inch baking pan layer ⅓ noodles, ½ ricotta filling, ½ shrimp, ½ sea stixs, ⅓ sauce and ⅓ Swiss cheese. Repeat layering. Top with remaining noodles, sauce and Swiss cheese. Cover with aluminum foil; bake 25 minutes. Uncover; continue baking for 15 to 20 minutes or until lightly browned around edges. Let stand 10 minutes. Garnish each serving with reserved shrimp and parsley sprigs.

Nutrition Information (1 serving)
• Calories 370 • Protein 28g • Carbohydrate 20g • Fat 18g
• Cholesterol 150mg • Sodium 483mg

Pasta & Vegetables in Wine Sauce (pictured)
Seafood Lasagna

Crisp Marinated Vegetables

4 hours 30 minutes

Crisp garden vegetables are subtly pickled in an easy marinade.

Marinade
½ cup chili sauce
¼ cup vegetable oil
2 tablespoons firmly packed brown sugar
3 tablespoons water
3 tablespoons tarragon vinegar *or* cider vinegar
½ teaspoon finely chopped fresh garlic

Vegetables
6 cups water
½ pound green *or* yellow beans, trimmed, cut into 2-inch pieces
1½ cups diagonally sliced ½-inch carrots
2 cups broccoli flowerets
1 cup (2 stalks) sliced 1-inch celery
1 cup small pitted ripe olives

8 servings

In small bowl stir together all marinade ingredients; set aside. In 4-quart saucepan bring 6 cups water to a full boil. Add beans; cook 2 minutes. Add carrots; continue cooking 3 minutes. Add broccoli and celery; continue cooking 2 minutes. Drain all vegetables; place in ice water to chill. Drain. Place vegetables and olives in large bowl; stir in marinade. Cover; refrigerate, stirring occasionally, for 4 hours or overnight. Serve with slotted spoon.

Nutrition Information (1 serving)
• Calories 70 • Protein 2g • Carbohydrate 8g • Fat 4g
• Cholesterol 0mg • Sodium 223mg

Buttered Vegetables With Fresh Mint

20 minutes

Crisp, colorful vegetables are seasoned with a hint of mint.

1 cup water
2 cups (4 medium) julienne strip carrots
1 cup sliced ¼-inch fresh mushrooms
6 ounces fresh pea pods, washed, remove tips and strings*

2 tablespoons butter *or* margarine
1 tablespoon chopped fresh mint leaves**

6 servings

In 2-quart saucepan bring water to a full boil; add carrots. Cover; cook over medium heat until carrots are crisply tender (4 to 5 minutes). Add mushrooms and pea pods. Continue cooking until pea pods are crisply tender (3 to 4 minutes); drain. Stir in butter and mint until vegetables are well coated.

*1 (6 ounce) package frozen pea pods can be substituted for 6 ounces fresh pea pods.

**1 teaspoon dried mint leaves can be substituted for 1 tablespoon chopped fresh mint leaves.

Microwave Directions: *Reduce 1 cup water to 2 tablespoons.* In 2-quart casserole place water and carrots. Cover; microwave on HIGH until carrots are crisply tender (3 to 5 minutes). Stir in pea pods and mushrooms. Cover; microwave on HIGH until vegetables are crisply tender (3 to 6 minutes). Drain. Stir in butter and mint until vegetables are well coated.

Nutrition Information (1 serving)
• Calories 65 • Protein 2g • Carbohydrate 7g • Fat 4g
• Cholesterol 10mg • Sodium 56mg

Crisp Marinated Vegetables (top)
Buttered Vegetables With Fresh Mint (bottom)

Seasoned Potato Wedges

1 hour 15 minutes

Dip these seasoned potatoes in a delicious chive dip.

Potatoes
⅓ cup all-purpose flour
⅓ cup freshly grated Parmesan cheese
1 teaspoon paprika
3 large baking potatoes, each cut into
　8 wedges
⅓ cup milk
¼ cup butter *or* margarine, melted

Dip
1 (16 ounce) carton (2 cups) dairy sour cream
8 slices crisply cooked bacon
½ teaspoon garlic powder
2 tablespoons chopped fresh chives

6 servings

Heat oven to 400°. In 9-inch pie pan stir together flour, Parmesan cheese and paprika. Dip potatoes into milk, then coat with flour mixture. Place on 15x10x1-inch jelly roll pan. Drizzle potatoes with butter. Bake, turning potatoes over after half the time, for 45 to 50 minutes or until potatoes are fork tender and

browned. Meanwhile, in medium bowl stir together all dip ingredients. Serve hot potatoes with dip.

Nutrition Information (1 serving)
• Calories 430 • Protein 11g • Carbohydrate 30g • Fat 30g
• Cholesterol 67mg • Sodium 370mg

Garlic Green Beans

20 minutes

These green beans are full of flavor when seasoned with garlic.

1½ cups water
¼ teaspoon salt
1 pound fresh green beans, trimmed
2 tablespoons olive oil *or* butter

½ teaspoon coarsely ground pepper
1 teaspoon finely chopped fresh garlic

4 servings

In 10-inch skillet bring water and salt to a full boil; add beans. Cook over medium heat, stirring occasionally, until beans are crisply tender (9 to 14 minutes). Drain. Stir in all remaining ingredients; continue cooking until garlic is tender (2 to 3 minutes).

Tip: 2 ounces shaved or freshly grated Parmesan cheese can be sprinkled over beans; let stand 2 minutes.

Microwave Directions: *Decrease 1½ cups water to ¼ cup.* In 2-quart casserole place beans and ¼ cup water. Cover; microwave on HIGH, stirring after half the time, until crisply tender (6 to 10 minutes). Drain. Stir in all remaining ingredients. Cover; microwave on HIGH, stirring after half the time, until garlic is tender (2 to 3 minutes).

Nutrition Information (1 serving)
• Calories 100 • Protein 2g • Carbohydrate 9g • Fat 7g
• Cholesterol 0mg • Sodium 4mg

Quilting Bees were a good way to get women together during the 1800s. They gave women hours of companionship, were usually accompanied by a potluck lunch or supper and at the end of the day they had something of beauty to display.

Seasoned Potato Wedges (pictured)
Garlic Green Beans

Sautéed Apple Wedges (top)
Magical Chocolate Bottom Cake (bottom)

Sautéed Apple Wedges

30 minutes

Serve these crisply tender cinnamon apples with vanilla ice cream.

1 cup firmly packed brown sugar
1 tablespoon butter *or* margarine
1 tablespoon lemon juice
¼ teaspoon cinnamon

3 tart red cooking apples, each cut into
  ¼-inch slices

Ice cream

6 servings

In 10-inch skillet combine all ingredients *except* apples and ice cream. Cook over medium heat, stirring constantly, until bubbly (4 to 7 minutes). Add apple slices. Reduce heat to low. Continue cooking, stirring occasionally, until apples are crisply tender (6 to 9 minutes). Serve warm with ice cream.

Nutrition Information (1 serving)
• Calories 190 • Protein 0g • Carbohydrate 46g • Fat 2g
• Cholesterol 5mg • Sodium 31mg

Magical Chocolate Bottom Cake

60 minutes

Pour chocolate on top of this cake before baking and it forms a moist, delicious layer on the bottom—magically!

½ cup chopped almonds

Cake
1 cup all-purpose flour
¾ cup sugar
½ cup butter *or* margarine, softened
½ cup milk
1 egg
1 teaspoon baking powder
½ teaspoon salt
½ teaspoon almond extract

Topping
⅔ cup sugar
2 (1 ounce) squares unsweetened chocolate
½ cup water
¼ cup butter *or* margarine
1 teaspoon almond extract
½ cup chopped almonds

Sweetened whipped cream

9 servings

Heat oven to 350°. Sprinkle ½ cup chopped almonds on bottom of greased and floured 9-inch square baking pan; set aside. In large mixer bowl combine all cake ingredients. Beat at low speed, scraping bowl often, until all ingredients are moistened. Beat at high speed, scraping bowl often, until smooth (2 to 3 minutes). Pour into prepared pan. In 1-quart saucepan combine ⅔ cup sugar, chocolate and water. Cook over medium heat, stirring occasionally, until mixture comes to a full boil (6 to 8 minutes). Remove from heat; stir in ¼ cup butter and 1 teaspoon almond extract until melted. Pour mixture evenly over cake batter. Sprinkle with ½ cup chopped almonds. Bake for 30 to 40 minutes or until top springs back when touched lightly in center. Serve with sweetened whipped cream.

Nutrition Information (1 serving)
• Calories 430 • Protein 6g • Carbohydrate 47g • Fat 26g
• Cholesterol 73mg • Sodium 327mg

Black Forest Pie

3 hours 30 minutes

This brownie fudge pie is topped with sour cream and cherries.

Single crust pie pastry

Filling
¾ cup butter *or* margarine
¾ cup sugar
6 tablespoons unsweetened cocoa
⅔ cup ground blanched almonds
2 tablespoons all-purpose flour
3 eggs, separated
2 tablespoons water
¼ cup sugar

Topping
⅓ cup dairy sour cream
2 tablespoons sugar
½ teaspoon vanilla

1 cup canned cherry pie filling

Glaze
½ cup semi-sweet real chocolate chips
1½ teaspoons shortening

10 servings

Heat oven to 350°. Line 9-inch pie pan with pastry; crimp or flute crust. Set aside. In 2-quart saucepan melt butter over medium heat (3 to 5 minutes). Stir in ¾ cup sugar and cocoa. Remove from heat; cool 5 minutes. Stir in almonds and flour. Stir in egg yolks, one at a time, until well mixed. Stir in water. In small mixer bowl beat egg whites at high speed, scraping bowl often, until foamy. Continue beating, gradually adding ¼ cup sugar, until soft peaks form (30 to 60 seconds). Fold chocolate mixture into egg whites just until blended. Pour into prepared pie shell. Bake for 35 to 45 minutes or until wooden pick inserted in center comes out clean. Cool 5 minutes. In medium bowl stir together all topping ingredients *except* cherry pie filling. Spread over warm pie; top with spoonfuls of cherry pie filling. Return pie to oven for 5 minutes. In 1-quart saucepan melt chocolate chips and shortening over low heat, stirring constantly, until melted (2 to 3 minutes). Drizzle over pie. Refrigerate at least 2 hours.

Nutrition Information (1 serving)
• Calories 460 • Protein 6g • Carbohydrate 47g • Fat 30g
• Cholesterol 120mg • Sodium 280mg

Iowa 1840: "Other social gatherings revolved around the settlers' own homes. Log-rollings to clear the land, house-raisings to build a dwelling and house-warmings to celebrate a home's completion all called for feasting, dancing and games. Cards, checkers, songfests or a Saturday night dance in someone's cabin to the local fiddler brought friends and neighbors together."

Black Forest Pie

Salted Peanut Ice Cream Squares   4 hours 30 minutes

A sure hit, the flavors in this frozen dessert are similar to a popular candy bar.

½ cup light corn syrup
½ cup chunky style peanut butter
3 cups crisp rice cereal
½ gallon vanilla *or* your favorite ice cream, slightly softened

1 cup chopped salted peanuts

Caramel ice cream topping

12 servings

In large bowl stir together corn syrup and peanut butter. Stir in cereal. Press on bottom of buttered 13x9-inch pan; freeze until firm (about 10 minutes). Spread ice cream on top of crust; sprinkle with chopped peanuts. Pat into ice cream. Cover; freeze until firm (2 to 4 hours). To serve, in 1-quart saucepan heat caramel topping. Cut ice cream into squares; serve caramel topping over ice cream.

Nutrition Information (1 serving)
• Calories 410 • Protein 10g • Carbohydrate 48g • Fat 21g
• Cholesterol 40mg • Sodium 294mg

Mocha Brownie Sundae   1 hour 30 minutes

Top this tempting dessert with your choice of "goodies."

Brownie
2 teaspoons instant coffee granules
1 tablespoon warm water
½ cup butter *or* margarine
2 (1 ounce) squares unsweetened chocolate
1 cup sugar
¾ cup all-purpose flour
2 eggs

Sauce
2 teaspoons instant coffee granules
⅓ cup warm water
½ cup sugar

¼ cup butter *or* margarine
2 tablespoons light corn syrup
6 (1 ounce) squares semi-sweet chocolate, chopped

Toppings
Vanilla *or* chocolate ice cream
Chopped chocolate-coated toffee candy bars
Chopped nuts
Chocolate chips *or* candy coated milk chocolate pieces

12 servings

Heat oven to 350°. In small bowl dissolve 2 teaspoons coffee granules in 1 tablespoon warm water. In 2-quart saucepan combine ½ cup butter and 2 ounces unsweetened chocolate. Cook over medium heat, stirring constantly, until melted (4 to 6 minutes). Remove from heat. Stir in all remaining brownie ingredients and dissolved coffee until well mixed. Spread into greased 12-inch pizza pan. Bake for 15 to 17 minutes or until brownie begins to pull away from sides of pan. Cool completely. Meanwhile, in 2-quart saucepan dissolve 2 teaspoons coffee granules in ⅓ cup warm water. Add ½ cup sugar, ¼ cup butter and corn syrup. Cook over medium heat, stirring constantly, until mixture comes to a full boil (5 to 8 minutes). Boil, stirring constantly, 3 minutes. Remove from heat. Immediately add chopped semi-sweet chocolate; stir with wire whisk or rotary beater until smooth. To serve, cut brownie into 12 wedges; top each wedge with two scoops ice cream. Drizzle sauce over ice cream; sprinkle each wedge with a heaping tablespoon chopped candy bars, nuts, chocolate chips or candy coated chocolate pieces.

Nutrition Information (1 serving)
• Calories 540 • Protein 6g • Carbohydrate 65g • Fat 31g
• Cholesterol 97mg • Sodium 192mg

Salted Peanut Ice Cream Squares (pictured)
Mocha Brownie Sundae

Lemon Fingers With Sherbet (pictured)
Rich Chocolate Fruit Dip

Lemon Fingers With Sherbet
60 minutes

A colorful assortment of sherbets is garnished with a crisp, buttery cookie.

Cookies
⅔ cup powdered sugar
1 cup butter *or* margarine, softened
2 eggs
1⅔ cups all-purpose flour
¼ cup cornstarch
2 tablespoons grated lemon peel
2 tablespoons lemon juice
½ teaspoon vanilla

Large crystal sugar

Lemon Glaze
1 cup powdered sugar
1 to 2 tablespoons lemon juice
2 teaspoons grated lemon peel

Sherbet
1 pint lemon sherbet
1 pint orange sherbet
1 pint raspberry sherbet

6 servings (4 dozen cookies)

Heat oven to 350°. In large mixer bowl combine ⅔ cup sugar and butter. Beat at low speed, scraping bowl often, until light and fluffy (1 to 2 minutes). Continue beating, adding eggs one at a time, until well mixed (2 to 4 minutes). In small bowl stir together flour and cornstarch. Continue beating, gradually adding flour mixture alternately with lemon peel, lemon juice and vanilla, until well mixed (1 to 2 minutes). Spoon into pastry bag with wide (Number 6) star tip. On greased cookie sheets pipe dough into 3-inch slightly curved fingers; sprinkle with large crystal sugar. Bake for 8 to 12 minutes or until edges are lightly browned. Cool completely. Meanwhile, in medium bowl stir together all glaze ingredients. Dip 1 inch of cookies into glaze; let stand until glaze is set. To serve, place one scoop of each flavor of sherbet into individual dessert dishes; place 2 cookies in each dish.

Tip: Cookie press with star disc can be used in place of pastry bag.

Nutrition Information (1 serving)
• Calories 360 • Protein 3g • Carbohydrate 53g • Fat 16g
• Cholesterol 69mg • Sodium 175mg

Rich Chocolate Fruit Dip
30 minutes

Dip fresh fruit in this rich, delicious chocolate.

2 cups powdered sugar
1 (6 ounce) package (1 cup) semi-sweet real chocolate chips
½ cup butter *or* margarine
1 (12 ounce) can evaporated milk
1 teaspoon vanilla

¼ cup your favorite liqueur, if desired

Your favorite fresh fruit, cut into bite-size pieces

2 cups

In 2-quart saucepan combine all ingredients *except* vanilla, liqueur and fruit. Cook over medium heat, stirring occasionally, until mixture comes to a full boil (13 to 15 minutes). Boil, stirring constantly, 3 minutes. Stir in vanilla and liqueur. Serve warm with fresh fruit. Store refrigerated.

Tip: Dip can be used as a sauce over cake or ice cream.

Nutrition Information (1 tablespoon)
• Calories 90 • Protein 1g • Carbohydrate 10g • Fat 6g
• Cholesterol 11mg • Sodium 41mg

Peppermint n' Chocolate Bars

3 hours 30 minutes

Refreshing peppermint complements chocolate in these easy to make bars.

Crust
½ cup butter *or* margarine
½ cup sugar
⅓ cup unsweetened cocoa
1 teaspoon vanilla
1½ cups graham cracker crumbs
1 cup flaked coconut
½ cup chopped nuts

Filling
2 cups powdered sugar
½ cup butter *or* margarine, softened
2 tablespoons milk
1 teaspoon peppermint extract
3 drops red *or* green food coloring, optional

Frosting
⅓ cup semi-sweet real chocolate chips
1 teaspoon vegetable oil

4 dozen

In 2-quart saucepan combine butter, sugar, cocoa and vanilla. Cook over medium heat, stirring constantly, until butter is melted and mixture is smooth (1 to 2 minutes). Stir in all remaining crust ingredients. Press firmly on bottom of 13x9-inch pan. Refrigerate until firm (15 to 20 minutes). In small mixer bowl combine all filling ingredients. Beat at medium speed, scraping bowl often, until smooth (2 to 3 minutes). Spread evenly over crust; refrigerate 15 minutes. In 1-quart saucepan combine chocolate chips and oil. Cook over low heat, stirring constantly, until chocolate is melted (2 to 4 minutes). Drizzle evenly over bars. Cover; refrigerate until firm (2 to 3 hours). Cut into bars; store refrigerated.

Nutrition Information (1 bar)
• Calories 90 • Protein 1g • Carbohydrate 10g • Fat 6g
• Cholesterol 10mg • Sodium 62mg

Spicy Oatmeal Raisin Bars

60 minutes

Chock full of surprises, these bars will delight young and old alike.

½ cup firmly packed brown sugar
½ cup sugar
1 cup butter *or* margarine, softened
2 eggs
2 teaspoons vanilla
1½ cups quick-cooking oats
1 cup all-purpose flour
1 teaspoon baking soda
1 teaspoon cinnamon
½ teaspoon salt
½ teaspoon ginger
¼ teaspoon nutmeg
1 cup shredded coconut
1 cup raisins
½ cup coarsely chopped pecans
1 (6 ounce) package (1 cup) semi-sweet chocolate chips

40 bars

Heat oven to 375°. In large mixer bowl combine brown sugar, sugar, butter, eggs and vanilla. Beat at medium speed, scraping bowl often, until light and fluffy (1 to 2 minutes). Add oats, flour, baking soda, cinnamon, salt, ginger and nutmeg. Beat at low speed, scraping bowl often, until well mixed (1 to 2 minutes). By hand, stir in all remaining ingredients. Spread dough on bottom of greased 15x10x1-inch jelly roll pan. Bake for 15 to 20 minutes or until lightly brown.

Nutrition Information (1 bar)
• Calories 130 • Protein 2g • Carbohydrate 13g • Fat 8g
• Cholesterol 23mg • Sodium 107mg

Peppermint n' Chocolate Bars (left)
Spicy Oatmeal Raisin Bars (right)

ELEGANT ENTERTAINING

In the late 1700s, Thomas Jefferson was famous for his elegant White House dinner parties. Although Washington, D.C. was still a small, rough town with muddy streets, the meals on our third president's table were haute cuisine prepared by a French chef under Jefferson's close personal supervision. He even went shopping with his chef! Jefferson had long been interested in fine food. As America's first ambassador to France, he spent a great deal of time in Parisian restaurants and enrolled his valet in a French cooking school.

In the 1960s, Jackie Kennedy brought back elegant 18th Century entertaining. On one memorable evening, she floated a whole dinner party down the Potomac River on the presidential yacht to Mount Vernon, George Washington's ancestral home, where the guests dined beautifully by candlelight.

We all have occasions in our lives worth cleaning the silver, bringing out the good dishes and getting all dressed up for. On the next pages we've collected some fancy foods for these special occasions that are truly worth your best efforts. Some take a bit of time, some just look fussy but are really easy to make. But all of our menus are designed for elegant entertaining, with foods that make a great impression and a grand time even grander.

ELEGANT ENTERTAINING
MENU

Before the Show

You'll get rave reviews for this meal that opens with Brie baked in a flaky pastry shell and features a colorful pasta with roasted red peppers and scallops. The last act is a beautiful raspberry crowned chocolate torte. Take a bow!

Baked Brie With Pastry p.357
Roasted Red Pepper & Scallop Fettuccine p.374   Fresh Orange Salad p.378
Raspberry Crowned Chocolate Torte p.388

ELEGANT ENTERTAINING
MENU

For Special Guests

The perfect meal for company . . . elegant beef tenderloin crowned with smooth Béarnaise sauce and served proudly with herbed Brussels sprouts and carrots, tender, homemade crescent rolls and a delicious Bavarian apple tart.

Elegant Beef Tenderloin With Béarnaise Sauce p.368
Crescent Dinner Rolls p.364   Herbed Brussels Sprouts & Carrots p.386
Bavarian Apple Tart p.388

351

ELEGANT ENTERTAINING
MENU

Spring Is in the Air

The fresh foods of spring in a perfect meal for guests – grilled lamb kabobs in a rosemary marinade, nutty wild rice salad, tender artichokes with lemon and lime butter sauces. Poppy seed torte makes a great finish.

Grilled Rosemary Lamb Kabobs p.370
Nutty Wild Rice Pilaf p.382   Tender Artichoke With Butter Sauces p.385
Orange Glazed Poppy Seed Torte p.394

ELEGANT ENTERTAINING
MENU
Best Dressed Affair

Serve fresh mushroom bisque for openers, then Cornish game hens, beautifully dressed in orange glaze. Add hot crescent dinner rolls and a colorful endive-broccoli-olive-red pepper salad. For dessert, a light and refreshing key lime cheesecake.

Fresh Mushroom Bisque p.361
Orange Glazed Cornish Game Hens p.367   Endive-Broccoli Salad p.378
Crescent Dinner Rolls p.364   Refreshing Key Lime Cheesecake p.390

Fresh Summer Fare

To start, serve chilled cucumber soup with French bread croutons. Next come salmon steaks, grilled and topped with a lime butter. Flaky rosemary biscuits and fresh peach butter follow. Then bring on the grand finale ... chocolate caramel truffle torte.

Fresh Cucumber Soup p.361   Northwest Salmon Steaks p.377
Flaky Rosemary Biscuits With Peach Butter p.362
Chocolate Caramel Truffle Torte p.393

ELEGANT ENTERTAINING
MENU

Summertime Elegance

Baked tuna steaks are stuffed with herbed feta cheese. The salad is made with tomatoes, olives, cucumber and lettuce, then served with a vinaigrette. Mini brioches are served as an accompaniment. Fresh berries and a custard cream finish the meal.

Feta-Stuffed Tuna Steaks p.377
Tomato & Cucumber in Vinaigrette p.380   Mini Brioche p.362
Fresh Berries Over Cookies & Cream p.393

Baked Brie With Pastry

2 hours 30 minutes

A golden, flaky pastry surrounds this warm Brie appetizer.

¾ cup all-purpose flour
¼ cup butter *or* margarine, softened
1 (3 ounce) package cream cheese, softened
1 (8 ounce) 4¼-inch diameter round Brie cheese
1 egg
1 teaspoon water

Apple *or* pear slices
Crackers

8 servings

In large mixer bowl combine flour, butter and cream cheese. Beat at low speed, scraping bowl often, until mixture leaves sides of bowl and forms a dough (2 to 3 minutes). Divide dough in half; wrap in waxed paper. Refrigerate 30 to 60 minutes. *Heat oven to 400°.* On lightly floured surface roll each half of dough to ⅛-inch thickness. Cut a 7-inch circle from each half. Place one circle on cookie sheet. Place Brie cheese on center of pastry circle and top with other pastry circle. Pinch edges of pastry to seal. Flute edges as desired. Decorate top with small pastry cutouts. In small bowl beat egg with water; brush over top and sides of pastry. Bake for 15 to 20 minutes or until golden brown. Remove from cookie sheet immediately. Let stand 30 minutes to allow cheese to set. Cut into small wedges and serve with apple slices and crackers.

Nutrition Information (1 serving)
• Calories 240 • Protein 9g • Carbohydrate 10g • Fat 18g
• Cholesterol 90mg • Sodium 278mg

To Prepare Pastry:

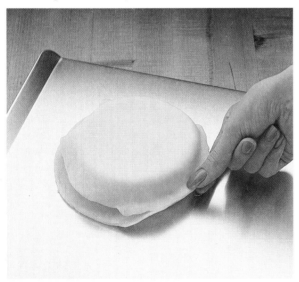

1. Place one circle on cookie sheet. Place Brie cheese on center of pastry circle and top with other pastry circle. Pinch edges of pastry to seal.

2. Flute edges as desired. Decorate top with small pastry cutouts.

Blue Cheese n' Walnut Dip

2 hours 15 minutes

A blue cheese dip with the unique flavor and crunch of walnuts.

1 cup mayonnaise
1 (8 ounce) carton (1 cup) dairy sour cream
½ cup chopped walnuts, *reserve 1 tablespoon*
¼ cup crumbled blue cheese
1 tablespoon chopped green onion
¼ teaspoon salt
½ teaspoon Worcestershire sauce

Fresh vegetable sticks
Tortilla chips
Crusty bread
Apple and pear slices

2 cups

In medium bowl stir together all ingredients *except* reserved 1 tablespoon chopped walnuts, vegetable sticks, chips, crusty bread and fruit slices. Spoon into serving dish; garnish with reserved walnuts. Cover; refrigerate at least

2 hours. Serve with vegetable sticks, chips, crusty bread or fruit slices.

Nutrition Information (1 tablespoon dip)
• Calories 80 • Protein 1g • Carbohydrate 1g • Fat 9g
• Cholesterol 8mg • Sodium 75mg

Avocado Crab Dip

45 minutes

Serve this crab and avocado dip warm or cold.

2 large avocados, peeled, cubed
2 tablespoons lemon juice
1 (8 ounce) package cream cheese, softened
2 tablespoons sliced ⅛-inch green onions
1 teaspoon finely chopped fresh garlic
½ teaspoon Worcestershire sauce
¼ teaspoon hot pepper sauce

1 (6 ounce) package frozen crab meat, thawed, drained

Assorted crackers, tortilla chips *or* corn chips

3 cups

In medium bowl toss avocados with *1 table-spoon* lemon juice; set aside. In medium bowl stir together cream cheese and remaining lemon juice. Stir in all remaining ingredients *except* crab meat, avocados and crackers. Gently fold in crab meat and avocados. Serve warm or cold. To serve warm, *heat oven to 350°.* Place dip in ovenproof serving dish. Bake for 15 to 20 minutes or until heated through. Stir gently before serving. Serve with crackers, tortilla chips or corn chips.

Microwave Directions: Prepare dip as directed above; place in 9-inch square baking dish or pie plate. Microwave on HIGH, stirring after half the time, until heated through (2½ to 4 minutes). Stir gently before serving. Serve with crackers, tortilla chips or corn chips.

Nutrition Information (1 tablespoon dip)
• Calories 34 • Protein 1g • Carbohydrate 1g • Fat 3g
• Cholesterol 7mg • Sodium 54mg

In the 1700s in Virginia, landed gentry copied the English and entertained at fox hunting, horse races and coach parties that started early and lasted into the evening.

Blue Cheese n' Walnut Dip (left)
Avocado Crab Dip (right)

Fresh Cucumber Soup (pictured)
Fresh Mushroom Bisque

Fresh Cucumber Soup
1 hour 15 minutes

Colorful vegetables garnish this fresh cucumber soup.

Soup
3 cups (3 medium) pared, seeded, cubed
  cucumbers
1 (16 ounce) carton (2 cups) dairy sour
  cream
1 (14½ ounce) can chicken broth
¼ teaspoon pepper
¼ teaspoon finely chopped fresh garlic
1 tablespoon white wine vinegar

Croutons
2 cups cubed ½-inch French bread
¼ cup butter *or* margarine, melted

Chopped tomato, green onions and green
  pepper

8 servings

In 5-cup blender container combine cucumbers, sour cream, ½ *cup* chicken broth, pepper, garlic and vinegar. Cover; blend at High speed until smooth (30 to 60 seconds). In medium bowl stir together cucumber mixture and remaining chicken broth. Refrigerate at least 1 hour. Meanwhile, *heat oven to 400°.* In medium bowl toss together bread and butter. Place on cookie sheet. Bake for 5 to 7 minutes or until lightly browned; cool. Top each serving of soup with tomato, green onions, green pepper and croutons.

Nutrition Information (1 serving)
• Calories 220 • Protein 4g • Carbohydrate 11g • Fat 18g
• Cholesterol 41mg • Sodium 319mg

Fresh Mushroom Bisque
45 minutes

Crisply tender carrots add color to this creamy mushroom soup.

½ cup butter *or* margarine
2 cups (8 ounces) sliced fresh mushrooms
⅓ cup finely chopped onion
1 teaspoon finely chopped fresh garlic
½ cup all-purpose flour
¼ teaspoon pepper
2 (14½ ounce) cans chicken broth

1 cup (2 medium) shredded carrots
2 cups half-and-half
⅛ to ¼ teaspoon hot pepper sauce

Chopped fresh parsley

8 servings

In 4-quart saucepan melt butter. Add mushrooms, onion and garlic. Cook over medium heat, stirring occasionally, until mushrooms and onion are tender (4 to 5 minutes). Stir in flour and pepper until smooth and bubbly (1 minute). Add chicken broth and carrots. Cook over medium heat, stirring occasionally, until carrots are crisply tender (8 to 10 minutes). Add half-and-half and hot pepper sauce; continue cooking, stirring occasionally, until heated through (7 to 9 minutes). Sprinkle with parsley.

Microwave Directions: In 3-quart casserole melt butter on HIGH (1 to 1½ minutes). Stir in mushrooms, onion and garlic. Microwave on HIGH, stirring once after half the time, until mushrooms and onion are tender (4 to 6 minutes). Stir in flour and pepper until smooth; microwave on HIGH until bubbly (30 to 60 seconds). Stir in chicken broth and carrots. Cover; microwave on HIGH, stirring after half the time, until mixture thickens (18 to 22 minutes). Stir in half-and-half and hot pepper sauce. Cover; microwave on HIGH, stirring after half the time, until heated through (3 to 5 minutes). Sprinkle with parsley.

Nutrition Information (1 serving)
• Calories 240 • Protein 5g • Carbohydrate 12g • Fat 19g
• Cholesterol 53mg • Sodium 475mg

Mini Brioche

1 day

1 (¼ ounce) package active dry yeast
¼ cup warm water (105 to 115°F)
2 tablespoons sugar
1 teaspoon salt
4 eggs
1 egg white, *reserve yolk*

1 cup butter *or* margarine, softened
3½ cups all-purpose flour

1 reserved egg yolk
1 tablespoon water

2 dozen

In large mixer bowl dissolve yeast in warm water. Add sugar, salt, 4 eggs, egg white, butter and *2 cups* flour. Beat at low speed, scraping bowl constantly, 30 seconds. Increase speed to medium. Continue beating, scraping bowl often, 10 minutes. By hand, stir in remaining flour; scrape batter from sides of bowl. Cover with plastic wrap; let rise in warm place until double in size (about 1 hour). Stir down dough by beating about 25 strokes. Cover bowl tightly with plastic wrap; refrigerate at least 8 hours. Divide dough into 2 halves. Shape one half into 7½-inch log-shaped roll; cut into 15 (½-inch) slices. With floured hands shape 12 of the slices into balls. Place one ball into each cup of greased muffin pan; flatten and make deep indentation in center of each. Cut each of the remaining 3 slices into 4 equal parts; shape each part into a small ball. Place a small ball on each indentation in dough in muffin pan. Repeat with remaining half of dough. Let rise until double in size (about 2 hours). *Heat oven to 375°.* In small bowl stir together reserved egg yolk and water; brush over top of rolls, being careful not to let egg mixture run down sides. Bake for 13 to 17 minutes or until golden brown. Immediately remove from pans.

Nutrition Information (1 brioche)
• Calories 160 • Protein 4g • Carbohydrate 15g • Fat 9g
• Cholesterol 68mg • Sodium 182mg

Flaky Rosemary Biscuits With Peach Butter

30 minutes

Biscuits
2 cups all-purpose flour
2 tablespoons sugar
4 teaspoons baking powder
½ teaspoon cream of tartar
¼ teaspoon salt
⅓ cup butter *or* margarine, cut into pieces
⅔ cup milk
1 teaspoon chopped fresh rosemary leaves*

Peach Butter
½ cup butter *or* margarine, softened
3 tablespoons peach preserves

8 biscuits, ⅔ cup peach butter

Heat oven to 400°. In large bowl combine flour, sugar, baking powder, cream of tartar and salt. Cut in ⅓ cup butter until crumbly. Stir in milk and rosemary just until moistened. Turn dough onto lightly floured surface; knead until smooth (15 seconds). Roll dough to ½-inch thickness. Cut into 8 (2½-inch) round biscuits. Place 1 inch apart on cookie sheet. Bake for 10 to 15 minutes or until lightly browned. Meanwhile, in small bowl stir together ½ cup butter and peach preserves. Serve warm biscuits with peach butter.

*¼ teaspoon dried rosemary leaves can be substituted for 1 teaspoon chopped fresh rosemary leaves.

Tip: Substituting unsalted butter in the peach butter enhances the sweet peach flavor.

Nutrition Information
(1 biscuit with about 1 tablespoon peach butter)
• Calories 320 • Protein 4g • Carbohydrate 32g • Fat 20g
• Cholesterol 53mg • Sodium 424mg

Mini Brioche (top)
Flaky Rosemary Biscuits With Peach Butter (bottom)

Crescent Dinner Rolls

3 hours

This rich egg dough makes elegant crescent rolls.

1⅔ cups milk
¼ cup butter *or* margarine
1 (¼ ounce) package active dry yeast
¼ cup warm water (105 to 115° F)
6¼ to 7 cups all-purpose flour
¼ cup sugar

3 eggs
1 tablespoon salt

Butter *or* margarine, melted

4 dozen

In 1-quart saucepan heat milk until just comes to a boil (3 to 4 minutes); stir in butter until melted. Cool to lukewarm (105 to 115° F). In large mixer bowl dissolve yeast in warm water. Add milk mixture, *3 cups flour*, sugar, eggs and salt to yeast. Beat at medium speed, scraping bowl often, until smooth (1 to 2 minutes). By hand, stir in enough remaining flour to make dough easy to handle. Turn dough onto lightly floured surface; knead until smooth and elastic (about 10 minutes). Place in greased bowl; turn greased side up. Cover; let rise in warm place until double in size (about 1½ hours). Dough is ready if indentation remains when touched. Punch down dough; divide into 4 equal portions. Roll 1 portion into 12-inch circle. Brush with melted butter. Cut into 12 wedges. Roll up, beginning at rounded edge. Place rolls, points underneath, on greased cookie sheets; curve slightly. Repeat with remaining dough. Cover; let rise until double in size (about 30 minutes). *Heat oven to 400°.* Bake for 12 to 14 minutes or until lightly browned. If desired, brush tops of rolls with butter.

Nutrition Information (1 roll)
• Calories 80 • Protein 2g • Carbohydrate 14g • Fat 2g
• Cholesterol 21mg • Sodium 153mg

To Prepare Rolls:

1. Roll 1 portion into 12-inch circle. Brush with melted butter. Cut into 12 wedges.

2. Roll up, beginning at rounded edge. Place rolls, points underneath, on greased cookie sheets; curve slightly.

Crescent Dinner Rolls

Apricot Glazed Chicken (pictured)
Orange Glazed Cornish Game Hens

Apricot Glazed Chicken

40 minutes

The delicate flavors and rich colors of dried apricots and currants blend together for a wonderful country taste.

⅓ cup butter *or* margarine
4 whole, boneless chicken breasts, skinned, halved, cut into 3x½-inch strips
¾ cup dried currants *or* raisins
1 cup orange marmalade
1 cup orange juice

1 (6 ounce) package (1 cup) dried apricots, halved
1 teaspoon ginger

Cooked rice

8 servings

In 10-inch skillet melt butter until sizzling. Cook chicken strips over medium high heat, stirring occasionally, until chicken is browned and fork tender (10 to 15 minutes). Stir in all remaining ingredients *except* rice. Continue cooking, stirring occasionally, until sauce is thickened (6 to 8 minutes). Serve over rice.

Nutrition Information (1 serving)
• Calories 500 • Protein 30g • Carbohydrate 70g • Fat 12g
• Cholesterol 96mg • Sodium 158mg

Orange Glazed Cornish Game Hens

2 hours

Orange and ginger flavor the moist stuffing in these glazed Cornish hens.

Stuffing
3 cups dried bread cubes
2 cups (4 stalks) sliced ¼-inch celery
½ cup (1 medium) chopped onion
½ cup butter *or* margarine, melted
2 (11 ounce) cans mandarin orange segments, drained
1 teaspoon salt
½ teaspoon pepper

¼ teaspoon ginger
¼ cup orange juice
8 Cornish game hens

Glaze
⅔ cup orange marmalade
¼ teaspoon ginger
¼ cup dry white wine *or* orange juice

8 servings

Heat oven to 375°. In large bowl stir together all stuffing ingredients *except* hens. Stuff hens with stuffing; secure opening with wooden picks. Tuck under wings of hens. Place 4 hens, breast side up, in each of 2 (13x9-inch) baking pans. Bake for 45 minutes. Meanwhile, in 1-quart saucepan combine all glaze ingredients. Cook over medium heat, stirring occasionally, until melted (2 to 3 minutes). Brush hens with half of glaze. Continue baking, basting with remaining glaze every 15 minutes, until hens are fork tender (30 to 45 minutes). Loosely cover with aluminum foil if browning too quickly. If necessary, add water to basting glaze.

Nutrition Information (1 serving)
• Calories 430 • Protein 27g • Carbohydrate 38g • Fat 19g
• Cholesterol 107mg • Sodium 592mg

Elegant Beef Tenderloin With Béarnaise Sauce 60 minutes

Mouth-watering beef served with an exquisite tarragon flavored sauce.

Sauce
¾ cup butter
¼ cup white wine vinegar
¼ cup dry white wine
2 tablespoons chopped green onions
1 tablespoon chopped fresh tarragon leaves
3 egg yolks
⅛ teaspoon salt
⅛ teaspoon white pepper
1 tablespoon finely chopped fresh parsley

Tenderloin
3 to 3½ pounds beef tenderloin
2 tablespoons butter, softened
1 teaspoon white wine vinegar
½ teaspoon finely chopped fresh garlic

8 servings

To clarify butter, in 1-quart saucepan over low heat melt ¾ cup butter until white solids separate from fat (10 to 13 minutes). Remove from heat; skim off foam. Cool to lukewarm; set aside. In heavy 1-quart saucepan combine ¼ cup vinegar, wine, green onions and tarragon. Cook over medium heat until reduced to 3 tablespoons liquid and solids (15 to 20 minutes); cool. *Heat oven to 425°.* In small bowl stir together 2 tablespoons softened butter, 1 teaspoon vinegar and garlic. Brush tenderloin with butter mixture; place on rack in shallow roasting pan. Bake for 20 to 25 minutes or until meat thermometer reaches 140°F (Rare). Meanwhile, whisk egg yolks, salt and pepper into cooled onion mixture until frothy. Place

pan over low heat, whisking constantly, until mixture thickens slightly. The pan should not be hot to the touch. Remove from heat; very slowly whisk in clarified butter leaving behind the milk solids residue in the bottom of the pan. Stir in parsley. Serve with tenderloin.

Tip: If sauce begins to separate, remove from heat and whisk in 1 tablespoon cold water; return to heat.

Nutrition Information (1 serving)
• Calories 490 • Protein 37g • Carbohydrate 1g • Fat 37g
• Cholesterol 266mg • Sodium 318mg

Beef	Internal Cooking Temperature
Rare	140°F
Medium	160°F
Well	170°F

To Prepare Sauce:

1. Melt ¾ cup butter until white solids separate from fat. Remove from heat; skim off foam.

2. Place pan with onion mixture and egg yolks over low heat, whisking constantly, until mixture thickens slightly. The pan should not be hot to the touch.

3. Remove from heat; very slowly whisk in clarified butter leaving behind the milk solids residue in the bottom of the pan.

Elegant Beef Tenderloin With Béarnaise Sauce

Grilled Rosemary Lamb Kabobs

3 hours

Marinade
1 cup olive *or* vegetable oil
⅓ cup lemon juice
2 tablespoons chopped fresh rosemary
  leaves*
1 tablespoon finely chopped onion
1 teaspoon finely chopped fresh garlic

Kabobs
6 (12-inch) metal skewers
2½ pounds lamb cubes for kabobs
1 medium green pepper, cut into 1½-inch pieces
1 medium red *or* yellow pepper, cut into
  1½-inch pieces
1 large red onion, cut into 12 wedges
12 large fresh mushroom caps

6 servings

In medium bowl combine all marinade ingredients. Place lamb in plastic food bag. Pour marinade into bag; seal tightly. Place in 13x9-inch pan. Refrigerate, turning once or twice, for 2 to 4 hours. *Prepare grill;* heat until coals are ash white. To assemble kabobs, on metal skewers alternate lamb pieces with green and red pepper pieces, onion wedges and mushroom caps. Place kabobs on grill.

Grill, turning occasionally, until lamb is fork tender and desired doneness (10 to 15 minutes for medium).

  *2 teaspoon dried rosemary leaves, crushed, can be substituted for 2 tablespoons chopped fresh rosemary leaves.

Nutrition Information (1 serving)
• Calories 300 • Protein 27g • Carbohydrate 5g • Fat 19g
• Cholesterol 98mg • Sodium 67mg

Hearty Olive & Tomato Veal Cutlets

45 minutes

Cutlets
⅓ cup all-purpose flour
½ teaspoon salt
¼ teaspoon pepper
2 tablespoons olive *or* vegetable oil
1 pound veal cutlets

Sauce
1 tablespoon chopped fresh fennel weed,
  if desired
2 teaspoons chopped fresh rosemary leaves*
1 teaspoon finely chopped fresh garlic
¼ cup dry white wine *or* chicken broth
½ cup chicken broth
½ cup sliced ripe olives
1 medium ripe tomato, cut into 12 wedges

4 servings

In 9-inch pie pan combine flour, salt and pepper. In 10-inch skillet heat *1 tablespoon* oil (1 to 2 minutes). Coat veal with flour mixture; shake off excess. Place ½ of veal in skillet. Cook over medium heat, turning once, until lightly browned and cooked through (2 to 3 minutes on each side). Place on serving platter; keep warm. Repeat with remaining 1 tablespoon oil and veal. Reduce heat to low. In same skillet add fennel, rosemary and garlic. Cook over low heat, stirring constantly, until garlic just begins to brown (2 to 3 minutes). Increase heat to high. Stir in wine; bring mixture to a full boil. Continue

cooking, stirring constantly, until reduced to a glaze (about 1 minute). Stir in chicken broth; bring mixture to a full boil. Continue cooking, stirring constantly, until reduced by half (about 2 minutes). Stir in olives and tomato; continue cooking until heated through (about 1 minute). Serve sauce over veal.

  *½ teaspoon dried rosemary leaves, crushed, can be substituted for 2 teaspoons chopped fresh rosemary leaves.

Nutrition Information (1 serving)
• Calories 330 • Protein 24g • Carbohydrate 10g • Fat 20g
• Cholesterol 82mg • Sodium 557mg

Grilled Rosemary Lamb Kabobs (pictured)
Hearty Olive & Tomato Veal Cutlets

Honey Mustard Glazed Swordfish (pictured)
Pork Loin Roast With Pears

Honey Mustard Glazed Swordfish

30 minutes

A sweet and tangy sauce glazes grilled swordfish steaks.

Glaze
¼ cup firmly packed brown sugar
1 teaspoon honey
3 tablespoons Dijon-style mustard
2 teaspoons cider vinegar
½ teaspoon vegetable oil

Swordfish
4 (about 8 ounces each) swordfish steaks
¼ cup sliced almonds, toasted

4 servings

Prepare grill; heat until coals are ash white. Meanwhile, in 1-quart saucepan stir together all glaze ingredients. Place swordfish on grill. Grill, basting with glaze and turning after half the time, until fish flakes with a fork (6 to 10 minutes). Place on serving platter; sprinkle with almonds. In 1-quart saucepan cook remaining glaze over low heat, stirring occasionally, until mixture just comes to a boil (2 to 3 minutes). Serve over swordfish.

Nutrition Information (1 serving)
• Calories 340 • Protein 39g • Carbohydrate 16g • Fat 12g
• Cholesterol 75mg • Sodium 509mg

Pork Loin Roast With Pears

2 hours

A savory pork loin roast is garnished with pears and toasted pecans,
then served with a rich demi-glacé sauce.

Roast
3 pound boneless center cut pork loin roast (2 loins tied)
2 teaspoons dried thyme leaves
1 teaspoon dried rosemary leaves, crushed
¼ teaspoon salt
¼ teaspoon coarsely ground pepper
2 tablespoons olive *or* vegetable oil

Sauce
½ cup pecan halves
2 medium ripe red pears, cored, sliced ¼-inch
¼ teaspoon dried thyme leaves
2 tablespoons brandy *or* apple juice
¼ cup chopped fresh parsley

8 servings

Heat oven to 325°. Place roast in 9-inch square baking pan. In small bowl stir together all remaining roast ingredients. Spoon oil mixture over roast. Bake for 1 hour 30 minutes to 1 hour 40 minutes or until meat thermometer reaches 160°F (Medium). Remove roast to carving board; *reserve pan juices.* Let roast stand 15 minutes. Meanwhile, pour pan juices into 1-cup measure; set aside. Place pecans in same pan. Bake for 10 to 15 minutes or until toasted. Add enough water to reserved pan juices to equal ½ cup. Place pan juice mixture in 10-inch skillet. Cook over medium heat, stirring occasionally, until mixture comes to a full boil (3 to 5 minutes). Add all remaining sauce ingredients *except 2 tablespoons* parsley. Continue cooking, stirring occasionally, until pears are crisply tender (2 to 3 minutes). To serve, place roast on serving platter. Place pears from sauce around roast; garnish with toasted pecans and remaining 2 tablespoons parsley. Serve with sauce.

Nutrition Information (1 serving)
• Calories 470 • Protein 37g • Carbohydrate 8g • Fat 30g
• Cholesterol 121mg • Sodium 156mg

Roasted Red Pepper & Scallop Fettuccine

1 hour 30 minutes

Roasted red pepper sauce adds color and flavor to scallops served over pasta.

2 whole red peppers
1 (16 ounce) package uncooked dried fettuccine
¼ cup butter *or* margarine
2 teaspoons finely chopped fresh garlic
½ cup sliced green onions
1½ pounds fresh *or* frozen large scallops

1 (16 ounce) carton (2 cups) dairy sour cream

Salt
Coarsely ground pepper

8 servings

Heat oven to 400°. Place whole red peppers on cookie sheet. Bake, turning occasionally, for 25 to 35 minutes or until skins are blackened. Cool; remove skins and seeds. In 5-cup blender container puree peppers on High until smooth (30 to 45 seconds). Set aside. Prepare fettuccine according to package directions; drain. In 10-inch skillet melt butter; add garlic. Cook over medium heat, stirring occasionally, 1 minute. Add green onions and scallops. Continue cooking, stirring occasionally, until scallops are tender (5 to 7 minutes). Stir in sour cream and red pepper puree until well mixed. Continue cooking until heated through (4 to 6 minutes). In large bowl toss together scallop mixture and cooked fettucine. Season to taste.

Microwave Directions: Prepare red peppers as directed above. Cook fettucine according to package directions; drain. In 2½-quart casserole melt butter on HIGH (1 to 1½ minutes). Stir in garlic. Cover; microwave on HIGH 1 minute. Stir in green onions and scallops. Cover; microwave on HIGH, stirring after half the time, until scallops are tender (6 to 9 minutes). Stir in sour cream and red pepper puree. Microwave on HIGH until heated through (2 to 4 minutes). In large bowl toss together scallop mixture and cooked fettuccine. Season to taste.

Nutrition Information (1 serving)
• Calories 470 • Protein 24g • Carbohydrate 50g • Fat 19g
• Cholesterol 69mg • Sodium 229mg

To Prepare Fettuccine:

1. Place whole red peppers on cookie sheet. Bake, turning occasionally, for 25 to 35 minutes or until skins are blackened.

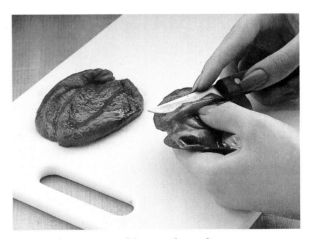

2. Cool; remove skins and seeds.

Roasted Red Pepper & Scallop Fettuccine

Northwest Salmon Steaks (pictured)
Feta-Stuffed Tuna Steaks

Northwest Salmon Steaks

20 minutes

Fresh salmon, grilled and served with a lime butter.

Lime Butter
1 cup butter *or* margarine, softened
2 teaspoons lime juice
2 teaspoons chopped fresh dill weed*
¼ teaspoon pepper

8 (1-inch thick) salmon steaks
2 limes, each cut into 8 slices

8 servings

In medium bowl stir together all lime butter ingredients. Place salmon steaks on greased broiler pan. Spread top side of each steak with 2 teaspoons lime butter. Broil 5 inches away from heat until lightly browned (5 to 6 minutes). Turn steaks over and top each steak with 2 lime slices. Continue broiling until salmon flakes with a fork (5 to 6 minutes). To serve, place lime slices beside steak and top each with 1 tablespoon lime butter.

*½ teaspoon dried dill weed can be substituted for 1 teaspoon fresh dill weed.

Grill Directions: Grease grill. Prepare grill; heat until coals are ash white. Prepare lime butter as directed. Place salmon on grill; spread top side of each steak with 2 teaspoons lime butter. Grill over medium hot coals for 5 to 6 minutes. Turn steaks over; top each steak with 2 lime slices. Continue grilling until salmon flakes with a fork (6 to 8 minutes). To serve, place lime slices beside each steak and top each with 1 tablespoon lime butter.

Nutrition Information (1 serving)
• Calories 420 • Protein 30g • Carbohydrate 0g • Fat 33g
• Cholesterol 144mg • Sodium 300mg

Feta-Stuffed Tuna Steaks

45 minutes

Tuna steaks are stuffed with an herbed feta cheese mixture, then baked until fork tender.

1 (8 ounce) package Feta cheese
2 tablespoons chopped fresh dill*
2 tablespoons chopped fresh oregano leaves**
2 tablespoons finely chopped onion

⅛ teaspoon pepper
4 (about 8 ounces each) tuna steaks
½ cup dry white wine *or* water

4 servings

Heat oven to 400°. In small bowl combine Feta cheese, *1 tablespoon* dill, *1 tablespoon* oregano, onion and pepper. Using fork, break up cheese and combine well. Cut a pocket in each tuna steak. Stuff each pocket with about ½ cup cheese mixture. In small bowl combine remaining dill and oregano; rub over both sides of tuna steaks. Place tuna steaks in 15x10x1-inch jelly roll pan; pour wine into pan. Bake for 20 to 25 minutes or until fish flakes with a fork.

*2 teaspoons dried dill weed can be substituted for 2 tablespoons chopped fresh dill.

**2 teaspoons dried oregano leaves can be substituted for 2 tablespoons chopped fresh oregano leaves.

Nutrition Information (1 serving)
• Calories 450 • Protein 53g • Carbohydrate 4g • Fat 22g
• Cholesterol 124mg • Sodium 711mg

Endive-Broccoli Salad

30 minutes

A warm herb dressing is served over this colorful salad.

Salad
4 cups broccoli flowerets, blanched
4 cups torn curly endive greens
½ cup pitted ripe olives
1 medium red pepper, cut into
   julienne strips

Dressing
½ cup olive *or* vegetable oil
¼ cup white wine vinegar
½ teaspoon sugar
½ teaspoon salt
⅛ teaspoon coarsely ground pepper
1 teaspoon chopped fresh basil leaves*
1 teaspoon finely chopped fresh garlic

8 servings

In large bowl toss together all salad ingredients. In 1-quart saucepan combine all dressing ingredients. Cook over medium heat, whisking occasionally, until mixture just comes to a boil (1 to 2 minutes). Cool 10 minutes. Pour warm dressing over salad. Serve immediately.

*¼ teaspoon dried basil leaves can be substituted for 1 teaspoon fresh basil leaves.

Tip: To blanch broccoli, place in boiling water for 4 to 5 minutes. Rinse with cold water.

Microwave Directions: Prepare salad as directed above. In 2-cup measure combine all dressing ingredients. Microwave on HIGH, beating after half the time with wire whisk, until mixture just comes to a boil (2 to 3 minutes). Cool 10 minutes. Pour warm dressing over salad. Serve immediately.

Nutrition Information (1 serving)
• Calories 150 • Protein 2g • Carbohydrate 5g • Fat 15g
• Cholesterol 0mg • Sodium 225mg

Fresh Orange Salad

30 minutes

A fresh orange dressing complements this refreshing salad.

Dressing
1 (8 ounce) carton (1 cup) dairy sour cream
1 tablespoon sugar
1 teaspoon poppy seed
2 to 3 tablespoons orange juice
½ teaspoon grated orange peel

Salad
8 cups torn red leaf lettuce
2 oranges, pared, sectioned, drained
¼ cup sliced almonds, toasted

8 servings

In medium bowl stir together all dressing ingredients. In large bowl toss together all salad ingredients. Serve dressing with salad.

Nutrition Information (1 serving)
• Calories 110 • Protein 3g • Carbohydrate 10g • Fat 8g
• Cholesterol 13mg • Sodium 21mg

When gold was discovered in California, foods may not have been elegant but they were certainly expensive. Peaches were $3, turnips $1 and whiskey was $1500 a barrel.

Endive-Broccoli Salad (pictured)
Fresh Orange Salad

Spinach Stuffed Pasta Shells

45 minutes

12 uncooked dried jumbo pasta shells
¼ cup butter *or* margarine
2 tablespoons pinenuts *or* sliced almonds
7 ounces fresh spinach, washed, torn
1 cup sliced ¼-inch fresh mushrooms
½ teaspoon fennel seed
½ teaspoon finely chopped fresh garlic

½ cup crushed croutons *or* dried crumbly style herb seasoned stuffing
½ cup (2 ounces) shredded Cheddar cheese

1 tablespoon butter *or* margarine, melted
Freshly grated Parmesan cheese
Paprika

4 servings

Heat oven to 375°. Prepare pasta shells according to package directions; drain. Rinse; set aside. In 10-inch skillet melt ¼ cup butter over medium heat. Add pinenuts; cook until toasted (2 to 4 minutes). Add spinach, mushrooms, fennel and garlic; continue cooking until spinach is wilted (2 to 3 minutes). Stir in croutons and Cheddar cheese. Fill each cooked pasta shell with about 2 tablespoons spinach mixture. Place in 9-inch square baking pan. Brush with 1 tablespoon melted butter. Sprinkle with Parmesan cheese and paprika. Cover with aluminum foil; bake 12 minutes. Uncover; continue baking for 2 to 4 minutes or until lightly browned.

Microwave Directions: Prepare pasta shells according to package directions; drain.

Rinse; set aside. In 2½-quart casserole melt ¼ cup butter on HIGH (50 to 60 seconds). Stir in pinenuts. Microwave on HIGH, stirring every minute, until light golden brown (2 to 3 minutes). Add spinach, mushrooms, fennel and garlic. Cover; microwave on HIGH, stirring after half the time, until spinach is wilted (3 to 5 minutes). Stir in croutons and Cheddar cheese. Fill each cooked pasta shell with about 2 tablespoons spinach mixture. Place in 9-inch square baking dish. Brush with 1 tablespoon melted butter. Sprinkle with Parmesan cheese and paprika. Cover with plastic wrap; microwave on HIGH, turning dish ½ turn after half the time, until heated through (4 to 6 minutes).

Nutrition Information (1 serving)
• Calories 470 • Protein 15g • Carbohydrate 49g • Fat 24g
• Cholesterol 55mg • Sodium 480mg

Tomato & Cucumber in Vinaigrette

30 minutes

Vinaigrette
⅓ cup olive *or* vegetable oil
1 tablespoon chopped fresh chives*
1 teaspoon chopped fresh mint leaves**
½ teaspoon sugar
¼ teaspoon salt
¼ teaspoon pepper
2 tablespoons red wine vinegar

Salad
6 Boston lettuce leaves, radicchio leaves *or* leaf lettuce leaves
3 ripe tomatoes, cut into ¼-inch slices
1 medium cucumber, cut into ¼-inch slices
½ cup sliced ripe olives

6 servings

In jar with lid combine all vinaigrette ingredients; shake well. Refrigerate until ready to serve. On individual salad or dinner   plates place 1 lettuce leaf. Arrange 3 to 4 slices tomato and 4 to 5 slices cucumber on each lettuce leaf. Sprinkle with olives. Just before serving, drizzle with vinaigrette.

*1 teaspoon dried chives can be substituted for 1 tablespoon chopped fresh chives.

**¼ teaspoon dried mint leaves can be substituted for 1 teaspoon chopped fresh mint leaves.

Nutrition Information (1 serving)
• Calories 140 • Protein 1g • Carbohydrate 4g • Fat 14g
• Cholesterol 0mg • Sodium 186mg

Spinach Stuffed Pasta Shells (pictured)
Tomato & Cucumber in Vinaigrette

Nutty Wild Rice Pilaf

60 minutes

Sweet raisins and crunchy almonds complement nutty wild rice.

1 cup uncooked wild rice, rinsed
3 cups water
2 teaspoons instant chicken bouillon granules
½ cup slivered almonds
¼ cup butter *or* margarine

¼ cup golden raisins
¼ cup sliced green onions
2 teaspoons grated orange peel

8 servings

In 2-quart saucepan combine rice, water and chicken bouillon. Cook over high heat until mixture comes to a full boil (6 to 10 minutes). Reduce heat to low. Cover; simmer until rice is tender and fluffy (40 to 45 minutes). Drain. In same pan with wild rice stir in all remaining ingredients. Cook over medium heat, stirring occasionally, until heated through (5 to 6 minutes).

Microwave Directions: In 3-quart casserole combine rice, water and chicken bouillon. Cover; microwave on HIGH, stirring after half the time, until rice is tender (45 to 60 minutes). Drain. In same casserole with wild rice stir in all remaining ingredients. Cover; microwave on HIGH until heated through (2½ to 3½ minutes).

Nutrition Information (1 serving)
• Calories 180 • Protein 5g • Carbohydrate 21g • Fat 10g
• Cholesterol 16mg • Sodium 155mg

Asparagus With Orange & Pecans

20 minutes

Crunchy pecans and a hint of orange accent this fresh spring asparagus side dish.

2½ pounds fresh asparagus spears, trimmed
¼ cup butter *or* margarine
⅓ cup pecan halves

1 teaspoon grated orange peel
1 teaspoon orange juice

8 servings

In 10-inch skillet place asparagus spears; add enough water to cover. Bring to a full boil. Cook over medium heat until asparagus is crisply tender (5 to 7 minutes). Drain; set aside. In same skillet melt butter; add pecans. Cook over medium heat until pecans are toasted (1 to 2 minutes). Stir in remaining ingredients *except* asparagus. Spoon over warm asparagus.

Microwave Directions: In 12x8-inch baking dish arrange asparagus with tips toward center. Add ¼ cup water. Cover; microwave on HIGH, moving outer spears to the center of the dish after half the time, until asparagus is crisply tender (12 to 14 minutes). Let stand 1 minute. Drain; set aside. In same baking dish microwave butter on HIGH until melted (40 to 60 seconds); add pecans. Microwave on HIGH until pecans are toasted (2 to 3 minutes). Stir in remaining ingredients *except* asparagus. Spoon over warm asparagus.

Nutrition Information (1 serving)
• Calories 110 • Protein 5g • Carbohydrate 6g • Fat 9g
• Cholesterol 16mg • Sodium 62mg

Nutty Wild Rice Pilaf (top)
Asparagus With Orange & Pecans (bottom)

Tender Artichoke With Butter Sauces

45 minutes

Tender artichokes served with lemon or lime butter.

4 medium artichokes
   Lemon juice
3 quarts (12 cups) water

Lemon Butter Sauce
¾ cup butter *or* margarine
3 tablespoons chopped fresh parsley
3 tablespoons lemon juice

Lime Butter Sauce
¾ cup butter *or* margarine
3 tablespoons chopped fresh parsley
2 tablespoons lime juice

8 servings

Wash, trim stems and remove bruised outer leaves of artichokes. Cut off 1 inch of tops and sharp leaf tips. Brush cut edges with lemon juice. In 5-quart Dutch oven bring water to a full boil; add artichokes. Cover; cook over low heat until leaf pulls out easily from artichoke (20 to 30 minutes). Remove artichokes; drain upside down on wire rack. Slice artichokes in half; gently remove choke. Meanwhile, in 1-quart saucepan melt ¾ cup butter. Stir in remaining ingredients for desired sauce. Cook over medium heat, stirring occasionally, until heated through (1 to 2 minutes). Serve warm artichokes with butter sauce spooned into center of each artichoke half. Pass additional sauce.

Microwave Directions: Trim artichokes as directed above. Rinse artichokes with water; shake off excess. Brush cut edges with lemon juice. Wrap each artichoke in plastic wrap. Microwave on HIGH, rearranging artichokes after half the time, until leaf pulls out easily from artichoke (10 to 12 minutes). Let stand 3 minutes. Slice artichokes in half; gently remove choke. Meanwhile, place ¾ cup butter in 4-cup measure. Microwave on HIGH, stirring after half the time, until melted (1½ to 2 minutes). Stir in remaining ingredients for desired sauce. Cover; microwave on HIGH until heated through (30 to 60 seconds). Serve warm artichokes with butter sauce spooned into center of each artichoke half. Pass additional sauce.

Nutrition Information (1 serving)
• Calories 220 • Protein 4g • Carbohydrate 16g • Fat 17g
• Cholesterol 47mg • Sodium 275mg

To Prepare Artichokes:

1. Wash, trim stems and remove bruised outer leaves of artichokes. Cut off 1 inch of tops and sharp leaf tips.

2. Slice artichokes in half; gently remove choke.

Herbed Brussels Sprouts & Carrots

40 minutes

Fresh rosemary enhances these garden vegetables.

1 cup water
1 pound Brussels sprouts, trimmed*
3 cups (6 medium) carrots, cut into
   2x¼-inch strips
⅓ cup butter *or* margarine

3 tablespoons slivered almonds
½ teaspoon chopped fresh rosemary leaves**
¼ teaspoon salt

8 servings

In 2-quart saucepan bring 1 cup water to a full boil. Add Brussels sprouts. Cover; cook over medium heat 4 minutes. Add carrots. Cover; continue cooking until crisply tender (6 to 8 minutes). Drain; set aside. In same pan place butter and almonds. Cook over medium heat, stirring constantly, until almonds are golden brown (3 to 4 minutes). Stir in vegetables and remaining ingredients. Cover; continue cooking, stirring occasionally, until heated through (4 to 5 minutes).

*2 (10 ounce) packages frozen Brussels sprouts can be substituted for 1 pound Brussels sprouts.

**⅛ teaspoon dried rosemary leaves, crushed, can be substituted for ½ teaspoon chopped fresh rosemary leaves.

Nutrition Information (1 serving)
• Calories 130 • Protein 3g • Carbohydrate 11g • Fat 10g
• Cholesterol 21mg • Sodium 179mg

Cauliflower Dijon

45 minutes

For a unique presentation, this whole cauliflower is served cut into wedges.

¾ cup water
1 medium head cauliflower

Sauce
3 tablespoons butter *or* margarine
3 tablespoons all-purpose flour
1 cup half-and-half
½ cup water

½ teaspoon instant chicken bouillon granules
⅛ teaspoon coarsely ground pepper
2 tablespoons Dijon-style mustard
2 teaspoons white wine vinegar
⅓ cup coarsely chopped salted pistachios, toasted*

8 servings

In 3-quart saucepan bring ¾ cup water to a full boil. Add whole cauliflower. Cover; cook over medium heat until cauliflower is fork tender (20 to 25 minutes). Drain. Meanwhile, in 2-quart saucepan melt butter over medium heat. Stir in flour until smooth and bubbly (1 minute). Add half-and-half, ½ cup water and bouillon. Cook over medium heat, stirring constantly, until mixture comes to a full boil (3 to 5 minutes). Reduce heat to low. Continue cooking, stirring occasionally, until mixture thickens

(4 to 5 minutes). Remove from heat. Whisk in pepper, mustard and vinegar until smooth. Pour 1 cup sauce over cauliflower. Sprinkle with pistachios. Cut into wedges; serve with additional sauce.

*⅓ cup coarsely chopped salted cashews can be substituted for ⅓ cup pistachios.

Nutrition Information (1 serving)
• Calories 140 • Protein 3g • Carbohydrate 7g • Fat 11g
• Cholesterol 23mg • Sodium 196mg

Herbed Brussels Sprouts & Carrots (pictured)
Cauliflower Dijon

Bavarian Apple Tart

2 hours 30 minutes

Moist, sweet apples are nestled in a cream cheese layer atop a sweet crust.

Crust
1 cup all-purpose flour
⅓ cup sugar
½ cup butter *or* margarine, softened
¼ teaspoon vanilla

Filling
½ cup sugar
2 (8 ounce) packages cream cheese, softened
2 eggs
1 teaspoon vanilla

Topping
4 cups (4 medium) peeled, sliced ¼-inch tart cooking apples
⅓ cup sugar
½ teaspoon cinnamon
½ teaspoon nutmeg
Dash cardamom

¼ cup sliced almonds

Sweetened whipped cream

12 servings

Heat oven to 375°. In small mixer bowl combine all crust ingredients. Beat at medium speed until dough leaves sides of bowl (2 to 3 minutes). Press on bottom of 10-inch springform pan. In same small mixer bowl combine all filling ingredients. Beat at medium speed until smooth (2 to 3 minutes). Spread over crust. In large bowl toss together apples, ⅓ cup sugar, cinnamon, nutmeg and cardamom. Arrange apples over filling. Bake for 35 to 45 minutes or until apples are fork tender. Sprinkle with almonds; continue baking for 5 to 10 minutes. Cool completely. Remove rim from springform pan. Cut into wedges; serve with whipped cream.

Nutrition Information (1 serving)
• Calories 360 • Protein 6g • Carbohydrate 34g • Fat 23g
• Cholesterol 108mg • Sodium 202mg

Raspberry Crowned Chocolate Torte

5 hours

Brownie-like layer topped with glistening raspberry preserves and a crown of whipped cream.

3 eggs, separated
⅛ teaspoon cream of tartar
⅛ teaspoon salt
1½ cups sugar
1 cup butter *or* margarine, melted
1½ teaspoons vanilla
½ cup all-purpose flour

½ cup unsweetened cocoa
3 tablespoons water
¾ cup finely chopped almonds
⅓ cup raspberry preserves
Sweetened whipped cream
Fresh raspberries

12 servings

Heat oven to 350°. Grease 9-inch round cake pan. Line with aluminum foil leaving excess foil over edges; grease foil. In small mixer bowl combine egg whites, cream of tartar and salt. Beat at high speed until soft peaks form (1 to 2 minutes). In large mixer bowl combine egg yolks, sugar, butter and vanilla. Beat at medium speed, scraping bowl often, until well mixed (1 to 2 minutes). Add flour, cocoa and water. Continue beating until well mixed (1 to 2 minutes). Stir in chopped almonds. Fold beaten egg whites into chocolate mixture. Spread into prepared pan. Bake for 40 to 55 minutes or until firm to the touch. (Do not overbake.) Cool on wire rack 1 hour; remove from pan by lifting aluminum foil. Cover; refrigerate until cool (3 hours). Place on serving plate. Spread raspberry preserves on top. Garnish with whipped cream and raspberries.

Nutrition Information (1 serving)
• Calories 350 • Protein 5g • Carbohydrate 38g • Fat 22g
• Cholesterol 111mg • Sodium 226mg

Bavarian Apple Tart (top)
Raspberry Crowned Chocolate Torte (bottom)

Refreshing Key Lime Cheesecake

4 hours

This refreshing dessert will bring oohs and aahs from your guests.

Crust
1 cup graham cracker crumbs
¼ cup sugar
⅓ cup butter *or* margarine, melted

Filling
1 cup lime juice
¼ cup water
2 (¼ ounce) envelopes unflavored gelatin
1½ cups sugar

5 eggs, slightly beaten
1 tablespoon grated lime peel
½ cup butter *or* margarine, softened
2 (8 ounce) packages cream cheese, softened
½ cup whipping cream

Sweetened whipped cream
Lime slices

12 servings

In medium bowl stir together all crust ingredients. Press on bottom of 9-inch springform pan; set aside. In 2-quart saucepan combine lime juice, water and gelatin. Let stand 5 minutes to soften. Add sugar, eggs and lime peel. Cook over medium heat, stirring constantly, until mixture just comes to a boil (7 to 8 minutes). DO NOT BOIL. In large mixer bowl combine ½ cup butter and cream cheese. Beat at medium speed, scraping bowl often, until well mixed (1 to 2 minutes). Gradually beat in hot lime mixture until well mixed (1 to 2 minutes). Refrigerate, stirring occasionally, until cool (about 1 hour). In chilled small mixer bowl beat chilled whipping cream at high speed, scraping bowl often, until stiff peaks form (3 to 4 minutes). Fold into lime mixture. Pour into prepared crust. Cover; refrigerate until firm (1½ to 3 hours). Loosen edge of cheesecake with knife; remove pan. Garnish top of cheesecake with sweetened whipped cream. If desired, garnish with lime slices.

Nutrition Information (1 serving)
• Calories 460 • Protein 8g • Carbohydrate 38g • Fat 32g
• Cholesterol 179mg • Sodium 321mg

To Prepare Refreshing Key Lime Cheesecake:

1. Fold into lime mixture.

2. Loosen edge of cheesecake with knife; remove pan.

Refreshing Key Lime Cheesecake

Fresh Berries Over Cookies & Cream (pictured)
Chocolate Caramel Truffle Torte

Fresh Berries Over Cookies & Cream

3 hours

Cookie
1 cup all-purpose flour
2 tablespoons sugar
⅓ cup butter *or* margarine
1 egg yolk
1 tablespoon water
1 tablespoon sugar

Custard Cream
½ cup sugar
1 cup milk

1 egg, slightly beaten
1 tablespoon cornstarch
1 teaspoon vanilla
1 cup whipping cream, whipped

Berry Sauce
1 (10 ounce) package frozen raspberries in syrup, thawed
1 tablespoon raspberry liqueur, optional
3 cups assorted berries

8 servings

Heat oven to 400°. In large bowl combine flour and 2 tablespoons sugar; cut in butter until crumbly. In small bowl beat egg yolk and water together; stir into flour mixture until moistened. Using floured hands, form into ball. On lightly floured surface roll dough to ¼-inch thickness. Using 3-inch round cookie or biscuit cutter cut dough into eight rounds, rerolling dough scraps as necessary. Place on cookie sheet. Sprinkle with 1 tablespoon sugar. Bake for 8 to 10 minutes. Cool. Meanwhile, in 2-quart saucepan combine all custard ingredients *except* vanilla and whipping cream. Cook over medium heat until mixture comes to a full boil. Boil 1 minute. Remove from heat; stir in vanilla. Cover surface with plastic wrap; refrigerate until cooled completely (2 hours). Fold whipped cream into custard. In large bowl mash raspberries in syrup; stir in liqueur. Fold in assorted berries. To serve, spread about ⅓ cup custard cream in center of each of 8 individual dessert plates; top each with cookie. Spoon about ⅓ cup berry sauce over each cookie.

Nutrition Information (1 serving)
• Calories 390 • Protein 5g • Carbohydrate 48g • Fat 21g
• Cholesterol 132mg • Sodium 117mg

Chocolate Caramel Truffle Torte

3 hours

Crust
1¾ cups very finely chopped pecans
⅔ cup sugar
¼ cup butter *or* margarine, melted

Filling
16 ounces high quality semi-sweet real chocolate, coarsely chopped
2 cups (1 pint) whipping cream

Caramel Sauce
¾ cup firmly packed brown sugar
¾ cup sugar
½ cup light corn syrup
⅓ cup butter *or* margarine
⅔ cup whipping cream

Garnish
1⅓ cups whipping cream, whipped

16 servings

Heat oven to 350°. In medium bowl stir together all crust ingredients. Firmly press on bottom and up sides of 12-inch tart pan with removable bottom. Place on cookie sheet. Bake for 15 to 18 minutes. Cool. In 2-quart saucepan cook 2 cups whipping cream over medium heat until just comes to a boil. Remove from heat; stir in chocolate until melted. Pour into cooled crust. Refrigerate until set (2 hours). Twenty minutes before serving, in 2-quart saucepan combine all caramel sauce ingredients *except* ⅔ cup whipping cream. Cook over medium heat, stirring occasionally, until mixture comes to a full boil. Cool 5 minutes; stir in ⅔ cup whipping cream. Garnish torte with whipped cream; serve with warm caramel sauce.

Nutrition Information (1 serving)
• Calories 630 • Protein 4g • Carbohydrate 56g • Fat 47g
• Cholesterol 100mg • Sodium 102mg

Orange Glazed Poppy Seed Torte   2 hours 30 minutes

Curls of orange peel add an elegant touch to this layered torte.

Cake
1½ cups cake flour*
 3 tablespoons poppy seed
¾ teaspoon baking powder
¼ teaspoon salt
1 cup sugar
1 cup butter *or* margarine, softened
1 tablespoon grated orange peel
1 teaspoon vanilla
3 eggs

Glaze
½ cup strained orange juice
 2 tablespoons sugar
1½ teaspoons cornstarch

Frosting
 3 cups powdered sugar
 1 (8 ounce) package cream cheese, softened
 1 tablespoon grated orange peel

2 tablespoons orange juice

Curls of orange peel

12 servings

Heat oven to 350°. In small bowl stir together flour, poppy seed, baking powder and salt; set aside. In large mixer bowl combine 1 cup sugar, butter, 1 tablespoon orange peel and vanilla. Beat at medium speed, scraping bowl often, until light and fluffy (3 to 5 minutes). Continue beating, adding eggs one at a time, until well mixed (2 to 3 minutes). Reduce speed to low; add flour mixture. Continue beating, scraping bowl often, until well blended (1 to 2 minutes). Spread into 2 greased and floured 8-inch round cake pans. Bake for 20 to 30 minutes or until wooden pick inserted in center comes out clean. Cool in pan 10 minutes. Remove from pan; cool completely. In 1-quart saucepan combine all glaze ingredients. Cook over medium heat, stirring constantly, until mixture thickens and comes to a full boil (3 to 4 minutes). Cool to room temperature (20 to 30 minutes). In small mixer bowl combine all frosting ingredients *except* 2 tablespoons orange juice and curls of orange peel. Beat at medium speed, scraping bowl often, until light and fluffy (2 to 3 minutes). Meanwhile, split each cake in half horizontally. On serving plate place 1 split cake half; sprinkle with *2 teaspoons* orange juice. Spread with about ½ cup frosting. Repeat with remaining layers. Do not sprinkle or frost top. Spread sides of cake with remaining frosting forming slight ridge at top of cake. Spread cooled glaze over top of cake; garnish with curls of orange peel. Store refrigerated.

*1⅓ cups all-purpose flour can be substituted for 1½ cups cake flour.

Nutrition Information (1 serving)
• Calories 450 • Protein 4g • Carbohydrate 55g • Fat 24g
• Cholesterol 116mg • Sodium 293mg

The 1890s were so much fun, Americans called them the Gay Nineties. Meals were lavish and society hostesses guarded menus for simple little 12-course meals that did not require the services of a French chef.

Orange Glazed Poppy Seed Torte

How To: Fold Napkins

Fancy fold napkins are an easy, quick way to give your table a dramatic new look.

Experiment with these ideas to determine the best fold for each occasion.

Some other ideas with napkins: roll up and tie with ribbons . . . tuck into wine glasses . . . fold in silverware . . . tuck in a fresh flower . . . use unusual fabrics such as bandana squares or linen dish towels.

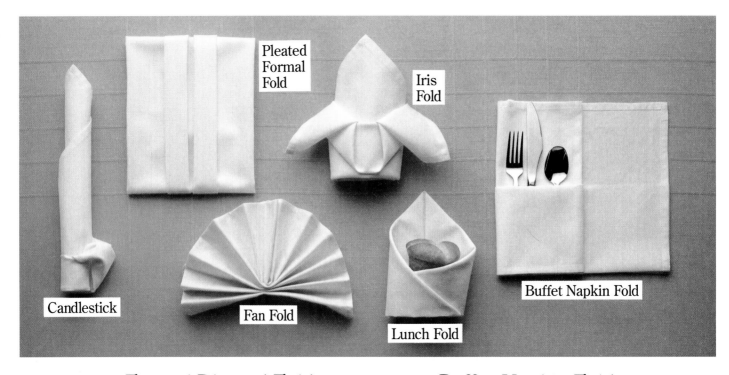

Pleated Formal Fold

Iris Fold

Candlestick

Fan Fold

Lunch Fold

Buffet Napkin Fold

Formal Pleated Fold

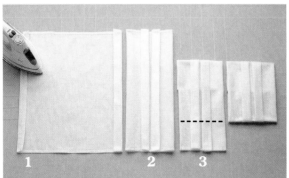

1. Turn opposite edges of square napkin in 1 inch; press with warm iron. Fold in again 1 inch.
2. Turn napkin over. Fold each side to center, leaving a slight gap.
3. Fold top and bottom under to meet in back.

Buffet Napkin Fold

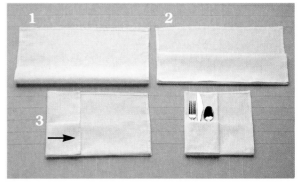

1. Place napkin, folded into halves, with the open edge at top and folded edge at bottom.
2. Fold the top edge down to folded edge at bottom; turn napkin over.
3. Fold left edge into center of napkin; fold left side over 2 more times to form a pocket for silverware.

Candlestick

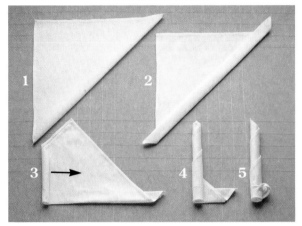

1. Fold napkin into triangle.
2. Turn up 1½ inches at bottom.
3. Turn napkin over to position shown in photo.
4. Roll up from bottom point.
5. Leave 1 inch at end and tuck into hem to secure. Stand candle up.

Lunch Fold

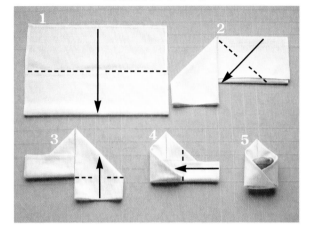

1. Fold napkin into 3 equal parts.
2. Fold down both left and right corners along dashed line.
3. Turn up bottom edge bringing lower corners together.
4. Tuck in corners to form a cylinder.
5. Use pocket to hold a dinner roll.

Fan Fold

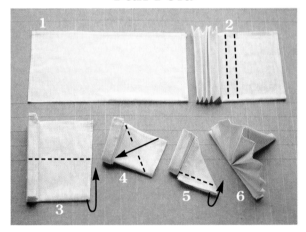

1. Fold napkin in half.
2. Make 1-inch accordion folds from bottom to a third of way from end.
3. Fold in half with pleats on the outside.
4. Fold all right corners into a triangle that overlaps 1 inch at side.
5. Fold 1-inch overlap under to make a base.
6. Stand napkin up on base and it will fan out.

Iris Fold

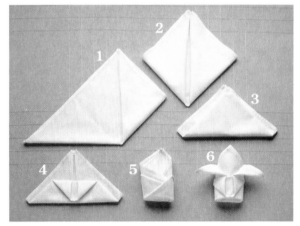

1. Fold napkin into triangle. Fold right corner up to center.
2. Fold left corners up to make diamond, leaving a slight gap.
3. Fold to make triangle, leaving a bit at the top.
4. Fold center tip down.
5. Tuck left corner into right one in back.
6. Stand napkin up and turn petals down.

CELEBRATIONS

In 1941, Congress passed laws making our two All-American celebrations, Thanksgiving and the Fourth of July, official holidays. But there are almost as many kinds of celebrations in this country as there are Americans.

Each state and community in America celebrates special times, from Mardi Gras in New Orleans to Winter Carnival in St. Paul, Cherry Blossom Days in Washington, D.C. to The Rose Parade in Pasadena. We do love a big party.

Within our families, we get together to celebrate homecomings and graduations, new jobs and retirements. Most families celebrate births and birthdays, and we all celebrate weddings, even in wartimes. In 1944, a young Midwestern girl wrote:

"Our next-door neighbor is home from the South Pacific and he's getting married Saturday. The whole neighborhood is saving ration points for dinner. There's going to be a big cake with real butter, real sugar and chocolate. And Dad gave him some of our gas coupons for their honeymoon."

Whatever the reason for celebrating, great food is a big part of the festivities, the fun of the day. The recipes on the next pages, like your celebrations, are very, very special indeed.

Holiday Feast

Start with pureed sweet potato soup and create a new kind of holiday magic with glazed crown roast of pork, apricot sausage stuffing, and all the delicious go-withs. The flaming finish is an old tradition . . . steamed plum pudding.

Glazed Crown Roast of Pork p.428   Apricot Sausage Stuffing p.448
Pureed Sweet Potato Soup p.418   Cranberry Orange Relish p.448
Crusty Hard Rolls p.416   Festive Vegetable Sauté p.442   Steamed Plum Pudding p.450

CELEBRATIONS MENU

Old-Fashioned Christmas

Orange eggnog opens a masterful British feast! Yorkshire pudding and garlic prime rib are great with mustard-sauced vegetables and a blue cheese pear salad. An old-fashioned sweet ending . . . marmalade mincemeat tart.

Garlic Prime Rib p.426   Vegetable Yorkshire Pudding p.416
Holiday Orange Eggnog p.411   Winter Vegetables With Mustard Sauce p.440
Pear & Walnut Salad With Blue Cheese p.433   Marmalade Mincemeat Tart p.479

Easter Celebration

A dinner to celebrate ... cheesecake tart followed by a tender leg of lamb surrounded by spring vegetables, served with hot rolls, spring fruit salad, and boiled new potatoes. A light, minted fruit trifle ends this truly memorable holiday meal!

Savory Cheesecake Tart p.406   Leg of Lamb With Garland of Spring Vegetables p.426
Boiled New Potatoes   Assorted Rolls
Fruits of the Season Salad p.434   Summertime Minted Trifle p.476

CELEBRATIONS
MENU

Spring Shower

Start with a sparkling punch cooled by a colorful fruit ice ring. Then offer shower guests a trio of springtime salads, spiced nuts and garlic toast. Phyllo pastry pie petals hold fresh berries and whipped cream for a beautiful dessert.

Sparkling Punch With Fruit Ice Ring p.411   Cardamom Spiced Nuts p.406
Refreshing Summer Salads With Garlic Toast p.437
Crisp Phyllo Petals With Berries p.464

Gouda Vegetable Spread (top)
Crackers Piped With Garlic Cream Cheese (bottom)

Gouda Vegetable Spread

3 hours

Gouda cheese and chopped vegetables flavor this unique spread served in its own shell.

1 (7 ounce) Gouda cheese round
1 (8 ounce) carton (1 cup) dairy sour cream
¼ teaspoon garlic powder
1 tablespoon Dijon-style mustard
½ teaspoon Worcestershire sauce
¼ cup shredded carrot

¼ cup finely chopped celery
2 tablespoons finely chopped red pepper

Crackers

2¼ cups

Cut thin slice wax from top of Gouda. Carefully scoop out cheese, leaving wax shell intact. Chop cheese into small (about ¼-inch) pieces. In medium bowl stir together sour cream, garlic powder, mustard and Worcestershire sauce. Stir in cheese, carrot, celery and red pepper.

Cover; refrigerate at least 2 hours to blend flavors. To serve, fill wax shell with spread; refill as necessary. Serve with crackers.

Nutrition Information (1 tablespoon dip)
• Calories 34 • Protein 2g • Carbohydrate 1g • Fat 3g
• Cholesterol 9mg • Sodium 62mg

Crackers Piped With Garlic Cream Cheese

60 minutes

Cream cheese is seasoned with garlic and pepper, then piped on a cracker with summer sausage.

1 (8 ounce) package cream cheese, softened
½ teaspoon poppy seed
½ teaspoon coarsely ground pepper
¼ teaspoon finely chopped fresh garlic

24 (⅛-inch) slices summer sausage*
24 (2-inch) specialty crackers
½ cup chopped fresh parsley
½ cup chopped pecans

2 dozen

In small mixer bowl beat cream cheese, poppy seed, pepper and garlic at medium speed, scraping bowl often, until light and fluffy (2 to 3 minutes). Refrigerate 30 minutes. Place 1 slice summer sausage on each cracker. Place cream cheese mixture in pastry bag with star tip. Pipe cream cheese mixture on summer sausage. Garnish each with chopped pecans and chopped parsley.

*12 slices prosciutto ham, halved, can be substituted for 24 (⅛-inch) slices summer sausage. Fold to fit crackers.

Nutrition Information (1 cracker)
• Calories 140 • Protein 5g • Carbohydrate 3g • Fat 12g
• Cholesterol 28mg • Sodium 350mg

 Labor Day is the traditional end of summer and was declared an official holiday by President Grover Cleveland to honor working Americans.

Savory Cheesecake Tart

2 hours

Serve this appetizer cheesecake tart warm with crackers and fresh fruit.

Pastry
1½ cups all-purpose flour
¼ cup butter *or* margarine
2 tablespoons shortening
2 tablespoons crumbled blue cheese
4 to 5 tablespoons ice water

Filling
1 (8 ounce) package cream cheese, softened
2 tablespoons crumbled blue cheese
¼ cup whipping cream

1 egg, slightly beaten
2 teaspoons chopped fresh rosemary leaves*
1 teaspoon chopped fresh thyme leaves**
¼ teaspoon coarsely ground pepper
1 teaspoon grated lemon peel
1 tablespoon lemon juice
1 medium ripe tomato, cut into 6 (¼-inch) slices
½ cup coarsely chopped walnuts

16 servings

Heat oven to 375°. In large bowl place flour; cut in butter, shortening and 2 tablespoons blue cheese until crumbly. With fork mix in water just until moistened; form into ball. On lightly floured surface roll out dough into 12-inch circle. Place in 10-inch tart pan, pressing firmly against bottom and sides of pan; cut away excess pastry. Prick with fork. Bake for 17 to 22 minutes or until very lightly browned. Meanwhile, in large mixer bowl combine cream cheese and 2 tablespoons blue cheese. Beat at medium speed, scraping bowl often, until creamy (1 to 2 minutes). Continue beating, gradually adding whipping cream and egg, until blended (1 to 2 minutes). Stir in

1 teaspoon rosemary and all remaining ingredients *except* tomato and walnuts. Spread into baked pastry. Arrange tomato slices on filling; sprinkle with walnuts and remaining rosemary. Bake for 20 to 25 minutes or until filling is set. Let stand 20 minutes; serve warm.

*½ teaspoon dried rosemary leaves, crushed, can be substituted for 2 teaspoons chopped fresh rosemary leaves.

**½ teaspoon dried thyme leaves can be substituted for 1 teaspoon chopped fresh thyme leaves.

Nutrition Information (1 serving)
• Calories 180 • Protein 4g • Carbohydrate 11g • Fat 14g
• Cholesterol 43mg • Sodium 107mg

Cardamom Spiced Nuts

45 minutes

*The delicate flavor of cardamom blends with caramelized sugar
to enhance the flavor of this nut assortment.*

¼ cup butter
1 cup salted cashews
1 cup salted peanuts
1 cup pecan halves

½ cup sugar
3 tablespoons sugar
1 teaspoon cardamom

3 cups (24 servings)

In 10-inch skillet melt butter; stir in nuts and ½ cup sugar. Cook over medium heat, stirring occasionally, until sugar is melted and nuts are browned and caramelized (8 to 12 minutes). Meanwhile, in large bowl combine 3 tablespoons sugar and cardamom. Stir in hot

caramelized nuts; toss to coat. Spread on waxed paper; cool completely. Break into clusters. Store in tightly covered container.

Nutrition Information (1 serving)
• Calories 140 • Protein 3g • Carbohydrate 10g • Fat 10g
• Cholesterol 5mg • Sodium 82mg

Savory Cheesecake Tart (pictured)
Cardamom Spiced Nuts

Old-Fashioned Soft Popcorn Balls   1 hour 30 minutes

These chewy popcorn balls will be a hit at Halloween or during the winter holidays.

20 cups popped popcorn
2 cups sugar
1½ cups water
½ cup light corn syrup
½ teaspoon salt
1 teaspoon vinegar

1 cup candy corn, small gumdrops, raisins
or salted peanuts

15 balls

In large bowl or roasting pan place popcorn; set aside. In 2-quart saucepan combine all remaining ingredients *except* candy. Cook over medium heat, stirring occasionally, until candy thermometer reaches 250°F or small amount of mixture dropped in ice water forms a hard ball (40 to 45 minutes). Remove from heat; pour over popcorn. Stir until all popcorn is coated. Gently stir in candy. Using buttered hands shape about 1 cup popcorn into a ball. Place on waxed paper. Repeat with remaining popcorn. Cool completely; wrap in waxed paper or plastic wrap.

Nutrition Information (1 serving)
• Calories 260 • Protein 3g • Carbohydrate 62g • Fat 1g
• Cholesterol 0mg • Sodium 108mg

Chocolate Drizzled Pecan Caramel Corn   2 hours

Pecans and chocolate make this caramel corn extra special.

20 cups popped popcorn
2 cups firmly packed brown sugar
1 cup butter
½ cup light corn syrup
½ teaspoon salt

½ teaspoon baking soda
2 cups pecan halves

6 ounces chocolate-flavored candy coating

18 cups

Heat oven to 200°. In roasting pan place popcorn; set aside. In 3-quart saucepan combine brown sugar, butter, corn syrup and salt. Cook over medium heat, stirring occasionally, until mixture comes to a full boil (12 to 14 minutes). Continue cooking, stirring occasionally, until candy thermometer reaches 238°F or small amount of mixture dropped into ice water forms a soft ball (4 to 6 minutes). Remove from heat; stir in baking soda. Pour over popcorn; sprinkle pecans over caramel mixture. Stir until all popcorn is coated. Bake 20 minutes; stir. Continue baking 25 minutes. Remove from oven; immediately place caramel corn on waxed paper. In 1-quart saucepan melt candy coating over low heat, stirring occasionally, until smooth (3 to 5 minutes). Drizzle chocolate over caramel corn, cool completely; break into pieces. Store in tightly covered container.

Nutrition Information (1 cup)
• Calories 400 • Protein 4g • Carbohydrate 51g • Fat 22g
• Cholesterol 28mg • Sodium 209mg

 In the South, as long as the Yule log burned, servants were freed from their duties. No wonder they usually wetted down the log before lighting it!

Old-Fashioned Soft Popcorn Balls (top)
Chocolate Drizzled Pecan Caramel Corn (bottom)

Sparkling Punch With Fruit Ice Ring (pictured)
Holiday Orange Eggnog

Sparkling Punch With Fruit Ice Ring 8 hours 30 minutes

Festive fruit, frozen in an ice ring, adds color to this sparkling punch.

2 cups crushed ice
4 small clusters seedless green grapes
4 (¼-inch) orange slices
1 cup fresh *or* frozen whole cranberries
3 (32 ounce) bottles cranberry juice cocktail, chilled

2 (25 ounce) bottles nonalcoholic sparkling white grape juice, chilled

24 servings

In 6-cup ring mold place crushed ice. Arrange fruit over ice. Pour 2 cups cranberry juice over fruit. Freeze ring at least 8 hours or overnight. To serve, dip mold into warm water for 10 to 15 seconds. Carefully unmold and place ring, fruit side up, in punch bowl. Add remaining cranberry and grape juice.

Nutrition Information (1 serving)
• Calories 110 • Protein 1g • Carbohydrate 27g • Fat 0g
• Cholesterol 0mg • Sodium 10mg

Holiday Orange Eggnog 20 minutes

Orange juice adds extra flavor to this celebration eggnog.

8 cups (2 quarts) prepared eggnog
2 cups milk
1 (12 ounce) can frozen orange juice concentrate, thawed
¼ cup sugar

4 cups (1 quart) vanilla ice cream

Nutmeg

16 servings

In large punch bowl stir together eggnog, milk, orange juice concentrate and sugar. Float scoops of ice cream in eggnog mixture. Sprinkle with nutmeg.

Nutrition Information (1 serving)
• Calories 300 • Protein 8g • Carbohydrate 38g • Fat 14g
• Cholesterol 92mg • Sodium 114mg

 In the 1700s, Christmas and New Year's Day were celebrated in the South with rich eggnog or syllabub, a milk and wine punch.

Festive Orange Nut Bread (top)
Glazed Chocolate Mini Loaves (bottom)

Festive Orange Nut Bread

1 hour 30 minutes

Make this flavorful bread in mini loaf pans for an easy hostess gift.

2 cups all-purpose flour
¾ cup sugar
½ cup milk
½ cup orange juice
1 egg, slightly beaten
2 tablespoons butter *or* margarine, melted

2 tablespoons grated orange peel
1 teaspoon baking powder
½ teaspoon baking soda
¼ teaspoon salt
½ cup chopped walnuts

1 loaf (12 servings)

Heat oven to 350°. In large bowl combine all ingredients *except* walnuts; stir just until moistened. Stir in walnuts. Pour into greased 8x4-inch loaf pan. Bake for 50 to 60 minutes or until wooden pick inserted in center comes out clean. Cool 10 minutes; remove from pan.

Tip: 4 greased 5½x3-inch mini loaf pans can be substituted for 8x4-inch loaf pan. Bake for 35 to 42 minutes.

Nutrition Information (1 serving)
• Calories 190 • Protein 4g • Carbohydrate 31g • Fat 6g
• Cholesterol 29mg • Sodium 149mg

Glazed Chocolate Mini Loaves

1 hour 20 minutes

Mini loaves of rich chocolate bread are glazed with additional chocolate.

Bread
⅔ cup firmly packed brown sugar
½ cup butter *or* margarine, softened
1 cup miniature semi-sweet real chocolate chips, melted
2 eggs
2½ cups all-purpose flour
1½ cups applesauce
1 teaspoon baking powder
1 teaspoon baking soda
2 teaspoons vanilla
½ cup miniature semi-sweet real chocolate chips

Glaze
½ cup miniature semi-sweet real chocolate chips
1 tablespoon butter *or* margarine
5 teaspoons water
½ cup powdered sugar
¼ teaspoon vanilla
  Dash salt

5 mini loaves (25 servings)

Heat oven to 350°. In large mixer bowl combine brown sugar and ½ cup butter. Beat at medium speed, scraping bowl often, until creamy (1 to 2 minutes). Add 1 cup melted chocolate chips and eggs; continue beating until well mixed (1 to 2 minutes). Add flour, applesauce, baking powder, baking soda and 2 teaspoons vanilla. Reduce speed to low; continue beating, scraping bowl often, until creamy (1 to 2 minutes). By hand, stir in ½ cup chocolate chips. Spoon batter into 5 greased 5½x3-inch mini loaf pans or aluminum foil pans. Bake for 35 to 42 minutes or until center crack is dry

when touched. Cool 10 minutes. Remove from pans; do not remove if using aluminum foil pans. (Bread can be frozen unfrosted. Remove from freezer; bring to room temperature before frosting.) Meanwhile, in 2-quart saucepan combine ½ cup chocolate chips, 1 tablespoon butter and water. Cook over low heat, stirring constantly, until melted and smooth. Remove from heat. Stir in powdered sugar, ¼ teaspoon vanilla and salt until smooth and creamy. Frost each loaf with glaze. Cool completely.

Nutrition Information (1 serving)
• Calories 190 • Protein 2g • Carbohydrate 27g • Fat 10g
• Cholesterol 34mg • Sodium 114mg

Festive Julekage

4 hours

This holiday bread is filled with candied fruit, raisins and almonds.

Bread
- 1 (¼ ounce) package active dry yeast
- ¼ cup warm water (105 to 115°F)
- 3¼ to 3¾ cups all-purpose flour
- ⅔ cup chopped mixed candied fruit
- ½ cup golden raisins
- ⅓ cup slivered almonds
- ¼ cup sugar
- ¾ cup milk
- ¼ cup butter *or* margarine, softened
- 1 egg
- ½ teaspoon salt
- ½ teaspoon cardamom
- ½ teaspoon grated lemon peel

  Butter *or* margarine

Glaze
- 1 cup powdered sugar
- 3 to 4 teaspoons milk

  Candied cherries

1 loaf (24 servings)

In large mixer bowl dissolve yeast in warm water. Add *2 cups* flour, candied fruit, raisins, almonds, sugar, milk, butter, egg, salt, cardamom and lemon peel. Beat at medium speed, scraping bowl often, until smooth (1 to 2 minutes). By hand, stir in enough remaining flour to make dough easy to handle. Turn dough onto lightly floured surface; knead until smooth and elastic (about 5 minutes). Place in greased bowl; turn greased side up. Cover; let rise in warm place until double in size (about 1½ hours). Dough is ready if indentation remains when touched. Punch down dough; shape into round loaf. Place in greased 9-inch round cake pan. Brush top of bread with melted butter. Cover; let rise until double in size (about 1 hour). *Heat oven to 350°.* Bake for 35 to 45 minutes or until golden brown. Remove from pan immediately. Cool completely. In small bowl stir together powdered sugar and 3 to 4 teaspoons milk to reach desired consistency. Spread over cooled bread. If desired, garnish with candied cherries.

Nutrition Information (1 serving)
- Calories 300 • Protein 6g • Carbohydrate 52g • Fat 7g
- Cholesterol 36mg • Sodium 178mg

Sparkling Cranberry Orange Muffins

45 minutes

Sugar sparkles on top of these special cranberry muffins.

- 1 cup chopped fresh cranberries
- 2 tablespoons sugar

- 2 cups all-purpose flour
- ⅓ cup sugar
- 2 teaspoons baking powder
- ½ teaspoon salt
- ½ cup butter *or* margarine
- ¾ cup orange juice
- 1 egg, slightly beaten

- ¼ cup butter *or* margarine, melted
- ¼ cup sugar

1 dozen

Heat oven to 400°. In small bowl combine cranberries and 2 tablespoons sugar; set aside. In large bowl stir together flour, ⅓ cup sugar, baking powder and salt. Cut in ½ cup butter until mixture is crumbly. Stir in orange juice and egg just until moistened; fold in cranberry mixture. Spoon batter into greased muffin pan. Bake for 20 to 25 minutes or until golden brown. Cool 5 minutes; remove from pan. Dip top of each muffin in ¼ cup melted butter, then in ¼ cup sugar. Serve warm.

Nutrition Information (1 muffin)
- Calories 240 • Protein 3g • Carbohydrate 31g • Fat 12g
- Cholesterol 54mg • Sodium 265mg

Festive Julekage (pictured)
Sparkling Cranberry Orange Muffins

Vegetable Yorkshire Pudding

1 hour 15 minutes

Serve this updated version of an English favorite with roasted prime rib.

½ cup water
2 cups broccoli flowerets

1¾ cups all-purpose flour
1 cup milk
1 cup cold water
4 eggs

1½ teaspoons seasoned salt
¼ teaspoon pepper

⅓ cup butter *or* beef drippings
½ cup thin carrot peel

8 servings

Heat oven to 400°. In 2-quart saucepan bring ½ cup water to a full boil. Add broccoli. Cover; cook over medium heat until crisply tender (2 to 3 minutes). Rinse with cold water. Drain; set aside. In large mixer bowl combine flour, milk, 1 cup water, eggs, salt and pepper. Beat at low speed, scraping bowl often, just until smooth (1 to 2 minutes). Meanwhile, in 13x9-inch baking pan melt butter in oven (3 to 5 minutes). Pour batter into hot baking pan. Sprinkle with broccoli and carrot. Bake for 35 to 45 minutes or until edges are dark golden brown and center is set. Serve immediately.

Tip: Make thin carrot peel by pulling vegetable peeler across length of carrot.

Tip: Batter can be made 1 hour ahead. Cover; refrigerate. Stir well before pouring into hot pan.

Tip: For a traditional Yorkshire pudding, omit broccoli and carrots.

Nutrition Information (1 serving)
• Calories 230 • Protein 8g • Carbohydrate 25g • Fat 11g
• Cholesterol 160mg • Sodium 431mg

Crusty Hard Rolls

3 hours

These rolls have a crusty outside with a chewy texture inside.

2½ cups warm water (105 to 115°F)
2 (¼ ounce) packages active dry yeast
1 tablespoon butter *or* margarine, softened
5 to 6 cups all-purpose flour

2 teaspoons salt
1 egg white
1 tablespoon water

1½ dozen

In medium bowl stir together 2½ cups warm water and yeast until dissolved; stir in butter until melted. In large bowl stir together *3 cups* flour and salt. Stir in yeast mixture. Stir in remaining flour, ½ cup at a time, until soft dough forms. Turn dough onto lightly floured surface; knead until smooth and elastic (about 8 minutes). Place in greased bowl; turn greased side up. Cover; let rise in warm place until double in size (about 1 hour). Dough is ready if indentation remains when touched. Punch down dough; divide in half. With floured hands divide each half into 9 pieces. Shape into 4x2-inch individual rolls; place on greased cookie sheets. With serrated knife slit center of each roll. Cover; let rise until double in size (about 30 minutes). *Heat oven to 400°.* Bake for 15 to 20 minutes or until lightly browned. Meanwhile, in small bowl stir together egg white and 1 tablespoon water. Remove rolls from oven; brush tops with egg white mixture. Return to oven; continue baking for 5 minutes or until golden brown. Remove from cookie sheets; cool on wire racks.

Nutrition Information (1 roll)
• Calories 140 • Protein 4g • Carbohydrate 27g • Fat 1g
• Cholesterol 2mg • Sodium 250mg

Vegetable Yorkshire Pudding (pictured)
Crusty Hard Rolls

Yuletide Oyster Stew With Buttery Croutons   45 minutes

Croutons
2 cups (3 to 4 slices) cubed ½-inch bread
¼ cup butter *or* margarine
2 tablespoons freshly grated Parmesan
   cheese

Stew
½ cup butter *or* margarine
1 cup (2 medium) shredded carrots
¼ cup chopped onion

1 pound fresh shucked oysters, undrained
¼ cup all-purpose flour
2 cups milk
2 cups (1 pint) whipping cream
½ teaspoon salt
¼ teaspoon pepper

   Fresh cracked pepper

6 servings

Heat oven to 400°. In small bowl toss together all crouton ingredients. Place on cookie sheet. Bake for 5 to 7 minutes or until browned; set aside. In 3-quart saucepan melt ½ cup butter. Add carrots, onion and undrained oysters. Cook over medium heat, stirring occasionally, until edges of oysters curl and vegetables are crisply tender (8 to 10 minutes). With slotted spoon remove oysters and vegetables; set aside. Gradually whisk flour into liquid in pan until smooth. Continue cooking until bubbly (1 to 3 minutes). Gradually stir in milk, cream, salt and ¼ teaspoon pepper. Continue cooking, stirring occasionally, until mixture comes to a full boil (10 to 12 minutes). Add oyster and vegetable mixture. Continue cooking until heated through (2 to 3 minutes). To serve, in individual bowls ladle soup; sprinkle with croutons and cracked pepper.

Nutrition Information (1 serving)
• Calories 450 • Protein 13g • Carbohydrate 23g • Fat 57g
• Cholesterol 221mg • Sodium 689mg

Pureed Sweet Potato Soup   60 minutes

4 cups water
2 pounds (4 medium) sweet potatoes *or*
   yams, peeled, cut into 1-inch pieces
¼ cup butter *or* margarine
1 cup quartered, sliced ¼-inch leek
1 (14½ ounce) can chicken broth
1¾ cups whipping cream

1 teaspoon chopped fresh thyme leaves*
½ teaspoon coarsely ground pepper
¼ teaspoon salt

   Leek greens, chopped
¼ cup whipping cream

8 servings

In 3-quart saucepan bring water to a full boil; add sweet potatoes. Continue cooking over medium heat until sweet potatoes are fork tender (10 to 15 minutes). Drain; place in food processor bowl. In same saucepan melt butter until sizzling; stir in leek. Cook over medium heat, stirring occasionally, until leek is tender (2 to 3 minutes). Meanwhile, process sweet potatoes until smooth (1 to 2 minutes). Continue processing, gradually adding chicken broth through tube, until well blended (30 to 60 seconds). Add leek mixture; continue processing 30 seconds. Pour back into saucepan; stir in 1¾ cups whipping cream, thyme, pepper and salt. Cook over medium heat, stirring occasionally, until heated through (10 to 15 minutes). To serve, in individual bowls ladle soup; with spoon swirl about 2 teaspoons whipping cream on surface of each serving of soup. Garnish with leek greens.

*¼ teaspoon dried thyme leaves can be substituted for 1 teaspoon chopped fresh thyme leaves.

Nutrition Information (1 serving)
• Calories 400 • Protein 5g • Carbohydrate 33g • Fat 29g
• Cholesterol 97mg • Sodium 331mg

Yuletide Oyster Stew With Buttery Croutons (pictured)
Pureed Sweet Potato Soup

Classic Bouillabaisse

2 hours

Fish and shellfish simmer in a rich, flavorful tomato broth.

Broth

1 cup (1 medium) chopped onion
1 cup (1 bulb) sliced ¼-inch fresh fennel,
   separated into rings
½ cup chopped fresh fennel weed
¼ cup cornmeal
1 (8 ounce) bottle (1 cup) clam juice
2 (14½ ounce) cans chicken broth
1 (28 ounce) can Italian-style tomatoes
1 (6 ounce) can tomato paste
2 bay leaves
1 tablespoon dried basil leaves
½ teaspoon salt
½ teaspoon coarsely ground pepper

2 tablespoons olive *or* vegetable oil
2 tablespoons red wine vinegar
1 teaspoon finely chopped fresh garlic

Seafood

1 pound (about 24 medium) fresh *or* frozen
   raw shrimp
1 pound swordfish steaks, cut into 1½-inch
   pieces
1 pound red snapper fillets, skinned, cut into
   1½-inch pieces
1 pound (about 16) mussels, in shell, scrubbed

8 servings

In Dutch oven stir together all broth ingredients. Cook over medium heat, stirring occasionally, until slightly thickened and flavors are blended (1 hour 15 minutes to 1 hour 30 minutes). Meanwhile, peel and devein shrimp, leaving tails intact; set aside. (If shrimp is frozen, do not thaw; peel under running cold water.) Add swordfish, red snapper and mussels to broth mixture. Continue cooking, stirring occasionally, until seafood flakes with a fork and mussels open (10 to 15 minutes). Stir in shrimp; continue cooking until shrimp turn pink (4 to 6 minutes). Remove bay leaves. Discard any mussels that do not open.

Nutrition Information (1 serving)
• Calories 350 • Protein 46g • Carbohydrate 19g • Fat 10g
• Cholesterol 146mg • Sodium 1235mg

In Charleston, Passover is celebrated in the traditional way, but there are often milk, meat and shrimp dishes served.

Rosemary Orange Turkey With Corn Bread Stuffing

6 hours

A traditional stuffed turkey is served with an extra-rich orange cream sauce.

Stuffing

6 cups (½ loaf) torn bread pieces
4 cups crumbled corn bread*
1 cup (2 stalks) sliced ¼-inch celery
1 cup (2 medium) coarsely chopped onions
½ cup chopped fresh parsley
½ cup orange juice
½ cup butter *or* margarine, melted
1 (14½ ounce) can chicken broth
1 egg, slightly beaten
2 teaspoons dried thyme leaves
1 teaspoon dried rosemary leaves, crushed
1 teaspoon dried sage leaves, rubbed
½ teaspoon coarsely ground pepper
¼ teaspoon salt
1 medium orange, sliced ¼-inch, quartered

Turkey

18 to 22 pound fresh *or* frozen turkey, thawed
2 tablespoons olive *or* vegetable oil
2 teaspoons grated orange peel
1 teaspoon finely chopped fresh garlic
1 teaspoon salt
1 teaspoon coarsely ground pepper
1 teaspoon dried rosemary leaves, crushed
1 teaspoon dried thyme leaves

Sauce

½ cup orange juice
2 teaspoons grated orange peel
1 cup whipping cream

16 servings

In large bowl stir together all stuffing ingredients except orange quarters. Stir in orange quarters. Rinse turkey thoroughly in cold water; drain well. Stuff neck and body cavities lightly; reserve remaining stuffing. *Heat oven to 325°.* Place turkey, breast side up, in shallow roasting pan. In small bowl stir together oil, 2 teaspoons orange peel and garlic; brush on turkey. In small bowl combine all remaining turkey ingredients; sprinkle over turkey. Bake as directed on turkey package directions or approximately 4½ to 6 hours for 18 to 22 pound stuffed turkey. Meat thermometer should reach 180°F in thigh. Meanwhile, in greased 2-quart casserole place remaining stuffing. Bake, basting stuffing occasionally with pan juices, until heated through (45 to 60 minutes). Remove roasted turkey to serving platter; *reserve pan juices.* Skim off fat from pan juices. In 2-quart saucepan cook 2 cups reserved pan juices, ½ cup orange juice and 2 teaspoons orange peel over medium heat until slightly reduced and flavors are intensified (10 to 15 minutes). Do not boil. Gradually stir in whipping cream. (Sauce will be thin.) Serve with roasted turkey and stuffing.

*9-inch square baking pan corn bread will make 4 cups crumbled corn bread or 1 (8 ounce) package crumbly style corn bread stuffing can be substituted for 4 cups crumbled corn bread.

Nutrition Information (1 serving)
• Calories 700 • Protein 79g • Carbohydrate 25g • Fat 30g
• Cholesterol 268mg • Sodium 847mg

422

Rosemary Orange Turkey With Corn Bread Stuffing

Cranberry Stuffed Holiday Goose

3 hours

Stuffing
1 cup fresh *or* frozen cranberries
¼ cup sugar
½ cup orange juice
3 cups dried bread cubes
1 cup (2 stalks) sliced ½-inch celery
⅓ cup butter *or* margarine, melted
1 medium onion, chopped
1 teaspoon salt

¼ teaspoon pepper
⅛ teaspoon allspice
8 to 12 pound goose

Sauce
1 (10 ounce) package frozen cranberry-orange sauce
¼ cup orange juice

6 servings

In 2-quart saucepan stir together cranberries, sugar and ½ cup orange juice. Cook over medium high heat, stirring occasionally, until cranberries pop and sugar dissolves (5 to 6 minutes); cool 15 minutes. Meanwhile, in large bowl stir together all remaining stuffing ingredients *except* goose. Stir in cranberry mixture. *Heat oven to 350°.* Stuff goose with stuffing. Place goose on rack in roasting pan. Cover; bake 45 minutes. Remove excess fat from baking pan. Continue baking, uncovered, basting occasionally and removing excess fat

from baking pan, for 1½ to 2 hours or until meat thermometer reaches 180° F. Meanwhile, in 2-quart saucepan stir together sauce ingredients. Cook over medium high heat, stirring occasionally, until melted (2 to 3 minutes). Baste goose with sauce during last 30 minutes of baking time. Loosely cover goose with aluminum foil if browning too quickly. Heat remaining sauce; serve over goose.

Nutrition Information (1 serving)
• Calories 770 • Protein 59g • Carbohydrate 52g • Fat 36g
• Cholesterol 212mg • Sodium 782mg

Mushroom Stuffed Chicken Breasts

45 minutes

¼ cup butter *or* margarine
3 cups (2 medium) leeks, cut into thin julienne strips
2 cups (8 ounces) sliced ¼-inch fresh mushrooms
4 whole boneless chicken breasts, skinned, halved, pounded to flatten

8 (¼-inch) slices prosciutto ham *or* thinly sliced ham
½ teaspoon finely chopped fresh garlic
Salt and pepper

8 servings

Heat oven to 350°. In 10-inch skillet melt *2 tablespoons* butter until sizzling; add leeks and mushrooms. Cook over medium high heat, stirring occasionally, until vegetables are tender (4 to 5 minutes). Lay 1 slice prosciutto on each chicken breast. Place about 2 tablespoons vegetable mixture in center of each chicken breast. *Reserve remaining vegetable mixture.* Roll up chicken breasts; secure with wooden picks. In same skillet melt remaining 2 tablespoons butter and garlic until sizzling. Place

4 rolled chicken breasts in skillet; sprinkle with salt and pepper. Cook over medium high heat, turning once, until browned (3 to 5 minutes); place in 13x9-inch baking pan. Repeat with remaining chicken breasts. Remove wooden picks. Bake for 15 to 20 minutes or until fork tender. Sprinkle with reserved vegetable mixture. Continue baking for 4 to 5 minutes or until vegetables are heated through.

Nutrition Information (1 serving)
• Calories 240 • Protein 31g • Carbohydrate 6g • Fat 10g
• Cholesterol 95mg • Sodium 333mg

Cranberry Stuffed Holiday Goose (pictured)
Mushroom Stuffed Chicken Breasts

Leg of Lamb With
Garland of Spring Vegetables

2 hours 30 minutes

Lamb

3 tablespoons white wine vinegar
2 tablespoons olive *or* vegetable oil
2 tablespoons chopped fresh mint
2 tablespoons chopped fresh watercress
1 tablespoon chopped fresh dill weed
½ teaspoon salt
½ teaspoon coarsely ground pepper
1 teaspoon finely chopped fresh garlic
4 to 5 pound leg of lamb, sirloin half
1 cup dry white wine *or* water

Vegetables

1½ cups water
1 (12 ounce) package baby carrots, peeled
1 pound (24) asparagus spears, trimmed
8 ounces fresh pea pods, washed, remove tips and strings
2 tablespoons butter *or* margarine, melted
2 tablespoons chopped fresh mint
1 tablespoon chopped fresh watercress
1 tablespoon chopped fresh dill weed

10 servings

Heat oven to 325°. In small bowl stir together vinegar, oil, 2 tablespoons mint, 2 tablespoons watercress, 1 tablespoon dill weed, ½ teaspoon salt, pepper and garlic. Place lamb in shallow roasting pan. Brush oil mixture over lamb. Bake 1 hour. Pour ½ *cup* wine over lamb; baste with pan juices. Continue baking 30 minutes. Pour remaining ½ cup wine over lamb; baste with pan juices. Continue baking for 30 to 45 minutes or until meat thermometer reaches 160° F (Medium). Meanwhile, in 10-inch skillet bring water to a full boil; add carrots. Cook over medium heat until crisply tender (6 to 8 minutes). Add asparagus; continue cooking until crisply tender (2 to 3 minutes). Add pea pods; continue cooking until crisply tender (1 minute). Drain; rinse vegetables with cold water. Place lamb on serving platter; let stand 10 to 15 minutes. Place drained vegetables in pan with pan juices; pour melted butter over vegetables. Sprinkle with 2 tablespoons mint, 1 tablespoon watercress, 1 tablespoon dill weed and ¼ teaspoon salt; spoon pan juices over vegetables. Bake for 10 to 15 minutes or until heated through. Serve vegetables around lamb.

Nutrition Information (1 serving)
• Calories 260 • Protein 28g • Carbohydrate 8g • Fat 11g
• Cholesterol 95mg • Sodium 210mg

Garlic Prime Rib

2 hours

4 to 5 pound rolled beef prime rib roast
6 cloves garlic, each cut lengthwise into thirds
4 medium carrots, cut into 1-inch pieces
2 medium onions, each cut into 8 wedges
½ cup chopped fresh parsley

1 cup water
2 bay leaves
2 teaspoons chopped fresh thyme leaves
1 teaspoon coarsely ground pepper
½ teaspoon salt

10 servings

Heat oven to 450°. In 13x9-inch baking pan place roast; with tip of sharp knife, cut 18 slits through fat and into meat just large enough for garlic thirds. Insert garlic third into each slit. Place carrots, onions, parsley and bay leaves around roast; pour water over vegetables. In small bowl stir together thyme, pepper and salt; sprinkle mixture over roast. Bake 30 minutes to brown outside of roast. *Reduce temperature to 325°.* Bake for 1 hour to 1 hour 15 minutes or until meat thermometer reaches 130° F. Let stand 10 minutes or until meat thermometer reaches 140° F.

Nutrition Information (1 serving)
• Calories 250 • Protein 26g • Carbohydrate 5g • Fat 13g
• Cholesterol 76mg • Sodium 188mg

Leg of Lamb With Garland of Spring Vegetables (pictured)
Garlic Prime Rib

Baked Ham With Sweet Cherry Sauce

3 hours

A spiced cherry sauce is served over slices of baked ham.

5 to 7 pound fully cooked smoked bone-in
half ham

Cherry Sauce
2 (16 ounce) cans pitted dark sweet red
cherries, drained, *reserve liquid*
Water
1 cup sugar

2 tablespoons cornstarch
¼ teaspoon salt
½ cup butter *or* margarine
2 cinnamon sticks
12 whole cloves
2 tablespoons lemon juice

14 servings

Heat oven to 325°. Place ham, fat side up, on rack in roasting pan. Bake for 1 hour 30 minutes to 2 hours 30 minutes (18 to 24 minutes per pound) or until meat thermometer reaches 130°F. Meanwhile, if necessary, in 2-cup measure add water to reserved cherry liquid to equal 1½ cups. In 2-quart saucepan combine sugar, cornstarch and salt. Add 1½ cups cherry liquid. Cook over medium heat, stirring occasionally, until sugar is dissolved (1 to 2 minutes). Stir in butter, cinnamon sticks, cloves and lemon juice. Continue cooking, stirring constantly, until mixture thickens and comes to a full boil (4 to 6 minutes). Boil 1 minute. Remove cinnamon sticks and cloves. Stir in cherries. Remove

ham from oven when thermometer reaches 130°F. If desired, cut fat surface in a diamond pattern to help cherry sauce penetrate; brush some cherry sauce over surface. Return ham to oven. Continue baking, brushing with cherry sauce every 10 minutes, until meat thermometer reaches 140°F (20 to 30 minutes). Serve with remaining cherry sauce.

Tip: ¼ teaspoon *each* ground cinnamon and ground cloves can be substituted for 2 cinnamon sticks and 12 whole cloves.

Nutrition Information (1 serving)
• Calories 290 • Protein 21g • Carbohydrate 27g • Fat 11g
• Cholesterol 62mg • Sodium 1170mg

Glazed Crown Roast of Pork

3 hours

Impress your family and friends with this magnificent crown roast.

½ cup apricot preserves
½ cup lemon juice
2 tablespoons finely chopped fresh shallots
or onion
2 teaspoons dried thyme leaves
1 teaspoon coarsely ground pepper

½ teaspoon salt
1 teaspoon finely chopped fresh garlic

5 to 6 pound crown roast of pork

8 servings

Heat oven to 325°. In medium bowl combine all ingredients *except* roast. Line shallow roasting pan with aluminum foil. Place roast, bone end up, in roasting pan. Brush apricot mixture over roast. Bake, basting with apricot mixture every 20 minutes, for 1 hour 40 minutes to 2 hours 30 minutes or until meat thermometer reaches 160°F (Medium). Let roast stand 15 minutes before carving.

Nutrition Information (1 serving)
• Calories 360 • Protein 35g • Carbohydrate 15g • Fat 17g
• Cholesterol 98mg • Sodium 193mg

Pork	Internal Cooking Temperature
Medium	160°F
Well	170°F

Elegant Julienne Salad

60 minutes

Julienne strips of beets, carrots and cucumber are served with a dill dressing.

2 medium (1 cup) beets, peeled, cut into
   very thin julienne strips
2 medium (1 cup) carrots, cut into very
   thin julienne strips
1 medium (1 cup) cucumber, halved, peeled,
   sliced ¼-inch
¼ cup olive *or* vegetable oil
¼ cup lime juice

½ teaspoon coarsely ground pepper
¼ teaspoon salt
1 tablespoon chopped fresh dill*
2 teaspoons grated lime peel
12 leaves (2 heads) Boston Bibb lettuce
18 leaves (2 heads) Belgian endive
½ cup fresh watercress

6 servings

Place beets, carrots and cucumbers in separate medium bowls. In small bowl stir together oil, lime juice, pepper, salt, dill and lime peel. Pour 2 tablespoons dressing over each vegetable. On individual salad plates arrange 2 leaves Bibb lettuce and 3 leaves Belgian endive. Place

about 2 tablespoons of each vegetable on lettuce leaves; garnish with watercress.

*1 teaspoon dried dill weed can be substituted for 1 tablespoon chopped fresh dill.

Nutrition Information (1 serving)
• Calories 110 • Protein 1g • Carbohydrate 7g • Fat 9g
• Cholesterol 0mg • Sodium 120mg

Asparagus Salad With Toasted Sesame Dressing

1 hour 30 minutes

Asparagus spears, new potatoes and fresh green beans make a unique salad.

Vegetables
2 cups water
½ teaspoon salt
8 small new red potatoes, halved
½ pound fresh green beans, trimmed
1 pound (24) asparagus spears, trimmed

Dressing
⅓ cup olive *or* vegetable oil
¼ cup red wine vinegar
½ teaspoon salt
½ teaspoon coarsely ground pepper
2 tablespoons country-style Dijon mustard

Salad
4 cups torn Romaine lettuce
2 teaspoons sesame seed, toasted

8 servings

In 10-inch skillet place water and ½ teaspoon salt; bring to a full boil. Add potatoes; cook over medium high heat until fork tender (13 to 18 minutes). Remove potatoes with slotted spoon. Add beans; cook until crisply tender (9 to 14 minutes). Remove beans with slotted spoon. Add asparagus spears; cook until crisply tender (2 to 3 minutes). Drain. Keep vegetables separate; place in ice water to chill. Drain. Meanwhile,

in small bowl stir together all dressing ingredients. Place potatoes in medium bowl. Pour 2 tablespoons dressing over potatoes; toss to coat. On serving platter place lettuce; arrange potatoes, beans and asparagus on lettuce. Drizzle with ¼ cup dressing; sprinkle with toasted sesame seed. Serve with remaining dressing.

Nutrition Information (1 serving)
• Calories 160 • Protein 4g • Carbohydrate 16g • Fat 10g
• Cholesterol 0mg • Sodium 385mg

Elegant Julienne Salad (pictured)
Asparagus Salad With Toasted Sesame Dressing

Pear & Walnut Salad With Blue Cheese (top)
Salad of Spinach, Apples & Pecans (bottom)

Pear & Walnut Salad With Blue Cheese   20 minutes

Select ripe pears to make this salad tossed with walnuts and blue cheese.

2 tablespoons olive *or* vegetable oil
1 tablespoon red wine vinegar
1 teaspoon Dijon-style mustard
¼ teaspoon coarsely ground pepper
2 medium ripe pears, sliced ¼-inch

2 tablespoons crumbled blue cheese
2 tablespoons coarsely chopped walnuts
2 tablespoons chopped fresh parsley

4 servings

In medium bowl stir together all ingredients *except* pears, blue cheese, walnuts and parsley. Add remaining ingredients; toss to coat.

Nutrition Information (1 serving)
• Calories 150 • Protein 2g • Carbohydrate 14g • Fat 11g
• Cholesterol 3mg • Sodium 97mg

Salad of Spinach, Apples & Pecans   20 minutes

A sweet honey mustard dressing is poured over this salad of torn spinach and apples.

Dressing
3 tablespoons olive *or* vegetable oil
1 tablespoon country-style Dijon mustard
1 tablespoon honey
1 tablespoon lemon juice

Salad
4 cups torn fresh spinach leaves
1 medium red apple, cored, sliced ⅛-inch
½ cup pecan halves

6 servings

In small bowl whisk together all dressing ingredients. In large bowl toss together all salad ingredients. Pour dressing over salad; toss to coat. Serve immediately.

Nutrition Information (1 serving)
• Calories 160 • Protein 2g • Carbohydrate 10g • Fat 13g
• Cholesterol 0mg • Sodium 103mg

Pioneer gatherings were well attended, because they helped ease the long-distance loneliness of the prairie. There was always a Strawberry Festival and a Fourth of July picnic.

Fruits of the Season Salad

30 minutes

A delicately spiced ginger orange dressing is tossed with salad greens.

Dressing
¼ cup orange juice
2 tablespoons olive *or* vegetable oil
1 tablespoon red wine vinegar
1 tablespoon honey
1 teaspoon grated fresh gingerroot*

Salad
4 cups torn romaine lettuce
3 tangerines, tangelos *or* oranges, pared, sectioned, drained
2 kiwi, peeled, sliced ⅛-inch
1 cup raspberries, strawberries, sliced *or* pomegranate seeds

8 servings

In small bowl stir together all dressing ingredients. In large bowl place torn lettuce. Pour 2 tablespoons dressing over lettuce; toss to coat. On individual salad plates place tossed lettuce. Arrange tangerine sections and kiwi on lettuce. Arrange raspberries, sliced strawberries or pomegranate seeds on salads. Drizzle with remaining dressing.

*¼ teaspoon ground ginger can be substituted for 1 teaspoon fresh gingerroot.

Nutrition Information (1 serving)
• Calories 81 • Protein 1g • Carbohydrate 12g • Fat 4g
• Cholesterol 0mg • Sodium 4mg

In New Mexico, Christmas is celebrated both with Midnight Mass and the dance rituals of the Indian winter-solstice festival. On Christmas Day, the buffalo dance is often performed, lasting about 4 hours.

Fruits of the Season Salad

Refreshing Summer Salads With Garlic Toast   3 hours

Cool, crisp salads of melon, shrimp and cucumber make a beautiful luncheon plate.

Shrimp Salad
⅛ teaspoon coarsely ground pepper
   Pinch of salt
3 tablespoons mayonnaise
¼ cup sliced ¼-inch green onions
3 hard-cooked eggs, chopped
1 pound cooked deveined shrimp, each cut
   in half
1 tablespoon chopped fresh dill*

Cucumber Salad
⅛ teaspoon salt
⅛ teaspoon coarsely ground pepper
2 tablespoons dairy sour cream
1 teaspoon grated lemon peel
1 teaspoon lemon juice
2 cups (2 medium) coarsely chopped, seeded
   cucumber
¼ cup thinly sliced red onion, cut in half
1 tablespoon chopped fresh mint leaves

Melon Salad
2 tablespoons plain yogurt
1 teaspoon grated lime peel
1 tablespoon lime juice
½ teaspoon grated fresh gingerroot**
2½ cups cantaloupe balls
½ cup coarsely chopped fresh watercress

Garlic Toast
16 slices cocktail rye bread
16 slices cocktail pumpernickel bread
⅓ cup butter *or* margarine, melted
1 teaspoon finely chopped fresh garlic
½ cup freshly grated Parmesan cheese

8 servings
(4 cups shrimp salad, 2 cups cucumber salad
and 2 cups melon salad)

In medium bowl stir together ⅛ teaspoon pepper, pinch of salt and mayonnaise. Stir in green onions, eggs, shrimp and dill weed. Cover; refrigerate at least 1 hour. In medium bowl stir together ⅛ teaspoon salt, ⅛ teaspoon pepper, sour cream, lemon peel and lemon juice. Stir in cucumber, red onion and mint. Cover; refrigerate at least 1 hour. In medium bowl stir together yogurt, lime peel, lime juice and gingerroot. Stir in cantaloupe and watercress. Cover; refrigerate at least 1 hour. *Heat oven to 400°.* Meanwhile, with 2-inch heart cookie cutter, cut heart shapes out of rye and pumpernickel bread. In small bowl combine melted butter and garlic. Brush on both sides of hearts. Place in 15x10x1-inch jelly roll pan. Bake 5 minutes. Turn hearts over; sprinkle with Parmesan cheese. Continue baking for 4 to 5 minutes or until toasted. Serve salads with garlic toast.

*1 teaspoon dried dill weed can be substituted for 1 tablespoon chopped fresh dill.

**⅛ teaspoon ground ginger can be substituted for ½ teaspoon grated fresh gingerroot.

Nutrition Information (1 serving)
• Calories 310 • Protein 20g • Carbohydrate 21g • Fat 16g
• Cholesterol 243mg • Sodium 584mg

The arrival of a steamboat on the St. Paul levee was a good reason for a celebration. It took boats 14 days to get up from St. Louis and the first steamboat in the spring was cause for a real party.

Green Beans With Orange

40 minutes

When fresh green beans are in season, try this recipe with its hint of orange.

1½ cups water
⅛ teaspoon salt
 1 pound fresh green beans, trimmed
 3 tablespoons butter *or* margarine

 2 tablespoons slivered almonds
 1 tablespoon orange peel zest *or* strips

4 servings

In 10-inch skillet bring water and salt to a full boil. Add beans. Cook over medium heat, stirring occasionally, until beans are crisply tender (15 to 20 minutes). Drain; set aside. In same skillet melt butter. Add slivered almonds; cook over medium heat, stirring constantly, until golden brown (3 to 4 minutes). Add beans and orange peel. Cover; cook over medium heat, stirring occasionally, until heated through (5 to 6 minutes).

Microwave Directions: *Reduce 1½ cups water to ½ cup.* In 3-quart casserole combine water, salt and beans. Cover; microwave on HIGH, stirring after half the time, until beans are crisply tender (8 to 10 minutes). Drain. In 1-cup measure melt butter on HIGH (30 to 40 seconds). Stir in almonds. Microwave on HIGH, stirring after half the time, until almonds are golden brown (1½ to 2½ minutes). Stir in orange peel; pour over beans.

Nutrition Information (1 serving)
• Calories 140 • Protein 3g • Carbohydrate 10g • Fat 11g
• Cholesterol 23mg • Sodium 159mg

Pistachio Sprinkled Brussels Sprouts

30 minutes

Pistachio nuts are a great flavor complement to Brussels sprouts.

 1 pound Brussels sprouts, trimmed
 3 tablespoons butter *or* margarine
¼ teaspoon pepper

¼ cup (2 ounces) coarsely chopped salted pistachio nuts *or* cashews

6 servings

In 2-quart saucepan place Brussels sprouts; add enough water to cover. Bring to a full boil. Cook over medium heat until Brussels sprouts are crisply tender (12 to 15 minutes); drain. Return to pan; add butter and pepper. Cook over medium heat, stirring occasionally, until butter is melted (1 to 2 minutes). Sprinkle with pistachio nuts.

Tip: 2 (10 ounce) packages frozen Brussels sprouts can be substituted for fresh Brussels sprouts. Cook according to package directions.

Microwave Directions: In 2-quart casserole place Brussels sprouts and ¼ cup water. Cover; microwave on HIGH until crisply tender (3 to 4 minutes). Drain. Return to casserole; stir in butter and pepper until butter is melted. Sprinkle with pistachio nuts.

Nutrition Information (1 serving)
• Calories 120 • Protein 3g • Carbohydrate 8g • Fat 9g
• Cholesterol 16mg • Sodium 78mg

Green Beans With Orange (pictured)
Pistachio Sprinkled Brussels Sprouts

Almond-Glazed Sweet Potatoes

1 hour 15 minutes

Almond liqueur adds a smooth, rich flavor to glazed sweet potatoes.

4 (2 pounds) large sweet potatoes, peeled,
    quartered
½ cup firmly packed brown sugar
½ cup butter *or* margarine
¼ cup almond flavored liqueur*
⅛ teaspoon salt

8 servings

In 3-quart saucepan place potatoes. Add enough water to cover; bring to a full boil. Cook over medium heat, stirring occasionally, until potatoes are fork tender (20 to 25 minutes); drain. Set aside; keep warm. In 10-inch skillet place brown sugar and butter. Cook over medium heat until butter is melted and glaze is formed (4 to 6 minutes). Stir in almond flavored liqueur and salt. Continue cooking until mixture comes to a full boil and glaze is slightly thickened (1 to 2 minutes). Gently stir in sweet potatoes. Continue cooking, stirring occasionally, until heated through (5 to 8 minutes).

*2 tablespoons water and ½ teaspoon almond extract can be substituted for ¼ cup almond flavored liqueur.

Nutrition Information (1 serving)
• Calories 300 • Protein 2g • Carbohydrate 48g • Fat 12g
• Cholesterol 31mg • Sodium 170mg

Winter Vegetables With Mustard Sauce

40 minutes

A country-style mustard sauce flavors this hearty vegetable dish.

2 cups (6 medium) cubed 1-inch new red
    potatoes
1 cup (1 medium) sliced ¼-inch carrot
2 cups water
1 pound Brussels sprouts, trimmed*
⅓ cup butter *or* margarine, melted
4 teaspoons country-style Dijon mustard
4 teaspoons vinegar
½ teaspoon salt
¼ teaspoon pepper
2 to 3 drops hot pepper sauce

6 servings

In 3-quart saucepan combine potatoes, carrots and water; bring to a full boil. Cover; cook over medium heat 8 minutes. Add Brussels sprouts. Continue cooking, stirring occasionally, until vegetables are crisply tender (10 to 12 minutes). Drain. Meanwhile, in small bowl stir together all remaining ingredients; pour over vegetables. Toss to coat.

*2 (10 ounce) packages frozen Brussels sprouts can be substituted for 1 pound Brussels sprouts.

Microwave Directions: *Reduce 2 cups water to ¼ cup.* In 2½-quart casserole combine potatoes, carrots and ¼ cup water. Cover; microwave on HIGH 4 minutes. Stir in Brussels sprouts. Cover; microwave on HIGH, stirring after half the time, until vegetables are crisply tender (10 to 14 minutes). Meanwhile, in small bowl stir together all remaining ingredients; pour over vegetables. Toss to coat.

Nutrition Information (1 serving)
• Calories 250 • Protein 6g • Carbohydrate 36g • Fat 11g
• Cholesterol 28mg • Sodium 416mg

Almond-Glazed Sweet Potatoes (top)
Winter Vegetables With Mustard Sauce (bottom)

Festive Vegetable Sauté

45 minutes

These crisp, colorful vegetables are the perfect accompaniment for roasted meat.

5 cups water
2 cups (4 medium) 3x¼x¼-inch strips carrots
2 cups (4 medium) peeled, cut lengthwise into 3x½x½-inch strips parsnips
½ pound fresh green beans, trimmed
1 medium red pepper, cut into ¼-inch strips

1 yellow summer squash, cut into 3x¼x¼-inch strips
3 tablespoons butter *or* margarine
¼ teaspoon salt
¼ teaspoon coarsely ground pepper

8 servings

In 3-quart saucepan bring water to a full boil. To blanch vegetables add one kind at a time to boiling water; cook 1 minute for all vegetables *except* 7 minutes for green beans. Drain; set aside. In 10-inch skillet melt butter until sizzling; stir in salt, pepper and blanched vegetables. Cook over medium high heat, stirring occasionally, until vegetables are crisply tender (10 to 12 minutes).

Tip: Vegetables can be blanched up to 1 day ahead; store refrigerated.

Microwave Directions: *Reduce 5 cups water to ½ cup.* In 3-quart casserole place beans and water. Cover; microwave on HIGH until beans begin to cook (3 to 5 minutes). Stir in carrots and parsnips. Cover; microwave on HIGH, stirring after half the time, until vegetables are crisply tender (9 to 12 minutes). Stir in red pepper and squash. Cover; microwave on HIGH until squash is crisply tender (2 to 3 minutes). Stir in butter, salt and pepper.

Nutrition Information (1 serving)
• Calories 100 • Protein 2g • Carbohydrate 16g • Fat 5g
• Cholesterol 12mg • Sodium 129mg

Garlic Roasted Summer Vegetables

45 minutes

Zucchini and yellow squash are sliced the entire length of the vegetable for an attractive presentation.

2 medium zucchini, cut lengthwise into ⅛-inch slices
2 medium yellow summer squash, cut lengthwise into ⅛-inch slices
1 cup thinly sliced red onion, separated into rings
1 medium red pepper, cut into ⅛-inch rings

3 tablespoons butter *or* margarine, melted
1½ teaspoons chopped fresh rosemary leaves*
⅛ teaspoon salt
⅛ teaspoon coarsely ground pepper
1 teaspoon finely chopped fresh garlic

6 servings

Heat oven to 375°. In 13x9-inch baking pan alternately place zucchini and yellow summer squash slices side by side. Arrange red onion and red pepper on top of zucchini slices. In small bowl stir together all remaining ingredients; pour butter mixture over vegetables. Bake, basting with butter every 5 minutes, for 15 to 20 minutes or until vegetables are crisply tender.

*½ teaspoon dried rosemary leaves, crushed, can be substituted for 1½ teaspoons chopped fresh rosemary leaves.

Nutrition Information (1 serving)
• Calories 80 • Protein 2g • Carbohydrate 6g • Fat 6g
• Cholesterol 16mg • Sodium 107mg

Festive Vegetable Sauté (top)
Garlic Roasted Summer Vegetables (bottom)

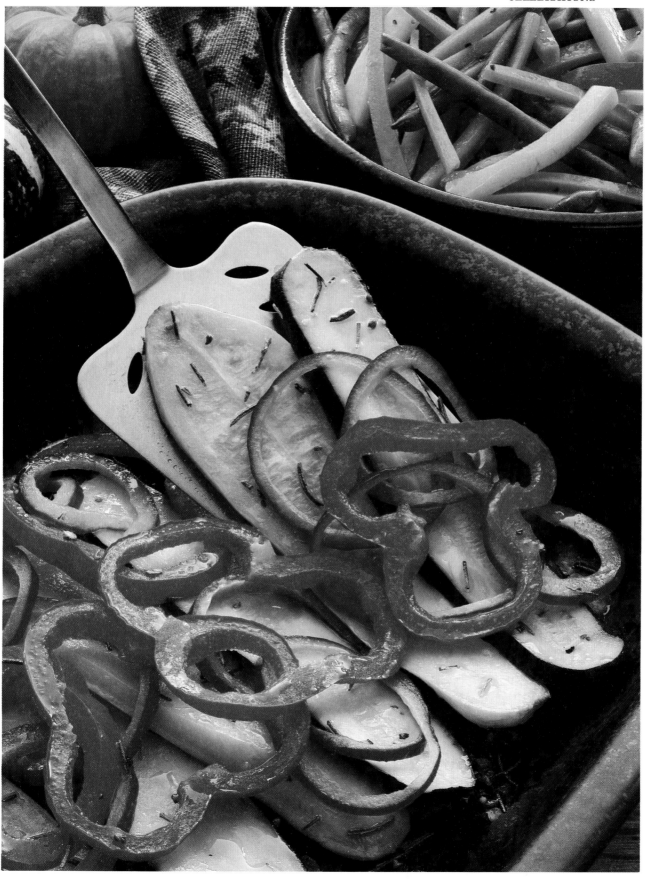

Gingered Acorn Squash (pictured)
Carrots in Butter Wine Sauce

Gingered Acorn Squash

60 minutes

Fresh gingerroot and maple syrup add a unique flavor to acorn squash.

2 medium acorn squash, quartered,
  remove seeds
  Water

¼ cup butter *or* margarine
2 tablespoons maple syrup
1 teaspoon grated fresh gingerroot*
¼ cup flaked coconut, toasted

8 servings

Heat oven to 375°. In 13x9-inch baking pan place squash, cut side up. Add water to pan to a depth of ¼ inch. Cover with aluminum foil; bake for 35 to 45 minutes or until fork tender. Place squash on serving platter. Meanwhile, in 1-quart saucepan combine butter, maple syrup and gingerroot. Cook over low heat, stirring occasionally, until butter is melted (1 to 2 minutes). Pour hot syrup mixture into each quartered squash; sprinkle with toasted coconut.

*½ teaspoon ground ginger can be substituted for 1 teaspoon grated fresh gingerroot.

Microwave Directions: In 13x9-inch baking dish place squash, cut side down. Add ¼ cup water. Cover with plastic wrap; microwave on HIGH 8 minutes. Turn squash, cut side up. Cover with plastic wrap; microwave on HIGH until squash is fork tender (8 to 12 minutes). Let stand 5 minutes. Meanwhile, in 2-cup measure combine butter, maple syrup and gingerroot. Microwave on HIGH, stirring after half the time, until butter is melted (1 to 2 minutes). Stir to mix well. Place squash on serving platter. Pour hot syrup mixture into each quartered squash; sprinkle with toasted coconut.

Nutrition Information (1 serving)
• Calories 120 • Protein 1g • Carbohydrate 16g • Fat 7g
• Cholesterol 16mg • Sodium 63mg

Carrots in Butter Wine Sauce

40 minutes

Raisins add a touch of sweetness to this carrot and onion mixture.

3 tablespoons butter *or* margarine
3 cups (6 medium) julienne strip carrots
3 small onions, each cut into eight wedges
¼ cup raisins

⅓ cup dry white wine *or* apple juice
½ teaspoon dried thyme leaves
2 bay leaves

6 servings

In 10-inch skillet melt butter; add carrots and onions. Cook over medium heat, stirring occasionally, 4 minutes. Add all remaining ingredients. Cover; reduce heat to low. Continue cooking, stirring occasionally, until vegetables are crisply tender (15 to 20 minutes). Remove bay leaves.

Microwave Directions: In 2½-quart casserole melt butter on HIGH (50 to 60 seconds). Stir in all remaining ingredients. Cover; microwave on HIGH, stirring after half the time, until vegetables are crisply tender (8 to 12 minutes). Let stand 2 minutes.

Nutrition Information (1 serving)
• Calories 120 • Protein 1g • Carbohydrate 14g • Fat 6g
• Cholesterol 16mg • Sodium 86mg

Herb Wild Rice

2 hours

Serve this wild rice stuffed inside game or alongside roasted meats.

1½ cups uncooked wild rice
2 cups water
1 (14½ ounce) can chicken broth
1 cup (2 medium) sliced ¼-inch carrots
1 cup (2 stalks) sliced ¼-inch celery
1 cup (2 medium) chopped onions
1½ teaspoons dried thyme leaves

1 teaspoon salt
½ teaspoon coarsely ground pepper
2 bay leaves
½ cup whipping cream
½ cup chopped fresh parsley

8 servings

Rinse wild rice. In 3-quart saucepan combine wild rice and all remaining ingredients *except* whipping cream and parsley. Cook over high heat until mixture comes to a full boil (6 to 10 minutes). Reduce heat to medium low. Cover; continue cooking until rice is tender (45 to 50 minutes). (Do not drain off excess liquid.) Stir in whipping cream. Continue cooking until heated through (2 to 3 minutes). Remove bay leaves. Stir in parsley.

Tip: ½ cup sliced almonds, chopped filberts or hazelnuts can be sprinkled over rice just before serving.

Nutrition Information (1 serving)
• Calories 180 • Protein 6g • Carbohydrate 27g • Fat 6g
• Cholesterol 20mg • Sodium 458mg

Spinach Rice Pilaf

50 minutes

Fresh spinach adds flavor and color to rice pilaf.

2 tablespoons butter *or* margarine
1 cup uncooked long grain rice
½ cup chopped onion
½ cup dry white wine *or* water
1 (14½ ounce) can chicken broth

¼ teaspoon dried thyme leaves
¼ teaspoon coarsely ground pepper
10 ounces spinach leaves, washed

6 servings

In Dutch oven melt butter; add rice and onion. Cook over medium heat, stirring constantly, until rice is golden (8 to 10 minutes). Slowly add wine, chicken broth, thyme and pepper. Continue cooking until mixture comes to a full boil (4 to 8 minutes); reduce heat to low. Cover; continue cooking until rice is tender (15 to 20 minutes). Stir in spinach; continue cooking, stirring occasionally, until spinach is wilted (2 to 3 minutes).

Microwave Directions: In 3-quart casserole melt butter on HIGH (40 to 50 seconds).

Stir in rice and onion. Microwave on HIGH until rice is golden (4 to 6 minutes). Stir in wine, chicken broth, thyme and pepper. Cover with plastic wrap; microwave on HIGH until mixture comes to a full boil (6 to 9 minutes). Reduce power to MEDIUM (50% power). Microwave, stirring after half the time and stirring in ¼ cup additional wine if needed, until rice is tender (15 to 20 minutes). Stir in spinach. Microwave on HIGH, stirring after half the time, until spinach is wilted (3 to 5 minutes).

Nutrition Information (1 serving)
• Calories 190 • Protein 5g • Carbohydrate 28g • Fat 5g
• Cholesterol 10mg • Sodium 297mg

Herb Wild Rice (pictured)
Spinach Rice Pilaf

Cranberry Orange Relish

2 hours 30 minutes

This traditional relish, with the crunch of pecans, is the perfect accompaniment to turkey.

1 orange
4 cups fresh *or* frozen cranberries, thawed
⅔ cup sugar

¼ cup chopped pecans
2 tablespoons chopped crystallized ginger

24 servings

Peel orange; reserve fruit for other use. Cut up peel into 1-inch pieces. In food processor bowl finely grind orange peel (about 15 seconds). Add half of cranberries; process slightly. Add remaining cranberries and process until coarsely chopped. Place in large bowl; stir in pecans and ginger. Cover; refrigerate until flavors are blended (at least 2 hours).

Tip: A blender or grinder can be used in place of food processor.

Nutrition Information (1 serving)
• Calories 44 • Protein 0g • Carbohydrate 9g • Fat 1g
• Cholesterol 0mg • Sodium 1mg

Apricot Sausage Stuffing

1 hour 30 minutes

Present this stuffing in the center of a crown roast or stuffed in turkey or game hen.

1 cup (2 medium) chopped onions
1 cup (2 stalks) chopped celery
1 pound bulk sweet Italian sausage
1 teaspoon finely chopped fresh garlic
1 cup chopped fresh parsley
1 (14½ ounce) can chicken broth
1 (6 ounce) package (1 cup) dried apricots, coarsely chopped

1 pound loaf white bread, torn, dried
1 egg, slightly beaten
1 teaspoon dried thyme leaves
1 teaspoon dried sage leaves, rubbed
½ teaspoon salt
½ teaspoon coarsely ground pepper
1 tablespoon grated lemon peel

8 servings

Heat oven to 325°. In 10-inch skillet cook onions, celery, sausage and garlic over medium high heat, stirring occasionally, until browned (8 to 10 minutes); drain off fat. In large bowl stir together sausage mixture and all remaining ingredients. Spoon stuffing into 3-quart casserole. Bake for 55 to 60 minutes or until heated through.

Microwave Directions: In 3-quart casserole combine onions, celery, sausage and garlic. Cover; microwave on HIGH, stirring after half the time, until sausage is no longer pink (9 to 12 minutes); drain off fat. In same casserole combine sausage mixture and all remaining ingredients. Cover with waxed paper. Microwave on HIGH, stirring after half the time, until heated through (11 to 15 minutes).

Nutrition Information (1 serving)
• Calories 320 • Protein 13g • Carbohydrate 46g • Fat 10g
• Cholesterol 57mg • Sodium 857mg

Cranberries, a Thanksgiving tradition, were actually named craneberries by the Pilgrims because their white stems and blossoms resembled the neck and head of a crane.

Cranberry Orange Relish (top)
Apricot Sausage Stuffing (bottom)

Steamed Plum Pudding

3 hours 30 minutes

This moist fruit-studded steamed pudding is crowned with a rum hard sauce.

Plum Pudding
¾ cup firmly packed brown sugar
½ cup butter *or* margarine, softened
3 eggs
¾ cup dry bread crumbs
½ cup all-purpose flour
1 teaspoon cinnamon
½ teaspoon baking soda
½ teaspoon nutmeg
¼ teaspoon salt
¼ teaspoon cloves
1 cup (2 medium) shredded carrots

1 cup golden raisins
½ cup dried currants
1 (30 ounce) can purple plums, drained, pitted, chopped
1 (8 ounce) package chopped dates
1 tablespoon grated orange peel

Hard Sauce
½ cup butter *or* margarine, softened
3 cups powdered sugar
¼ cup dark rum *or* orange juice

12 servings

In large mixer bowl combine brown sugar, ½ cup butter and eggs. Beat at medium speed, scraping bowl often, until well mixed (1 to 2 minutes). In small bowl stir together bread crumbs, flour, cinnamon, baking soda, nutmeg, salt and cloves. Beat at low speed, gradually adding flour mixture, until smooth and creamy (1 to 2 minutes). By hand, fold in all remaining plum pudding ingredients. Pour into well-greased 6 to 9-cup metal mold or casserole. Place double thickness of greased waxed paper on top, then cover with double thickness of aluminum foil. Tie tightly with heavy string. Trim paper and aluminum foil leaving 1-inch overhang. Place rack in Dutch oven or roasting pan; add boiling water to 2-inch level. Place mold on rack. Bring water to a full boil; cover with lid. Reduce heat to low; continue cooking over simmering water for 2½ hours or until center springs back when touched lightly. Remove from Dutch oven; let stand 3 to 5 minutes. Remove covers and unmold. Meanwhile, in small mixer bowl combine

all hard sauce ingredients. Beat at medium speed, scraping bowl often, until smooth and creamy (2 to 3 minutes). Serve with steamed pudding. If desired, place hard sauce in pastry bag; pipe on and around steamed pudding.

Tip: Plum pudding is best when made ahead. Cool 1 hour; wrap tightly. Store refrigerated for 3 to 5 days. To reheat, wrap plum pudding in aluminum foil; bake at 350° for 30 to 40 minutes or until heated through.

Tip: To flame pudding, heat ¼ cup brandy in 1-quart long-handled saucepan. Being very careful, use a long-handled fireplace match to ignite brandy; pour over warm pudding. (The flavor of the alcohol will remain after the alcohol burns off.)

Nutrition Information (1 serving)
• Calories 500 • Protein 4g • Carbohydrate 84g • Fat 17g
• Cholesterol 110mg • Sodium 322mg

1870 Christmas: "When the door opened, we marched in and clear around the tree, taking in the beauty of the candles and the tree festooned with strings of cranberries and popcorn and gay colored ribbons. There was the delightful odor of scorching cedar . . . Father would keep walking around and around the tree smothering every smoking stem and keeping the candles burning safely."

Steamed Plum Pudding

Chocolate Mint Layered Torte

4 hours

This elegant four-layer torte can be made with either chocolate-mint or mocha.

Cake

- 2 cups all-purpose flour
- 1½ cups sugar
- ½ cup unsweetened cocoa
- ½ cup butter *or* margarine, softened
- 1 cup water
- 3 eggs
- 1¼ teaspoons baking powder
- 1 teaspoon baking soda
- 1 teaspoon vanilla

Filling

- 2 cups (1 pint) whipping cream
- 1½ teaspoons mint extract
- 2 tablespoons sugar

Glaze

- 2 tablespoons butter *or* margarine
- ½ cup semi-sweet real chocolate chips
- 2 tablespoons light corn syrup
- ¼ teaspoon mint extract

16 servings

Heat oven to 350°. Grease 2 (9-inch) round cake pans. Line each pan with 9-inch round piece of waxed paper; grease waxed paper. Set aside. In large mixer bowl combine all cake ingredients. Beat at medium speed, scraping bowl often, until smooth (2 to 3 minutes). Pour batter into prepared pans. Bake for 20 to 25 minutes or until wooden pick inserted in center comes out clean. Cool 10 minutes; remove from pans. Remove waxed paper; cool completely. In chilled small mixer bowl combine chilled whipping cream and 1½ teaspoons mint extract. Beat at high speed, scraping bowl often, until soft peaks form. Gradually add sugar; continue beating until stiff peaks form (1 to 2 minutes). *Reserve ½ cup filling* for garnish; refrigerate. Using serrated knife, cut each cake

layer horizontally in half. To assemble torte, place one split cake layer on serving plate; spread with ⅓ of filling. Repeat with remaining cake layers and filling, ending with cake layer. Refrigerate torte at least 1 hour. In 1-quart saucepan melt 2 tablespoons butter. Stir in chocolate chips and corn syrup. Cook over low heat, stirring constantly, until chocolate chips are melted (2 to 3 minutes). Remove from heat; stir in ¼ teaspoon mint extract. Spread glaze over top of torte, allowing glaze to drizzle down sides. Garnish with reserved ½ cup filling. Refrigerate until ready to serve.

Nutrition Information (1 serving)
- Calories 480 • Protein 6g • Carbohydrate 52g • Fat 29g
- Cholesterol 150mg • Sodium 287mg

Variation

Chocolate Mocha Torte: Omit 1½ teaspoons mint extract in filling and ¼ teaspoon mint extract in glaze. Add 3 tablespoons coffee flavored liqueur to filling and 1 teaspoon coffee flavored liqueur to glaze.

The Pennsylvania Dutch had a custom of serving seven sweets and seven sours at every holiday meal.

Ice Cream Filled Lace Cookie Cups

2 hours

Make these cookie cups a day ahead; just before serving
fill with ice cream and drizzle with chocolate for an elegant dessert.

Cups
½ cup light corn syrup
½ cup butter
1 cup all-purpose flour
½ cup firmly packed brown sugar
½ cup slivered almonds, finely chopped

Favorite ice cream
Chocolate syrup

2 dozen

Heat oven to 300°. In 2-quart saucepan bring corn syrup to a full boil (2 to 3 minutes). Add butter. Cook over low heat, stirring occasionally, until butter is melted (3 to 5 minutes). Remove from heat; stir in flour, brown sugar and almonds. Drop by tablespoonfuls 4 inches apart onto greased cookie sheets. (Bake only 4 cookies per cookie sheet.) Bake for 11 to 15 minutes or until cookies bubble all over. *Let cool on cookie sheets 1 minute.* Working quickly, remove and shape cookies over inverted small custard cups to form cups. Cool completely;

remove from custard cups. Just before serving, fill each cup with large scoop of ice cream. If desired, drizzle with chocolate syrup.

Tip: Make desired number of cups. With remaining dough, bake as directed above *except* shape into cones or leave flat. Serve as cookies.

Nutrition Information (1 cookie)
• Calories 240 • Protein 4g • Carbohydrate 30g • Fat 12g
• Cholesterol 40mg • Sodium 104mg

To Prepare Ice Cream Filled Lace Cookie Cups:

1. Bake for 11 to 15 minutes or until cookies bubble all over. *Let cool on cookie sheets 1 minute.*

2. Working quickly, remove and shape cookies over inverted small custard cups to form cups.

3. Cool completely; remove from custard cups.

On the frontier, a wedding was attended by the whole neighborhood and was the only celebration that wasn't work related, like barn raising or crop reaping.

Ice Cream Filled Lace Cookie Cups

Date Baklava

2 hours

This traditional Greek pastry takes on a new twist with the addition of dates.

Filling
2 cups finely chopped walnuts
⅓ cup sugar
2 (8 ounce) packages chopped dates, finely chopped

1½ to 1¾ cups butter *or* margarine, melted
1 pound frozen phyllo dough, thawed, trimmed to 15x10-inch

Syrup
½ cup sugar
¾ cup orange juice
½ cup honey

Glaze
¾ cup powdered sugar
1 tablespoon milk

4 dozen

Heat oven to 325°. In large bowl stir together all filling ingredients; set aside. Brush 15x10x1-inch jelly roll pan with butter. Layer 8 phyllo sheets, lightly brushing each with butter, in prepared pan. Sprinkle with 1¾ cups filling mixture. Top with 4 more phyllo sheets, lightly brushing each with butter. Repeat layering filling mixture and 4 phyllo sheets twice. Top with remaining 8 phyllo sheets, lightly brushing each with butter. Cut diagonally through first phyllo layer to make 4 dozen diamond shapes. Bake for 60 to 70 minutes or until golden brown. Meanwhile, in 2-quart saucepan combine all syrup ingredients. Cook over medium heat, stirring frequently, until mixture comes to a full boil (4 to 5 minutes). Reduce heat to low; simmer until slightly thickened (30 to 40 minutes). Pour syrup over warm dessert. In small bowl stir together glaze ingredients until smooth. Drizzle over warm pastry.

Nutrition Information (1 baklava)
• Calories 170 • Protein 2g • Carbohydrate 22g • Fat 9g
• Cholesterol 16mg • Sodium 125mg

To Prepare Date Baklava:

1. Layer 8 phyllo sheets, lightly brushing each with butter, in prepared pan. Sprinkle with 1¾ cups filling mixture. Top with 4 more phyllo sheets, lightly brushing each with butter.

2. Cut diagonally through first phyllo layer to make 4 dozen diamond shapes.

3. Pour syrup over warm dessert.

Date Baklava

Frosted Jack-O-Lanterns (pictured)
Frothy Orange Smoothy

Frosted Jack-O-Lanterns

3 hours

Serve ice cream in these special Halloween orange jack-o-lanterns.

4 large oranges
2 to 3 cups chocolate ice cream

4 green gum drops

4 servings

If necessary, cut off thin slice of peel from bottom of oranges so they sit level. For each jack-o-lantern cut a slice off top of orange; reserve. Cut around top edge of orange and membrane. Keeping shell intact remove orange sections (save and use for juice). Starting ¼ inch below top cut edge, cut out eyes, nose and mouth from orange shell. Fill orange shell with chocolate ice cream, mounding slightly. Replace top of orange. Use green gumdrop for stem. Freeze 2 hours or until ready to serve.

Nutrition Information (1 serving)
• Calories 140 • Protein 2g • Carbohydrate 17g • Fat 7g
• Cholesterol 30mg • Sodium 59mg

Frothy Orange Smoothy

15 minutes

This frothy orange juice will be a sure winner with kids of all ages.

½ cup sugar
1 cup milk
1 cup orange juice*
1 (6 ounce) can frozen orange juice
    concentrate

12 ice cubes
1 teaspoon vanilla

6 servings

In 5-cup blender container combine all ingredients. Blend at High speed until ice dissolves and mixture is frothy (30 to 60 seconds).

*1 cup water can be substituted for 1 cup orange juice.

Nutrition Information (1 serving)
• Calories 160 • Protein 2g • Carbohydrate 37g • Fat 1g
• Cholesterol 3mg • Sodium 20mg

 The first successful harvest in the Plymouth Colony was in 1621 and was celebrated with a thanksgiving feast that lasted an entire week.

Rocky Road Fudge Pops

5 hours

Frozen pudding pops are made extra special with the addition of peanuts, chocolate chips and marshmallow creme.

1 (3⅝ ounce) package chocolate flavored pudding and pie filling*
2 cups milk
1 cup marshmallow creme
⅓ cup chopped salted peanuts
¼ cup miniature semi-sweet chocolate chips

8 (5 ounce) wax coated paper cups
8 flat wooden sticks

8 servings

In 2-quart saucepan combine pudding and pie filling and milk. Cook over low heat, stirring constantly, until mixture thickens (4 to 6 minutes). Cool to room temperature. Fold in marshmallow creme to create marbled appearance. In small bowl stir together peanuts and chocolate chips. Place about 1 tablespoon peanut mixture in each paper cup. Add 1 tablespoon pudding to each cup; stir well. Divide remaining pudding into cups; insert flat wooden stick in each. Freeze until firm (about 4 hours). To serve, peel cups from frozen pops.

*1 (4⅛ ounce) package instant chocolate flavored pudding and pie filling can be substituted for 1 (3⅝ ounce) package chocolate flavored pudding and pie filling. Prepare according to package directions. Let stand 2 minutes. Fold in marshmallow creme to create marbled appearance. Continue as directed above.

Tip: ¼ cup chopped semi-sweet chocolate chips can be substituted for ¼ cup miniature semi-sweet chocolate chips.

Microwave Directions: In 4-cup measure combine pudding mix and pie filling and milk. Microwave on HIGH, stirring every 3 minutes, until mixture thickens (6 to 8 minutes). Cool to room temperature. Continue as directed above.

Nutrition Information (1 serving)
• Calories 180 • Protein 4g • Carbohydrate 30g • Fat 6g
• Cholesterol 5mg • Sodium 150mg

To Prepare Pops:

1. Fold in marshmallow creme to create marbled appearance.

2. Divide remaining pudding into cups; insert flat wooden stick in each. Freeze until firm (about 4 hours).

3. To serve, peel cups from frozen pops.

Rocky Road Fudge Pops

Chocolate-Coated Ice Cream Bon Bons

5 hours

Garnish this chocolate-coated strawberry ice cream with fresh strawberries and whipped cream.

2 cups strawberry ice cream*
¼ cup butter
1 (6 ounce) package (1 cup) semi-sweet
   real chocolate chips

3 tablespoons milk
   Sweetened whipped cream
   Fresh strawberries

6 servings

Line cookie sheet with aluminum foil; place in freezer 10 minutes. Scoop 6 (⅓ cup) ice cream balls; place on cookie sheet. Freeze until very firm (2 to 3 hours). In 1-quart saucepan melt butter and chocolate chips over low heat, stirring occasionally, until smooth (4 to 5 minutes). Stir in milk; cool to room temperature. Working quickly with one ice cream ball at a time, lift frozen ice cream ball from cookie sheet with large spoon. Hold over chocolate; spoon chocolate over ice cream ball evenly coating all sides. Carefully slide ice cream ball from spoon back onto cookie sheet. Return to freezer until ready to serve (at least 1 hour). If ice cream becomes too soft while coating, return to freezer. On individual dessert plates place ice cream bon bons; garnish with whipped cream and strawberries.

*2 cups your favorite flavor ice cream can be substituted for 2 cups strawberry ice cream.

Tip: Chocolate-Coated Ice Cream Bon Bons can be prepared up to 7 days in advance. Cover; store frozen.

Nutrition Information (1 serving)
• Calories 310 • Protein 3g • Carbohydrate 27g • Fat 23g
• Cholesterol 41mg • Sodium 122mg

To Prepare Bon Bons:

1. Working quickly with one ice cream ball at a time, lift frozen ice cream ball from cookie sheet with large spoon. Hold over chocolate; spoon chocolate over ice cream ball evenly coating all sides.

2. Carefully slide ice cream ball from spoon back onto cookie sheet.

Chocolate-Coated Ice Cream Bon Bons

Crisp Phyllo Petals With Berries   1 hour 30 minutes

The pastry of this luscious pie is made from phyllo dough, the filling from sweetened whipped cream blended with summer's berries.

Crust
6 sheets frozen phyllo dough, thawed
¼ cup butter *or* margarine, melted
2 tablespoons powdered sugar

Filling
1 cup whipping cream
¼ cup powdered sugar

2 tablespoons orange juice
½ teaspoon vanilla
4 cups (1 quart) strawberries, hulled, sliced ¼-inch
1 cup raspberries
1 cup blueberries
   Powdered sugar

6 servings

Heat oven to 400°. Lay one sheet of phyllo over 9-inch pie pan, gently gathering to form ruffled and uneven rim. Fit into pan, allowing ends to hang over. (Keep remaining phyllo sheets covered while assembling crust.) Brush phyllo with about *2 teaspoons* melted butter; sprinkle with about *1 teaspoon* powdered sugar. Fit second sheet of phyllo in pan perpendicular to first. Brush with *2 teaspoons* butter; sprinkle with *1 teaspoon* powdered sugar. Repeat layering, buttering and sugaring with remaining phyllo sheets, butter and powdered sugar. Bake for 7 to 12 minutes or until golden brown. Let stand 5 minutes; remove from pan. Place on serving plate. Sprinkle powdered sugar over crust. Just before serving, in chilled small mixer bowl beat chilled whipping cream at high speed, scraping bowl often, until soft peaks form (1 to 2 minutes). Continue beating, gradually adding ¼ cup powdered sugar, until stiff peaks form (1 to 2 minutes). Fold in orange juice and vanilla. Fold in *2 cups* strawberries, *½ cup* raspberries and *½ cup* blueberries. Spoon whipped cream mixture into center of crust. Arrange remaining berries on top of whipped cream mixture; sprinkle with powdered sugar.

Nutrition Information (1 serving)
• Calories 308 • Protein 3g • Carbohydrate 26g • Fat 23g
• Cholesterol 75mg • Sodium 151mg

To Prepare Crisp Phyllo Petals With Berries:

1. Lay one sheet of phyllo over 9-inch pie pan, gently gathering to form ruffled and uneven rim. Fit into pan, allowing ends to hang over.

2. Brush phyllo with about *2 teaspoons* melted butter; sprinkle with about *1 teaspoon* powdered sugar.

3. Fit second sheet of phyllo in pan perpendicular to first. Brush with *2 teaspoons* butter; sprinkle with *1 teaspoon* powdered sugar. Repeat layering, buttering and sugaring with remaining phyllo sheets, butter and powdered sugar.

Crisp Phyllo Petals With Berries

Chocolate Sugar Plum Torte

2 days

Torte
½ cup coarsely chopped dried apricots
½ cup coarsely chopped walnuts
½ cup golden raisins
¼ cup ¼-inch pieces dried pineapple
¼ cup brandy *or* water
2¼ cups (14 ounces) semi-sweet real chocolate chips
¼ cup water
1 cup butter *or* margarine
6 eggs, separated
1⅓ cups sugar
1 cup finely ground almonds
9 tablespoons cake flour
Dash salt

Piping & Glaze
2 cups (12 ounces) semi-sweet real chocolate chips
2 cups (1 pint) whipping cream

Sugar Plums
¼ cup dried apricots
¼ cup walnuts
2 tablespoons golden raisins
2 tablespoons flaked coconut
2 tablespoons dried dates
1 tablespoon brandy *or* water

Sugar
Large crystal sugar

16 servings

Butter 10-inch professional cake pan or spring-form pan; line bottom with waxed paper. Butter and flour waxed paper. In medium bowl place ½ cup dried apricots, ½ cup walnuts, ½ cup raisins, dried pineapple and ¼ cup brandy. Cover; let stand at least 6 hours. *Heat oven to 350°.* In 2-quart saucepan cook 2¼ cups chocolate chips, water and butter over low heat, stirring occasionally, until melted (5 to 7 minutes). In large bowl whisk egg yolks with sugar until creamy. Whisk in melted chocolate mixture. Whisk in almonds and cake flour. Fold in brandied fruit mixture (do not drain). In small mixer bowl beat egg whites and salt at high speed, scraping bowl often, until stiff peaks form (1 to 3 minutes). Fold egg whites into chocolate mixture until blended. Pour batter into prepared pan. Bake for 45 to 50 minutes or until torte just begins to pull away from sides of pan. (Torte will be moist in center.) Let stand 15 minutes. Remove from pan; place on flat plate. Cool completely. Wrap tightly in plastic wrap; refrigerate at least 6 hours. In 2-quart saucepan cook *1 cup* chocolate chips and *1 cup* whipping cream over low heat, stirring constantly, until melted and mixture just comes to a boil (5 to 7 minutes). Cover; refrigerate at least 6 hours or until chocolate is firm enough to pipe through pastry bag.

To Decorate Torte: Prepare chocolate for glaze. In 2-quart saucepan cook remaining 1 cup chocolate chips and 1 cup whipping cream over low heat, stirring constantly, until melted and mixture just comes to a boil (5 to 7 minutes). Refrigerate, stirring occasionally, 1 hour or until chocolate is just beginning to thicken. Meanwhile, in food processor bowl or 5-cup blender container place all sugar plum ingredients *except* 1 tablespoon brandy, sugar and large crystal sugar. Process until mixture is finely chopped (1 minute); place in medium bowl. Stir in 1 tablespoon brandy; shape into 20 (1-inch) balls. Roll in sugar. Place ⅓ of firm piping chocolate mixture into pastry bag with star decorating tip. Pipe ends of balls with small star garnish; set aside. Pour thin layer of glaze over cake, spreading sides with glaze that has drizzled from top of torte; refrigerate 30 minutes. With knife, design chocolate by making lines through chocolate 1 inch apart, horizontally and vertically, to form diamond shapes. With remaining firm piping chocolate mixture, pipe rosettes around edge of torte. Sprinkle with large crystal sugar. Refrigerate 1 to 2 hours before serving. Place on serving plate; arrange sugar plums on torte.

Nutrition Information (1 serving)
• Calories 700 • Protein 8g • Carbohydrate 65g • Fat 49g
• Cholesterol 153mg • Sodium 167mg

Chocolate Sugar Plum Torte

Fruited Pound Cake (pictured)
Rum Hazelnut Fruited Cake

Fruited Pound Cake   1 hour 30 minutes

This buttery pound cake is filled with candied fruit.

2¼ cups all-purpose flour
1½ cups sugar
　1 cup butter *or* margarine, softened
　1 (8 ounce) package cream cheese, softened
　4 eggs

1½ teaspoons baking powder
1½ teaspoons vanilla
1½ cups mixed, chopped candied fruit
　½ cup chopped walnuts

                              6 loaves (60 servings)

Heat oven to 350°. In large mixer bowl combine *1¼ cups* flour and all ingredients *except* candied fruit and walnuts. Beat at medium speed, scraping bowl often, until well mixed (2 to 3 minutes). By hand, stir in remaining 1 cup flour, candied fruit and nuts. Pour into 6 greased 5½x3-inch mini loaf pans. Bake for 45 to 55 minutes or until wooden pick inserted in center comes out clean. Cool 10 minutes; remove from pan. Cool completely.

Tip: 2 greased 8x4-inch loaf pans can be substituted for mini loaf pans. Bake for 50 to 60 minutes.

Nutrition Information (1 serving)
• Calories 100 • Protein 1g • Carbohydrate 11g • Fat 5g
• Cholesterol 31mg • Sodium 55mg

Rum Hazelnut Fruited Cake   3 days

A rich, moist fruit cake filled with apricots, figs, pears, cherries and raisins, then soaked in rum.

¾ cup sugar
¾ cup firmly packed brown sugar
　1 cup butter *or* margarine, softened
　3 eggs
　2 cups all-purpose flour
　½ cup dairy sour cream
¾ cup dark rum
¼ cup light molasses
　1 teaspoon baking powder
　1 teaspoon baking soda

　1 teaspoon cinnamon
　1 teaspoon nutmeg
　2 tablespoons grated orange peel
　1 tablespoon grated lemon peel
　2 cups coarsely chopped dried apricots
　2 cups coarsely chopped hazelnuts
　1 cup coarsely chopped dried figs *or* pitted dates
　1 cup halved candied red cherries
　1 cup coarsely chopped dried pears

                              2 loaves (36 servings)

Heat oven to 325°. In large mixer bowl combine sugar, brown sugar and butter. Beat at low speed, scraping bowl often, until creamy (2 to 3 minutes). Continue beating, adding eggs one at a time, until creamy (1 to 2 minutes). Add flour, sour cream, *½ cup* rum, molasses, baking powder, baking soda, cinnamon, nutmeg, orange peel and lemon peel. Continue beating, scraping bowl often, until well mixed (1 to 2 minutes). By hand, fold in all remaining ingredients *except* ¼ cup rum. Spread batter into 2 greased and floured 9x5-inch loaf pans. Bake for 55 to 70 minutes or until wooden pick inserted in center comes out clean. Cool 30 minutes; remove from pans. Place remaining ¼ cup rum in medium bowl; soak 2 (20-inch) squares of cheesecloth (large enough to completely wrap cakes) in rum. For each fruit cake spread rum-soaked cheesecloth on large sheet of aluminum foil; place cakes in center. Wrap tightly with cheesecloth and aluminum foil. Place in refrigerator to mellow for 3 days; store refrigerated. To serve, slice thinly.

Nutrition Information (1 serving)
• Calories 240 • Protein 3g • Carbohydrate 34g • Fat 11g
• Cholesterol 33mg • Sodium 115mg

Raspberry Laced Wedding Cake

2 days

Cake
12 (1½ cups) egg whites
3⅓ cups sugar
6¼ cups cake flour
3 tablespoons baking powder
2 teaspoons salt
4 cups cold water
1½ cups vegetable oil
1 tablespoon grated lemon peel
1 tablespoon grated orange peel
1 tablespoon vanilla
1 tablespoon raspberry flavored liqueur, if desired

Raspberry Glaze
1 (¼ ounce) envelope unflavored gelatin
3 tablespoons water
⅓ cup sugar
½ cup water
2 tablespoons raspberry flavored liqueur, if desired
4 drops red food coloring

Frosting
1 cup shortening
¾ cup butter, softened
12 cups sifted powdered sugar
⅔ to ¾ cup lemon juice
3 tablespoons grated lemon peel

36 servings

Heat oven to 350°. In large mixer bowl beat egg whites at high speed, scraping bowl often, until soft peaks form (3 to 4 minutes). Continue beating, gradually adding *1⅓ cups* sugar, until stiff, but not dry, peaks form (1 to 2 minutes). Set aside. In another large mixer bowl stir together remaining 2 cups sugar, cake flour, baking powder and salt. Stir in *3 cups* water and all remaining cake ingredients. Beat at low speed, scraping bowl often, until smooth (1 to 2 minutes). Pour batter into 8-quart bowl; fold in egg whites. Gradually fold in remaining 1 cup water. Lightly spray bottoms of 2 (10-inch) round and 2 (8-inch) round professional cake pans with no-stick cooking spray. Pour about 6 cups batter into each 10-inch prepared pan and about 4 cups batter into each 8-inch prepared pan. Pound pans on counter top 2 to 3 times to remove air bubbles from batter. Bake for 25 to 30 minutes or until cake pulls away from sides of pan. (If necessary, rotate pans in oven for even browning.) Let stand 10 minutes; remove from pans. With fingertips brush all browned crumbs from surfaces of cake. Cool completely on wire racks. Decorate or wrap tightly in plastic wrap and freeze up to 5 days.

To Decorate: In small bowl soften gelatin in 3 tablespoons water. In 1-quart saucepan stir together softened gelatin and all remaining glaze ingredients. Cook over medium high heat until gelatin is dissolved (3 to 4 minutes). Refrigerate, stirring occasionally, for 1 to 2 hours or until gelatin mounds with a spoon. In large mixer bowl beat shortening and butter at low speed,

scraping bowl often, until well mixed (2 to 3 minutes). Continue beating, gradually adding powdered sugar alternately with lemon juice and 3 tablespoons lemon peel, until fluffy (8 to 10 minutes). Remove any crumbs from cakes. On 10-inch cake cardboard rounds place 1 (10-inch) layer, bottom side up. Spread with thin, smooth layer of frosting; top with thin layer of raspberry glaze to within ½ inch of edge of cake. Refrigerate 30 minutes or until slightly set. Meanwhile, on 8-inch cake cardboard rounds place 1 (8-inch) layer, bottom side up. Spread with thin, smooth layer of frosting; top with thin layer of raspberry glaze. Refrigerate 30 minutes or until set. Place remaining cake layers, rounded side up, on matching bottom layer. Frost sides and top of each cake. Spread so that frosting is smooth. If necessary, dip metal spatula into water, spread over cake to smooth frosting. Place some of remaining frosting in pastry bag with ribbon decorating tip; pipe ½-inch ribbons around outer edge of 8-inch cake and across top of cake to form decorative lines. Change decorating tip; pipe tiny dots or V design on decorative ribbons. To present, remove from cake rounds. Place 10-inch cake on large platter or tiered cake stand. Center 8-inch cake on top of 10-inch cake. Place remaining frosting in pastry bags with choice of decorating tips. Pipe tiny dots to form V's on sides of each cake or decorate as desired. If desired, garnish with raspberries, mint leaves and fresh cut flowers.

Nutrition Information (1 serving)
• Calories 430 • Protein 3g • Carbohydrate 66g • Fat 19g
• Cholesterol 10mg • Sodium 250mg

Raspberry Laced Wedding Cake

Petits Fours

4 hours

These dainty icing coated miniature cakes add a special touch to showers, open houses or teas.

Cake
1 (18½ ounce) package white cake mix
½ teaspoon almond extract

Icing
3 cups sugar
¼ teaspoon cream of tartar
1½ cups water
1 teaspoon almond extract *or* vanilla
1 cup powdered sugar, sifted
3 drops food coloring

Candy flowers
Frosting flowers

4 dozen

Heat oven to 350°. Prepare cake mix according to package directions adding ½ teaspoon almond extract with water and baking in 2 greased and floured 9-inch square baking pans. Bake for 20 to 30 minutes or until wooden pick inserted in center comes out clean. Cool 10 minutes; remove from pans. Cool completely. Trim edges from cake; cut each cake into 24 pieces. In 3-quart saucepan combine sugar, cream of tartar and water. Cook over medium heat, stirring occasionally, until mixture comes to a full boil (12 to 14 minutes). Cover; boil 3 minutes. Uncover; continue cooking until candy thermometer reaches 226° F or small amount of mixture dropped into ice water forms a thin syrup (10 to 15 minutes). Remove from heat; cool to 110° F (do not stir). Stir in 1 teaspoon almond extract, powdered sugar and food coloring. Place wire rack on cookie sheet. Place cake pieces on wire rack. Using ladle or large spoon carefully spoon icing over cake pieces; spread over edges if desired. Repeat, coating each piece twice. If icing becomes too thick reheat over low heat until pouring consistency (2 to 3 minutes). Scrape icing from cookie sheet; reuse if needed. Garnish each petit four with candied flowers or frosting flowers.

Nutrition Information (1 petit four)
• Calories 100 • Protein 1g • Carbohydrate 21g • Fat 2g
• Cholesterol 1mg • Sodium 40mg

To Prepare Petits Fours:

1. Trim edges from cake; cut each cake into 24 pieces.

2. Uncover; continue cooking until candy thermometer reaches 226° F or small amount of mixture dropped into ice water forms a thin syrup (10 to 15 minutes).

3. Place cake pieces on wire rack. Using ladle or large spoon carefully spoon icing over cake pieces; spread over edges if desired. Repeat, coating each piece twice.

Raspberry Truffle Ice Cream Cake

9 hours

*A truffle-like cake is layered with vanilla ice cream and
raspberry sorbet, then covered with chocolate.*

2½ cups semi-sweet real chocolate chips
½ cup butter *or* margarine
1½ tablespoons all-purpose flour
1½ tablespoons sugar
 1 teaspoon hot water
 4 eggs, separated
 4 cups (1 quart) vanilla ice cream, slightly
   softened

2 cups (1 pint) raspberry sorbet *or* sherbet
½ cup semi-sweet real chocolate chips
½ cup whipping cream

Raspberries

12 servings

Heat oven to 400°. Grease bottom and sides of 8-inch springform pan; dust with powdered sugar. In 2-quart saucepan cook chocolate chips and butter over low heat, stirring constantly, until chocolate is melted (4 to 5 minutes). Stir in flour, sugar and hot water. Stir egg yolks into chocolate mixture. In small mixer bowl beat egg whites at high speed, scraping bowl often, just until stiff peaks form (2 to 3 minutes). By hand, fold egg whites into chocolate mixture. Pour into prepared pan. Bake for 22 to 28 minutes or until cake pulls away from sides of pan. Let stand 10 minutes; run knife along sides and bottom to loosen cake from springform pan. Cool completely in pan. Spread ice cream on top of cake in springform pan. Freeze 1 hour. Spread sorbet on top of ice cream. Freeze 1 hour. Meanwhile, in 1-quart saucepan cook

chocolate chips and whipping cream over low heat, stirring constantly, until mixture just comes to a boil (3 to 5 minutes). Cool 15 minutes. Pour over sorbet. Freeze 6 hours or overnight until firm. With knife, design chocolate by making lines through chocolate 1 inch apart, horizontally and vertically, to form diamond shapes. Garnish with raspberries.

Tip: 9-inch square baking pan can be substituted for 8-inch springform pan. Line with aluminum foil, extending excess aluminum foil over edges. Bake for 18 to 22 minutes or until cake pulls away from sides of pan.

Nutrition Information (1 serving)
• Calories 490 • Protein 6g • Carbohydrate 48g • Fat 34g
• Cholesterol 128mg • Sodium 159mg

*The first American Independence Day was celebrated in Philadelphia and not
on the 4th but on the 8th of July.*

Summertime Minted Trifle

4 hours

A light, refreshing trifle made with orange flavored cake,
fresh mint custard, strawberry puree and summertime fruits.

Cake

4 eggs, separated
¾ cup sugar
1 teaspoon grated orange peel
½ teaspoon vanilla
¾ cup all-purpose flour
¼ cup butter *or* margarine, melted, cooled
(but not solidified)

Custard

½ cup sugar
1 (¼ ounce) envelope unflavored gelatin
2½ cups half-and-half
4 egg yolks, slightly beaten

2 tablespoons white crème de menthe*
1 teaspoon grated orange peel
½ teaspoon vanilla
⅓ cup coarsely chopped fresh mint leaves

Strawberry Puree

1 pint (2 cups) strawberries, hulled
⅓ cup powdered sugar

Fruit

1 pint (2 cups) strawberries, hulled, halved
1 nectarine *or* peach, thinly sliced
Mint leaves

10 servings

Heat oven to 350°. In small mixer bowl beat 4 egg whites at high speed, scraping bowl often, until stiff peaks form (1 to 2 minutes). Set aside. In large bowl whisk together 4 egg yolks, ¾ cup sugar, 1 teaspoon orange peel and ½ teaspoon vanilla until thick and light. Gradually fold in egg whites alternately with flour; gradually fold in cooled butter. Pour into greased and floured 9-inch round cake pan. Bake for 25 to 30 minutes or until cake begins to pull away from sides of pan. Let stand 15 minutes; remove from pan. Cool completely. Meanwhile, in 2-quart saucepan combine ½ cup sugar and gelatin. Gradually stir in *1½ cups* half-and-half. Cook over medium heat, stirring constantly, until mixture just comes to a boil (10 to 15 minutes). In medium bowl place 4 egg yolks. Stir half of heated half-and-half mixture into egg yolks. Return to saucepan with remaining half-and-half mixture. Continue cooking, stirring occasionally, 1 minute. Stir in crème

de menthe, 1 teaspoon orange peel and ½ teaspoon vanilla. Cover; refrigerate until thickened (about 1½ hours). Gradually whisk in remaining 1 cup half-and-half and ⅓ cup mint leaves. Meanwhile, in 5-cup blender container place 1 pint strawberries. Blend on High speed until pureed (1 to 2 minutes). Continue blending, gradually adding powdered sugar, until dissolved (1 to 2 minutes). Refrigerate about 1 hour. Tear cake into bite-size pieces; place ½ of pieces in medium-size glass serving bowl. Pour about ½ strawberry puree over cake; top with ½ custard and ½ halved strawberries. Repeat with remaining cake pieces, strawberry puree and custard. Garnish with remaining strawberries, sliced nectarine and mint leaves.

*½ teaspoon mint extract can be substituted for 2 tablespoons crème de menthe.

Nutrition Information (1 serving)
• Calories 360 • Protein 8g • Carbohydrate 46g • Fat 16g
• Cholesterol 230mg • Sodium 105mg

Common wedding presents in pioneer days were fancy butter dishes. A woman often served her butter in these special molded shapes when company came. Land O'Lakes has a collection of over 150 of these antique butter dishes.

Summertime Minted Trifle

Marmalade Mincemeat Tart

2 hours

Candied orange peel glistens on top of a twisted lattice mincemeat tart.

Pastry
2 cups all-purpose flour
3 tablespoons sugar
1 tablespoon grated orange peel
¾ cup butter, cut into 2 tablespoon pieces
2 egg yolks, slightly beaten
4 to 5 tablespoons ice water

Filling
1 (3 ounce) package cream cheese, softened
2 tablespoons orange juice
1 (27 ounce) jar mincemeat
2 cups (2 medium) cored, peeled, sliced
¼-inch tart cooking apples

Candied Orange
1 medium orange
½ cup water
¼ cup sugar

10 servings

Heat oven to 375°. In large bowl stir together flour, 3 tablespoons sugar and 1 tablespoon orange peel. Cut in butter until crumbly. With fork mix in egg yolks and 4 to 5 tablespoons ice water just until moistened. Divide dough into 2 balls making 1 ball one-fourth larger than the other ball. Wrap smaller ball in plastic wrap; refrigerate. On lightly floured surface roll out larger ball into 14-inch circle. Place in 10-inch tart pan, pressing firmly against bottom and sides of pan. Cut away excess pastry. In small bowl whisk together cream cheese and orange juice. Spread over bottom of unbaked tart. In large bowl stir together mincemeat and apples. Pour into tart. Roll remaining pastry ball into 12-inch circle. With sharp knife or pastry wheel, cut circle into 10 (½-inch) strips. Twist each strip 5 times; place 5 twisted strips, 1 inch apart, across filling in tart pan. Place remaining 5 twisted strips, 1 inch apart, at right angles to strips already in place. With thumb seal ends of strips and cut away excess dough. Bake for 40 to 50 minutes or until golden brown. Meanwhile, with vegetable peeler, peel large strips of orange peel (colored part only); cut into thin julienne strips. In 1-quart saucepan bring ¼ *cup* water to a full boil; add orange strips. Cook over medium high heat until orange strips are blanched (1 to 2 minutes); drain. In same saucepan stir together remaining ¼ cup water, ¼ cup sugar and blanched orange strips. Cook over medium heat, stirring occasionally, until orange is glazed and candied (12 to 15 minutes). Remove orange strips; separate on waxed paper. Arrange on baked mincemeat tart.

Nutrition Information (1 serving)
• Calories 460 • Protein 5g • Carbohydrate 70g • Fat 19g
• Cholesterol 101mg • Sodium 367mg

Norwegian Christmas Eve features lutefisk, usually a cod that has been soaked in lye, skinned, boned and boiled. It's served with boiled potatoes and lefse. For dessert, 7 different kinds of cookies are offered to honor the 7 phases of the moon.

Ice Cream Cone Cakes

1 hour 30 minutes

Great for children's parties — frosted cake baked in ice cream cones.

Cake

 2 cups all-purpose flour
 1¼ cups sugar
 ½ cup butter *or* margarine, softened
 1 cup milk
 3 eggs
 3½ teaspoons baking powder
 ½ teaspoon salt
 2 teaspoons vanilla
 2 tablespoons multicolored candy sprinkles
 18 to 20 flat-bottom ice cream cones

Frosting

 1 cup milk
 3 tablespoons all-purpose flour
 ⅛ teaspoon salt
 1 cup sugar
 1 cup butter *or* margarine, softened
 2 teaspoons vanilla

 ½ cup semi-sweet real chocolate chips, melted
 1 teaspoon vegetable oil

 Chopped peanuts
 Maraschino cherries
 Assorted candies

2½ dozen

Heat oven to 350°. Line muffin pans with paper liners. In large mixer bowl combine all cake ingredients *except* candy sprinkles and ice cream cones. Beat at medium speed, scraping bowl often, until smooth (2 to 3 minutes). Stir in candy sprinkles. Fill paper-lined muffin cups ½ full. For each cupcake place 1 ice cream cone upside down on batter. Bake for 18 to 20 minutes or until wooden pick inserted in cupcake comes out clean. Cool completely. Meanwhile, in 1-quart saucepan combine 1 cup milk, 3 tablespoons flour and ⅛ teaspoon salt. Cook over medium heat, stirring constantly, until mixture thickens and comes to a full boil (4 to 7 minutes). Boil 1 minute. Cover surface with plastic wrap; cool completely. In small mixer bowl combine 1 cup sugar, 1 cup butter and 2 teaspoons vanilla. Beat at medium speed,

scraping bowl often, until light and fluffy (1 to 2 minutes). Continue beating, gradually adding cooked, thickened flour mixture, until light and fluffy (6 to 7 minutes). Remove paper liner from cupcakes. Frost all cake surfaces. Decorate frosted cupcakes as desired or for sundae-style cakes stir oil into melted chocolate, spoon 2 teaspoons melted chocolate over top of each frosted cupcake; sprinkle with peanuts and top with cherry.

Tip: Bake as many Ice Cream Cone Cakes as desired, bake remaining batter as cupcakes.

Tip: If cakes are lopsided, trim cakes to shape.

Nutrition Information (1 ice cream cone cake)
• Calories 230 • Protein 3g • Carbohydrate 30g • Fat 12g
• Cholesterol 47mg • Sodium 206mg

The Fourth of July has always been America's premier party. In the 1900s, it was an all-day affair that started with church services and ended, after speeches, parades, ice cream socials and band concerts, with fireworks.

Ice Cream Cone Cakes

Carrot Bunny Cookies (left)
Favorite Teddy Bear Cookies (right)

Carrot Bunny Cookies

1 hour 30 minutes

These carrot-filled cookies are shaped like little bunnies with fluffy white tails.

1 cup butter *or* margarine, softened
1 cup sugar
1 egg
1 teaspoon vanilla
1 cup (1 medium) shredded carrot
3 cups all-purpose flour
2 teaspoons cream of tartar

1 teaspoon baking soda
¼ teaspoon salt
1 teaspoon grated orange peel

30 miniature marshmallows

2½ dozen

Heat oven to 350°. In large mixer bowl combine butter, sugar, egg and vanilla. Beat at medium speed, scraping bowl often, until well mixed (1 to 2 minutes). Add all remaining ingredients *except* marshmallows. Reduce speed to low. Continue beating, scraping bowl often, until well mixed (2 to 3 minutes). To shape bunnies, roll ⅓ dough into 30 (1-inch) balls, ⅓ into 30 (¾-inch) balls and remaining ⅓ into 60 (1 x ¼-inch) logs to resemble ears. On greased cookie sheets for each bunny place 1 (1-inch) ball; place 1 (¾-inch) ball next to, and touching, 1-inch ball. Place 2 logs for ears next to, and touching, ¾-inch ball. Bunny is formed during baking. Bake for 11 to 15 minutes or until top springs back when touched lightly in center. Remove from oven; place 1 marshmallow on each bunny to resemble tail. Continue baking for 1 to 2 minutes or until marshmallows are slightly melted.

Tip: If desired, decorate cookies with frosting.

Nutrition Information (1 cookie)
• Calories 130 • Protein 2g • Carbohydrate 17g • Fat 7g
• Cholesterol 26mg • Sodium 122mg

Favorite Teddy Bear Cookies

1 hour 30 minutes

Cookies become a special treat when shaped into cute little teddy bears.

1 cup sugar
¾ cup butter *or* margarine, softened
1 egg
2 teaspoons vanilla
2¼ cups all-purpose flour

1 teaspoon baking powder
¼ teaspoon salt
2 (1 ounce) squares unsweetened chocolate, melted

1½ dozen

Heat oven to 375°. In large mixer bowl combine sugar, butter, egg and vanilla. Beat at medium speed, scraping bowl often, until well mixed (1 to 2 minutes). Add flour, baking powder and salt. Continue beating, scraping bowl often, until well mixed (1 to 2 minutes). Divide dough in half. Place half of dough in medium bowl; by hand, stir in chocolate. For each teddy bear, form a portion of either color dough into a large ball (1-inch) for body, a medium ball (¾-inch) for head, four small balls (½-inch) for arms and legs, two smaller balls for ears and one small ball for nose. If desired, add additional balls for eyes and mouth. Repeat with remaining dough, making either vanilla or chocolate teddy bears or mixing the doughs to make two-toned teddy bears. To form each cookie, place large ball (body) on cookie sheet; flatten slightly. Attach head, arms, legs and ears by overlapping slightly onto body. Add nose, eyes and mouth. Bake for 7 to 8 minutes or until body is set. Cool 1 minute. Remove from cookie sheet; cool completely.

Tip: If desired, decorate cookies with frosting.

Nutrition Information (1 cookie)
• Calories 190 • Protein 2g • Carbohydrate 24g • Fat 10g
• Cholesterol 33mg • Sodium 129mg

Trim-the-Tree Christmas Cookies

4 hours

These cut-out sugar cookies are delicious to eat or make beautiful tree ornaments.

Cookies
2½ cups all-purpose flour
 1 cup sugar
 1 cup butter *or* margarine, softened
 1 egg
 1 teaspoon baking powder
 2 tablespoons orange juice
 1 tablespoon vanilla

Frosting
 4 cups powdered sugar
 ½ cup butter *or* margarine, softened
 3 to 4 tablespoons milk
 2 teaspoons vanilla

Decorations
 Colored sugars
 Food coloring

3 dozen

In large mixer bowl combine all cookie ingredients. Beat at low speed, scraping bowl often, until well mixed (1 to 2 minutes). Divide dough into thirds. Wrap in waxed paper; refrigerate until firm (2 to 3 hours). *Heat oven to 400°.* Roll out dough, ⅓ at a time, on well-floured surface to ¼-inch thickness. Cut with 3-inch cookie cutters. Place 1 inch apart on cookie sheets. If desired, sprinkle with colored sugars and bake, or bake and decorate later. Bake for 6 to 10 minutes or until edges are lightly browned. While still warm use wooden pick to make hole for string to hang as ornament. Cool completely. In small mixer bowl combine all frosting ingredients. Beat at low speed, scraping bowl often, until fluffy (1 to 2 minutes). If desired, color frosting with food coloring. Frost or decorate cookies. Serve cookies or use as tree ornaments.

Nutrition Information (1 serving)
• Calories 170 • Protein 1g • Carbohydrate 23g • Fat 8g
• Cholesterol 28mg • Sodium 89mg

Chocolate-Dipped Shortbread

1 hour 30 minutes

Traditional shortbread dipped in semi-sweet chocolate and almonds.

1¼ cups all-purpose flour
 ½ cup powdered sugar
 ⅔ cup butter *or* margarine, softened
 ½ teaspoon almond extract

 ½ cup semi-sweet real chocolate chips
 2 teaspoons vegetable oil
 ½ cup finely chopped almonds

32 cookies

Heat oven to 325°. In large mixer bowl combine flour, sugar, butter and almond extract. Beat at medium speed, scraping bowl often, until mixture leaves sides of bowl and forms a ball (3 to 4 minutes). With floured fingers press dough evenly on bottom of 9-inch square baking pan. Score dough in 16 squares; score each square into 2 triangles. Prick each triangle twice with fork. Bake for 18 to 22 minutes or until set and edges are very lightly browned. Let cool 5 minutes. Cut into triangles; cool completely in pan. In 1-quart saucepan combine chocolate chips and vegetable oil. Cook over medium low heat, stirring constantly, until chocolate is melted (4 to 5 minutes). Remove from heat. Dip one cut edge of each triangle ¼ inch into melted chocolate; scrape against side of pan to remove excess chocolate. Dip chocolate-coated edge into chopped almonds; place on wire rack. Let stand until chocolate is firm.

Nutrition Information (1 serving)
• Calories 86 • Protein 1g • Carbohydrate 7g • Fat 6g
• Cholesterol 10mg • Sodium 39mg

Trim-the-Tree Christmas Cookies (top)
Chocolate-Dipped Shortbread (bottom)

Coconut Date Balls

2 hours

These moist cookies are filled with dates and rolled in coconut.

½ cup butter *or* margarine
1 cup sugar
1 (8 ounce) package chopped dates
1 egg, slightly beaten
½ teaspoon salt
2 tablespoons milk

1 teaspoon vanilla
2 cups crushed cornflakes
½ cup chopped pecans
½ cup chopped maraschino cherries, drained
1½ cups flaked coconut

4 dozen

In 10-inch skillet melt butter over medium heat (3 to 4 minutes). Stir in sugar and dates. Remove from heat; stir in egg, salt, milk and vanilla. Cook over medium heat, stirring occasionally, until mixture comes to a full boil (4 to 7 minutes). Boil, stirring constantly, 1 minute. Remove from heat; stir in cornflakes, pecans and cherries. Shape into 1-inch balls; roll in coconut. Place on waxed paper. Refrigerate until set (1 to 2 hours).

Nutrition Information (1 cookie)
• Calories 85 • Protein 1g • Carbohydrate 13g • Fat 4g
• Cholesterol 11mg • Sodium 80mg

Almond Strawberry Bars

1 hour 30 minutes

A touch of almond flavors these delicious bars.

Crumb Mixture
1¼ cups all-purpose flour
⅓ cup firmly packed brown sugar
½ cup butter *or* margarine

Topping
½ cup all-purpose flour
½ cup firmly packed brown sugar
¼ cup butter *or* margarine, softened
½ teaspoon almond extract
¾ cup strawberry preserves

Glaze
½ cup powdered sugar
1 to 2 teaspoons milk
½ teaspoon almond extract

3 dozen

Heat oven to 350°. In small mixer bowl combine all crumb mixture ingredients. Beat at low speed, scraping bowl often, until mixture is crumbly (1 to 2 minutes). Press on bottom of greased and floured 9-inch square baking pan. Bake for 15 to 20 minutes or until edges are lightly browned. Meanwhile, in same bowl combine all topping ingredients *except* preserves. Beat at low speed, scraping bowl often, until well mixed (1 to 2 minutes); set aside. Spread preserves to within ⅛ inch from edge of hot crust. Sprinkle topping over preserves. Return to oven; continue baking for 20 to 25 minutes or until edges are lightly browned. Meanwhile, in small bowl stir together all glaze ingredients. Cool bars completely; drizzle with glaze. Cut into bars.

Nutrition Information (1 bar)
• Calories 100 • Protein 1g • Carbohydrate 16g • Fat 4g
• Cholesterol 11mg • Sodium 42mg

Coconut Date Balls (top)
Almond Strawberry Bars (bottom)

Melt-In-Your-Mouth Truffles

1 day

These rich chocolate truffles are pure indulgence.

½ cup whipping cream
8 ounces dark sweet chocolate, coarsely chopped*
¼ cup butter *or* margarine, softened
2 teaspoons vanilla**

Finely chopped nuts
Unsweetened cocoa
Powdered sugar

3 dozen

In 2-quart saucepan combine whipping cream and chocolate. Cook over low heat, stirring constantly, until chocolate is melted and mixture is smooth (2 to 4 minutes). Stir in butter until melted. Cool to room temperature (about 30 minutes). Stir in vanilla. Cover; refrigerate until firm enough to shape (at least 8 hours). Mixture can be kept in refrigerator for up to 3 days. To make truffles shape about 1 teaspoon chocolate mixture into 1-inch ball. (Mixture will be soft.) Roll in finely chopped nuts, cocoa or powdered sugar. Refrigerate until firm (2 to 4 hours). Store refrigerated or frozen.

*8 (1 ounce) squares semi-sweet chocolate, coarsely chopped, can be substituted for 8 ounces dark sweet chocolate, coarsely chopped.

**½ teaspoon mint extract or 4 teaspoons your favorite liqueur can be substituted for 2 teaspoons vanilla.

Nutrition Information (1 candy)
• Calories 55 • Protein 0g • Carbohydrate 4g • Fat 5g
• Cholesterol 8mg • Sodium 16mg

Chocolate Swirl Divinity

2 hours

Swirls of chocolate make this divinity extra special.

3 cups sugar
¾ cup light corn syrup
¾ cup water
⅛ teaspoon salt
3 egg whites

1 (12 ounce) package (2 cups) semi-sweet real chocolate chips
2 teaspoons vanilla

3 dozen

In 2-quart saucepan combine sugar, corn syrup, water and salt. Cook over low heat, stirring constantly, until sugar is dissolved (5 to 8 minutes). Without stirring, continue cooking until candy thermometer reaches 260°F or small amount of mixture dropped into ice water forms a hard ball (30 to 60 minutes). Meanwhile, in large mixer bowl beat egg whites at high speed until stiff peaks form (2 to 3 minutes). Reduce to medium speed; continue beating while slowly pouring hot syrup into egg whites in a thin stream. Beat at high speed, scraping bowl often, until mixture loses gloss and starts to hold shape (4 to 6 minutes). By hand, stir in chocolate chips and vanilla just until chocolate melts and forms swirls. Quickly drop by tablespoonfuls onto buttered cookie sheets. Cool completely.

Tip: Divinity should be made with a standing mixer; a hand held mixer does not have the power to beat the syrup to a stiff consistency.

Nutrition Information (1 candy)
• Calories 130 • Protein 1g • Carbohydrate 27g • Fat 3g
• Cholesterol 0mg • Sodium 17mg

489

Cashew Butter Crunch (top)
Dark Chocolate Fudge (bottom)

Cashew Butter Crunch
60 minutes

No one will have to dig to the bottom of the bowl to find the cashews in this toffeelike candy.

1 cup sugar
1 cup butter

1 tablespoon light corn syrup
1½ cups salted cashew pieces

1¼ pounds (20 servings)

In 2-quart saucepan combine sugar, butter and corn syrup. Cook over low heat, stirring occasionally, until candy thermometer reaches 290°F or small amount of mixture dropped into ice water forms brittle strands (25 to 30 minutes). Remove from heat; stir in cashews. Spread to ¼-inch thickness on waxed paper lined 15x10x1-inch jelly roll pan. Cool completely; break into pieces.

Tip: 1½ cups your favorite salted nuts can be substituted for 1½ cups salted cashew pieces.

Nutrition Information (1 serving)
• Calories 180 • Protein 2g • Carbohydrate 14g • Fat 14g
• Cholesterol 25mg • Sodium 160mg

Dark Chocolate Fudge
2 hours 15 minutes

This dark fudge can be flavored 4 luscious ways.

2 cups miniature marshmallows
3 (6 ounce) packages semi-sweet real chocolate chips

1 (14 ounce) can sweetened condensed milk
1½ teaspoons vanilla

2 pounds (64 servings)

In 2-quart saucepan combine marshmallows, chocolate chips and sweetened condensed milk. Cook over low heat, stirring often, until melted and smooth (7 to 9 minutes). Remove from heat; stir in vanilla. Pour into greased 8 or 9-inch square pan. Refrigerate at least 2 hours or until firm. Cut into squares.

Variations

Peanut Butter Swirl Fudge: Reduce 1½ teaspoons vanilla to 1 teaspoon. Prepare fudge as directed; stir in ½ cup chopped salted peanuts and ½ cup peanut butter until peanut butter just begins to melt. Swirls of peanut butter will be visible. Pour into greased 8 or 9-inch square pan. Continue as directed.

Almond Fudge: Reduce 1½ teaspoons vanilla to 1 teaspoon. Prepare fudge as directed; stir in

1 teaspoon almond extract. Pour into greased 8 or 9-inch square pan. Continue as directed.

Macadamia Nut Fudge: Prepare fudge as directed. Stir in ½ cup coarsely chopped macadamia nuts. Pour into greased 8 or 9-inch square pan. Continue as directed.

Microwave Directions: In 1½-quart casserole or medium glass bowl combine marshmallows, chocolate chips and sweetened condensed milk. Microwave on HIGH, stirring after half the time, until melted (3 to 4 minutes). Stir until smooth; stir in vanilla. Pour into greased 8 or 9-inch square pan. Refrigerate at least 2 hours or until firm. Cut into squares.

Nutrition Information (1 serving)
• Calories 65 • Protein 1g • Carbohydrate 9g • Fat 3g
• Cholesterol 2mg • Sodium 9mg

Chocolate Covered Cherries

4 days

A candy store favorite you can make at home.

⅓ cup butter *or* margarine
⅓ cup light corn syrup
¼ teaspoon salt
½ teaspoon almond extract
4 cups powdered sugar

2 (10 ounce) jars maraschino cherries
  without stems, drained
  Chocolate for dipping*

6 dozen

In large mixer bowl combine butter, corn syrup, salt and almond extract. Beat at medium speed, scraping bowl often, until well mixed (1 to 2 minutes). By hand, gradually stir in *3 cups* powdered sugar. Turn mixture onto lightly powdered sugar dusted surface. Knead in remaining 1 cup powdered sugar. Continue kneading until mixture is smooth (1 to 2 minutes). Using about 1 teaspoon mixture, completely enclose each cherry. Place on waxed paper lined cookie sheets. Loosely cover; refrigerate until firm (2 to 4 hours). Coat cherries

with dipping chocolate. Store at room temperature until centers soften (3 to 5 days). For longer storage freeze or refrigerate.

*See Celebrations page 499 for Chocolate For Dipping recipe.

Tip: Maraschino cherries with stems can be used. Carefully seal sugar mixture around stems.

Nutrition Information (1 serving)
• Calories 65 • Protein 0g • Carbohydrate 16g • Fat 1g
• Cholesterol 2mg • Sodium 29mg

Buttercreams

5 hours

These homemade buttercream candies bring back memories of years gone by.

½ cup butter, softened
1 (3 ounce) package cream cheese, softened
1½ teaspoons vanilla
4 cups powdered sugar

Chocolate for dipping*

5 dozen

In large mixer bowl combine butter and cream cheese. Beat at medium speed, scraping bowl often, until smooth (1 to 2 minutes). Add vanilla; continue beating until well mixed. Reduce speed to low; continue beating, gradually adding powdered sugar, until well mixed (4 to 5 minutes). If mixture is too soft, cover; refrigerate until firm enough to form balls (45 to 60 minutes). Shape rounded teaspoonfuls of mixture into 1-inch balls. Place on waxed paper lined cookie sheets. Cover loosely; refrigerate until firm (2 hours or overnight).

Coat buttercreams with dipping chocolate. Store frozen or refrigerated.

*See Celebrations page 499 for Chocolate For Dipping recipe.

Tip: 1½ teaspoons almond extract, orange extract or rum extract can be added with vanilla for additional flavor variations.

Nutrition Information (1 serving)
• Calories 70 • Protein 0g • Carbohydrate 14g • Fat 2g
• Cholesterol 6mg • Sodium 32mg

Chocolate Covered Cherries (pictured)
Buttercreams

Peanut Butter Cups

3 hours

A great gift idea or a fun addition to your holiday dessert plate.

Cups
1 (11½ ounce) package real milk chocolate chips
2 tablespoons shortening

Filling
½ cup butter *or* margarine
½ cup crunchy style peanut butter
1 cup powdered sugar
⅔ cup graham cracker crumbs

30 (1¾x1¼-inch) mini paper cups

2½ dozen

In 1-quart saucepan combine chocolate chips and shortening. Cook over low heat, stirring occasionally, until melted and smooth (3 to 5 minutes). Loosen top paper cup from stack, but leave in stack for greater stability while being coated. With small paintbrush coat inside of top cup evenly with about 1 teaspoon melted chocolate to about ⅛-inch thickness, bringing coating almost to top of cup but not over edge. Repeat until 30 cups are coated; refrigerate cups. In 2-quart saucepan combine butter and peanut butter. Cook over medium heat, stirring occasionally, until melted (4 to 6 minutes). Stir in powdered sugar and graham cracker crumbs. Press about ½ tablespoon filling into each chocolate cup. Spoon about ½ teaspoon melted chocolate on top of filling; spread to cover. Freeze until firm (about 2 hours); carefully peel off paper cups. Store refrigerated.

Nutrition Information (1 candy)
• Calories 140 • Protein 2g • Carbohydrate 12g • Fat 10g
• Cholesterol 11mg • Sodium 75mg

To Prepare Peanut Butter Cups:

1. With small paintbrush coat inside of top cup evenly with about 1 teaspoon melted chocolate to about ⅛-inch thickness, bringing coating almost to top of cup but not over edge.

2. Press about ½ tablespoon filling into each chocolate cup.

3. Spoon about ½ teaspoon melted chocolate on top of filling; spread to cover.

Peanut Butter Cups

Buffet parties, always popular, are among the easiest for busy hosts and hostesses. For a successful buffet party, keep the following tips in mind as you do your planning.

• Choose foods that can be prepared ahead.

• Unless guests will be seated at tables, prepare foods that are easy to eat. It's difficult to cut meat with a tray balanced on your lap.

• Consider having a theme. It can add to the fun and make food and centerpiece choices easier.

• Always be aware of food safety. Keep cold foods cold (40° F) and hot foods hot (140° F). Bowls of ice and heated serving trays make this job easier.

• Place foods in medium-size serving dishes and replace as needed. Large dishes that are half empty are unappetizing.

• Arrange dessert on a side table or clear the buffet and arrange the dessert, plates and silverware on the same table.

One-line buffet set on a table in the center of the room allows plenty of space for food and beverage. It's a good choice when your table is small because it uses four sides.

Two-line buffet speeds serving for a large group. Beverage may be served from the end of the table or a separate table. Provide two serving dishes of each food item, so the table is the same on both sides.

497

How To: Decorate & Garnish Desserts

If desired, create stunning desserts by combining these decorating and garnishing ideas.

To Make Chocolate Curls:

1. Curls will work better if chocolate is slightly warm. To warm, microwave chocolate on HIGH until slightly warm (10 to 30 seconds).

2. Using even pressure, pull a vegetable peeler across the chocolate to desired thickness of curl.

3. Use a wooden pick to lift curl onto a waxed paper lined plate or tray.

4. Refrigerate until firm.

To Make Chocolate Leaves:

1. Heavy veined leaves (such as lemon leaves or rose leaves) give the most definition. Wash and dry leaves thoroughly.

2. Using small pastry brush, paint melted chocolate on underside of each leaf. Be careful not to get chocolate onto the front of leaf, making it more difficult to remove.

3. Place leaves on waxed paper lined plate or tray; refrigerate until firm.

4. Carefully pull back on leaf, separating leaf from chocolate. Be careful not to handle chocolate too long.

5. Refrigerate leaves until ready to use.

To Use a Pastry Bag:

1. Fold back bag about 5 inches.

2. Fit selected tip tightly into bag.

3. Spoon frosting or other mixture into bag, filling it ½ full.

4. Unfold bag; roll up open end of bag to close.

5. Hold bag with one hand and squeeze out frosting. Use the other hand to guide the tip.

6. Roll up bag as you work for easier handling and better control.

Other items for garnishing: Fresh flowers, fresh or dried fruit slices, nuts, powdered sugar, grated chocolate, mint leaves, lemon or orange peel.

Chocolate for Dipping

1½ cups semi-sweet miniature real chocolate
  chips
2 tablespoons shortening*
        Coats about 2½ dozen 1-inch centers

Remove candy centers to be dipped from refrigerator about 10 minutes before coating; dipping cold centers may result in cracked coating or bloom (white crystals) on the coating. Chop 1½ teaspoons chocolate chips; set aside. In 2-cup measure place remaining chocolate chips and shortening. Place measure in large bowl which contains very warm (100 to 110° F) water that reaches halfway up 2-cup measure. *Don't let even 1 drop of water mix with chocolate.* Stir mixture constantly with rubber spatula until chocolate is melted and mixture is smooth (18 to 22 minutes). (Do not rush melting process.) If necessary, replace water with more very warm water. Remove 2-cup measure from water; continue stirring until chocolate is cooled slightly (2 to 3 minutes). Stir reserved chopped chocolate chips into melted chocolate until smooth (1 to 2 minutes). Set one center on tines of fondue fork or 2-pronged fork. Completely dip center into melted chocolate. Gently tap fork against side of 2-cup measure to remove excess melted chocolate. Invert candy onto waxed paper lined cookie sheet. Repeat with remaining centers. If melted chocolate becomes too thick for dipping, place 2-cup measure containing chocolate back into bowl of very warm water until desired consistency.

*Do not use butter, margarine or oil.

TIP: Do not dip chocolate on humid days.

To Work With Dipping Chocolate:

• Avoid all types of moisture when melting chocolate. Steam or drops of moisture can cause mixture to "seize" or become very firm, crumbly and grainy. If this occurs, it may be corrected by stirring in 1 teaspoon shortening for each 2 ounces of melted chocolate.

• Always melt chocolate over low heat, in a double boiler or on MEDIUM (50% power) in microwave. If chocolate is melted at too high a temperature it will become crumbly and grainy. This can be corrected as directed above.

• Chop chocolate into small pieces for smooth and even melting.

• Store chocolate tightly wrapped, in a cool, dry place. Do not refrigerate.

INDEX

A

APPETIZER
(See also Dip; Snack; Spread)
Baked Brie With Pastry 357
Cheese n' Spinach Pinwheels 297
Crackers Piped With Garlic
  Cream Cheese 405
Crunchy Blue Cheese Ball 294
Garlic Pepper Toast 229
Gouda Vegetable Spread 405
Grilled Lemonade Drummies 230
Homemade Salsa & Chips 301
Honey-Glazed Snack Mix 301
Marinated Antipasto Platter 292
Oven-Baked Chicken Wings 298
Parmesan Twists 302
Pizza Breadsticks 298
Savory Cheesecake Tart 406
Spicy Cajun Shrimp 230
Sweet & Sour Meatballs 291
Tortilla Wedges 297

APPLE
Apple Butter 26
Apple Cheese Coffee Cake 34
Apple Cheese n' Turkey Grill 126
Bavarian Apple Tart 388
Cinnamon Apple Baked Pancake 20
Grandma's Apple Blueberry
  Cake 212
Grilled Ham With Apple
  Chutney 318
Ham n' Apple Bagels 45
Marmalade Mincemeat Tart 479
Salad of Spinach, Apples
  & Pecans 433
Sautéed Apple Wedges 339
Spinach Apple Toss 199

APRICOT
Apricot Cream Coffee Cake 34
Apricot Glazed Chicken 367
Apricot Sausage Stuffing 448
Chocolate Sugar Plum Torte 466
Glazed Crown Roast of Pork 428

ARTICHOKE
Curried Chicken Rice Salad 323
Layered Artichoke & Tomato
  Bake 63
Pasta With Artichoke Hearts 201
Shrimp & Artichoke Kabobs 248
Spinach & Artichoke Rolled
  Flank Steak 243
Tender Artichoke With Butter
  Sauces 385

ASPARAGUS
Asparagus Salad With Toasted
  Sesame Dressing 430
Asparagus With Orange
  & Pecans 382

Canadian Bacon n' Egg Stack 118
Fresh Tomato & Asparagus
  Frittata 51
Leg of Lamb With Garland of
  Spring Vegetables 426
Pasta & Vegetables in Wine
  Sauce 332
Red Snapper Baked With
  Asparagus 190
Vegetables With Chili
  Mayonnaise 270

AVOCADO
Avocado Crab Dip 358
Lemon Chili Chicken Breasts
  in Tortillas 262

B

BACON
Barbecued Chicken Bundles 239
Cheese & Mushroom Oven
  Omelet 52
Chicken Coq Au Vin 312
Chunky Chicken n' Corn
  Chowder 88
Egg & Bacon Topped Croissant 45
Fresh Tomato & Asparagus
  Frittata 51
Quiche Lorraine Squares 51
Rigatoni With Eggplant &
  Parmesan Cheese 136
Savory Bacon Muffins 31
Seasoned Potato Wedges 336
Smoked Bacon Red Sauce
  Over Spaghetti 134
Spinach Apple Toss 199

BANANA
Banana-Nut Pancakes 18
Chocolate Chip Banana Muffins 28
Chocolate Chip Biscuits With
  Strawberries n' Bananas 274
Custard Cream With Oranges
  & Bananas 146

BARBECUE
Beef
  Barbecued Beef Brisket 176
  Barbecued Beef Sandwiches 328
  Grilled Steaks With Garden
    Tomato Basil Sauce 243
  Hamburgers With Cucumber
    Relish 244
  Spinach & Artichoke Rolled
    Flank Steak 243
  Western Barbecued Rib
    Sampler 244
Breads
  Grilled Cheese Bread 236
  Grilled Sourdough Bread With
    Garden Tomatoes 236

Chicken
  Barbecued Chicken Bundles 239
  Grilled Lemonade Drummies 230
  Light Barbecue Chicken 239
  Spinach Ricotta Chicken
    Breasts 240
Fish
  Grilled Garden Vegetables
    & Sole 252
  Grilled Halibut With Pineapple
    Salsa 251
  Lemon Pepper Grilled Fish
    Steaks 251
Lamb
  Grilled Rosemary Lamb
    Kabobs 370
  Mint Pesto Lamb Chops 248
Sausage
  Grilled German Dip Sandwich 260
  Grilled Salami & Onion
    Sandwich 262
Seafood
  Shrimp & Artichoke Kabobs 248
  Spicy Cajun Shrimp 230
Vegetables
  Blue Cheese Grilled Potatoes 268
  Grilled Corn With Herb Butter 267
  Grilled Vegetable Kabobs 268

BEANS
Brown Sugar Baked Beans 264
Corn Bread Topped Casserole 183
Mixed-Up Bean Soup 167
Sausage n' Pasta Stew 88
Spicy Red Beans Over Rice 264

BEEF
(See also Ground Beef; Hamburgers)
Main Dish, One Dish Meal
  Beef With Mushrooms &
    Pea Pods 101
  Corn Bread Topped Casserole 183
  Santa Fe Supper 104
  Skillet Beef n' Vegetables 102
Main Dish, Roasted
  Barbecued Beef Brisket 176
  Elegant Beef Tenderloin With
    Béarnaise Sauce 368
  Garlic Prime Rib 426
  Pot Roast With Winter
    Vegetables 178
  Roasted Beef With Horseradish 176
Main Dish, Steak
  Blue Cheese & Onion Baked
    Steak 181
  Family Swiss Steak 178
  Grilled Steaks With Garden
    Tomato Basil Sauce 243
  Horseradish Steak With
    Cream Sauce 315
  Peppered Minute Steak 102

Rolled Burgundy Steak 181
Spinach & Artichoke Rolled
  Flank Steak 243
Sandwiches
  Barbecued Beef Sandwiches 328
  Giant Corned Beef & Swiss
    Hero 331
  Stroganoff Beef Sandwich 128
Other
  Western Barbecued Rib
    Sampler 244

BEET
Elegant Julienne Salad 430

BEVERAGE
Cold
  Citrus Iced Tea 232
  Cranberry Citrus Sparkler 291
  Frothy Orange Smoothy 459
  Holiday Orange Eggnog 411
  Minted Lemon Ginger Ale 232
  Peach & Berry Shake 149
  Sparkling Juice With Fruit
    Kabobs 15
  Sparkling Punch With Fruit
    Ice Ring 411
Warm
  Flavored Coffees 17
  Mixed Fruit Warmer 15

BISCUIT
Cheddar Cheese Pan Biscuits 305
Chocolate Chip Biscuits With
  Strawberries n' Bananas 274
Flaky Rosemary Biscuits With
  Peach Butter 362

BLACKBERRIES
Berries With Orange Cream 274
Blackberry Cobbler 210
Mixed Berry Almond Pie 210

BLUE CHEESE
Blue Cheese & Onion Baked
  Steak 181
Blue Cheese Grilled Potatoes 268
Blue Cheese n' Walnut Dip 358
Crunchy Blue Cheese Ball 294
Pear & Walnut Salad With Blue
  Cheese 433
Savory Cheesecake Tart 406

BLUEBERRY
Berries With Orange Cream 274
Blueberry Pancakes 18
Crisp Phyllo Petals With
  Berries 464
Fresh Berries Over Cookies
  & Cream 393
Grandma's Apple Blueberry
  Cake 212
Mixed Berry Almond Pie 210
Prize Winning Blueberry Muffins 28

BREAD, QUICK
Biscuits
  Cheddar Cheese Pan Biscuits 305
  Flaky Rosemary Biscuits With
    Peach Butter 362
Muffins
  Chocolate Chip Banana Muffins 28
  Cinnamon Topped Rhubarb
    Muffins 83
  Good Morning Muffins 31
  Oatmeal Pecan Muffins 161
  Prize Winning Blueberry
    Muffins 28
  Savory Bacon Muffins 31
  Sparkling Cranberry Orange
    Muffins 414
Pancakes & Waffles
  Cinnamon Apple Baked Pancake 20
  Sun Honey Waffles 23
  Tender Yogurt Pancakes 18
  Wild Rice Breakfast Cakes 64
  Wild Rice Pecan Waffles 23
Sweet Breads
  Festive Orange Nut Bread 413
  Glazed Chocolate Mini Loaves 413
  Lemon Nut Bread 32
  Old-Fashioned Poppy Seed
    Tea Bread 68
Other
  Basil Lemon Garlic Bread 81
  Buttery Herbed Breadsticks 306
  Country Custard Skillet Corn
    Bread 305
  French Toast Croissants 20
  Garlic Pepper Toast 229
  Grilled Cheese Bread 236
  Grilled Sourdough Bread With
    Garden Tomatoes 236
  Hearty Parmesan Soda Bread 161
  Jalapeño Corn Scones 84
  Old-Fashioned Spoon Bread
    With Maple Butter 162
  Onion Crusted Whole Grain
    Bread 84
  Orange Raisin Scones 32
  Parmesan Basil Puffs 83
  Peach Melba Crepes 18
  Rosemary Breadstick Twists 81
  Vegetable Yorkshire Pudding 416

BREAD, YEAST
Bread
  Festive Julekage 414
  Hearty Caraway Rye Bread 306
  Onion Dill Picnic Bread 235
  Orange Almond Braided
    Coffee Cake 39
Frozen Dough
  Buttery Cinnamon-Nut Bread 37
  Cheesy Snack Bread 302
  Garlic Pull-Apart Bread 308

Parmesan Twists 302
Spinach Swirl Whole Wheat
  Bread 164
Rolls
  Crescent Dinner Rolls 364
  Crusty Hard Rolls 416
  Honey n' Wheat Potato Rolls 164
  Mini Brioche 362
  Onion Hamburger Buns 235
Other
  Country Flat Bread 308
  Old World Kolachi 40

BROCCOLI
Broccoli Beer Cheese Soup 310
Broccoli n' Cheese Oven
  Omelet 52
Chicken Divan Pasta 136
Chicken Vegetable Sauté 94
Creamy Marinated Vegetable
  Salad 257
Crisp Marinated Vegetables 334
Endive-Broccoli Salad 378
Ham & Broccoli Fettuccine 134
Ham & Broccoli Strata 47
Hearty Turkey Divan Bake 169
Sausage & Vegetable Melt 321
Sausage n' Pasta Stew 88
Vegetable Yorkshire Pudding 416
Vegetables With Chili
  Mayonnaise 270

BROWNIES
Crazy-Topped Brownies 278
Mocha Brownie Sundae 342

BRUSSELS SPROUTS
Herbed Brussels Sprouts
  & Carrots 386
Pistachio Sprinkled Brussels
  Sprouts 438
Winter Vegetables With
  Mustard Sauce 440

BUTTERS
Apple Butter 26
How To: Flavor Butter 71
Savory 331, 377, 385
Sweet 20, 32, 162, 362

BUTTERSCOTCH
Butterscotch Refrigerator
  Cookies 217
Choco-Scotch Bars 276

C

CABBAGE
Braised Pork Chops & Cabbage 187
Crunchy Cabbage Salad 320
Stuffed Hamburger-Cabbage
  Buns 326
Sweet n' Tangy Slaw 257
Vegetable Ground Beef Soup 91

INDEX

CAKE

Fruit

Fruited Pound Cake ... 469
Rum Hazelnut Fruited Cake ... 469

Layered

Chocolate Mint Layered Torte ... 453
Orange Glazed Poppy Seed
Torte ... 394
Raspberry Laced Wedding
Cake ... 470

Other

Buttery Coconut Pecan Cake ... 212
Grandma's Apple Blueberry
Cake ... 212
Ice Cream Cone Cakes ... 480
Magical Chocolate Bottom
Cake ... 339
Petits Fours ... 472
Raspberry Truffle Ice Cream
Cake ... 475

CANDY

Almond Fudge ... 491
Buttercreams ... 492
Cashew Butter Crunch ... 491
Chocolate Covered Cherries ... 492
Chocolate Drizzled Pecan
Caramel Corn ... 408
Chocolate Swirl Divinity ... 488
Dark Chocolate Fudge ... 491
Macadamia Nut Fudge ... 491
Melt-In-Your-Mouth Truffles ... 488
Old-Fashioned Soft Popcorn
Balls ... 408
Peanut Butter Cups ... 494
Peanut Butter Swirl Fudge ... 491

CARAMEL

Chocolate Caramel Truffle
Torte ... 393
Chocolate Drizzled Pecan
Caramel Corn ... 408

CARROT

Main Dish

Chicken Coq Au Vin ... 312
Cheese n' Vegetable Linguine ... 131
Festive Vegetable Sauté ... 442
Garden Skillet Chicken ... 94
Grilled Garden Vegetables
& Sole ... 252
Leg of Lamb With Garland
of Spring Vegetables ... 426
Pot Roast With Winter
Vegetables ... 178
Roasted Beef With Horseradish ... 176

Salads

Carrot n' Turnip Salad With
Mustard Dressing ... 196
Creamy Marinated Vegetable
Salad ... 257
Elegant Julienne Salad ... 430

Vegetables

Buttered Vegetables With
Fresh Mint ... 334
Carrots in Butter Wine Sauce ... 445
Creamed Dilly Peas ... 141
Crisp Marinated Vegetables ... 334
Herbed Brussels Sprouts
& Carrots ... 386
Parmesan Potato & Carrot
Bundles ... 267
Tangy Mustard Carrots ... 205
Vegetables With Chili
Mayonnaise ... 270

Other

Carrot Bunny Cookies ... 483
Good Morning Muffins ... 31

CASSEROLE

(See One Dish Meal)

CAULIFLOWER

Cauliflower Dijon ... 386
Creamy Marinated Vegetable
Salad ... 257

CHEESE

(See also Blue Cheese)

Appetizers

Baked Brie With Pastry ... 357
Cheese n' Spinach Pinwheels ... 297
Cheesy Snack Bread ... 302
Crunchy Blue Cheese Ball ... 294
Garlic Pepper Toast ... 229
Gouda Vegetable Spread ... 405
Hot Pepper Cheese Party Dip ... 292
Marinated Antipasto Platter ... 292
Pizza Breadsticks ... 298
Tortilla Wedges ... 297

Bread

Cheddar Cheese Pan Biscuits ... 305
Grilled Cheese Bread ... 236

Eggs

Broccoli n' Cheese Oven Omelet ... 52
Cheese & Mushroom Oven
Omelet ... 52
Country Provence Eggs ... 117
Dijon Chicken With Double
Cheese Bake ... 42
Enchilada-Style Scrambled
Eggs ... 118
Fresh Tomato & Asparagus
Frittata ... 51
Ham & Broccoli Strata ... 47
Quiche Lorraine Squares ... 51
Spinach-Filled Puff Pancake ... 54
Zucchini, Tomato & Cheese
Frittata ... 117

Main Dish, Beef

Corn Bread Topped Casserole ... 183
Double Crust Pizza Pie ... 315
Fiesta Taco Bake ... 183
Layered Mexicana Casserole ... 317
Santa Fe Supper ... 104

Skillet Pizza Casserole ... 101
Stuffed Hamburger-Cabbage
Buns ... 326

Main Dish, Chicken

Barbecued Chicken Bundles ... 239
Chicken Divan Pasta ... 136
Garlic n' Lime Chicken Fajitas ... 324
Spinach Ricotta Chicken
Breasts ... 240

Main Dish, Fish & Seafood

Feta-Stuffed Tuna Steaks ... 377
Florentine-Style Fish ... 318
Grilled Garden Vegetables
& Sole ... 252
Seafood Lasagna ... 332

Main Dish, Pork

Ham & Cheese Potato Pie ... 54
Sausage & Vegetable Pasta
Supper ... 108
Stuffed Eggplant ... 187

Main Dish, Turkey

Cheese & Tomato Turkey
Cutlets ... 92
Hearty Turkey Divan Bake ... 169

Main Dish, Other

Cheese n' Vegetable Linguine ... 131
Country Vegetable Lasagna ... 192
Mixed Grill Whole Wheat
Pizza ... 194
Quick Tortellini Supper ... 131
Spinach & Cheese Mostaccioli ... 201

Salads

Fresh Herb Tomato-Jack Salad ... 259
Spinach Apple Toss ... 199

Sandwiches

Apple Cheese n' Turkey Grill ... 126
Giant Corned Beef & Swiss
Hero ... 331
Grilled German Dip Sandwich ... 260
Grilled Salami & Onion
Sandwich ... 262
Ham n' Apple Bagels ... 45
Open-Faced Salami n' Relish
Sandwich ... 128
Picnic Peppered Hoagie ... 260
Sausage & Vegetable Melt ... 331
Super Sloppy Subs ... 328

Soups

Broccoli Beer Cheese Soup ... 310
Hearty Potato & Sausage
Chowder ... 86

Vegetables

Easy Southwestern Potatoes ... 64
Garden Harvest Stuffed
Peppers ... 208
Hearty Twice-Baked Potatoes ... 206
Skillet Zucchini Sauté ... 141

Other

Apple Cheese Coffee Cake ... 34
Pasta With Artichoke Hearts ... 201
Spinach Stuffed Pasta Shells ... 380

INDEX

CHEESECAKE
Refreshing Key Lime
Cheesecake 390
Savory Cheesecake Tart 406

CHERRY
Baked Ham With Sweet Cherry
Sauce 488
Black Forest Pie 340
Chocolate Covered Cherries 492

CHICKEN
Appetizers
Grilled Lemonade Drummies 230
Oven-Baked Chicken Wings 298
Main Dish, Baked
Cashew Rice & Chicken
Casserole 169
Chicken Coq Au Vin 312
Dijon Chicken With Double
Cheese Bake 42
Honey Nut Baked Chicken 170
Layered Mexicana Casserole 317
Lemon Honey Glazed Chicken 170
Mushroom Stuffed Chicken
Breasts 424
Oven-Baked Parmesan
Chicken 172
Paella 312
Roasted Chicken n' Vegetables 172
Main Dish, Barbecued
Barbecued Chicken Bundles 239
Light Barbecue Chicken 239
Spiced Orange Chicken 240
Spinach Ricotta Chicken
Breasts 240
Main Dish, Fried
Peppery Fried Chicken
& Potatoes 175
Southern Fried Peanut
Chicken 175
Main Dish, Stove-Top
Apricot Glazed Chicken 367
Chicken & Vegetables Over
Fettuccine 92
Chicken Divan Pasta 136
Chicken Vegetable Sauté 94
Garden Skillet Chicken 94
Garden Vegetable Skillet
Dinner 98
Hearty Shrimp Jambalaya 188
Skillet Chicken & Potato
Dinner 97
Skillet Sesame Chicken 98
Tomato Patch Chicken 97
Salads
Chicken Caesar Salad 120
Crisp Cucumber n' Melon
Chicken Salad 42
Curried Chicken Rice Salad 323

Garden Chicken Salad 120
Vinaigrette Chicken &
Spinach Salad 323
Sandwiches
Garlic n' Lime Chicken Fajitas 324
Grilled Chicken Sandwich
With Spinach 126
Lemon Chili Chicken Breasts
in Tortillas 262
Whole Wheat Chicken
Sandwich 324
Soups
Cajun Gumbo Soup 91
Chunky Chicken n' Corn
Chowder 88

CHILI
Chili For a Crowd 317

CHOCOLATE
(See also Chocolate Chip)
Cakes
Chocolate Mint Layered Torte 453
Magical Chocolate Bottom
Cake 339
Candy
Buttercreams 492
Chocolate Covered Cherries 492
Chocolate Drizzled Pecan
Caramel Corn 408
Melt-In-Your-Mouth Truffles 488
Cookies
Chewy Crunch Bars 150
Choco-Scotch Bars 276
Crazy-Topped Brownies 278
Favorite Teddy Bear Cookies 483
No-Bake Chocolate Cookies 150
Peppermint n' Chocolate Bars 346
Desserts
Chocolate Caramel Truffle
Torte 393
Mocha Brownie Sundae 342
Raspberry Crowned Chocolate
Torte 388
Pies
Black Forest Pie 340
Choco-Peanut Butter
Ice Cream Pie 214
Other
How To: Decorate & Garnish
Desserts 498
How To: Work With Dipping
Chocolate 499

CHOCOLATE CHIP
Cakes
Chocolate Mint Layered Torte 453
Ice Cream Cone Cakes 480
Raspberry Truffle Ice Cream
Cake 475

Candy
Chocolate Swirl Divinity 488
Dark Chocolate Fudge 491
Peanut Butter Cups 494
Cookies
Chocolate-Dipped Shortbread 484
Peanut Chocolate Swirl Bars 278
Peppermint n' Chocolate Bars 346
Spicy Oatmeal Raisin Bars 346
Desserts
Chocolate Chip Biscuits With
Strawberries n' Bananas 274
Chocolate Sugar Plum Torte 466
Chocolate-Coated Ice Cream
Bon Bons 462
Strawberries With Orange
Chocolate 149
Pie
Black Forest Pie 340
Sauce
Special Hot Fudge Sauce 273
Other
Chocolate Chip Banana
Muffins 28
Chocolate Mocha Pastry 37
Glazed Chocolate Mini Loaves 413
Rich Chocolate Fruit Dip 345
Rocky Road Fudge Pops 460

CHOWDER
Chunky Chicken n' Corn
Chowder 88
Corn Chowder With Red
Pepper 310
Hearty Potato & Sausage
Chowder 86

CHUTNEY
Grilled Ham With Apple
Chutney 318

COBBLER
Blackberry Cobbler 210

COCONUT
Buttery Coconut Pecan Cake 212
No-Bake Chocolate Cookies 150

COFFEE
Chocolate Mocha Pastry 37
Chocolate Mocha Torte 453
Flavored Coffees 17
Mocha Brownie Sundae 342

COFFEE CAKE
Apple Cheese Coffee Cake 34
Apricot Cream Coffee Cake 34
Chocolate Mocha Pastry 37
Old-Fashioned Poppy Seed
Tea Bread 68
Orange Almond Braided
Coffee Cake 39

COLESLAW
Crunchy Cabbage Salad 320
Sweet n' Tangy Slaw 257

COMPOTE
Orange Laced Fruit Compote 60

COOKIES
Bars
Almond Strawberry Bars 486
Chewy Crunch Bars 150
Chocolate-Dipped Shortbread 484
Choco-Scotch Bars 276
Crazy-Topped Brownies 278
Peanut Chocolate Swirl Bars 278
Peppermint n' Chocolate Bars 346
Spicy Oatmeal Raisin Bars 346
Cutout
Trim-the-Tree Christmas
Cookies 484
Drop
Delicate Cookie Cones With
Orange Cream 68
Ice Cream Filled Lace
Cookie Cups 454
Molded
Butterscotch Refrigerator
Cookies 217
Carrot Bunny Cookies 483
Coconut Date Balls 486
Favorite Teddy Bear Cookies 483
Lemon Fingers With Sherbet 345
No-Bake Chocolate Cookies 150
Old-Fashioned Chewy
Molasses Cookies 217

CORN
Chunky Chicken n' Corn
Chowder 88
Corn Chowder With Red
Pepper 310
Enchilada-Style Scrambled Eggs 118
Fiesta Taco Bake 183
Garden Chicken Salad 120
Garden Harvest Stuffed Peppers 208
Grilled Corn With Herb Butter 267
Jalapeño Corn Scones 84
Pork Chops Stuffed With
Corn Relish 246
Pronto Pasta Dinner 107

CORN BREAD
Corn Bread Topped Casserole 183
Country Custard Skillet Corn
Bread 305
Jalapeño Corn Scones 84
Rosemary Orange Turkey With
Corn Bread Stuffing 422

CORNISH HEN
Orange Glazed Cornish
Game Hens 367

CORNMEAL
Corn Bread Topped Casserole 183
Country Custard Skillet Corn
Bread 305
Jalapeño Corn Scones 84
Old-Fashioned Spoon Bread
With Maple Butter 162

CRAB
Avocado Crab Dip 358
Crab, Mushroom & Leek Tart 48

CRANBERRY
Cranberry Citrus Sparkler 291
Cranberry Orange Relish 448
Cranberry Stuffed Holiday
Goose 424
Sparkling Cranberry Orange
Muffins 414
Sparkling Punch With Fruit
Ice Ring 411

CREPE
Peach Melba Crepes 18

CUCUMBER
Crisp Cucumber n' Melon
Chicken Salad 42
Elegant Julienne Salad 430
Fresh Cucumber Soup 361
Hamburgers With Cucumber
Relish 244
Refreshing Summer Salads
With Garlic Toast 437
Tomato & Cucumber in
Vinaigrette 380

CUSTARD
Aunt Emma's Rhubarb Custard
Dessert 214
Custard Cream With Oranges
& Bananas 146

D

DATE
Coconut Date Balls 486
Date Baklava 456
Steamed Plum Pudding 450

DESSERT
(See also Cake; Pie)
Cheesecake
Refreshing Key Lime
Cheesecake 390
Custard
Custard Cream With Oranges
& Bananas 146
Frozen
Chocolate-Coated Ice Cream
Bon Bons 462
Frosted Jack-O-Lanterns 459

Rocky Road Fudge Pops 460
Salted Peanut Ice Cream
Squares 342
Fruit
Aunt Emma's Rhubarb Custard
Dessert 214
Berries With Orange Cream 274
Blackberry Cobbler 210
Fresh Berries Over Cookies
& Cream 393
Orange Laced Fruit Compote 60
Rich Chocolate Fruit Dip 345
Sautéed Apple Wedges 339
Strawberries With Orange
Chocolate 149
Tender Pears in Almond
Cream Sauce 146
Sauces
Special Hot Fudge Sauce 273
Toasted Pecan Ice Cream
Sauce 273
Other 18, 342, 393, 450
Tarts
Bavarian Apple Tart 388
Marmalade Mincemeat Tart 479
Strawberry n' Cream Tart 66
Other
Chocolate Caramel Truffle
Torte 393
Chocolate Chip Biscuits With
Strawberries n' Bananas 274
Chocolate Sugar Plum Torte 466
Date Baklava 456
Delicate Cookie Cones With
Orange Cream 68
Ice Cream Filled Lace
Cookie Cups 454
Lemon Fingers With Sherbet 345
Mocha Brownie Sundae 342
Raspberry Crowned Chocolate
Torte 388
Summertime Minted Trifle 476

DIP
Avocado Crab Dip 358
Blue Cheese n' Walnut Dip 358
Garlic Eggplant Dip 294
Hot Pepper Cheese Party Dip 292
Peanut Butter n' Honey
Fruit Dip 227
Piña Colada Fruit Dip 57
Pineapple Pepper Dip 227
Rich Chocolate Fruit Dip 345
Sour Cream Pesto Dip 229
Other 260, 270

E

EGG
Broccoli n' Cheese Oven Omelet 52
Canadian Bacon n' Egg Stack 118

Country Provence Eggs 117
Dijon Chicken With Double
  Cheese Bake 42
Egg & Bacon Topped Croissant 45
Enchilada-Style Scrambled Eggs 118
Fresh Tomato & Asparagus
  Frittata 51
Ham & Broccoli Strata 47
Quiche Lorraine Squares 51
Zucchini, Tomato & Cheese
  Frittata 117

EGGNOG
Holiday Orange Eggnog 411

EGGPLANT
Garlic Eggplant Dip 294
Potato Ratatouille 142
Rigatoni With Eggplant &
  Parmesan Cheese 136
Stuffed Eggplant 187

F

FENNEL
Classic Bouillabaisse 421
Red Snapper Baked With
  Asparagus 190

FISH
Main Dish, Baked
  Baked Fish With Herbed
    Vegetables 110
  Feta-Stuffed Tuna Steaks 377
  Florentine-Style Fish 318
  Red Snapper Baked With
    Asparagus 190
Main Dish, Barbecued
  Grilled Garden Vegetables
    & Sole 252
  Grilled Halibut With Pineapple
    Salsa 251
  Honey Mustard Glazed
    Swordfish 373
  Lemon Pepper Grilled
    Fish Steaks 251
Main Dish, Broiled
  Broiled Sole Parmesan 113
  Northwest Salmon Steaks 377
Main Dish, Stove-Top
  Cracker Coated Walleye Pike 114
  Fresh Citrus Fish Sauté 110
  Orange Roughy With
    Caramelized Onions 113
  Rosemary Rainbow Trout 188
Salad
  Tuna Salad With Corn Crisps 123
Soup
  Classic Bouillabaisse 421
Other
  Salmon Pinwheels With Melon
    Puree 47

FRENCH TOAST
French Toast Croissants 20

FROSTINGS, GLAZES & ICINGS
Frostings   212, 278, 346, 394,
                 470, 480, 484
Glazes   32, 34, 39, 345, 367,
                 373, 394, 413, 414,
                 453, 456, 466, 470,
Icings   486, 472

FRUIT
(See also specific fruit)
Appetizers
  Peanut Butter n' Honey
    Fruit Dip 227
Beverages
  Mixed Fruit Warmer 15
  Sparkling Juice With Fruit
    Kabobs 15
Desserts
  Delicate Cookie Cones With
    Orange Cream 68
  Fruited Pound Cake 469
  Rich Chocolate Fruit Dip 345
  Rum Hazelnut Fruited Cake 469
Salads
  Devonshire-Style Fruit 58
  Fruits of the Season Salad 434
  Ginger Glazed Fruit 58
  Glazed Fruit Cups 66
  Lemon Zest Dressing Over
    Fresh Fruit 124
  Orange Laced Fruit Compote 60
  Orange Poppy Seed Fruit
    Salad 60
  Summer Fruit With Lime
    Ginger Dressing 250

FUDGE
Almond Fudge 491
Dark Chocolate Fudge 491
Macadamia Nut Fudge 491
Peanut Butter Swirl Fudge 491

G

GELATIN
Molded Raspberry Peach Salad 320

GINGERROOT
Country Rice With Shrimp 114
Fruits of the Season Salad 434
Ginger Chive Green Beans 205
Ginger Glazed Fruit 58
Gingered Acorn Squash 445
Gingered Pea Pods & Red
  Pepper 138
Grilled Halibut With Pineapple
  Salsa 251
Grilled Ham With Apple
  Chutney 318

GOOSE
Cranberry Stuffed Holiday
  Goose 424

GRAPEFRUIT
Grapefruit Salad Tossed
  With Peas 196

GREEN BEANS
Crisp Green Beans With Red
  Pepper 270
Crisp Marinated Vegetables 334
Fresh Green Beans With
  Mushrooms & Celery 63
Garlic Green Beans 336
Ginger Chive Green Beans 205
Green Beans With Orange 438
Herbed Green Beans 138
Skillet Chicken & Potato Dinner 97
Vegetables With Chili
  Mayonnaise 270

GREEN PEPPER
Festive Vegetable Sauté 442
Garden Harvest Stuffed
  Peppers 208
Pineapple Pepper Dip 227

GROUND BEEF
(See also Hamburgers)
Chili For a Crowd 317
Double Crust Pizza Pie 315
Market Meat Loaf 184
Stuffed Hamburger-Cabbage
  Buns 326
Sweet & Sour Meatballs 291
Vegetable Ground Beef Soup 91

GUACAMOLE
Lemon Chili Chicken Breasts
  in Tortillas 262

H

HAM
Baked Ham With Sweet Cherry
  Sauce 428
Canadian Bacon n' Egg Stack 118
Grilled Ham With Apple
  Chutney 318
Ham & Broccoli Fettuccine 136
Ham & Broccoli Strata 47
Ham & Cheese Potato Pie 54
Ham n' Apple Bagels 45
Mixed-Up Bean Soup 167
Mushroom Stuffed Chicken
  Breasts 424
Pronto Pasta Dinner 107

HAMBURGERS
Hamburgers With Cucumber
  Relish 244
Onion Stuffed Hamburgers
  With Sloppy Joe Sauce 104

INDEX

HONEY

Date Baklava ... 456
Harvest Honey Thyme Squash ... 208
Honey Lime Marinated Pork
  Tenderloin ... 246
Honey Mustard Glazed
  Swordfish ... 373
Honey n' Wheat Potato Rolls ... 164
Honey Nut Baked Chicken ... 170
Honey-Glazed Snack Mix ... 301
Lemon Honey Glazed Chicken ... 170
Orange Roughy With
  Carmelized Onions ... 113
Peanut Butter n' Honey
  Fruit Dip ... 227
Summer Fruit With Lime
  Ginger Dressing ... 254
Sun Honey Waffles ... 23

HORSERADISH

Hearty Twice-Baked Potatoes ... 206
Horseradish Steak With
  Cream Sauce ... 315
Roasted Beef With Horseradish ... 176
Rosemary Rainbow Trout ... 188

HOW TO:

How To: Decorate & Garnish
  Desserts ... 498
How To: Flavor Butter ... 71
How To: Flavor Cream
  Cheese ... 70
How To: Fold Napkins ... 396
How To: Set a Buffet Table ... 496
How To: Work With Dipping
  Chocolate ... 499

I

ICE CREAM

Chocolate-Coated Ice Cream
  Bon Bons ... 462
Choco-Peanut Butter
  Ice Cream Pie ... 214
Frosted Jack-O-Lanterns ... 459
Holiday Orange Eggnog ... 411
Ice Cream Filled Lace
  Cookie Cups ... 454
Lemon Ribbon Ice Cream Pie ... 276
Mocha Brownie Sundae ... 342
Peach & Berry Shake ... 149
Raspberry Truffle
  Ice Cream Cake ... 475
Salted Peanut Ice Cream
  Squares ... 342
Sautéed Apple Wedges ... 339

J

JAM

Homemade Berry Jam ... 25
Homemade Raspberry Jam ... 25

JAMBALAYA

Hearty Shrimp Jambalaya ... 188

K

KABOB

Grilled Rosemary Lamb Kabobs ... 370
Grilled Vegetable Kabobs ... 268
Shrimp & Artichoke Kabobs ... 248
Sparkling Juice With Fruit
  Kabobs ... 15
Spicy Cajun Shrimp ... 230

L

LAMB

Grilled Rosemary Lamb Kabobs ... 370
Leg of Lamb With Garland
  of Spring Vegetables ... 426
Mint Pesto Lamb Chops ... 248

LASAGNA

Country Vegetable Lasagna ... 192
Seafood Lasagna ... 332

LEEKS

Crab, Mushroom & Leek Tart ... 48
Mushroom Stuffed Chicken
  Breasts ... 424
Pureed Sweet Potato Soup ... 418
Roasted Beef With Horseradish ... 176

LEMON

Beverages
  Citrus Iced Tea ... 232
  Minted Lemon Ginger Ale ... 232
Bread
  Basil Lemon Garlic Bread ... 81
  Lemon Nut Bread ... 32
Desserts
  Lemon Fingers With Sherbet ... 345
  Lemon Ribbon Ice Cream Pie ... 276
Main Dish
  Broiled Sole Parmesan ... 113
  Fresh Citrus Fish Sauté ... 110
  Lemon Honey Glazed Chicken ... 170
  Lemon Pepper Grilled Fish
    Steaks ... 251
  Lemon Pork Picatta ... 108
Other
  Grilled Lemonade Drummies ... 230
  Lemon Chili Chicken Breasts
    in Tortillas ... 262
  Lemon Zest Dressing Over
    Fresh Fruit ... 124
  Lemon Zest Rice ... 133
  Vegetable n' Cracked Wheat
    Salad ... 254

LENTIL

Smoked Turkey Lentil Soup ... 167

LIME

Cranberry Citrus Sparkler ... 291
Fresh Citrus Fish Sauté ... 110
Garlic n' Lime Chicken Fajitas ... 324
Grilled Halibut With Pineapple
  Salsa ... 251
Honey Lime Marinated Pork
  Tenderloin ... 246
Northwest Salmon Steaks ... 377
Refreshing Key Lime
  Cheesecake ... 390
Summer Fruit With Lime
  Ginger Dressing ... 254

M

MAPLE

Gingered Acorn Squash ... 445
Old-Fashioned Spoon Bread
  With Maple Butter ... 162

MARINADE

Beef ... 102, 243
Chicken ... 230, 239
Vegetable ... 334

MEAT LOAF

Market Meat Loaf ... 184

MEATBALL

Sweet & Sour Meatballs ... 291

MELON

Crisp Cucumber n' Melon
  Chicken Salad ... 42
Refreshing Summer Salads
  With Garlic Toast ... 437
Salmon Pinwheels With
  Melon Puree ... 47

MENUS

Breakfasts & Brunches
  Easy & Quick Brunch ... 8
  Make-Ahead Brunch ... 10
  Rise & Shine Breakfast ... 12
  Seafood Lover's Brunch ... 9
  Special Occasion Brunch ... 11
  Springtime Brunch ... 13
Casual Entertaining
  Appetizer Buffet ... 285
  Casual Winter Get-Together ... 288
  Light Summer Supper ... 287
  Southwestern Fare ... 287
  Summertime Outdoor BBQ ... 282
  Sunday Evening Entertaining ... 283
  3-Alarm Chili Dinner ... 284
  When Good Friends Gather ... 289
Celebrations
  Easter Celebration ... 402
  Holiday Feast ... 400
  Old-Fashioned Christmas ... 401
  Spring Shower ... 403

Elegant Entertaining
Before the Show 350
Best Dressed Affair 353
For Special Guests 351
Fresh Summer Fare 354
Spring Is in the Air 352
Summertime Elegance 355
Hearty Dinners
Bubbling Kettle Dinner 159
Fall Harvest Dinner 155
Family Favorite 157
Fisherman's Delight 154
Homemade Pot Roast 156
Touch of the Southwest 158
Picnics & BBQ
Catch of the Day 224
Company's Coming BBQ 223
Grilled Hamburger Special 221
Picnic Basket Time 225
Southwestern BBQ 220
Summertime Steak Grill 222
Simple Suppers
Chicken Express Dinner 74
Country Spaghetti Supper 75
Down Home Cooking 78
Lakeside Supper 77
Quick Family Dinner 76
Simmering Supper 79

MINCEMEAT
Marmalade Mincemeat Tart 479

MINT
Buttered Vegetables With
Fresh Mint 334
Chocolate Mint Layered Torte 453
Mint Pesto Lamb Chops 248
Minted Lemon Ginger Ale 232
Summertime Minted Trifle 476

MOLASSES
Old-Fashioned Chewy Molasses
Cookies 217

MUFFIN
Chocolate Chip Banana Muffins 28
Cinnamon Topped Rhubarb
Muffins 83
Good Morning Muffins 31
Oatmeal Pecan Muffins 161
Prize Winning Blueberry Muffins 28
Savory Bacon Muffins 31
Sparkling Cranberry Orange
Muffins 414

MUSHROOM
Cheese & Mushroom Oven
Omelet 52
Crab, Mushroom & Leek Tart 48
Fresh Green Beans With
Mushrooms & Celery 63
Fresh Mushroom Bisque 361

Mushroom Stuffed Chicken
Breasts 424

MUSTARD
Carrot n' Turnip Salad With
Mustard Dressing 196
Cauliflower Dijon 386
Dijon Chicken With Double
Cheese Bake 42
Grilled German Dip Sandwich 260
Honey Mustard Glazed
Swordfish 373
Mustard Cream Pork Chops 107
Potato Salad With Mustard
Mayonnaise 259
Tangy Mustard Carrots 205
Winter Vegetables With
Mustard Sauce 440

N

NUTS
Buttery Cinnamon-Nut Bread 37
Cardamom Spiced Nuts 406
Cashew Butter Crunch 491
Date Baklava 456
Festive Orange Nut Bread 413
Honey-Glazed Snack Mix 301
Honey Nut Baked Chicken 170
Lemon Nut Bread 32
Macadamia Nut Fudge 491
Nutty Wild Rice Pilaf 382
Nutty Wild Rice Salad 199
Pecan Pancakes 18
Toasted Pecan Ice Cream
Sauce 273

O

OATMEAL
No-Bake Chocolate Cookies 150
Oatmeal Pecan Muffins 161
Spicy Oatmeal Raisin Bars 346

OMELET
Broccoli n' Cheese Oven Omelet 52
Cheese & Mushroom Oven
Omelet 52

ONE DISH MEAL
Beef
Corn Bread Topped Casserole 183
Fiesta Taco Bake 183
Santa Fe Supper 104
Skillet Beef n' Vegetables 102
Skillet Pizza Casserole 101
Chicken
Cashew Rice & Chicken
Casserole 169
Chicken Vegetable Sauté 94
Garden Skillet Chicken 94
Garden Vegetable Skillet
Dinner 98

Layered Mexicana Casserole 317
Roasted Chicken n' Vegetables 172
Skillet Chicken & Potato
Dinner 97
Pasta
Pronto Pasta Dinner 107
Quick Tortellini Supper 131
Rigatoni With Eggplant &
Parmesan Cheese 136
Pork
Country Provence Eggs 117
Ham & Broccoli Fettuccine 134
Sausage & Vegetable Pasta
Supper 108
Turkey
Hearty Turkey Divan Bake 169

ONION
Blue Cheese & Onion Baked
Steak 181
Grilled Salami & Onion
Sandwich 262
Onion Crusted Whole Grain
Bread 84
Onion Dill Picnic Bread 235
Onion Hamburger Buns 235
Onion Stuffed Hamburgers
With Sloppy Joe Sauce 104
Orange Roughy With
Caramelized Onions 113

ORANGE
Beverages
Citrus Iced Tea 232
Frothy Orange Smoothy 459
Holiday Orange Eggnog 411
Mixed Fruit Warmer 15
Bread
Festive Orange Nut Bread 413
Orange Almond Braided
Coffee Cake 39
Orange Raisin Scones 32
Sparkling Cranberry Orange
Muffins 414
Desserts
Berries With Orange Cream 274
Delicate Cookie Cones With
Orange Cream 68
Frosted Jack-O-Lanterns 459
Marmalade Mincemeat Tart 479
Orange Glazed Poppy Seed
Torte 394
Strawberries With Orange
Chocolate 149
Main Dish
Apricot Glazed Chicken 367
Orange Glazed Cornish Game
Hens 367
Rosemary Orange Turkey With
Corn Bread Stuffing 422
Spiced Orange Chicken 240

Salads
Baked Ambrosia in a Cup 57
Fresh Orange Salad 378
Glazed Fruit Cups 66
Orange Laced Fruit Compote 60
Orange Poppy Seed Fruit Salad 60
Vegetables
Asparagus With Orange
& Pecans 382
Green Beans With Orange 438
Other
Cranberry Orange Relish 448

OYSTER
Yuletide Oyster Stew With
Buttery Croutons 418

P

PANCAKES
Cinnamon Apple Baked Pancake 20
Spinach-Filled Puff Pancake 54
Tender Yogurt Pancakes 18
Wild Rice Breakfast Cakes 64

PARMESAN
Broiled Sole Parmesan 113
Ham & Broccoli Fettuccine 134
Hearty Parmesan Soda Bread 161
Oven-Baked Parmesan Chicken 172
Parmesan Basil Puffs 83
Parmesan Potato & Carrot
Bundles 267
Parmesan Twists 302
Rigatoni With Eggplant
& Parmesan Cheese 136
Seasoned Potato Wedges 336
Sour Cream Pesto Dip 229
Spinach & Cheese Mostaccioli 201

PARSNIP
Festive Vegetable Sauté 442

PASTA
Main Dish, Chicken & Turkey
Chicken & Vegetables Over
Fettuccine 92
Chicken Divan Pasta 136
Hearty Turkey Divan Bake 169
Main Dish, Meatless
Cheese n' Vegetable Linguine 131
Country Vegetable Lasagna 192
Pasta & Vegetables in
Wine Sauce 332
Pasta With Artichoke Hearts 201
Quick Tortellini Supper 131
Rigatoni With Eggplant &
Parmesan Cheese 136
Main Dish, Pork
Ham & Broccoli Fettuccine 134
Mustard Cream Pork Chops 107
Pronto Pasta Dinner 107

Sausage & Vegetable Pasta
Supper 108
Smoked Bacon Red Sauce
Over Spaghetti 134
Main Dish, Seafood
Angel Hair Pasta With Basil
& Shrimp 202
Roasted Red Pepper & Scallop
Fettuccine 374
Shrimp & Artichoke Kabobs 248
Soups
Easy Turkey Soup 86
Sausage n' Pasta Stew 88
Other
Butter Crumb Noodles 133
Spinach & Cheese Mostaccioli 201
Spinach Stuffed Pasta Shells 380

PASTRY
Chocolate Mocha Pastry 37

PEACH
Flaky Rosemary Biscuits With
Peach Butter 362
Molded Raspberry Peach Salad 320
Peach & Berry Shake 149
Peach Melba Crepes 18
Summertime Minted Trifle 476

PEANUT
Chewy Crunch Bars 150
Choco-Peanut Butter
Ice Cream Pie 214
Peanut Chocolate Swirl Bars 278
Salted Peanut Ice Cream
Squares 342
Southern Fried Peanut Chicken 175

PEANUT BUTTER
Choco-Peanut Butter
Ice Cream Pie 214
Crazy-Topped Brownies 278
Peanut Butter Cups 494
Peanut Butter n' Honey
Fruit Dip 227
Peanut Butter Swirl Fudge 491
Southern Fried Peanut Chicken 175

PEAR
Old-Fashioned Pear Conserve 26
Pear & Walnut Salad With
Blue Cheese 433
Pork Loin Roast With Pears 373
Tender Pears in Almond Cream
Sauce 146

PEAS (GREEN)
Beef With Mushrooms
& Pea Pods 101
Buttered Vegetables With
Fresh Mint 334
Creamed Dilly Peas 141
Garden Skillet Chicken 94

Gingered Pea Pods &
Red Pepper 138
Grapefruit Salad Tossed
With Peas 196
Leg of Lamb With Garland
of Spring Vegetables 426
Mashed Potatoes With
Buttered Peas 206
Nutty Wild Rice Salad 199
Quick Tortellini Supper 131
Vegetable n' Cracked Wheat
Salad 254
Vegetable Rice Pilaf 202

PEPPER
(See Green Pepper; Red Pepper)

PEPPERONI
Pizza Breadsticks 298

PESTO
Mint Pesto Lamb Chops 248
Sour Cream Pesto Dip 229

PIE
Black Forest Pie 340
Choco-Peanut Butter
Ice Cream Pie 214
Crisp Phyllo Petals With
Berries 464
Double Crust Pizza Pie 315
Ham & Cheese Potato Pie 54
Lemon Ribbon Ice Cream Pie 276
Mixed Berry Almond Pie 210

PINEAPPLE
Baked Ambrosia in a Cup 57
Grilled Halibut With Pineapple
Salsa 251
Piña Colada Fruit Dip 57
Pineapple Pepper Dip 227
Sweet & Sour Meatballs 291

PIZZA
Double Crust Pizza Pie 315
Mixed Grill Whole Wheat Pizza 194
Pizza Breadsticks 298
Skillet Pizza Casserole 101

PLUM
Steamed Plum Pudding 450

POPCORN
Chocolate Drizzled Pecan
Caramel Corn 408
Old-Fashioned Soft Popcorn
Balls 408

PORK
(See also Bacon; Ham; Sausage)
Braised Pork Chops & Cabbage 187
Canadian Bacon n' Egg Stack 118
Chili Picante Roasted Pork Loin 184
Glazed Crown Roast of Pork 428

Honey Lime Marinated Pork
  Tenderloin | 246
Lemon Pork Picatta | 108
Market Meat Loaf | 184
Mustard Cream Pork Chops | 107
Pork Chops Stuffed With
  Corn Relish | 246
Pork Loin Roast With Pears | 373

POTATO
(See also Sweet Potato)
Bread
  Honey n' Wheat Potato Rolls | 164
Main Dish
  Chicken Coq Au Vin | 312
  Country Provence Eggs | 117
  Cracker Coated Walleye Pike | 114
  Ham & Cheese Potato Pie | 54
  Peppery Fried Chicken
    & Potatoes | 175
  Skillet Chicken & Potato Dinner | 97
Salad
  Potato Salad With Mustard
    Mayonnaise | 259
Soups
  Chunky Chicken n' Corn
    Chowder | 88
  Hearty Potato & Sausage
    Chowder | 86
Vegetables
  Blue Cheese Grilled Potatoes | 268
  Easy Southwestern Potatoes | 64
  Hearty Twice-Baked Potatoes | 206
  Mashed Potatoes With
    Buttered Peas | 206
  Mashed Potatoes With
    Sour Cream | 144
  Parmesan Potato & Carrot
    Bundles | 267
  Potato Ratatouille | 142
  Rosemary Garlic Potatoes | 144
  Seasoned Potato Wedges | 336
  Winter Vegetables With
    Mustard Sauce | 440

POULTRY
(See Chicken; Cornish Hen; Turkey)

PUDDING
Steamed Plum Pudding | 450

PUNCH
Sparkling Punch With Fruit
  Ice Ring | 411

Q

QUICHE
Quiche Lorraine Squares | 51

QUICK BREAD
(See Bread, Quick)

R

RAISIN
Apricot Glazed Chicken | 367
Grilled Ham With Apple Chutney | 318
Spicy Oatmeal Raisin Bars | 346
Steamed Plum Pudding | 450

RASPBERRY
Berries With Orange Cream | 274
Crisp Phyllo Petals With Berries | 464
Fresh Berries Over Cookies
  & Cream | 393
Homemade Raspberry Jam | 25
Mixed Berry Almond Pie | 210
Molded Raspberry Peach Salad | 320
Peach Melba Crepes | 18
Raspberry Crowned Chocolate
  Torte | 388
Raspberry Laced Wedding Cake | 470
Raspberry Truffle Ice Cream
  Cake | 475

RED PEPPER
Corn Chowder With Red Pepper | 310
Crisp Green Beans With
  Red Pepper | 270
Garlic Pepper Toast | 229
Gingered Pea Pods &
  Red Pepper | 138
Roasted Red Pepper & Scallop
  Fettuccine | 374

RELISH
Cranberry Orange Relish | 448
Hamburgers With Cucumber
  Relish | 244
Open-Faced Salami n' Relish
  Sandwich | 128
Pork Chops Stuffed With
  Corn Relish | 246

RHUBARB
Aunt Emma's Rhubarb Custard
  Dessert | 214
Cinnamon Topped Rhubarb
  Muffins | 83

RICE
(See also Wild Rice)
Cajun Gumbo Soup | 91
Cashew Rice & Chicken
  Casserole | 169
Country Rice With Shrimp | 114
Curried Chicken Rice Salad | 323
Hearty Shrimp Jambalaya | 188
Lemon Zest Rice | 133
Paella | 312
Santa Fe Supper | 104
Spicy Red Beans Over Rice | 264
Spinach Rice Pilaf | 446
Vegetable Rice Pilaf | 202
Wild Rice Breakfast Cakes | 64

ROLLS
Crescent Dinner Rolls | 364
Crusty Hard Rolls | 416
Honey n' Wheat Potato Rolls | 164

RUTABAGA
Pot Roast With Winter
  Vegetables | 178

S

SALADS
Fruit
  Baked Ambrosia in a Cup | 57
  Fresh Orange Salad | 378
  Fruits of the Season Salad | 434
  Ginger Glazed Fruit | 58
  Glazed Fruit Cups | 66
  Grapefruit Salad Tossed
    With Peas | 196
  Lemon Zest Dressing Over
    Fresh Fruit | 124
  Orange Poppy Seed Fruit Salad | 60
  Pear & Walnut Salad With
    Blue Cheese | 433
  Salad of Spinach, Apples
    & Pecans | 433
  Summer Fruit With Lime
    Ginger Dressing | 254
Main Dish
  Chicken Caesar Salad | 120
  Crisp Cucumber n' Melon
    Chicken Salad | 42
  Curried Chicken Rice Salad | 323
  Garden Chicken Salad | 120
  Refreshing Summer Salads
    With Garlic Toast | 437
  Tuna Salad With Corn Crisps | 123
  Turkey Wild Rice Salad | 123
  Vinaigrette Chicken & Spinach
    Salad | 323
Molded
  Molded Raspberry Peach Salad | 320
Vegetable
  Asparagus Salad With Toasted
    Sesame Dressing | 430
  Carrot n' Turnip Salad With
    Mustard Dressing | 196
  Creamy Marinated Vegetable
    Salad | 257
  Crisp Marinated Vegetables | 334
  Crunchy Cabbage Salad | 320
  Elegant Julienne Salad | 430
  Endive-Broccoli Salad | 378
  Fresh Herb Tomato-Jack Salad | 259
  Potato Salad With Mustard
    Mayonnaise | 259
  Spinach Apple Toss | 199
  Sweet n' Tangy Slaw | 257
  Tomato & Cucumber in
    Vinaigrette | 380

INDEX

Tossed Salad With Spicy
    Tomato Dressing   124
Other
    Nutty Wild Rice Salad   199
    Vegetable n' Cracked Wheat
        Salad   254

SALAD DRESSING
Savory   42, 120, 124, 196, 257, 259,
            320, 323, 378, 380, 430, 433
Sweet   124, 254, 378, 434

SALMON
Northwest Salmon Steaks   377
Salmon Pinwheels With
    Melon Puree   47

SALSA
Grilled Halibut With Pineapple
    Salsa   251
Homemade Salsa & Chips   301

SANDWICH
Beef
    Barbecued Beef Sandwiches   328
    Giant Corned Beef & Swiss
        Hero   331
    Stroganoff Beef Sandwich   128
Pork
    Egg & Bacon Topped Croissant   45
    Grilled German Dip Sandwich   260
    Grilled Salami & Onion
        Sandwich   262
    Ham n' Apple Bagels   45
    Open-Faced Salami n' Relish
        Sandwich   128
    Picnic Peppered Hoagie   260
    Sausage & Vegetable Melt   331
    Super Sloppy Subs   328
Poultry
    Apple Cheese n' Turkey Grill   126
    Garlic n' Lime Chicken Fajitas   324
    Grilled Chicken Sandwich
        With Spinach   126
    Whole Wheat Chicken
        Sandwich   324

SAUCE
(See also Dessert)
Barbecue   176, 244
Béarnaise   368
Butter   385
Cherry   428
Hollandaise   45
Mustard   386, 440
Pesto   248
Tomato   104, 243, 298

SAUSAGE
(See also Pepperoni)
Appetizer
    Crackers Piped With Garlic
        Cream Cheese   405

Sweet & Sour Meatballs   291
Tortilla Wedges   297
Main Dish
    Country Provence Eggs   117
    Double Crust Pizza Pie   315
    Hearty Shrimp Jambalaya   188
    Paella   312
    Sausage & Vegetable Pasta
        Supper   108
    Skillet Pizza Casserole   101
    Stuffed Eggplant   187
Sandwiches
    Grilled German Dip Sandwich   260
    Grilled Salami & Onion
        Sandwich   262
    Open-Faced Salami n' Relish
        Sandwich   128
    Picnic Peppered Hoagie   260
    Sausage & Vegetable Melt   331
    Super Sloppy Subs   328
Soups
    Cajun Gumbo Soup   91
    Hearty Potato & Sausage
        Chowder   86
    Sausage n' Pasta Stew   88
Other
    Apricot Sausage Stuffing   448

SCALLOP
Roasted Red Pepper & Scallop
    Fettuccine   374

SCONE
Jalapeño Corn Scones   84
Orange Raisin Scones   32

SEAFOOD
(See also specific seafood)
Classic Bouillabaisse   421
Crab, Mushroom & Leek Tart   48
Paella   312
Roasted Red Pepper & Scallop
    Fettuccine   374
Seafood in Patty Shells   48
Seafood Lasagna   332

SHRIMP
Angel Hair Pasta With Basil
    & Shrimp   202
Classic Bouillabaisse   421
Country Rice With Shrimp   116
Hearty Shrimp Jambalaya   188
Paella   312
Refreshing Summer Salads
    With Garlic Toast   437
Seafood in Patty Shells   48
Seafood Lasagna   332
Shrimp & Artichoke Kabobs   248
Spicy Cajun Shrimp   230

SNACK
Cheesy Snack Bread   302
Honey-Glazed Snack Mix   301

SOUP
(See also Chowder; Stew)
Broccoli Beer Cheese Soup   310
Cajun Gumbo Soup   91
Easy Turkey Soup   86
Fresh Cucumber Soup   361
Fresh Mushroom Bisque   361
Mixed-Up Bean Soup   167
Pureed Sweet Potato Soup   418
Smoked Turkey Lentil Soup   167
Vegetable Ground Beef Soup   91

SPAGHETTI
Smoked Bacon Red Sauce
    Over Spaghetti   134

SPINACH
Main Dish
    Country Provence Eggs   117
    Florentine-Style Fish   318
    Spinach & Artichoke Rolled
        Flank Steak   243
    Spinach Ricotta Chicken
        Breasts   240
    Spinach-Filled Puff Pancake   54
Salad
    Spinach Apple Toss   199
    Vinaigrette Chicken & Spinach
        Salad   323
Other
    Cheese n' Spinach Pinwheels   297
    Garlic Spinach With Red Onion   142
    Grilled Chicken Sandwich
        With Spinach   126
    Spinach & Cheese Mostaccioli   201
    Spinach Rice Pilaf   446
    Spinach Stuffed Pasta Shells   380
    Spinach Swirl Whole Wheat
        Bread   164

SPREAD
Apple Butter   26
Gouda Vegetable Spread   405
How To: Flavor Butter   71
How To: Flavor Cream
    Cheese   70
Old-Fashioned Pear Conserve   26

SQUASH
(See also Zucchini)
Festive Vegetable Sauté   442
Garlic Roasted Summer
    Vegetables   442
Gingered Acorn Squash   445
Harvest Honey Thyme Squash   208
Pasta & Vegetables in Wine
    Sauce   332
Skillet Beef n' Vegetables   102

INDEX

STEAK

(See Beef)

STEW

Chicken Coq Au Vin 312
Classic Bouillabaisse 421
Hearty Shrimp Jambalaya 188
Sausage n' Pasta Stew 88
Yuletide Oyster Stew With
  Buttery Croutons 418

STRAWBERRY

Almond Strawberry Bars 486
Berries With Orange Cream 274
Chocolate Chip Biscuits With
  Strawberries n' Bananas 274
Crisp Phyllo Petals With
  Berries 464
Fresh Berries Over Cookies
  & Cream 393
Fresh Strawberry Syrup 25
Homemade Berry Jam 25
Mixed Berry Almond Pie 210
Peach & Berry Shake 149
Strawberries With Orange
  Chocolate 149
Strawberry n' Cream Tart 66
Summertime Minted Trifle 476

STUFFING

Apricot Sausage Stuffing 448
Bread 170
Corn Bread 422
Fruit 367, 424
Rice 446
Vegetables 181

SWEET POTATO

Almond-Glazed Sweet Potatoes 440
Pureed Sweet Potato Soup 418

SYRUP

Fresh Strawberry Syrup 25

T

TOMATO

Cheese & Tomato Turkey
  Cutlets 92
Fresh Herb Tomato-Jack Salad 259
Fresh Tomato & Asparagus
  Frittata 51
Garden Chicken Salad 120
Grilled Sourdough Bread With
  Garden Tomatoes 236
Grilled Steaks With Garden
  Tomato Basil Sauce 243

Hearty Olive & Tomato Veal
  Cutlets 370
Homemade Salsa & Chips 301
Layered Artichoke & Tomato
  Bake 63
Tomato & Cucumber in
  Vinaigrette 380
Tomato Patch Chicken 97
Tossed Salad With Spicy
  Tomato Dressing 124
Zucchini, Tomato & Cheese
  Frittata 117

TORTILLA

Enchilada-Style Scrambled Eggs 118
Garlic n' Lime Chicken Fajitas 324
Homemade Salsa & Chips 301
Lemon Chili Chicken Breasts
  in Tortillas 262
Tortilla Wedges 297
Tuna Salad With Corn Crisps 123

TUNA

Feta-Stuffed Tuna Steaks 377
Tuna Salad With Corn Crisps 123

TURKEY

Apple Cheese n' Turkey Grill 126
Cheese & Tomato Turkey
  Cutlets 92
Easy Turkey Soup 86
Hearty Turkey Divan Bake 169
Rosemary Orange Turkey
  With Corn Bread Stuffing 422
Smoked Turkey Lentil Soup 167
Turkey Wild Rice Salad 123

TURNIP

Carrot n' Turnip Salad With
  Mustard Dressing 196
Pot Roast With Winter
  Vegetables 178

V

VEAL

Hearty Olive & Tomato Veal
  Cutlets 370

VEGETABLE

(See specific vegetable)

W

WAFFLES

Sun Honey Waffles 23
Wild Rice Pecan Waffles 23

WHIPPING CREAM

Spicy Whipped Cream 17
Other 23, 68, 274

WILD RICE

Cashew Rice & Chicken
  Casserole 169
Herb Wild Rice 446
Nutty Wild Rice Pilaf 382
Nutty Wild Rice Salad 199
Turkey Wild Rice Salad 123
Wild Rice Breakfast Cakes 64
Wild Rice Pecan Waffles 23

WINE

Carrots in Butter Wine Sauce 445
Orange Laced Fruit Compote 60
Pasta & Vegetables in Wine
  Sauce 332
Rolled Burgundy Steak 181

Y

YAM

(See Sweet Potato)

YOGURT

Tender Yogurt Pancakes 18

Z

ZUCCHINI

Main Dish
  Baked Fish With Herbed
    Vegetables 110
  Cheese n' Vegetable Linguine 131
  Grilled Garden Vegetables
    & Sole 252
  Pronto Pasta Dinner 107
  Santa Fe Supper 104
  Zucchini, Tomato & Cheese
    Frittata 117
Salads
  Fresh Herb Tomato-Jack Salad 259
  Sweet n' Tangy Slaw 257
Vegetables
  Garlic Roasted Summer
    Vegetables 442
  Grilled Vegetable Kabobs 268
  Potato Ratatouille 142
  Skillet Zucchini Sauté 141
  Vegetables With Chili
    Mayonnaise 270
Other
  Cajun Gumbo Soup 91
  Open-Faced Salami n' Relish
    Sandwich 128

MEASURING MADE EASY : METRIC EQUIVALENTS

HOW TO MEASURE LIQUIDS

¼ cup	50 mL
⅓ cup	75 mL
½ cup	125 mL
¾ cup	175 mL
1 cup	250 mL
2 cups	500 mL
2½ cups	625 mL
4 cups	1 liter
(32 oz)	1 liter

HOW TO MEASURE SOLID INGREDIENTS

½ oz	15 g
1 oz	30 g
¼ lb	115 g
⅓ lb	150 g
½ lb	225 g
⅔ lb	300 g
¾ lb	350 g
1 lb	450 g
2 lbs	900 g

HOW TO MEASURE SPOONFULS

⅛ teaspoon	0.5 mL
¼ teaspoon	1 mL
½ teaspoon	2 mL
1 teaspoon	5 mL
1 tablespoon	15 mL
1½ tablespoons	25 mL
2 tablespoons	30 mL

HOW TO MEASURE LENGTH AND THICKNESS

¼ inch	5 mm
½ inch	1 cm
¾ inch	2 cm
1 inch	2.5 cm
2 inches	5 cm
2½ inches	6 cm
4 inches	10 cm
5 inches	12 cm
6 inches	15 cm
7 inches	18 cm
8 inches	20 cm
9 inches	22 cm
10 inches	25 cm
11 inches	28 cm
12 inches	30 cm

OVEN TEMPERATURES

°F	°C
200 °	100 °
250 °	120 °
300 °	150 °
325 °	160 °
350 °	180 °
375 °	190 °
400 °	200 °
425 °	220 °
450 °	230 °

For the girls of Road Trip 2001 to Salem:
Jen, Glendon, Kaitlin, Mollie, and Maddison
—J. Y. and H. E. Y. S.

For Marion Moskowitz
—R. R.

With thanks to Richard Trask for his keen historical insight.

A NOTE FROM THE ARTIST

The illustrations in this book were done in a series of stages. First I did tiny, rough "thumbnail" sketches. This is really the fun and creative part for me. Then from these thumbnails I made large, detailed pencil drawings, which I traced onto watercolor paper. Next I painted the pictures using transparent watercolors, adding pencil for detail and texture.

SIMON & SCHUSTER BOOKS FOR YOUNG READERS
An imprint of Simon & Schuster Children's Publishing Division
1230 Avenue of the Americas, New York, New York 10020
Text copyright © 2004 by Jane Yolen and Heidi Elisabet Yolen Stemple
Illustrations copyright © 2004 by Roger Roth
All rights reserved, including the right of reproduction in whole or in part in any form. SIMON & SCHUSTER BOOKS FOR YOUNG READERS is a trademark of Simon & Schuster, Inc.
Book design by Lucy Ruth Cummins
The text for this book is set in Minister Book. The illustrations for this book are rendered in graphite and watercolor.
Manufactured in China
1 2 3 4 5 6 7 8 9 10
CIP data for this book is available from the Library of Congress.
ISBN 0-689-84620-7

first edition

BIBLIOGRAPHY

BOOKS AND BOOKLETS

Boyer, Paul, and Stephen Nissenbaum, eds. *Salem-Village Witchcraft: A Documentary Record of Local Conflict in Colonial New England.* Boston: Northeastern University Press, 1993.

Breslaw, Elaine G. *Tituba, Reluctant Witch of Salem: Devilish Indians and Puritan Fantasies.* New York: New York University Press, 1996.

Fowler, Samuel P., Esquire. *An Account of the Life and Character of Rev. Samuel Parris of Salem Village and His Connection with the Witchcraft Delusion of 1692.* Salem, MA: The New England & Virginia Company, 1997.

Hansen, Chadwick. *Witchcraft at Salem.* New York: George Braziller, Inc., 1969.

Hill, Frances. *A Delusion of Satan: The Full Story of the Salem Witch Trials.* New York: Doubleday, 1995.

Richardson, Katherine W. *The Salem Witchcraft Trials.* Salem, MA: Essex Institute, 1983.

Roach, Marilynne K. *In the Days of the Salem Witchcraft Trials.* Boston: Houghton Mifflin, 1996.

Wilson, Lori Lee. *The Salem Witch Trials: How History Is Invented.* Minneapolis: Lerner Publications Company, 1997.

WEB SITES

"Timeline of the Salem Witch Trials."
http://www.salemwitchtrials.com/timeline.html
[February 13, 2001].

"Salem Witchcraft Hysteria: Ask the Expert."
http://www.nationalgeographic.com/features/97/salem/digest.html
[February 13, 2001].

"Life in Salem 1692: Puritan Children."
http://school.discovery.com/schooladventures/salemwitchtrials/life/children.html [October 25, 2001].

THE SALEM WITCH TRIALS

An Unsolved Mystery
from History

BY JANE YOLEN AND HEIDI ELISABET YOLEN STEMPLE
ILLUSTRATED BY ROGER ROTH

Simon & Schuster Books for Young Readers
New York   London   Toronto   Sydney

When I grow up, I want to be a detective, just like my dad.

He says I was born curious and that the most important quality a detective needs is curiosity.

Right now I'm curious about old mysteries that have never been solved. The police call them "open" cases, but Dad and I call them "unsolved mysteries from history." I am determined to figure out at least one of them.

For each mystery I collect as much information about the case as I can. As I learn the story, I organize the clues in my notebook. I always keep a list of words that are important to the case.

The Salem witch trials happened because the Puritans who settled in Massachusetts were afraid of witchcraft and evil spirits. They believed that several young girls who lived in Salem Village could point out which townspeople were witches. Today we have ideas—or theories—about what really happened in Salem, but no one is absolutely sure. Still, my dad says that no mystery is impossible to solve, as long as you have enough clues.

This is how the story goes.

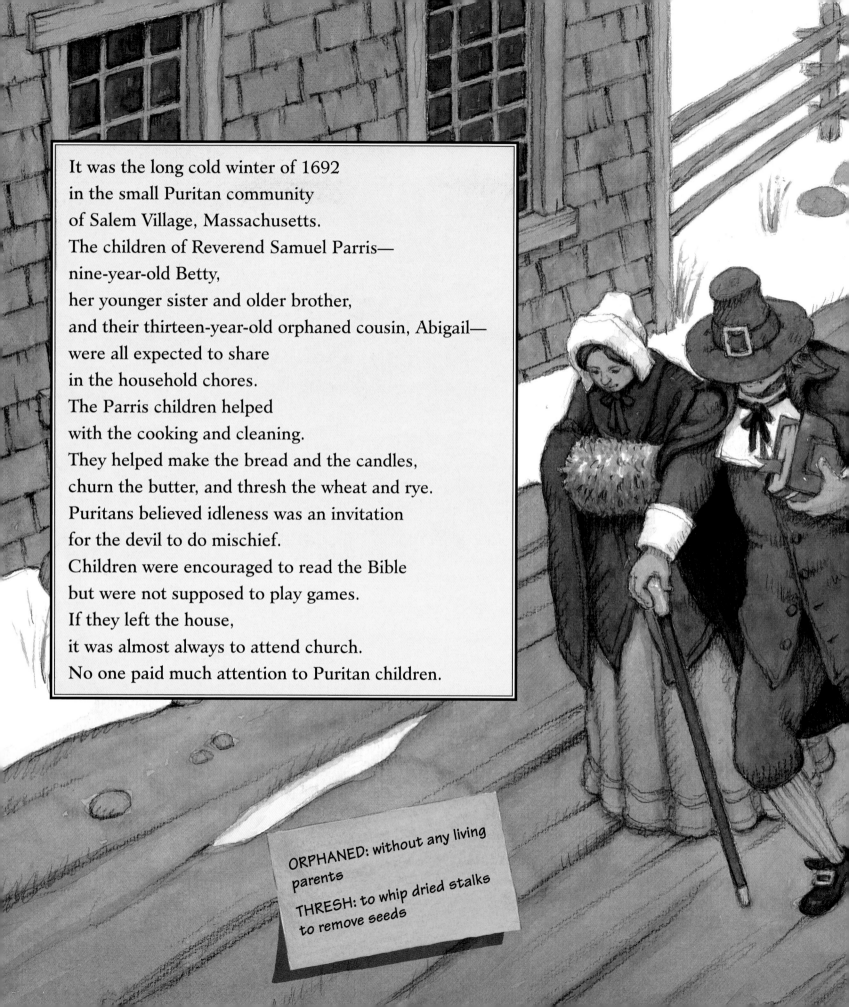

It was the long cold winter of 1692
in the small Puritan community
of Salem Village, Massachusetts.
The children of Reverend Samuel Parris—
nine-year-old Betty,
her younger sister and older brother,
and their thirteen-year-old orphaned cousin, Abigail—
were all expected to share
in the household chores.
The Parris children helped
with the cooking and cleaning.
They helped make the bread and the candles,
churn the butter, and thresh the wheat and rye.
Puritans believed idleness was an invitation
for the devil to do mischief.
Children were encouraged to read the Bible
but were not supposed to play games.
If they left the house,
it was almost always to attend church.
No one paid much attention to Puritan children.

ORPHANED: without any living parents

THRESH: to whip dried stalks to remove seeds

IDLENESS: inactivity or not doing any work

SECT: a group with religious beliefs different from the majority

MORAL CODE: rules for proper conduct

The Puritans who helped settle Massachusetts were members of a strict religious sect. They had faith that their simple ways were the purest form of Christianity. Children and adults were bound by a moral code. All were expected to work hard, and they believed that everything in their lives was preplanned by God.

Also living in the Parris household
were two slaves:
John Indian and his wife, Tituba.
Betty and Abigail were especially fond
of the stories Tituba told
about life in Barbados—
so different from life in Salem Village—
and Tituba told them about Barbadian magic.
The girls already knew a fortune-telling game
played by many English colonists.
To learn the identity of their future sweethearts,
they cracked eggs in well water
and "read" the floating white forms.
But now when Betty and Abigail talked
with other Salem Village girls,
they secretly whispered about Tituba's magic.

Tituba was likely a North or South American Indian and not of African blood. She was probably kidnapped by European slave traders and raised as a house slave on a Barbados plantation. There, surrounded by slaves from many cultures as well as the European masters, she would have learned many fantastic games and stories. Few records about Tituba exist, though, so what is known of her background is mostly guesswork.

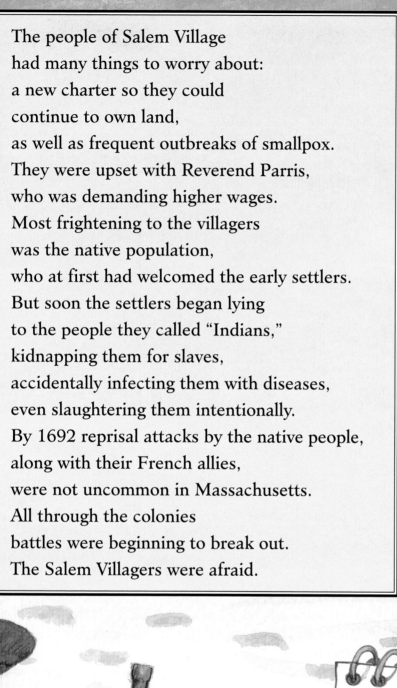

The people of Salem Village
had many things to worry about:
a new charter so they could
continue to own land,
as well as frequent outbreaks of smallpox.
They were upset with Reverend Parris,
who was demanding higher wages.
Most frightening to the villagers
was the native population,
who at first had welcomed the early settlers.
But soon the settlers began lying
to the people they called "Indians,"
kidnapping them for slaves,
accidentally infecting them with diseases,
even slaughtering them intentionally.
By 1692 reprisal attacks by the native people,
along with their French allies,
were not uncommon in Massachusetts.
All through the colonies
battles were beginning to break out.
The Salem Villagers were afraid.

Massachusetts was one of thirteen New World
colonies. Each was governed by a charter, or legal
paper, granted by the king of England. The charter
allowed the people living there to own all of their land,
which, to the Puritans, was the most important form
of wealth. In 1688 the original Massachusetts
charter had been revoked by the king, and in 1692 a
new one had not yet arrived.

SMALLPOX: a highly contagious and often fatal disease

INTENTIONALLY: on purpose

REPRISAL: repayment of an injury, insult, or other attack

ALLIES: people, countries, or populations who cooperate with one another

REVOKED: withdrawn, canceled, or taken back

One bitterly cold day in February,
Betty and Abigail both fell ill,
collapsing onto their small rope beds.
They convulsed.
They contorted.
Their arms and legs jerked about.
They shouted bizarre, unintelligible words.
They crouched under chairs
and cowered as if frightened.
In other houses in Salem Village
several of their friends began
to act the same way.

The other sick girls in Salem Village included Ann Putnam Jr. (age 12), Mercy Lewis (age 19), Mary Walcott (age 16), Elizabeth Hubbard (age 17), and Mary Warren (age 20). Like Abigail, Elizabeth and Mercy were orphans; Mercy may have witnessed her parents being killed in an Indian attack three years earlier in Maine. Mary Walcott had lost her mother when she was eight. Ann and Betty were daughters of landowners, but Mary Warren, Elizabeth, and Mercy were maidservants.

CONVULSED: shook violently

CONTORTED: twisted into unusual shapes

UNINTELLIGIBLE: impossible to understand

The local physician, Dr. Griggs,
was called in to examine Betty and Abigail.
He found no illness in his medical books
that matched the girls' symptoms.
As far as he could tell,
they had not been poisoned.
They did not need bleeding,
nor did their limbs need setting.
He knew no other way to heal them.
Dr. Griggs pronounced
Betty and Abigail "bewitched."
"The evil hand is upon them," he said.
His prescription:
prayer and fasting.

In the seventeenth century many illnesses were blamed on evil, and doctors often recommended religious cures. A country "doctor" (a title given to any healer, whether or not he had a medical degree) would sometimes use "bleeding"—draining patients of supposed excess blood—as a treatment. Most of today's common medicines had not yet been discovered or invented, and people regularly died of ordinary ailments such as strep throat, measles, and even dental problems.

PRONOUNCED: formally declared

BEWITCHED: under an evil spell

PRESCRIPTION: doctor's instructions

FASTING: going without food for a period of time

AILMENTS: sicknesses

Thinking Tituba might be able to help,
Mary Walcott's aunt, Mary Stibley,
asked Tituba to bake a witch cake—
made of rye and the girls' urine—
to feed to the Parrises' dog, which Mary Stibley
believed was an evil messenger.
When Reverend Parris heard about this,
he made Mary Stibley stand up in church
and admit what she had done.
He told his parishioners
never to use white magic,
even to break a bad magic spell.
Standing at the front of his church,
he warned of "a going to the Devil
for help against the Devil."

Most religious people of the seventeenth century believed in evil spirits, magic, and witches. They thought witches made a pact with the devil and were given certain powers such as the ability to curse a neighbor with a poor planting season or even smallpox. Witches could be male or female, young or old. It was also believed that each witch had an animal "familiar"—a dog, cat, toad, or owl—to help work the evil magic.

Everyone prayed.
Everyone fasted.
Important religious men
from other communities came
to say prayers over the girls.
But nothing worked.
The girls continued to weep,
faint, contort, and speak gibberish.
In a rare moment of calm,
the girls were asked
who was bewitching them.
They named three women.
One was Sarah Good.
One was Sarah Osbourn.
The third woman was Tituba.

Sarah Good was a poor, pregnant, pipe-smoking, bad-tempered woman with a young daughter. When Sarah Good was accused, her own husband stated in court that he thought she might be a witch. Sarah Osbourn was a sick, older woman who was gossiped about because she did not attend church, she had married a servant, and she had disputed land ownership in her first husband's will. Her first husband had owned land, which he had left in trust to Sarah Osbourn for his sons. She had contested the will to try to keep the land as her own.

The girls said they saw specters—floating spirits
no one else could see—doing bad things.
The specters pinched and pricked the girls,
who fell to the floor in shrieking fits.
On the first day of March
Tituba confessed to being a witch.
At first her story was simply an admission.
But soon she spoke of "sister witches,"
a mysterious man dressed in black,
and even flying upon a stick.
Everyone believed
she was speaking the truth.
And they believed the girls, too.

After being beaten and then questioned over and over again, Tituba finally confessed. This saved her life because it made her important to the court: Her accusers now believed she had special knowledge that could help them find other witches. Had she not confessed, it would have been assumed that she was lying, and she would surely have been executed.

Since Betty Parris was so young,
she was sent away
to stay with another family
in nearby Salem Town.
The girls who remained
became famous in the village.
Ann Putnam Jr. and Mary Walcott
were even asked to visit sick people
in other towns to see if their illnesses
had some relationship to the Devil.
Some of the girls were invited
to touch suspected witches
to see if they could feel evil spirits.
If the girls said they felt the Devil,
those people were accused of witchcraft.
Everyone was listening to the girls.

SUSPECTED: thought to be guilty, but without proof

ACCUSED: blamed for a crime or wrongdoing

After being hardly noticed their whole lives, the girls had become the center of attention. They were brought around to other towns to help adults there hunt for witches. It must have made them feel important, even powerful, to be recognized everywhere. Their names were on everyone's lips. Even people as far away as Boston had heard of them.

CONVICTED: proved guilty of a crime or wrongdoing in a court of law

INFLUENCE: the power to affect someone's beliefs or actions

Soon the courthouse
was filled with the accused,
the jailhouse with the convicted.
No one was safe,
not even those who were well thought of.
Martha Cory and her husband, Giles,
members of the church and landowners;
respected townswoman Rebecca Nurse;
and John and Elizabeth Procter,
who lived outside the village,
were all named as witches.
To be with her mother, Sarah Good,
five-year-old Dorcas Good confessed
to being a witch and was led away in chains.
Reverend George Burroughs,
who had preached in Salem Village years earlier,
was accused of committing murder
while under the Devil's influence.
More than 141 people were arrested.

HYSTERIA: wild and uncontrollable emotion

TESTIFY: to make a statement based on personal knowledge or belief

Finally, as 1692 was coming to an end,
the new Puritan governor of Massachusetts,
Sir William Phips,
came to see for himself
why the witchcraft hysteria
had overwhelmed the village.
Many important people—
even Phips's own wife—
were being accused of witchcraft
as other towns followed Salem's lead.
Phips declared that no person
would be allowed to stand up in court
and testify to seeing invisible spirits,
since such things could not be proven.
Without "spectral evidence"
no one else could be convicted of witchcraft.

SPECTRAL: ghostly; having to do with ghostly or invisible things

Only those who had not confessed to being witches were ever tried. When spectral evidence was introduced at a trial, the jury had to decide whether or not to believe the accusers, since no one could actually see the evidence.

PARDONED: canceled punishment for a crime

JAIL COSTS: fees from a person's stay in jail, charged as if it were a hotel, including costs for food, bedding, and a share of the jailer's pay

At the time of the witch trials, Salem Village had a population of 550 people within its twenty square miles. The village was in an area where streams ran through swampy land. There today are the towns of Danvers, Middleton, and Peabody. Together they have a combined population of around 70,000. Salem Town has become the city of Salem, and the witchcraft trials are its primary tourist attraction. In both Salem and Danvers there are historical museums (including Rebecca Nurse's house), a memorial to the victims, witchcraft-themed gift shops, and many popular ghost tours.

By the time the witch trials came to an end,
nineteen people had been hanged as witches.
One man was pressed to death
under a pile of rocks.
Four others died in jail, awaiting trial.
Governor Phips pardoned the people still in jail,
but they had to remain until their families
paid all of their jail costs.
Tituba was sold by Reverend Parris to cover her jail fees.
In 1712 payments were made
to some of the suffering families.
In 1752 Salem Village changed its name
to Danvers so as not to be associated with the trials.
In 1957 Massachusetts formally apologized
for the events of 1692.
But it wasn't until 1992—
300 years later—
that the Massachusetts House of Representatives
passed a resolution formally acknowledging
that the accused had been innocent of witchcraft.

RESOLUTION: formal statement of opinion or intent agreed upon by a group

ACKNOWLEDGING: recognizing that something is true or valid

So what really happened?

No one knows for sure.

But now that you have read the story and looked at my notes, maybe you can solve the mystery of the Salem witch trials. Maybe one of the theories about the bewitched girls and the witch trials seems right to you. Or maybe you have your own idea about what happened.

Just remember what my dad always tells me: Check your clues.

1. The girls were telling the truth about witches in Salem:

Tituba or one of the other accused witches really did cast a spell that forced the girls to see spirits and act bewitched.

Can you prove that such magic exists—or that it existed in Salem Village in the seventeenth century?

Was there proof, other than the girls' own words, that they could see spirits and witches?

Why would anyone confess to being a witch?

2. The girls were bored and seeking attention:

Starting with Betty and Abigail, the girls of Salem Village were just playacting in order to get attention, and the more attention they got, the more they wanted.

Did the girls have any other way of getting attention from their parents or neighbors?

Is it possible to fake symptoms of being bewitched?

Did the girls know a lot about witchcraft—enough to fool the adults?

3. The girls were playing a game and became too frightened to stop:

What started as a game turned serious when the first people were imprisoned and tortured. It all happened so quickly that the girls had no time to say they were just playing or to beg for forgiveness from the people they had accused.

How could Rebecca Nurse ever forgive them? Or Dorcas Good? Or any of the others?

Did the girls play other acting-out games? Had they taken acting lessons?

What would probably have happened if the girls had admitted to lying?

Were strict Puritans likely to forgive such wicked behavior, even from children?

Who would the girls have feared the most? Their parents? Reverend Parris? Governor Phips? Witches? The Devil? God?

4. The girls were suffering from a physical or mental ailment:

The problem was not witchcraft but some kind of disease, contamination, or mental problem. The most popular ideas have been: poisoning by ergot, a fungus found in rye grain; encephalitis, a disease carried by mosquitoes; and post-traumatic stress disorder, a mental reaction to witnessing horrible things such as war. All of these illnesses can cause hallucinations, twitching, spasms, and nervous behavior.

Was rye bread part of the Colonial meals?

Were there places for mosquitoes to breed near Salem?

Did the girls' families or any adults develop the same symptoms?

What was medicine like in the seventeenth century?

Would the doctor have recognized these illnesses or known how to treat them?

Had any of the girls witnessed raids, battles, or wars?

5. The girls were put up to their actions as part of town politics:

It has been suggested that the girls chose certain people to accuse because their families were in dispute with them over property or other town problems.

Were poor people with no property safe from the girls' accusations?

Did people own their property outright or was it owned by the king?

Were there any other problems in town?

Were any of the accused people enemies of the girls' families?